COSMIC PROBLEMS

COSMIC PROBLEMS

ESSAYS ON GREEK AND ROMAN
PHILOSOPHY OF NATURE

DAVID FURLEY

CHARLES EWING PROFESSOR OF GREEK LANGUAGE AND LITERATURE
PRINCETON UNIVERSITY

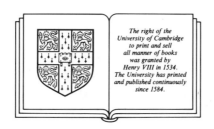

The right of the
University of Cambridge
to print and sell
all manner of books
was granted by
Henry VIII in 1534.
The University has printed
and published continuously
since 1584.

CAMBRIDGE UNIVERSITY PRESS

CAMBRIDGE

NEW YORK   NEW ROCHELLE   MELBOURNE   SYDNEY

Published by the Press Syndicate of the University of Cambridge
The Pitt Building, Trumpington Street, Cambridge CB2 1RP
32 East 57th Street, New York, NY 10022, USA
10 Stamford Road, Oakleigh, Melbourne 3166, Australia

© Cambridge University Press 1989

First published 1989

Printed in Great Britain at the University Press, Cambridge

British Library cataloguing in publication data
Furley, David
Cosmic problems: essays on Greek and Roman philosophy of nature
1. Classical cosmology
I. Title
113′.093

Library of Congress cataloguing in publication data
Furley, David J.
Cosmic problems: essays on Greek and Roman philosophy of nature/David Furley.
p.   cm.
Articles originally published 1966–1988.
Bibliography.
Includes index.
ISBN 0 521 33330 X
1. Philosophy of nature–History.   2. Philosophy, Ancient–History.   I. Title.
BD581.F87 1988
113′.0938 – dc19   88-11120 CIP

ISBN 0 521 33330 X

CONTENTS

Preface		*page* ix
Acknowledgements		xiii

1 THE GREEK THEORY OF THE INFINITE UNIVERSE — 1

2 THE DYNAMICS OF THE EARTH: ANAXIMANDER, PLATO, AND THE CENTRIFOCAL THEORY — 14

Introduction	14
The evidence of Aristotle concerning the Milesians	16
Other evidence about Anaximander	20
A note on the centrifocal theory and the spherical earth	23

3 NOTES ON PARMENIDES — 27

Parmenides goes to the House of Night	27
Mortals wrongly set up two separate and opposite forms	30
The hard-hitting refutation and the sense of ἔστι	33

4 TRUTH AS WHAT SURVIVES THE *ELENCHOS* — 38

5 ANAXAGORAS IN RESPONSE TO PARMENIDES — 47

Introduction	47
A difficulty in the conventional account of Anaxagoras	50
Nutrition and the homoiomerous bodies	51
Genesis and the seeds	55
Anaxagoras and Zeno	58
Anaxagoras compared with Plato	62

6   ANTIPHON'S CASE AGAINST JUSTICE   66

7   ARISTOTLE AND THE ATOMISTS ON MOTION   77
     IN A VOID

     Introduction   77
     Democritus' Theory of Motion   78
     Aristotle's criticism of the concept of void   81
     Arguments about speed of motion in a void   83
     Arguments about direction of motion in a void   84

8   WEIGHT AND MOTION IN DEMOCRITUS'   91
     THEORY

9   ARISTOTLE AND THE ATOMISTS ON INFINITY   103

     Time   103
     The debate about infinite divisibility   103
     The debate about the infinitely large   109

10   THE RAINFALL EXAMPLE IN *PHYSICS* II. 8   115

11   SELF-MOVERS   121

12   THE MECHANICS OF *METEOROLOGICA* IV: 132
     A PROLEGOMENON TO BIOLOGY

     Introduction   132
     Natural motions   134
     Hot and cold as causes of motion   136
     Evaporation of moisture by heat   137
     Solidification caused by cold   138
     How do bodies contract?   140
     Pores and qualities   141
     Attraction   144
     'Αντιπερίστασις   145
     Meteorologica IV and the biological works   145

13   STRATO'S THEORY OF THE VOID   149

14   KNOWLEDGE OF ATOMS AND VOID IN   161
     EPICUREANISM

15 VARIATIONS ON THEMES FROM EMPEDOCLES   172
    IN LUCRETIUS' PROEM

16 LUCRETIUS AND THE STOICS   183
    1.449–482. Properties and accidents   184
    1.615–626. Infinite divisibility   185
    1.635–704. Fire   185
    1.782–802. The four elements   187
    1.1052–1113. Geocentric cosmology   187
    II.167–183. Providence   195
    II.251–293. Free will and necessity   195
    II.886–972. The elements of sensation   196
    III.307–322. Character and philosophy   198
    III.350–369. The soul, the body, and sensation 198
    III.425–829. The survival of the soul   198
    III.847–861. Rebirth   199
    IV.823–857. Teleology   199
    V.55–234. Gods and the world   200
    V.306–350. The mortality of the cosmos   203
    Conclusion   204

17 LUCRETIUS THE EPICUREAN, ON THE   206
    HISTORY OF MAN

18 THE COSMOLOGICAL CRISIS IN CLASSICAL   223
    ANTIQUITY

    Bibliography   236

    Index locorum   245
    Index of modern scholars   253
    General index   255

PREFACE

Is the universe finite or without boundaries? Is it continuously filled with matter, or is there empty space in it? Is our world unique or one of many? Is it eternal or did it have a beginning in time? Is it directed in some fashion by a god or gods, or is it an autonomous material system? Have the forms of animals and plants in this world existed for ever, or did they come into existence at some time in the world's history? Is mind prior to and in control of the motions of matter, or is it derived from them? Does the study of the natural world teach us anything about the right way to live?

In the classical world, these questions and others closely related to them were keenly debated over a period greater than a millennium, beginning in Miletus soon after 600 B.C. To give shape to the debate, it is useful to regard it as a clash between two systems, which can conveniently be labelled Aristotelianism and Atomism. This choice of names is neither arbitrary nor accurate. It is not arbitrary, because in fact Aristotle gathered together the answers on one side, and the Atomists Democritus and Epicurus gave opposed answers; and there were no more representative figures than these. But it is not accurate, because the debate was from time to time carried on by those who did not wholly agree with either Aristotle or the Atomists, although it is easy to see that in general they belong in one camp rather than the other.

The essays in this collection, written over a period of twenty years, are all related to this debate. Some of the early ones, together with my book *Two Studies in the Greek Atomists* (1967), helped to form my picture of the debate; the rest have been written with the conscious intention of exploring certain details in order to fill out the picture. All of them can be regarded as companions to my attempt to write a history of the debate as a whole, in *The Greek Cosmologists*, vol. 1 (Cambridge University Press, 1987); vol. 2 forthcoming.

Chapter 1, 'The Greek Theory of the Infinite Universe', may serve as an introduction to the collection as a whole. It was composed for oral delivery to an audience of classicists, and although it deals with a particular problem – the problem of creating a unified theory of motion in the universe – it presents some of the outlines of the debate as a whole. As a kind of epilogue, chapter 18, which was also originally a lecture designed for a non-specialist audience, contains some general reflections on the nature of the debate, with examples taken particularly from a later period.

The arrangement of the rest of the book is roughly according to the chronology of the subject-matter.

First, there are four studies of the early Greek philosophers who preceded and led up to the formation of the atomic theory. Chapter 2 is an attempt – first published here and much against the grain of current scholarship on the subject – to show that Anaximander, the sixth-century Milesian, has been wrongly credited with an anachronistic dynamic theory concerning the position of the earth in the cosmos. Chapter 3 argues for some points in the interpretation of Parmenides that are crucial to my view of the immediately following stages of the cosmological argument, and to my analysis of the formation of the atomic theory. Chapter 4, on the Presocratic notion of *elenchos*, seeks to reinforce a point in this view of Parmenides by comparisons drawn from non-philosophical Greek texts, and I hope it may also be useful in giving some of the background of early Greek philosophical argument. Chapter 5 defends my interpretation of Anaxagoras' theory of matter and change – a theory that I believe to have been consciously intended to rehabilitate the concept of natural change after its attempted destruction by Parmenides.

Chapter 6 is concerned with the place of the concept of nature in morality. This chapter may seem to change the subject. The rest of the book is almost wholly concerned with cosmology in a fairly restricted sense – such subjects as the shape and order of the cosmos, matter and motion, the causes of large-scale and small-scale physical change, how we get our knowledge of the external physical world. But the relevance of one's view of the natural world to human choice and action is also a theme for cosmology – indeed, contemporary anthropology uses the term 'cosmology' more often in this context than in the purely physical sense. It is surprising, to my mind, that the cosmological controversies discussed in this book set up so few echoes in other genres of literature in Greece during the classical period. There might have been traces to be found in fifth-century drama, but in fact, apart from one or two well-known passages of Euripides and Aristophanes, the surviving plays show little knowledge of the work of earlier and contemporary philosophers of nature. (This may, however, be due to the fact that fifth-century cosmology was largely non-Athenian, whereas the surviving Greek drama of the period is wholly Athenian.) But in one important area there is some interaction between philosophy of nature and other kinds of literature: namely, in the antithesis between nature and convention that played a large part in the moral discussions of the last decades of the fifth century. The philosophers detached the operations of nature from the intentions of anthropomorphic gods, and increasingly freed themselves from the use of categories applicable to human society in discussing the natural world. But if the rules that govern human communities are not imbedded in the cosmos, what is the source of their authority? This question, which had overwhelming importance in shaping discussions in the fourth century, is raised for the first time in the work of the Athenian Sophist Antiphon, which by great good luck survives, in part, on some fragments of papyrus. In chapter 6, I show how he uses the concept of nature in criticisms of the arguments of conventional moralists.

The next four chapters are all to do with Aristotle's position vis-à-vis Democritus or those who held theories similar to his. Chapters 7 and 8 take up again some of the questions dealt with in chapter 2, about the facts that today would be brought together under the heading 'gravity'. Aristotle is the major source for Democritus' views on these questions (as he is also for Anaximander), and these essays are an attempt to reconstruct Democritus' theory from the evidence of Aristotle and others. Chapter 8 was written some while after chapter 7, and is explicitly concerned with defending the view of Democritus' theory presented there against the alternative proposed by D. O'Brien (1981). Chapter 9 reviews Aristotle's presentation of Democritus' arguments for the infinity of the universe, with his own criticisms of these arguments and his defence of the opposing case. Chapter 10, although it takes the form of a close examination of a short stretch of text in book II of Aristotle's *Physics*, raises a very large issue concerning the range of Aristotle's difference from the materialists on teleological explanation in physics. It has usually been thought, by scholars who have studied the subject in recent years, that Aristotle conceded to the materialists that a whole range of natural phenomena can be adequately explained on non-teleological principles. I argue that the passage in question requires us to ascribe to him a more all-embracing teleology than we had thought – although he was still a long distance from the providentialism of the Stoics.

Next come two essays on Aristotle's theory of motion. Chapter 11, 'Self-Movers', discusses the question of how we are to reconcile his assertion that animals and humans initiate their own motions with his claim that everything that moves requires a mover – the latter being an essential premiss in his argument for the existence of a divine Unmoved Mover. Chapter 12 studies motion at the opposite end, so to speak, of the hierarchy of nature: it examines the changes exhibited by the material components of organisms, according to Aristotelian theory, and the efficient causes of these.

Chapter 13 takes up again the theme of chapter 8, at a later stage in the chronology. Strato, the third head of the Peripatetic School, is said to have differed from Aristotle on several points in the philosophy of nature. This essay is an attempt to assess some complex and even contradictory evidence on Strato's views about the existence of void space in the world. I conclude that Strato did venture to contradict Aristotle on the existence of void space, and that he did so from within the general system of the Peripatetic School, rather than under the influence of the Epicureans, as some have believed.

Last comes a set of papers on Epicurean Atomism. Like most of the essays in this collection, they are polemical, in the sense that they were occasioned by my disagreement with some particular aspect of recent scholarship on the subject. This is particularly true of chapter 16, entitled 'Lucretius and the Stoics' –

perhaps somewhat misleadingly since its aim is to show that Lucretius took no notice of the Stoics. It is the text of a lecture, and perhaps adopts too much of the tone of an advocate rather than that of a judicial assessor; but since it has attracted critical attention in this form – and I still believe its thesis – I have decided not to make any changes in it for the present publication.

Although these Epicurean essays are directed at a variety of targets, they nevertheless hang together, in that they are all constituent elements of the overall picture that I have formed of Epicureanism and its relation to other philosophies. I hope to present that picture more fully and connectedly in the second volume of *The Greek Cosmologists*. Something of what I want to say has appeared already in the essay I wrote on Lucretius for *Ancient Writers: Greece and Rome* (New York: Charles Scribner's Sons, 1982).

The main concern of the historian of philosophy is with arguments and counterarguments. He aims to analyse the reasoning with which a philosopher persuades himself and seeks to persuade others that a particular view is to be accepted, and this usually entails criticism and rejection of an earlier view. This is a process that is internal to philosophy. Sometimes, it is true, it can be shown that external factors must be invoked to explain the course of events. For instance, progress in technology, a change in the political or social structure, contact with a hitherto unknown or little-known culture – these have all been held to be causes in the development of Greek philosophy. But such suggestions have on the whole proved less illuminating and have been less widely accepted than explanations framed in terms of philosophical arguments.

It must be admitted, however, that writing a history of this kind about classical philosophy involves an uncomfortable amount of conjecture. There are two compelling reasons for this: only a portion of the relevant texts have survived; and within those texts the opponents who are subjected to overt or tacit criticism are not always clearly identified. So there will never be a definitive history of classical philosophy. All contributions are tentative, and although they are put forward in the hope that they will be received with agreement, it is more likely that the response will be a critical one. Some of the papers in this volume have already received a fair amount of critical attention. I have thought of adding some replies, but perhaps it is best to hope that others will carry on the discussion. Critics have sometimes persuaded me that there is more to be said on the other side than I thought there was. But I have not included in this book anything of which I have been convinced that it does not deserve further discussion.

ACKNOWLEDGEMENTS

Most of the chapters of this book have been previously published as follows. I am grateful to the editors and publishers for permission to reprint them.

1   The Greek Theory of the Infinite Universe
    (*Journal of the History of Ideas* 42 (1981), 571–85)

2   The Dynamics of the Earth: Anaximander, Plato, and the Centrifocal
    Theory
    (Not previously published)

3   Notes on Parmenides
    (*Exegesis and Argument: Studies in Greek Philosophy Presented to Gregory
    Vlastos*, ed. E. N. Lee, A. P. D. Mourelatos, and R. Rorty. *Phronesis*,
    Supplementary volume no. 1 (Assen: Van Gorcum, 1973), pp. 1–15)

4   Truth as What Survives the *Elenchos*
    (Not previously published)

5   Anaxagoras in Response to Parmenides
    (*New Essays in Plato and the Pre-Socratics*, ed. Roger A. Shiner and John
    King-Farlow. *Canadian Journal of Philosophy*, Supplementary volume no. 2
    (1976), pp. 61–85)

6   Antiphon's Case against Justice
    (*The Sophists and Their Legacy*, Proceedings of the Fourth International
    Colloquium on Ancient Philosophy, ed. G. B. Kerferd. *Hermes Einzel-
    schriften* 44 (Wiesbaden: Franz Steiner, 1981), pp. 81–91)

7   Aristotle and the Atomists on Motion in a Void
    (*Motion and Time, Space and Matter*, ed. Peter K. Machamer and Robert J.
    Turnbull (Columbus: Ohio State University Press, 1976), pp. 83–100)

8   Weight and Motion in Democritus' Theory
    (*Oxford Studies in Ancient Philosophy* 1 (1983), 193–209)

9 Aristotle and the Atomists on Infinity
(*Naturphilosophie bei Aristoteles und Theophrast*, Proceedings of the Fourth Symposium Aristotelicum, ed. Ingemar Düring (Heidelberg: Lothar Stiehm Verlag, 1969), pp. 85–96)

10 The Rainfall Example in *Physics* II. 8
(*Aristotle on Nature and Living Things: Philosophical and Historical Studies presented to David M. Balme on his Seventieth Birthday*, ed. Allan Gotthelf (Pittsburgh, Duquesne University: Mathesis Publications, 1986), pp. 177–82)

11 Self-Movers
(*Aristotle on Mind and the Senses*, Proceedings of the Seventh Symposium Aristotelicum, ed. G. E. R. Lloyd and G. E. L. Owen (Cambridge University Press, 1978), pp. 165–79)

12 The Mechanics of *Meteorologica* IV: a Prolegomenon to Biology (*Zweifelhaftes im Corpus Aristotelicum: Studien zu einigen Dubia*, Akten des 9. Symposium Aristotelicum, ed. Paul Moraux and Jürgen Wiesner (Berlin/New York: De Gruyter, 1983), pp. 73–93)

13 Strato's Theory of the Void
(*Aristoteles Werk und Wirkung*, vol. 1: 'Aristoteles und seine Schule', Paul Moraux gewidmet, ed. Jürgen Wiesner (Berlin/New York: De Gruyter, 1985), pp. 594–609)

14 Knowledge of Atoms and Void in Epicureanism
(*Essays in Ancient Greek Philosophy*, ed. John P. Anton and George L. Kustas (Albany: SUNY Press, 1971), pp. 607–19)

15 Variations on Themes from Empedocles in Lucretius' Proem
(*Bulletin of the [London] Institute of Classical Studies*, 17 (1970), 55–64)

16 Lucretius and the Stoics
(*Bulletin of the [London] Institute of Classical Studies* 13 (1966), 13–33)

17 Lucretius the Epicurean, on the History of Man (*Lucrèce*, Entretiens sur l'Antiquité Classique 24 (Vandoeuvres Genève: Fondation Hardt, 1978 (actually 1979)), pp. 1–37)

18 The Cosmological Crisis in Classical Antiquity
(*Proceedings of the Boston Area Colloquium in Ancient Philosophy* 2 (1986) 1–19)

I

THE GREEK THEORY OF THE INFINITE UNIVERSE

[1981]

The picture of the world that was passed on by the classical civilizations to medieval Christian Europe was largely the work of Plato and Aristotle, with finishing touches from Ptolemy. It was a picture of a spherical world, with earth at the centre, motionless, and the stars wheeling round it at the circumference. Outside the sphere, there was either nothing at all, as Aristotle believed, or nothing of any interest. It was not until the sixteenth and seventeenth centuries that the picture changed comprehensively – a change that is accurately captured by the title of Alexander Koyré's book, *From the Closed World to the Infinite Universe.*[1]

Of course, the theory of the infinite universe was already anticipated in classical antiquity, in some of its essentials. But the classical theory was not the same as the one that displaced Aristotle in the seventeenth century. In particular, I believe the motivation was different, and I think the motivation of the classical theory could bear closer study. What did its proponents expect to get from the theory? What reasons did they have for holding it?

Let us begin with what seems obvious.

If we walk outside on a clear night, and then stop, and observe the position of the stars several times during the night, then two things may seem to us to be undeniable: first, that when we stop, then we are no longer moving but at rest; second, that the stars (except one, the Pole Star, perhaps) are moving, on arcs of circles. With just a little persistence and measurement, we work out that all the circles on which the stars move have their centre on the line that passes from the one stationary point, at the Pole, through the earth. And with an effort of imagination, because all the stars except a handful always keep fixed positions relative to each other, we conclude that these circles are not independent rings, but are all joined together on the surface of a great sphere, which rotates as a whole once a day.

From these apparently plain observations and this one immensely plausible inference, it follows that the size of the world must be limited. The whole sphere carrying the fixed stars completes a 360° rotation around its axis in twenty-four hours. If we imagine the radius of the sphere to increase, we must imagine the

---

[1] Koyré (1957).

speed of motion of the stars to increase proportionately. And if the radius increases to infinity, so does the speed. Aristotle produced a neat set of arguments, in *De caelo* I, to show that if the stars move round the earth they cannot be *infinitely* distant from the earth (*De caelo* 1.5.271 b 28ff).

So long as it is accepted, then, that the earth is at rest and the stars move, it must also be accepted that the world is a limited system, a very important fact to remember when we speak about Greek theories of the infinite. There is a difference in this respect between the Greek theory and the theory that has been held since the seventeenth century. Today, we can think of ourselves as being somewhere in the middle of a vast forest of stars, so to speak, that stretches interminably away in every direction. We can see some of the stars with the naked eye, and we believe some are comparatively close, and others further away. We know that telescopes will bring more stars into view – stars that were invisible to the naked eye not merely because they were too small or too dim to be seen, but also because they were too distant. So we come to think that what we see is the nearest region of a starscape that would continue indefinitely for as long as we could move our viewpoint further and further into it.

Greek theories of the infinite universe, however, present a significantly different picture. What they saw in the night sky was not the beginning of the infinite universe: it was rather the boundary beyond which the infinite universe began. This point stands out clearly enough in the most famous classical description of the infinite universe:

> ergo vivida vis animi pervicit, et extra
> processit longe flammantia moenia mundi,
> atque omne immensum peragravit mente animoque.
>
> Lucretius, *De rerum natura* I.73–5[2]

So Lucretius praises the achievement of Epicurus. His mind was powerful enough to range 'beyond the fiery ramparts of the world' into the boundless universe. The world is like a walled city with unknown country outside the walls.

Notice that this picture was even stamped on the vocabulary of the classical languages. *Mundus* in Latin and *kosmos* in Greek meant a limited, organized system, bounded by the stars: the universe as a whole was called by Greek writers τὸ πᾶν, and by Latin writers (cursing their language for the absence of a definite article) *omne quod est, omne immensum*, and so on. This is a distinction without a point in modern theory: *cosmology* is the study of the *universe*. But in this chapter I shall artificially reimpose the distinction in English, and use the word 'world' for the limited *kosmos* or *mundus*, and reserve the word 'universe' for the sum total of everything. The first point that I want to emphasize, because it is very often obscured or forgotten, is that no one in classical antiquity believed that the *world* is infinite. The controversy was not about the *existence* of a closed world, but about its status: is it all that there is, or is there something else too?

---

[2] 'And so his splendid strength of soul prevailed/Outside he went, beyond the flaming ramparts of the world/And ranged the infinite whole in mind and thought's imagining' (trans. A. D. Winspear).

Before we try to pursue Epicurus and others beyond the *flammantia moenia mundi* (the flaming ramparts of the world), it may be as well to pause first, and reconsider these opening moves. Was there nobody in antiquity who denied that the earth is stationary, and that the stars move round it, and who might therefore have been in a position to abandon the notion of a sphere of stars at the boundary of the world? The answer is, of course, that there were a few imaginative spirits who floated the idea that the earth moves, but they made curiously little impact on the classical picture of the stars. There were some Pythagoreans who claimed that the centre of the world is occupied by fire – the finest element in the finest place – and the earth moves cosily around the fire.[3] There was Heracleides of Pontus, who argued that the earth rotates on its own axis once a day, and the stars are stationary.[4] And there was Aristarchus of Samos, who was apparently the first to put up the idea that the earth is in orbit round the sun.[5] In all of these theories, the apparent daily motion of the stars is merely an effect of the earth's motion.

It would appear, then, that they had no need to posit a *sphere* of stars. So long as the stars are thought to be in motion while still keeping the same relative positions, it is natural to think of them as a vast *corps de ballet* – creating a single harmony, as in pseudo-Aristotle *De mundo*, 'as they sing and dance in concert round the sky' (399 a 12). But as soon as they are conceived to be stationary, there seems at first sight to be no cogent reason why they may not vary enormously in their distance from the earth. On this hypothesis, what reason is there to think of the stars that make up Orion's belt, for instance, as being located all at the same distance from us?

Well, there are reasons. First, there is the problem of parallax, which was known in antiquity. If the earth is moving in orbit round the sun, why do the stars not appear to change their relative positions as the earth moves from one extreme to the other of its orbit? Even if the earth is stationary but rotating, the same problem arises for an observer on the earth's surface, because he is in an orbit around the centre. There are two possible solutions. One is to retain the supposition that the stars are all equidistant from the centre of the world. That reduces the parallax to a minimum, which can easily be thought of as undetectable by the naked eye. This is the solution that is attested for Aristarchus.[6] The second is to suppose that the stars do vary in their distance from us, but *all* of them are so far away from the earth that no parallax is observable. One may guess that the reason for rejecting this is that the stars do not appear to the observer to differ much in magnitude and brightness.[7]

---

[3] Cf. Burkert (1972), IV.3 'The Cosmos of Philolaus'.
[4] Wehrli (1969), fragments 104–8. See Gottschalk (1980), 58–87.
[5] Heath (1913), 301–10.
[6] Archimedes, *Arenarius (Sand-Reckoner)* 1.4; translation in Cohen and Drabkin (1966), 108–9.
[7] Compare Kepler's arguments in *De stella nova serpentarii*, ch. 21 in his *Gesammelte Werke*, ed. Max Caspar (München: Beck, 1938), 1.253–4, quoted by Koyré (1957), 62–70. Kepler argues that however far away from the earth we suppose the stars to be, we must still accept that the region around the earth and the sun is peculiarly empty of stars, and different in this respect from the rest of the universe.

There are also reasons that one might say come more from the heart than from the head, or more from poetry than from science. Even the most mechanistic of Greek philosophers of nature retained elements of a different, non-mechanistic model of the world – the model that gets its most powerful expression in Plato's *Timaeus*. The world is a ZŌON, a living creature. But an animal needs a skin: the world's skin is its outer sphere. We find the analogy between the skin and the outer sphere of the cosmos drawn very explicitly in that strange and fascinating tract once thought to be by Hippocrates, *On Sevens*.[8] We find it in the words attributed to Leucippus and Democritus, who said that the world is enclosed in some kind of caul or membrane.[9] There is a tradition that Democritus was the first to call man a microcosm.[10] Lucretius substitutes the image of a walled city for that of the body, but that is not to be regarded as a very big shift, in view of the common association between the body and the social organization or body politic.[11]

There is just one hint in the direction of a quite different view that survives in the Doxographers, who say that according to Heracleides of Pontus every *star* is a world (*kosmos*) with its own earth and its own air.[12] This looks like a very promising theory, but unfortunately it is reported without any of its supporting context, and we are completely in the dark about its motivation. Heracleides is also credited with the statement that a man once fell to earth from the moon – the same origin that was assigned to the Nemean lion, and Helen.[13] Heracleides' star worlds may be equally lunatic. To be fair, it should be said that he wrote dialogues, and need not be thought of as subscribing to every view that is attributed to his pen.

We are justified, then, in leaving aside these eccentric viewpoints, and returning to the main theme: in classical times the antithesis to the Platonic–Aristotelian picture of the closed world was a view that itself accepted a kind of closed world, but asserted that this world is not the only thing that exists and not the only subject for philosophical inquiry. Some of the early Presocratics believed that outside the cosmos there is an unlimited supply of the stuff, whatever it was, from which the world grew.[14] The Stoics held that outside the cosmos there is an infinite extent of empty space. But the theory that has most significance is that outside the cosmos in which we live there is not only empty space but also matter, and moreover matter that forms itself into other worlds. This is the theory of Leucippus and Democritus, and Epicurus and Lucretius. It may perhaps have been held by earlier philosophers – that is a controversial point;[15]

---

[8] *De hebd.* 6. The relevant part of this text is most conveniently found, with commentary, in West (1971), 365–88.
[9] D–K 67A.1.32.
[10] D–K 68B.34.
[11] Lucretius, *De rerum natura* I.1102, II.1144, III.16, V.371.
[12] Wehrli (1969), fragment 113.
[13] *Ibid.* fragment 115.
[14] See Guthrie (1952), 87–104.
[15] I agree that infinite worlds should not be attributed to Anaximander or Anaxagoras: arguments in Kirk (1955), 21–38; Kahn (1960), 46–53; Vlastos (1959), 354–60.

I propose to concentrate on the Atomists.[16]

The significance of this introduction to their theory is this. We have now seen that even for those who believed in the infinite universe, direct evidence – the evidence of our eyes – is confined to the bounded world. Beyond the fiery ramparts of the world nothing can be *seen*, everything must be guessed. That is one way of looking at it. But the obverse of that thought must be considered too. If there is a boundary set between the visible world and the rest of the universe outside, what can be the *use* of speculating about what goes on outside? We are stuck where we are: the phenomena are what we want to explain. What help shall we get from a theory of what goes on beyond the stars? For Epicurus, who said that the only point of doing physics was to set the mind free from anxiety, the question appears to be a pressing one.[17]

But before we look directly at the ancient Atomists' theory, I propose to digress for a minute or two to introduce a character from the seventeenth century, who may ultimately prove to be illuminating.

The main work of rebutting the closed world of Aristotelian theory was done by Copernicus, Kepler, Galileo, and Newton. At the time, there was a great revival of interest in the rival Greek theories that had been defeated by Plato and Aristotle. One of the leaders of this revival was the Provençal priest Pierre Gassendi: but I want to quote from his English follower Walter Charleton, son of the Rector of Shepton Mallet, and physician to Charles the First. Apart from making a great and early reputation for himself as a physician, Charleton published specialized studies on two curiously assorted topics: Epicureanism and Stonehenge.

I want to quote briefly from the book Charleton published in 1654: *Physiologia Epicuro-Gassendo-Charletoniana: or a Fabrick of Science Natural upon the Hypothesis of Atoms, founded by Epicurus, repaired by Petrus Gassendus, augmented by Walter Charleton.*[18]

Charleton adopted the hypothesis of atoms; but he rejected just that feature of Greek Atomism that we are concerned with here. His second chapter has the title 'That this world is the Universe' (my distinction between the world and the universe has excellent seventeenth-century English authority). He concedes that there is 'an infinite Inanity or Ultramundane Space, yet can it *not* follow of necessity that there are Infinite Atoms contained in that Ultramundane Space, as Democritus and Epicurus preposterously infer: insomuch as it sounds much more concordant to reason, that there are no more Atoms, than those of which this single World was compacted'.

Charleton offers some criticism of what he takes to be the Greek Atomists' argument for an infinite universe containing many worlds, and then produces his

---

[16] Primary evidence for Democritus is collected in Luria (1970), fragments 343–66; for Epicurus, *Letter to Herodotus* 73–4; Lucretius II.1023–174.

[17] Epicurus, *Kyriai doxai* II.

[18] There is a fine reprint by the Johnson Reprint Corporation (New York, 1966). Cf. Osler (1979), 445–56.

own reasons for rejecting the idea: first, that there is no mention of it in the book of Genesis, which he calls 'Moses' inestimable diary or narrative of the Creation' and thus it is denied divine authority; and secondly, most of the ancient philosophers were against it, and so it lacks human authority.

He ends the chapter with a fine rhetorical paragraph, which is worth repeating:

> If any Curiosity be so immoderate, as to transgress the Limits of this All, break out of Trismegistus Circle, and adventure into the Imaginary Abyss of Nothing, vulgarly called the Extramundane Inanity; in the Infinity (or rather Indefinity) of which many long-winged Wits have, like seel'd Doves, flown to an absolute and total loss: the most promising Remedy we can prescribe for the reclaiming of such Wildness, is to advertise, that a serious Diversion of thought to the speculation of any the most obvious and sublunary natures will prove more advantageous to the acquisition of Science, than the most acute metaphysical Discourse, that can be hoped from the groveling and limited Reason of man, concerning that impervestigable Abstrusity; of which the more is said, the less is understood; and that the most inquisitive may find Difficulties more than enough within the little World of their own Nature, not only to exercize, but empuzle them. To which may be annexed that judicious Corrective of Pliny: 'Furor est, profecto furor est egredi ex hoc mundo, et tanquam interna eius cuncta plane iam sint nota, ita scrutari extera' ['It is madness, downright madness, to step out of this world, and to study whatever lies outside as if everything inside it were already well known.' (*Natural history* II.1.4)].

(p. 15)

Well, that gives point to our question: what was the motivation of this theory of a universe wholly beyond the reach of human senses? And if Charleton's Atomic Fabrick of Nature could do without the theory, why was it essential to the Greek Atomists?

The arguments of the earlier Greek Atomists, Leucippus and Democritus, as usual have to be retrieved from a largely hostile tradition. Aristotle mentions five arguments which, he says, are the plausible arguments in favour of the existence of an infinite.[19] The first is about the infinity of time, and the second about infinite divisibility; so these need not concern us now. Number three is that coming-to-be and passing away can be perpetual *only* if what comes-to-be is taken from an infinite source. Aristotle objects to this that it breaks down if coming-to-be and passing away are cyclical.[20] Since this is so obviously true, and was accepted by everyone who had been convinced by Parmenides that a thing that exists can never be annihilated, and the argument is not attributed to the Atomists, we can forget about it.

The fourth is this: that whatever is limited is always limited *against* something, and hence it follows that there *is* no ultimate limit, if one thing always has a limit against another. This is an argument with a venerable history going back at least as far as the Eleatic Melissus (that intellectual admiral who rather astonishingly

[19] Aristotle, *Physics* III.4.203 b 15–30.
[20] *Ibid.* 8.208 a 5–10.

defeated Pericles' navy at Samos in 441 B.C.).[21] A version of it was included by Epicurus in his 'elements of natural philosophy' in the *Letter to Herodotus*.[22]

The fifth, says Aristotle, is the principal argument, and the one that is most plausible. It is because there is no limit to the power of thinking of things that men attribute infinity to number, and to geometrical magnitude, and to the region outside the heavens. Archytas, the fourth-century Pythagorean, is credited with a picturesque version of this argument: 'If I were at the edge of the world, as it might be in the region of the fixed stars, could I stretch out my hand or a stick into the outer region or not?'[23] Lucretius uses the same argument, substituting a javelin for the prosaic stick.[24] The point is, of course, that if you *can't* throw the javelin out of the finite world, there must be something outside to stop it. If you *can* throw it, there must be somewhere outside for it to go.

However, both of these arguments, the fourth and the fifth, in so far as they are persuasive, prove only that there is *something* outside the cosmos. It might be totally empty space (perhaps a space inhabited by nothing but a few experimental javelins and triumphantly waving hands). We have not yet been told anything about the motivation of the more significant theory of a space containing innumerable worlds.

Aristotle continues the fifth reported argument in favour of the existence of the infinite with something more meaty: 'If what is outside the heavens is infinite, then it is thought that body is infinite too, and worlds. For why here, in the void, rather than there? Hence, if in one place, then in all places there should be bodily material.'

'Why here, in the void, rather than there?' It is an excellent question, and an essential clue to the true meaning of the theory. For Plato and for Aristotle, there is no problem here. We have a cosmos, in their theory, and it is an organized whole with a determinate boundary and therefore a determinate centre. The cosmos *has* no location: it *is* the location for everything else. There is no need to ask why it is here, rather than there.

But if anyone rejects Aristotle's arguments against the existence of void space, and accepts his opponents' arguments that there must be something outside the cosmos, then this question arises about the location of the cosmos as a whole. And it is a question with devastating impact in one respect above all: in the explanation of motion.

Aristotle based his theory of motion on the concept of the centre of the universe. He offered no explanation, but simply stated as an observed fact that heavy objects naturally move *towards* the centre of the universe, light objects move *away* from the centre, and the material of the heavens moves *around* the centre. This theory loses all plausibility when the centre of the universe – the focus of all this movement – is believed to be nothing but a point in a void. If the void is infinite,

[21] D–K 30B.6.
[22] *Letter to Herodotus* 41.
[23] Simplicius, *Physics* 467.26ff.
[24] Lucretius 1.968–79.

then it is doubtful if it makes any sense to talk about a centre at all. In any case, what can possibly be so special about one point in the void that makes *it* the focus of natural motion of the elements rather than any other place? 'Why here, in the void, rather than there?' People asked awkward questions about the behaviour of a piece of heavy matter in motion, when it reaches the centre of the universe, supposing that it could. Would it stop dead in its tracks? or go on for a while and then turn back, like a pendulum? Since it is supposed to be travelling through a void, which offers no resistance to anything, what possible reason can be given for its not continuing in the same direction? The centre cannot attract it, since it is just a point in the void, and the void has no attractive properties.

One way of solving this problem – the way taken by the Stoics, or some of them – was to suppose that all *matter* has a reciprocal attractive force. Since the void has no force whatever, and there is no counteracting force of repulsion, all the matter there is in the whole universe is naturally held together around a single centre. There is nothing special about the location of this centre in the void: it is simply the centre of gravity, so to speak, of all the matter in the universe, wherever it happens to be. What prevents the whole system from collapsing upon itself to form an extremely dense ball of matter (like the black holes of contemporary theory) is the natural tension of matter – a fairly mysterious property that keeps every kind of matter, in Stoic theory, at an approximately constant density.

So the Stoics were able to maintain the theory of a single, geocentric cosmos along with an infinite void. But this option was not available to the Atomists. It was not available because it would have meant attributing to matter a force of attraction that could not be reduced to collisions of atoms, whereas the only way in which atoms could interact, in Greek atomic theory, was by colliding with each other.

To the Atomists, then, it appeared that there was no answer to the question 'why here, rather than there, in the void?' The most plausible account seemed to be that matter is more or less evenly distributed *throughout* the void.

Now we come at last to the crucial question. The Atomists recognized the force of the arguments that showed, first, that outside the boundary of the world there is infinite empty space, and, second, that in this space there is an unlimited supply of matter, of the same kind as the matter of which our world is composed. The question is: what were they to suppose this matter does, what kind of motion were they to attribute to it?

Let us study this question for a moment from the epistemological point of view. It was a question about what lies beyond the phenomena. The phenomena we have to reckon with are the circular motions of the stars, the rectilinear motions of heavy and light bodies, together with the complexities of change of quality, and the growth, reproduction, and death of organic life. The Atomists reduced all of the latter to locomotions of atoms: they were left with what might appear to be an irreducible dualism – on the one hand, heavy bodies fall and light bodies rise in straight lines; on the other, the stars go round and round. The question they had to answer, then, was this: what is the relation between this observed dualism of circular and rectilinear motion, and the *un*observed motion of the atoms in the 'Extramundane Inanity'?

It is worth pausing briefly to reflect on the magnitude of this question of the two kinds of motion, and the way other philosophers handled it. For both Plato and Aristotle, this duality was of immense significance. Both made the contrast between circular and rectilinear motion a symbol of the contrast between the eternal and the transient, hence also between the psychical and the physical, even the divine and the mortal. By so doing, they were not necessarily taking the problem of the stars out of the realm of science altogether – one can be scientific about the soul and the gods, and to a degree they were – but they were at least setting up a *different* science of the stars, one in which the criteria for the acceptance of a conclusion were not the same as those in the science of perishable nature. The uniqueness of the cosmos, in their view, made it easier to do this. They did not have to work out the kind of explanation that would present our cosmos as an instance of a general law.

There is an argument of the Atomists that is relevant here.[25] It is an inductive argument. If we look around at the objects in the world of which we can get a clear view, we never find an instance that is the only one of its kind. Hence we should accept it as a universal truth that there is nothing unique. So if anything appears to be unique among the things that we cannot examine closely – for example, the sun, the moon, the earth – we should conclude that the appearance is misleading, and that there are other instances somewhere out of our view.

It is a consequence of this that our cosmos must be seen not as any kind of special case, but as a specimen of a kind. Any explanation of what goes on in the cosmos has to be capable of being generalized – given the same conditions elsewhere, the same results must be expected to follow.

How, then, are these considerations to be applied to the *dual* motions that are observed in the cosmos? It seems to be the circular motion that presents the main problem. A circle needs a centre, and there is no centre in the infinite void; so it is impossible to suppose, as Aristotle did, that there is a kind of matter which naturally moves in a circular orbit around a centre. The only possible conclusion was that the circular motion is a secondary, derivative motion: it depends on the formation of something with a centre.

In principle, it seems to me that there were just two options open to the Atomists when they faced the problem of inferring a theory of extramundane motion from the observed motion of matter inside the cosmos. Either they could accept rectilinear motion as basic, and try to show how circular motion could develop from it; or they could hold that there is *no* basic form of motion at all, and try to show how both circular motion and rectilinear motion due to weight might develop from the random wanderings or jostlings of atoms.

[25] Lucretius II.1077.

9

In principle, two options: but it seems perhaps too convenient and suspiciously neat that according to present-day orthodoxy Democritus chose the latter and Epicurus the former.

The evidence concerning Epicurus is much more direct and unambiguous, so we will take him first, out of chronological order.[26] In his theory, the basic motion is what we observe on earth as a rectilinear downward movement of free-falling heavy bodies. Upward motion, of fiery things (also basic and natural in Aristotle's system), was explained as being due to the pressure of more massive bodies crowding together – like a lemon pip squeezed between the fingers. The circular motion of the heavenly bodies is explained by analogy with various homely and familiar devices in which we see rectilinear motion translated into circular motion – basically, water-wheels.[27] The stars are part of a unified compound with earth at its centre, and the earth forms the hub of the star-wheels, which are blown or washed round by streams of atoms falling past in straight lines.

Now, viewed from some scientific points of view, this theory has all the marks of a disaster. In the first place, since there is no centre in the infinite void, no focal point at all, downward motion, which is basic, cannot be defined as in Aristotle's theory or the Stoic theory by its end point at the centre. It can be defined with the help of the axiom of parallels, but only if *some* line is taken as given. The Epicureans chose as the datum the line of free fall – that is to say, the line on which they observed things to fall, in the Garden at Athens – and asserted that everything that falls freely, anywhere in the infinite universe, falls parallel to this line. The disaster is, of course, that in fact Aristotle was right: a stone dropped at Athens does not fall parallel to a stone dropped at Stagira; they both fall towards the centre of the earth. The Epicurean theory demands that all downward fall should be parallel: that means that it works only if the earth is flat, since so far as can be observed, the line of fall is everywhere perpendicular to the earth's surface.

The second disaster was this: the chosen model (of water-wheels and sail-boats) offered no good explanation of the outstanding feature of star motion: its absolute regularity. Greek astronomy, with the help of the Near East, had already reached an advanced level of accuracy in predicting the positions of the stars, planets, sun and moon; they had already worked out sophisticated mathematical models for computing these positions. Now the Epicureans offered a theory that the heavens move because they are blown around – and the wind notoriously bloweth where it listeth, and never on schedule. The implausibility is compounded by the Epicurean habit of suggesting alternatives on matters that cannot be decided by direct inspection: perhaps it is a wind that blows outside, perhaps inside, perhaps it is more like a water-wheel. This kind of thing earned (and earns) contempt from astronomers.

[26] The most connected ancient account of the Epicurean theory is in Lucretius II.62–332.

[27] *Ibid.* v.509–33, 614–782. See Landels (1978), 16–27. Although water-wheels were familiar, there is no evidence for rotary windmills in classical antiquity. Lucretius imagines winds blowing the stars around, but quotes the analogy of water-wheels (516).

The situation illustrates a recurrent dilemma in ancient natural philosophy. Here we have a *physical* theory of the motion of stars that has the merits of needing no mythological props, and using nothing but familiar models drawn from the natural world – but it is a theory that is a mathematical disaster. On the other hand, we have a beautiful mathematical model, the model of concentric spheres, later patched up with epicycles, that is physically preposterous. The ancient world never succeeded in putting both models together.

Finally, back to Democritus, and to a problem which still seems extremely puzzling.

Practically no direct evidence survives. We hear from Aristotle that Democritus did not say what is the natural motion of bodies, but only that they move because of collisions.[28] That seems to mean that Democritus cannot have held the Epicurean theory of downward fall. We also hear that Democritus did not admit an *origin* of motion as a whole.[29] So it seems – this is the usual view nowadays – that according to Democritus the basic motion of atoms in the infinite void is a random jostling in which no factor but collision plays a part.

What interests us now is how Democritus derived from this formless jostling, if that is the correct picture, the two motions observable in our cosmos. We have some information about his derivation of circular motion. Instead of the water-wheel, Democritus chose the vortex or whirlpool – the *DINÊ* who Aristophanes said had usurped the kingdom of Zeus.[30] In certain conditions, we can observe water and wind spontaneously forming circular whirls, the most spectacular examples being the tornadoes and minor 'twisters' of the American Midwest, and similar phenomena in the Mediterranean world. We have to believe according to Democritus that star motions are the relic of such a whirl. One of the observed effects is that massive objects congregate at the centre of the whirl, where they are relatively exempt from the circular motion and come to a halt, while less sluggish objects fly out to the exterior and continue to whirl around. This is the model for the formation of the stationary, disc-shaped earth, with the heavenly bodies in circular orbits around it.

But does this model also explain why a stone dropped from a height falls of its own accord in a line perpendicular to this flat earth? Epicurus had no need to work out an explanation of this: it was the datum from which other motions were derived. But if Democritus did not follow that path, how *did* he explain the second one of the two motions in the cosmos?

Some of the standard modern books say that downward fall is one aspect of the tendency of heavy bodies to seek the centre of the whirl.[31] But that will not do. What needs to be explained is a linear motion at an angle to the central axis of the

---

[28] Aristotle, *De caelo* III.2.300 b 8.
[29] Aristotle, *Physics* VIII.1.250 b 18–21 (no names, but the attribution to the Atomists, confirmed by Simplicius, seems certain).
[30] D–K 68 B.167. Aristophanes, *Clouds* 380. See Ferguson (1971); Tigner (1974).
[31] For example, Guthrie II.410.

whirl, not from the circumference *to* the central axis.[32] It is true that some rectilinear up-and-down motions are produced by whirls: everyone has seen bits of paper rise vertically in a whirlwind, and notoriously boats get sucked down by whirlpools. But was that really the model that Democritus suggested to explain downward fall? Even if we concede that the initial whirl of atoms, at the time of the formation of the cosmos, might plausibly explain some features of the upward and downward distribution of matter in the cosmos, is there any plausibility in suggesting that the remainder of the original whirl, now confined to the outer shell of the cosmos, explains why a stone falls to earth here at the centre? If Democritus dropped a heavy pot to the floor of his house in Abdera, what could he say? He could not say, like Aristotle, that it is seeking the centre of the universe, as all heavy objects do; he could not say, like the Stoics, that it is attracted to the centre of all the material body in existence; he could not say, according to the orthodox account of his theory, like Epicurus, that this is just what every material body in the universe does if not prevented; could he really say, instead, that it fell down like that *because* the stars and the sun and moon out there are going round and round in a whirl? It seems very implausible.

Elsewhere I have offered some arguments for thinking that Democritus' view was after all similar to that of Epicurus, and included the idea of a natural downward motion of atoms, at right angles to the earth's flat surface.[33] But this is a very controversial position, which entails accusing Aristotle, our best source of information, of ignorance or of extremely ambiguous writing. For the present, this problem must be left undecided.

It can be asserted with confidence, however, that the problem of motion is what motivated the Atomists' theory of the infinite universe. Although it is not mentioned explicitly either in Aristotle's discussion of Democritus, or in Epicurus' *Letter to Herodotus*, it comes through clearly enough in Lucretius, especially in book v. And we can confirm it by reflecting on this question: what else in their philosophy of nature would the Atomists have had to give up, if they had abandoned the theory of an infinite universe containing plural worlds? I see no way in which they could have explained the dual motions of the cosmos without abandoning some vital first principle of their system. They would have had to abandon their simple theory of matter, and divide it into two different kinds, and in addition they would have had to attribute forces of attraction and repulsion to it, acting at a distance through the void or acting through some invisible, non-resistant material like the ether of early modern physics; or else they would have had to take an Aristotelian stance and treat the two motions as irreducible data of the universe; or else they would have had to reimport gods.

---

[32] Greek cosmologists who used the hypothesis of a vortex to explain the origin of the cosmos had to face the problem that the axis of the whirling stars is visibly not perpendicular to the horizon (in Greece). They commonly explained this by the *ad hoc* assumption that the heavens tilted somehow, after the formation of the earth. Democritus' version of this is reported by Aëtius II.12.2 (D–K 68A.96).

[33] See below, chapters 7 and 8.

It was this last option that enabled the seventeenth-century Atomist Walter Charleton to do without the postulate of plural worlds. In his view, God had created just that amount of matter needed for our world, and had endowed it with just those capacities for motion that enabled it to perform as it does. In a similar vein, Richard Bentley, in his *Confutation of Atheism*, argued at length against the Epicurean theory of the origin of our world in the infinite universe, because he saw it as a rival to the creation story.[34] The Epicurean theory was that given an infinite universe and infinite time, the matter in the universe, in random motion, must eventually produce everything that can be produced out of matter[35] – the argument later familiar with typewriting monkeys in the leading role. Bentley will not accept it: 'Let us suppose two ships, fitted with durable timber and rigging, but without pilot or mariners, to be placed in the vast Atlantic or the Pacific Ocean, as far asunder as may be; how many thousand years might expire before those solitary vessels should happen to strike one against the other?' By a calculation of his own, Bentley worked out that atoms are comparatively *further* apart from each other, and hence even less likely to collide. Hence, the infinite universe cannot give birth to the finite, organized cosmos without divine intervention.

Whatever may be thought of the plausibility of these two positions, there is at least this much to be said for the theory of the ancient Atomists – and it is something of great importance. They made the first bold effort to construct a unified theory of motion. They dispensed with the cosmic Mind of Anaxagoras, the forces of Love and Strife in Empedocles, the demiurge of Plato's *Timaeus* and the World Soul of the *Laws*. They had no need to postulate Aristotle's heavenly spheres, reeling with love for their divine Unmoved Mover, nor to add a fifth element endowed with natural spin. If unity and simplicity are virtues in an explanatory hypothesis, then those virtues can be set in the balance against the naiveté of some of the theory's detail.

[34] Richard Bentley, *Works*, ed. Alexander Dyce (London, 1836–8), III.158–62.
[35] Lucretius IV.416–31.

2

THE DYNAMICS OF THE EARTH: ANAXIMANDER, PLATO, AND THE CENTRIFOCAL THEORY

[1987]

INTRODUCTION

The world picture presented by the earliest surviving Greek literature is tolerably clear.[1] It consists of a flat earth, surrounded by the waters of the Ocean, with the solid dome of the heaven stretched over the top of all. Underneath is Tartarus, where the earth has its roots.[2] Tartarus is as far below the earth as the sky is above it. The sun makes a journey across the heavens every day and sinks into the Ocean at night, to make his way somehow around the earth and rise again in the east in the morning. The stars perform a similar journey at night, except that some of them, the Pole Star and those close to it, never dip into the Ocean at all.

The whole 'picture' shares a feature in common with non-metaphorical pictures: there is only one way in which it can be hung, so to speak. It has a top, the sky, and a bottom, Tartarus. In Hesiod's *Theogony*,

> An anvil made of bronze, falling from heaven,
> Would fall nine nights and days, and on the tenth
> Would reach the earth; and if the anvil fell
> From earth, would fall again nine nights and days
> And come to Tartarus upon the tenth.
>
> (*Theogony* 722–5, trans. Dorothea Wender)

The anvil *falls* downwards (κατιέναι is the verb); there is no doubt about its direction throughout.

But at the other chronological end of the history of Greek cosmology, the picture is of course quite different. The earth is no longer believed to be flat, but spherical. The sky is no longer a dome, but a sphere, with the earth situated at its centre. The sun, moon, planets, and stars circle around the earth once a day in orbits that are essentially circular, although the circles of the sun, moon, and planets shift their positions in complicated ways during the year. But the crucial

---

[1] The main texts are Homer, *Iliad* VIII.13 and XVIII.607; Hesiod, *Theogony* 116–34 and 726–45; Mimnermus, fragment 10 (Diehl); and Stesichorus VI.1–4 (Diehl).
[2] Hesiod, *Theogony* 728.

difference (for our present purposes) between this picture and the earlier one is that it is not possible now in the same way to assign a top and bottom to the picture. 'Up' and 'down' still have a meaning, but now 'up' means away from the centre towards the circumference, on a radius of the sphere, and 'down' means towards the centre. All points on the spherical surface of the sky are equally 'up' with respect to the earth.

It will be convenient to give names to these two contrasting world pictures. For the later one it is necessary to coin a name, because the existing words 'centrifugal' and 'centripetal' each capture only half of the point. So I shall coin the word 'centrifocal'. The other may be called 'linear' or 'parallel'; according to this model, the line of fall of any body is parallel to that of any other at any point on the earth's surface.

My introduction of falling bodies into cosmology at this early stage is quite deliberate: motion is a key concept in this field of speculation. It is this point that has been poorly appreciated, as it seems to me, in most earlier studies. The *shape* of the earth, the shape of the cosmos as a whole, and the position of the earth in the cosmos, constitute a set of questions that are habitually discussed together. Theory of motion is as a rule separated from these questions, and treated as if it were independent. But right from the beginning some experience of the phenomena of free fall must be presumed to form a part of the data. Builders knew how to build vertically to the earth's surface. As we shall see, one of the problems of early cosmology was presented by two observed facts that might appear to be inconsistent with each other: that a piece of earth, lifted up from the earth's surface, falls through the air if not supported, and that the whole earth, although perhaps surrounded by air, does not fall. Aristotle observes in this connection that it would be the mark of 'a rather lazy mind' (ἀλυποτέρας διανοίας: *De caelo* 294 a 13) not to raise this question, and in *De caelo* the theory of the motion of the sublunary elements occupies as much space as questions of the shape, size, and motion of the heavens.

In fact, the shift from the archaic world picture of Hesiod to the spherical cosmology of Aristotle constitutes a revolution of profound importance not only for the geometrical science of astronomy but also because of the accompanying radical change in ideas about motion. The Aristotelian centrifocal theory contained a feature that was to have great significance for many centuries: namely, a fundamental dualism in its theory of motion. In the region of the cosmos between the earth's surface and the moon's sphere the natural motions of the elements were in straight lines, either to or from the centre of the universe. In the region of the heavens, however, there was a different element, where natural motion was circular. These elements and their motions were not derivable from each other, and there was no interchange between them. They obeyed different laws. This was a dualism as important to Aristotle's philosophy as the dualism of soul and body was to Plato's.

The linear, parallel cosmology, on the other hand, was able to suggest a way in which linear motion could produce circular motion. One model was the watermill, in which the linear motion of the water is turned into a rotary motion in the wheel.[3] Perhaps there was some familiarity with similar devices operated by the wind, although windmills were a later invention. There were also circular swirls and eddies varying the linear motion of rivers, and tornadoes or 'twisters' produced by wind. Such models as these, projected on a scale that went beyond the range of the cosmos, showed how the cosmic vortex might get started in a situation where only linear motion prevailed.[4]

THE EVIDENCE OF ARISTOTLE CONCERNING THE MILESIANS

Thales, we are told by Aristotle himself, although not on his own authority, believed that the earth rests on water and stays where it is because it floats, like a piece of wood.[5] This is no great step away from the mythical picture of the world; we are in the frame of the linear cosmology. The earth is supported *underneath*; we live on the upper side. The earth needs support because it would otherwise fall downwards, like a piece of earth detached from the surface. Aristotle went on to object that Thales gave no reason why the supporting water itself did not fall – a good question, from his own point of view. But presumably for Thales the water constituted the bottom, like Tartarus in Hesiod's picture. Perhaps he retained a notion of the waters above and below the cosmos, as in the Near Eastern myths.

In the same chapter of his *De caelo*, Aristotle reports the theory of Anaximenes, that the earth is supported by air: being flat, 'it does not cut the air underneath but covers it like a lid' (ἐπιπωματίζειν: 294 b 16). It rides on the top of the air, says another source (ὀχεῖσθαι: Hippolytus, *Ref.* 1.7.4). Again there can be no doubt that Anaximenes set out to explain why the earth does not *fall*.

Xenophanes, from the nearby Ionian city of Colophon, is the first whose actual words on the subject have been preserved:

> Earth's upper limit here at our feet is seen,
> next to the air: the lower goes to infinity. (B28)

There is no support under the earth: the earth is its own foundation. The linear picture is still unmistakeable.

Anaximander, the middle one of the three famous Milesians, is not mentioned by Aristotle in company with the other two, but receives a brief and casual notice, in another context although still in the same chapter, *after* Aristotle has introduced his own theory of natural motion into the discussion. The passage must be quoted in full:

The majority, then, discourse about these causes [just described]. But some say that the earth remains where it is because of indifference (ὁμοιότης) – as, among the ancients,

---

[3] See Lucretius, *De rerum natura* V.513–16.
[4] See chapter 1.
[5] *De caelo* II.13.294 a 29.

Anaximander. For that which is set in the middle and is related all alike to the extremes is not obliged to move rather up or down or sideways; but it cannot move simultaneously in opposite directions; so of necessity it remains where it is.

Οἱ μὲν οὖν πλεῖστοι περὶ τὰς αἰτίας ταύτας διατρίβουσιν· εἰσὶ δέ τινες οἳ διὰ τὴν ὁμοιότητά φασιν αὐτὴν μένειν, ὥσπερ τῶν ἀρχαίων Ἀναξίμανδρος· μᾶλλον μὲν γὰρ οὐθὲν ἄνω ἢ κάτω ἢ εἰς τὰ πλάγια φέρεσθαι προσήκει τὸ ἐπὶ τοῦ μέσου ἱδρυμένον καὶ ὁμοίως πρὸς τὰ ἔσχατα ἔχον· ἅμα δ' ἀδύνατον εἰς τὸ ἐναντίον ποιεῖσθαι τὴν κίνησιν· ὥστ' ἐξ ἀνάγκης μένειν.

(De caelo II.13.295 b 10–16)

In a single clause in this passage Aristotle takes Anaximander out of the company of the Milesians and ranges him with more modern theorists, who were closer to his own centrifocal theory. What is described here is a theory that says the earth stays where it is because there is no *sufficient reason* for it to move in any direction. And Anaximander has received great praise in recent literature for his advanced ideas. 'He completely broke away from the popular idea that the earth must be supported by something concrete, that it must have "roots"; his theory of equilibrium was a brilliant leap into the a priori.'[6] 'Anaximander is clearly the precursor of the mathematical approach to astronomy developed later by the Pythagoreans, Eudoxus and Aristarchus.'[7]

In this chapter, I shall attempt to argue that such a theory at the time of Anaximander would be even more remarkable than has usually been supposed, and that the evidence for attributing it to Anaximander is not strong enough to bear so much weight.[8]

With regard to Aristotle's evidence, an obvious point must first be emphasized. Aristotle compares certain later thinkers, unnamed, with Anaximander as an example of the early philosophers, and his chief interest is in the later version of the theory. It happens that this later version can be identified, with something like certainty, as the theory advanced by Socrates in Plato's *Phaedo*, shortly before the concluding myth.

At 108c, Socrates claims that the earth is 'not of the form or size supposed by those who customarily talk about the earth', and adds that he has been persuaded of this by some unnamed person. He continues with a description of this unusual theory:

Well, I have been persuaded (he said) first that if it is in the middle of the heavens, being round in shape, then it has no need of air to prevent it from falling, nor of any other similar force, but the likeness of the heaven itself to itself everywhere suffices it, together with the equal balance of the earth itself. For something equally balanced, placed in the middle of

[6] Kirk and Raven (1957), 135.
[7] Kahn (1967).
[8] I know of two scholars who have taken the same view as myself: W. A. Heidel, and John Mansley Robinson. On the other side are most of the recent writers on the subject: Cornford, Kirk, Guthrie, Kahn, von Fritz, Classen, Dicks, West. For Freudenthal's view, see n. 20, below.

something all alike, will have no tendency to move any more or less in any direction, but being situated alike it will remain with no tendency to move.

Πέπεισμαι τοίνυν, ἦ δ' ὅς, ἐγώ ὡς πρῶτον μέν, ἐν μέσῳ τῷ οὐρανῷ περιφερὴς οὖσα, μηδὲν αὐτῇ δεῖν μήτε ἀέρος πρὸς τὸ μὴ πεσεῖν μήτε ἄλλης ἀνάγκης μηδεμιᾶς τοιαύτης, ἀλλὰ ἱκανὴν εἶναι αὐτὴν ἴσχειν τὴν ὁμοιότητα τοῦ οὐρανοῦ αὐτοῦ ἑαυτῷ πάντῃ καὶ τῆς γῆς αὐτῆς τὴν ἰσορροπίαν· ἰσόρροπον γὰρ πρᾶγμα ὁμοίου τινὸς ἐν μέσῳ τεθὲν οὐχ ἕξει μᾶλλον οὐδ' ἧττον οὐδαμόσε κλιθῆναι, ὁμοίως δ' ἔχον ἀκλινὲς μενεῖ.

(*Phaedo* 108E–109A)

The verbal parallels are too close to be coincidental.[9] It is theoretically possible that both Aristotle and Plato were drawing on a common source – perhaps the 'someone' who persuaded Socrates, if he is not a fiction. But this is unlikely: Aristotle has already alluded unmistakeably to *Phaedo* 99C in a rather similar context in chapter 1 of the same book (284 a 20). There are two differences between Aristotle's description and the *Phaedo* passage: Aristotle does not mention that the earth itself has the property of equilibrium or that it is 'round', and he locates the 'likeness' in the relation of the earth to the limits of heaven, rather than in the quality of the heaven itself. Perhaps his idea is that this relation is just what Plato meant when he spoke of the equilibrium of the earth. In any case, Simplicius was in no doubt that Aristotle had Plato in mind here, and that seems pretty clearly right.

Who was the 'someone' who persuaded Socrates? Not Anaximander, certainly. Plato never mentions or otherwise alludes to Anaximander. The perfect tense of the verb suggests a fairly recent 'conversion', from personal contact rather than by written work. The 'someone' may perhaps be no more than a fiction, designed to distance Socrates a little from this new theory, in view of his avowed lack of interest in cosmology (*Apol.* 19C), and perhaps for another reason that will be suggested below, in the last section of this chapter. Plato not infrequently has Socrates learning from others, as a device for putting non-typical material into Socrates' mouth.[10]

Aristotle's criticisms of the theory he describes make it clear that there are differences between it and his own centrifocal theory.

This [theory] is clever, but not true. According to this argument whatever is set in the middle should remain where it is: even fire will remain at rest, since the property described is not peculiar to earth.

---

[9] *Phaedo*
τὴν ὁμοιότητα
ὁμοίου τινὸς ἐν μέσῳ τεθέν

οὐχ ἕξει μᾶλλον οὐδ'ἧττον
οὐδαμόσε κλιθῆναι
ὁμοίως ἔχον

De caelo
τὴν ὁμοιότητα
ἐπὶ τοῦ μέσου ἱδρυμένον
ὁμοίως πρὸς τὰ ἔσχατα ἔχον
μᾶλλον ... οὐθὲν ἄνω ἢ κάτω
ἢ εἰς τὰ πλάγια φέρεσθαι προσήκει
ὁμοίως προς τὰ ἔσχατα ἔχον

[10] Diotima is of course the most striking example (*Symp.* 201 Dff). Other examples, more or less close, are *Phaedr.* 274C5; *Lysis* 215C4; *Gorgias* 493A2.

But in addition, it is superfluous, since the earth manifestly not only rests at the centre, but also moves to the centre. For wherever any part of it moves, the whole must move there also. And where it is natural for it to move to, there it is natural for it to rest. So it does not rest because it is related all alike to the extremes; that is a property shared by all the elements, but motion towards the centre is peculiar to earth.

τοῦτο δὲ λέγεται κομψῶς μέν, οὐκ ἀληθῶς δέ· κατὰ γὰρ τοῦτον τὸν λόγον ἀναγκαῖον ἅπαν, ὅ τι ἂν τεθῇ ἐπὶ τοῦ μέσου, μένειν, ὥστε καὶ τὸ πῦρ ἠρεμήσει· τὸ γὰρ εἰρημένον οὐκ ἴδιόν ἐστι τῆς γῆς. – ἀλλὰ μὴν οὐδ' ἀναγκαῖον. οὐ γὰρ μόνον φαίνεται μένουσα ἐπὶ τοῦ μέσου, ἀλλὰ καὶ φερομένη πρὸς τὸ μέσον. ὅπου γὰρ ὁτιοῦν φέρεται μόριον αὐτῆς, ἀναγκαῖον ἐνταῦθα φέρεσθαι καὶ τὴν ὅλην· οὖ δὲ φέρεται κατὰ φύσιν, καὶ μένει ἐνταυθοῖ κατὰ φύσιν. οὐκ ἄρα διὰ τὸ ὁμοίως ἔχειν πρὸς τὰ ἔσχατα· τοῦτο μὲν γὰρ πᾶσι κοινόν, τὸ δὲ φέρεσθαι πρὸς τὸ μέσον ἴδιον τῆς γῆς.

(295 b 16–25)

In this theory, Aristotle goes on to say, the earth stays where it is 'because of the compulsion (ἀνάγκη) of the likeness' (b 30). In his own cosmology the earth's motionlessness needs no explanation because it is in its natural place. He accuses Plato (assuming that the theory in question is that of the *Phaedo*) of offering a kind of mechanical explanation: the earth stays where it is because it is similarly related to the extremes. Perhaps he has in mind Plato's later views, as given in the *Timaeus*, where centripetal and centrifugal motions of the elements are due to like-to-like attraction: a part of earth or fire, detached from the mass of its element, is drawn towards the mass. Hence he interprets Plato's words in the *Phaedo*, 'the likeness of the heaven itself to itself everywhere suffices it, together with the equal balance of the earth itself', as meaning a dynamic relationship between earth at the centre and the heavens at the circumference.

And no doubt this is right. Plato may not yet have worked out the detail of the *Timaeus* theory, but he makes a point that would be equally true in the *Timaeus* theory: that whatever forces act on the earth owing to its own nature and that of the heavens are all equal in all directions from the centre. In that sense, the *Phaedo* too expresses a centrifocal dynamics. Fortunately, Plato makes it perfectly clear that he is not talking of a linear theory in which the earth is somehow supported in equilibrium in spite of a natural tendency to fall downwards; this is made clear by his statement: 'it has no need of air to prevent it from falling, nor of any other similar force' (108E5). He thus contrasts his new theory with the sort of thing that he had learnt from the earlier philosophers of nature (*Phaedo* 99B).

It follows that if this whole theory is to be attributed to Anaximander, including the proposition that the earth needs no underpropping, we must attribute to him some kind of centrifocal dynamics too. That is to say, we have no minor difference between him and his two Milesian colleagues, Thales and Anaximenes, but a difference of enormous significance: nothing less than the abandonment of the archaic world view, and the substitution of something that Plato presents as a surprising novelty nearly 200 years later.

Before moving on to other evidence about Anaximander, we may return briefly to Aristotle's text. This chapter of *De caelo* consists of a review of previous theories of the earth's position and shape, and its motion or motionlessness. On the latter subject, Aristotle mentions by name Xenophanes, Thales, Anaximenes, Anaxagoras, Democritus, and Empedocles, before he comes to Anaximander. All those mentioned earlier held some kind of theory of the underpropping of the earth, and Aristotle describes it. It is clear, therefore, that he is contrasting Anaximander with the others. If it were not for this context, we might suppose from his wording that Aristotle was perhaps attaching only the word 'likeness' to Anaximander, and not the whole of the *Phaedo* theory. Even given the context, I am inclined to think that the explanation lies somewhere in this area. Xenophanes mentioned the infinity of earth's lower limit, Thales claimed that it floats on water; Anaximenes, Anaxagoras, and Democritus spoke of its flatness, which allowed it to float on air like a frisbee, and Empedocles held that it was somehow supported by the vortex motion of the cosmos. But Anaximander singled out *likeness* as the cause of its motionlessness. Whether Aristotle knew this or not, it may be that Anaximander meant no more than that the earth, being supported on a cushion of air, is held in equilibrium by the air all round it. The earth is equally balanced in the sense that it is not heavier on one side than on another. The air is equally distributed on all sides of the earth. 'Likeness' may refer to either or perhaps to both of these factors.

This idea, although it may sound like a piece of special pleading, receives support from Simplicius' comment on the passage in question. He asks why Aristotle mentions Anaximander at all, since it is plainly the *Phaedo* that he has in mind, and answers that perhaps Aristotle felt qualms about criticizing Plato directly, but no such objection to criticizing Anaximander. At the end of his comment, he tells us that Anaximander held that the earth stays where it is *'because of the air that holds it up* and because of its equal balance and likeness'.[11] Confused, say the historians. But perhaps it is right after all.

OTHER EVIDENCE ABOUT ANAXIMANDER

Hippolytus, who is believed to follow Theophrastus on Presocratic doctrines, reports the following about Anaximander:

The earth is aloft, not held in the power of anything but remaining where it is because of its like distance from all things.

(*Ref.* 1.6.3)

The earth is 'aloft (μετέωρον)': that means it is up in the air, suspended somehow. 'Raised from off the ground' is the first English equivalent given in the Greek lexicon (Liddell–Scott–Jones). It has been claimed that the expression 'not held in the power of anything (ὑπὸ μηδενὸς κρατουμένην)' adds something that is not already to be found in Aristotle or Plato.[12] I think rather that the whole phrase

---

[11] Simplicius, *De caelo* 531.32ff.
[12] Kahn (1960a) p. 80.

means no more than Plato's expression, 'it has no need of air to prevent it from falling, nor of any other similar force (ἀνάγκη)'.[13] I conclude that Hippolytus' testimony is taken from Aristotle by someone who knew he was referring to our passage in the *Phaedo* – Theophrastus, no doubt. There is no reason to think Hippolytus adds anything that is not to be found in our passage of Aristotle. If the suggestion made at the end of my last section is right, it is not true of Anaximander, who would have to concede that the earth is 'in the power of' air.

Diogenes Laertius and the Suda (D–K 1.81.10 and 82.9) report that Anaximander put the earth in the centre, but they give no reason. Eudemus (fragment 145 Wehrli, *ap.* Theo Smyrnaeus) claims that Anaximander made the earth 'move around the centre of the cosmos'; but this unique statement, contradicted by the testimonia which say that Anaximander's earth is at rest, is often rejected as being textually corrupt.[14] It seems most likely to be wrong.

We have a very definite report of Anaximander's view of the shape of the earth: it is cylindrical, three times as wide as it is high.[15] This is confirmed by other sources which state that it is shaped like the drum of a pillar.[16] It has two surfaces, 'one on which we walk, and the other is opposed to this'.[17] It has sometimes been claimed that this quotation is defective, and it should continue with a mention of antipodeans walking on the opposed surface, but that is pure conjecture.

It is difficult to combine a flat earth with centrifocal dynamics. It would be easier to imagine some kind of reciprocal dynamics, in which heavy bodies fall vertically towards each of the two surfaces of the earth, but there is no evidence of the existence of such a theory. If lines of fall truly converge on the centre from all directions, and the earth, being flat, lies at the centre, it follows that falling bodies arrive at the earth's flat surface at all angles from horizontal to vertical. Even supposing the Greek world is the centre of the earth, so that at Delphi all lines of fall might be thought of as theoretically vertical, at the extremes of the known world falling bodies should have been observed to fall at an angle. The contradiction of the theory with observable phenomena seems too obvious for the theory to be credible.

At the beginning of the cosmos, 'a certain ball of flame grew around the air that is around the earth, like bark around the tree'. This report on Anaximander, from pseudo-Plutarch's *Stromateis* 2 (D–K A.10), carries some conviction as a genuinely archaic piece of cosmology. If it is genuine, it helps to align Anaximander with Thales and Anaximenes as being used to picture the world as an organism. Thales, Aristotle suggests, chose water as the origin of the world because the seed of all things is moist (*Metaph.* 1.3.983 b 21); Anaximenes chose air instead of water, thinking of the breath of life (fragment 2); Anaximander, according to this same

---

[13] The equivalence of ἀνάγκη and κρατεῖν in this context is shown neatly by the phrase attributed to Thales by the doxographers: ἰσχυρότατον ἀνάγκη, κρατεῖ γὰρ τοῦ παντός (Aëtius 1.25.1).
[14] D–K 12A.26n., κεῖται for κινεῖται; Burkert (1972), 345, n.38 suggests ἀκίνητος.
[15] Pseudo-Plutarch, *Stromateis* 2 = D–K A.10.
[16] Aëtius III.9.2 = D–K A.25; Hippolytus, *Ref.* 1.6.3 = D–K A.11.
[17] Hippolytus, following ref. in last note.

passage of the *Stromateis*, wrote that the first thing to be secreted in the Boundless was the seed of Hot and Cold, and it was from this that the ball of flame and the tree-like cosmos grew.

This is far from the imagery of geometry and the centrifocal cosmos. One might rather think that Anaximander's drum-shaped earth was held in its position in the middle of the cosmos in much the same way as the internal organs of the body are held in place, by being supported evenly all round.[18] This is in fact close to one of the images used later by the Epicureans for precisely this case in their own cosmology:

> For every man, his own members have no weight, and his head does not burden his neck; nor is the whole weight of the body felt to rest on the feet; whereas whatever weights are external and imposed on us – these are a pain to us, smaller though they often are. To that extent it matters much what role each thing has. So, then, is the earth no foreign body suddenly put in and thrust from elsewhere on the alien air.
>
> (Lucretius, *De rerum natura* V.540–7)

The earth floats as effortlessly in the air as the parts of the body are supported effortlessly (it is alleged) by each other.

It is important to be clear how this differs from the *Phaedo* cosmology and, still more, from the fully developed centrifocal dynamics of Aristotle. Holding a theory of this kind, it would be impossible for Anaximander to say, as Socrates says in the *Phaedo*, 'it has no need of air to prevent it from falling, nor of any other similar force'. The earth does indeed need air to prevent it from falling: it needs, and gets, *even* support from the air all round, and this keeps it in place in the middle. Anaximander's inspiration is not geometrical, if this is right, at least in this part of his cosmology. It is true that he wrote about the circles of the stars, and gives numerical values for the relative distances of the sun and the moon from the earth, in terms of the diameter of the earth's disc.[19]

But this is not enough to warrant the inference to a centrifocal dynamic theory. Moreover, Anaximander's argument does not depend on the Principle of Sufficient Reason, unless we are to suppose that every case of physical balance is an exercise of this principle. It is not that the earth has no reason to move, but that although there *is* reason for it to *fall* it is prevented from doing so by the equal support of the air all around.[20]

---

[18] Freudenthal (1986) suggests the earth is more like the root of the tree. But what is the tree rooted in?
[19] See Burkert (1963).
[20] Freudenthal (1986) reaches the right conclusion, that the equilibrium that keeps the earth in place arises from Anaximander's physics, not from an abstract metaphysical principle (p. 213). But he locates this equilibrium in the inertia that belongs to earth as a substance that is passive unless activated by heat. But the Milesian question was: Why does the earth not fall if it rests on nothing more substantial than air? I doubt if the earth could have been thought of as so passive that it could not even fall. That idea seems to belong to a rather sophisticated conception of weight.

A NOTE ON THE CENTRIFOCAL THEORY AND THE SPHERICAL EARTH

In our passage of the *Phaedo* Socrates presents the doctrine of the 'round' earth, which needs no support from the air because it is in equilibrium and situated in the middle of the uniform sky, as a new and strange doctrine. The Athenians of his time, according to Plato's testimony in the *Apology* (26D), were familiar with the cosmology of Anaxagoras, who supposed the earth was flat. Aristophanes' *Clouds* bears witness to their familiarity with Diogenes of Apollonia, who thought the earth was supported on air.[21] Herodotus clearly had a flat earth in mind when he wrote on the subject of the gold-digging ants (III.104). These giant ants are found in India, and the Persian king, he says, has some brought to him by hunters. When they dig their homes, they throw up gold dust along with the sand. The Indians go after this gold at the hottest time, when the ants burrow down to get out of the heat; and the hottest time of day in India is in the morning, not at noon as in Greece, and in the afternoon it is only as hot as it is in the morning elsewhere. In the East, it appears, the sun in his path across the sky arrives overhead earlier in the day and so warms the earth up earlier than elsewhere.

What is new in the *Phaedo* and dialogues of about the same date is an interest in the Italians. Presumably this followed upon Plato's first visit to South Italy. If we remove Anaximander from consideration, there are no centrifocalists among the Ionians. So it looks very likely that this kind of world picture originated in the West. Socrates, of course, paid no visit to Italy, but Plato has already, in the *Phaedo*, set up a scenario for acquainting him with Western ideas, in that he is described in conversation with Simmias and Kebes, both of whom have been listening to the Pythagorean Philolaus. Philolaus himself could hardly be quoted as a source for Socrates' new cosmological theory, because he was known for his doctrine of a central fire around which the earth moves.[22] So Socrates, having been moving in Pythagorean circles, has been persuaded by 'someone' of a new cosmology.

But before going any further, we should first split the issues. Perhaps it is possible that some cosmologist argued for a spherical earth without also embracing a centrifocal dynamic theory, or vice versa. We have already spoken of the conceptual difficulty of combining the two kinds of cosmology, but in considering the evidence it will be clearer if we keep the shape of the earth separate from the dynamics.

Concerning the early history of the problem of the earth's shape, one may be forgiven for despairing from the outset of the inquiry. Doxographers and scholars, ancient and modern, have committed themselves to statements that are as firm and unambiguous as they are contradictory. It would be tedious and pointless to go over the ground again: the evidence can be found collected by Heidel (1937), or

---

[21] D–K 64A.16a. But Diogenes Laertius says he thought it was 'round' (στρογγύλην) and fixed in the centre (IX.57).

[22] Aëtius III.11.3 = D–K 44A.17.

Burkert (1972). The first firm description we have of a spherical earth is in our passage of the *Phaedo*; those who have argued that even here the earth is not thought of as spherical but only as 'round' in some other way are not convincing. However, I see no reason to disbelieve the statement of Diogenes Laertius, based on Theophrastus as he declares it is, that Parmenides was the first to speak of the earth as spherical (IX.21–2).[23]

The matter is complicated by the strange Hippocratic text *De hebdomadibus*, about which there has been much controversy. It has been claimed (a) that the cosmology contained in this text is very early – as early as Anaximander himself;[24] and (b) that it regards the earth as spherical. As to (b), both the reading and the meaning of the text are very uncertain. What is particularly interesting is that it appears to regard 'up' and 'down', and also 'left' and 'right' as relative matters. The relativization of 'up' and 'down' does not immediately entail a centrifocal dynamic theory, but it is certainly in contradiction with the linear cosmology of Thales, Anaximenes, and the rest, who support the earth *underneath*. In fact the author of the *De hebdomadibus* asserts both that 'up' and 'down' are relative, and that the earth is supported on, or rather 'in', the air. In spite of Kranz's claim[25] that what is said in this chapter might apply equally to various 'round' shapes, such as cylinders or eggs, I think it likely that the author is presupposing a spherical earth.

This is, however, much less startling than it might once have seemed, since Jaap Mansfeld has argued very persuasively that the whole treatise belongs to a much later date, quite late in the Hellenistic period.[26] If this is correct, we need no longer allow ourselves to be confused by it.

If Parmenides remains as the best-attested pioneer of the spherical earth, he is also the strongest candidate for the honour of having invented the centrifocal dynamic theory. This is, in a way, thoroughly paradoxical, because he and his successors claimed that motion itself was no more than a matter of seeming, without status in true being. Nevertheless, his Way of Truth expresses the equations necessary for centrifocal dynamics. What is unclear is what we are to take the range of application of these equations to be; the subject of the following lines is nothing more specific than 'what is':

> But since there is an outermost limit, it is perfected
> from all sides, like the mass of a well rounded ball,
> equally balanced from the centre everywhere. For neither greater
> nor smaller must it be in one place or another.
> For neither is there Not-Being, which might stop it reaching
> its like, nor is there Being such as to be

[23] Not Thales, as Diogenes says elsewhere, less carefully. Morrison (1955) argues against a spherical earth in Parmenides.
[24] Roscher (1913), 117ff.
[25] Kranz (1944), 183.
[26] Mansfeld (1971); see also the review of Mansfeld's book by Thesleff (1973).

more than Being here, less there, since all is inviolate.
For equal to itself from all sides, it lies uniformly in its limits.

(B8.42–9)

αὐτὰρ ἐπεὶ πεῖρας πύματον, τετελεσμένον ἐστί
πάντοθεν, εὐκύκλου σφαίρης ἐναλίγκιον ὄγκωι,
μεσσόθεν ἰσοπαλὲς πάντηι. τὸ γὰρ οὔτε τι μεῖζον
οὔτε τι βαιότερον πελέναι χρεόν ἐστι τῆι ἢ τῆι.
οὔτε γὰρ οὐκ ἐὸν ἔστι, τό κεν παύοι μιν ἱκνεῖσθαι
εἰς ὁμόν, οὔτ' ἐὸν ἔστιν ὅπως εἴη κεν ἐόντος
τῆι μᾶλλον τῆι δ' ἧσσον, ἐπεὶ πᾶν ἐστιν ἄσυλον.
οἱ γὰρ πάντοθεν ἶσον, ὁμῶς ἐν πείρασιν κύρει.

There are several close parallels between this text and what Plato says of the οὐρανός in our passage of the *Phaedo*. We have in both texts a geometric concept of a sphere as the limit of all lines of equal length radiating from the centre. But more significantly we have the same ideas about the dynamics operative within the sphere, and they are explored in similar language. Plato stresses 'the likeness of the heaven itself to itself everywhere'; Parmenides says of his subject that it must be 'neither greater nor smaller in one place or another' and it cannot be 'more here, less there' than itself, but must be 'equal to itself from all sides'. Parmenides twice uses a word of the same root as Plato's 'likeness': Plato has the noun ὁμοιότης (likeness), the adjective ὅμοιος and the adverb ὁμοίως; Parmenides has a noun ὅμον and an adverb ὁμῶς.

Parmenides also says that it is 'equally balanced from the centre everywhere' (ἰσοπαλές). Whereas the rest of his description might be interpreted, without this word to guide us, as referring only to equality of spatial extension and uniformity in some unspecified quality, ἰσοπαλές implies equality of *force*. It is used of well-matched armies by Herodotus (I.82) and Thucydides (IV.94). The παλ- root is akin to παλαίειν, 'to wrestle': Pindar uses the compound adjective δυσπαλῆς, 'hard to wrestle'. I see no reason, in view of this etymology, to agree with those who devalue the word and take it to mean nothing more than 'equal'.[27]

This passage of Parmenides' Way of Truth gives us only an abstract framework for a centrifocal dynamic theory. The earth is not mentioned or implied. The reference of Parmenides' lines has aroused much controversy, and will no doubt continue to do so. Some take him to be making statements of the utmost abstractness about whatever has a claim to 'be', with no specific reference to the cosmos; thus the 'well-rounded ball' is just a simile.[28] Others, with whom I am more inclined to agree on this point, believe his subject is\not the properties of 'being' as such, but the properties of the whole of what *is* as a matter of fact: that is, the universe.

Whatever may be the truth about Parmenides' meaning in this respect, it is clear that it is only necessary to identify the 'well-rounded ball' with the universe and to

---

[27] For example, Guthrie II.43–4; but there are many who take the same view.
[28] E.g. Owen (1960).

supply the earth at the centre of it to have a centrifocal cosmology that coincides almost exactly with Socrates' 'new' cosmology described in our passage of the *Phaedo*. Since the 'balance' is equal in all directions around the centre, there will be no sufficient reason for the earth to incline in any direction. The Principle of Sufficient Reason, then, already introduced by Parmenides with regard to the origin of what *is* (B8.9–10), will explain why the earth stays where it is, or show why it needs no explaining.

3

NOTES ON PARMENIDES

[1973]

PARMENIDES GOES TO THE HOUSE OF NIGHT

There is a set of problems, much discussed in the literature, concerning the nature of the journey described in B1 of Parmenides, its destination, the revelation made to him by the goddess, and the connection between the symbolism of B1 and the two forms, Light and Night, which are the principles of the cosmology of the Way of *Doxa*. Some of these problems, I believe, have now been solved. The solution, which is mainly the work of scholars writing in German,[1] has been either overlooked or rejected by the English-speaking community,[2] and it seems worthwhile drawing attention to it and developing it.

The first essential point lies in the interpretation of B1.8–10:

> ... ὅτε σπερχοίατο πέμπειν
> Ἡλιάδες κοῦραι προλιποῦσαι δώματα Νυκτός
> εἰς φάος ὠσάμεναι κράτων ἄπο χερσὶ καλύπτρας.

Printed thus, without punctuation, the passage appears at first sight to contain two participial phrases describing the Sun-Maidens: they have previously (aorist) left the House of Night and come into the Light, and they have pulled their veils from their heads with their hands. Diels–Kranz, however, and other editors print commas before and after προλιποῦσαι δώματα Νυκτός; and then, of course, we can take εἰς φάος with the verb σπερχοίατο πέμπειν – 'the Sun-Maidens, having left the House of Night, hasten to escort me into the Light'.

Which is the more natural reading of the Greek? The elliptical construction λιπεῖν ... εἰς, 'to leave (and move) to ...', is well attested, as in the following examples listed in Kühner–Gerth:[3]

ἐβουλεύοντο ἐκλιπεῖν τὴν πόλιν εἰς τὰ ἄκρα τῆς Εὐβοίης

(Herodotus VI.100)

---

[1] The essential suggestion was made, without much argument, by Morrison (1955). For detailed arguments, see Mansfeld (1964) 222–61, and Burkert (1969).
[2] For example, by Guthrie II, Tarán (1965), myself (1967a), Kahn (1969), and Mourelatos (1970), 15 and n. 19.
[3] *Syntax* I, § 447. These examples are quoted by Mansfeld (1964), 238.

τὴν πόλιν ἐξέλιπον οἱ ἐνοικοῦντες εἰς χωρίον ὀχυρὸν ἐπὶ τὰ ὄρη.
(Xenophon, *Anabasis* 1.2.24)

ἐάν τις λίπῃ τὴν τάξιν εἰς τοὐπίσω.

(Lysias xiv.5)

There can be no doubt that it is relatively awkward and therefore implausible to construe εἰς φάος with πέμπειν.

Why, then, have so many editors followed Diels and read the lines in the less natural way? The motive lies, of course, in the presupposition that Parmenides' journey is *into the light*, and there is no way of allowing B1 to say this unless εἰς φάος is construed with πέμπειν. Sextus, our source for B1, although he gave an allegorical account of it, in fact took εἰς φάος neither with πέμπειν nor with προλιποῦσαι but with ὠσάμεναι; but he could do this only because of the complex details of his allegory – the Sun-Maidens stand for vision, and vision is impossible without light. Later interpreters, however, perhaps with Plato's cave or simply with the metaphor of *enlightenment* in mind, have determinedly insisted that the actual journey of Parmenides is from darkness into light.

It is a necessary consequence of this view that the topography described in B1 is vague: 'the topography of the journey is blurred beyond recognition' (Mourelatos (1970), 15). 'The journey is not narrated stage by stage, but the keypoints are brought out in an impressionistic manner' (Guthrie II.9). This ought perhaps to be more than a little embarrassing, since Parmenides' main concern is to chart a route – not this route, certainly; but one failure in map-reading leads to others.

Much of the difficulty vanishes when we accept that the destination of the journey is not the region of light. It is not Parmenides but the Sun-Maidens who leave the House of Night and come into the light, and they come to meet Parmenides and take him back home with them – back into the House of Night. The journey is not a new type of allegory but a *katabasis* of a familiar kind.[4]

The description of the journey can now be read in a reasonably straightforward manner. In general, Parmenides in this fragment uses present tenses for permanent features, imperfects to denote the continuing activities of his journey, aorists to denote events that took place before these activities, and then aorists for the particular actions involved in his reception by the goddess.[5] He set off from earth, pulled in a chariot by horses that take him 'as far as my heart might desire', on the road of the goddess – that is, the road that leads to the goddess, or leads the goddess to earth if she wants to come.[6] It is a road that takes 'the man who

---

[4] The most famous is Odysseus' journey to the underworld in search of information about his route in *Odyssey* XI; the connection between Parmenides B1 and *Odyssey* XI was pointed out most persuasively by Havelock (1958). Others are the experiences of Epimenides of Crete, Orpheus, and Pythagoras, for which see Burkert (1969), 16–29.

[5] There is only one journey. I was wrong about this in my article (1967a). The chief problem is the optatives in lines 1 and 8, which look like frequentative optatives. For the right explanation, see Mourelatos (1970), 17, n. 21.

[6] Cf. *Iliad* III.406.

knows' past all the cities.[7] The reading κατὰ πάντ' ἄστη has been thrown into doubt again by Coxon (1968): to avoid becoming tangled in controversy, let us say that the main idea is probably that of a long distance. The 'man who knows', as Burkert has convincingly shown, is the initiated man.[8] The word does not imply that he already knows what the goddess will tell him after he has arrived, but only that as an initiate he need not fear the journey into a mysterious place and is ready for the revelation.

The Sun-Maidens came into the region of light to escort him, having left the House of Night. 'Here' (ἔνθα; line 11), at or near the House of Night, 'are the gates of the roads of Night and Day'. The gates do not separate the road of Night from the road of Day, as some have thought; they are the gates through which both Day and Night pass when they emerge, alternately, from their home and go out along their 'roads' (sc. the same road, but traversed alternately by Night and Day) over all the earth. Justice holds the key;[9] the Maidens persuaded her with soft words to admit the stranger, and they led the chariot, with Parmenides aboard, through the open gates into the vast chasm (χάσμ' ἀχανές) beyond. The goddess, who is not named and probably not meant to be identified,[10] welcomed him and began her μῦθος (B2.1).

The chief importance of all this lies in Parmenides' destination. The House of Night has a clear place in Greek mythology, since Hesiod's Theogony (740ff). It lies on the edge of the world, where Earth, Tartarus, Sea, and Heaven have their sources, and where a mysterious bottomless chasm gapes open; even gods find it terrifying. That the sun, as well as Night, is at home here is proved by Stesichorus,[11] who writes that the sun in the evening hurries 'to cross the ocean to the depths of holy dark Night, to his Mother, his young wife and his children'. It was Darkness that gave birth to Light in Hesiod's Theogony (123ff); and the sun's children of course include Parmenides' escort.

The essential point about this place is that it is the meeting-place, where opposites are undivided. Here there is no meaning in the familiar oppositions between Earth and Sky, Earth and Tartarus, Earth and Sea, because this is their common origin. Parmenides makes reference to this point when he says that the great gate has a threshold of stone and aetherial doors. But most significantly of all, Night and Day are both at home here; it is here that they meet.

A rationalistic objector might say that since Day and Night are never at home together, the House of Night is just the obverse of the world outside. When it is dark outside, it is light inside, and vice versa. Inside the house there is the same

---

[7] Contra Mourelatos (1970), 17, n. 21, and Mansfeld (1964), 228, it seems clear to me that the relative pronoun ἥ refers to the road, not to the goddess; this is shown by the correlative τῇ φερόμην, where τῇ cannot refer to the goddess.
[8] Burkert (1969), 5.
[9] The similar image in Anaximander B1 and Heraclitus B94 has often been observed. Justice controls the exits and entrances of Night and Day.
[10] Almost the only thing reasonably certain about the goddess is that she is not Justice, as Sextus carelessly thought. She refers in line 28 to θέμις τε δίκη τε, in the third person.
[11] Fragment 8 (Page).

dualism as in the world outside. Hesiod indeed stresses, at some length, that they alternate both inside and outside.[12] Hence the opposites are just as much divided here as outside, and the House of Night could not symbolize the abolition of opposites.

There are two answers to this. First, we must notice that Parmenides describes, at great length, the Gate: ten lines of the twenty-one that describe the journey are about the Gate and its opening. It is here, at the Gate, that Night and Day meet, according to the myth. This is certain, and we need not worry too much about what happens inside. Secondly, the Roads of Day and Night are known from Homer, as well as Hesiod. The Laestrygonians live at the far edge of the world, and 'the roads of Night and Day are near'.[13] The feature of their way of life explained by this is that 'the shepherd driving his flocks in calls to the shepherd driving his flocks out, and he hears him; here a man who did not sleep could earn two wages, one herding cattle, the other tending sheep'. It might be said that this is the first recorded mention of 'moonlighting' – but I take the point to be that there is no difference between daylight and moonlight. Some have argued that we have here a fantasy based on information about the short nights in summer in the far north; but I see no reference to *short* nights at all. This is surely a mythical place where there is no difference between Day and Night.

Now we should turn to the world of mortal *doxa*.

MORTALS WRONGLY SET UP TWO SEPARATE AND OPPOSITE FORMS

μορφὰς γὰρ κατέθεντο δύο γνώμαις ὀνομάζειν,
τῶν μίαν οὐ χρεών ἐστιν, ἐν ᾧ πεπλανημένοι εἰσίν.

(B8.53–4)

First we may note that there is a variant reading in line 53: Simplicius quotes the line three times, once with γνώμας, once with γνώμαις, and once where one manuscript has the accusative and two the dative. I believe the dative is right, contrary to all the recent editors who construe μορφάς as the object of ὀνομάζειν. The expression μορφὰς γὰρ κατέθεντο is a metrical unit with a clear sense content; it is exactly similar to ὅσσα βροτοὶ κατέθεντο in B8.39. It seems intolerably harsh to separate the accusative μορφάς from the verb that at first hearing so obviously governs it, and postpone the fixing of its role until we have heard ὀνομάζειν. The proper meaning is: 'they set up two forms in their minds for naming'.[14]

That, however, is less important than the next line, which has probably aroused more comment than any other from Elea. I believe it means 'not one of which is it

---

[12] *Theogony* 748–57.
[13] *Odyssey* x.86: ἐγγὺς γὰρ νυκτός τε καὶ ἤματός εἰσι κέλευθοι. Some take ἐγγύς to mean 'close together', but see the article by Vos (1963) for an argument against this.
[14] I greatly admire the ingenuity of Mourelatos (1970), 228–31, who (while construing δύο with μορφάς) finds a clever *double entendre* in the group κατέθεντο δύο γνώμας; but I am not convinced.

right (sc. to set up for naming)' – i.e. *neither* is right. That the Greek *can* mean this, although many have denied it, is proved by a line from Aristophanes' *Thesmophoriazousae* (549): μίαν γὰρ οὐκ ἂν εἴποις / τῶν νῦν γυναικῶν Πηνελόπην – 'not a single one of today's women could you call Penelope'. This at least proves that μίαν … οὐ can mean οὐδεμίαν, and there seems to be no reason why it should not also mean οὐδετέραν, 'neither of two'. That οὐ χρεών ἐστι can mean 'it is not right', rather than 'it is not necessary', is proved by B8.44–5: τὸ γὰρ οὔτε τι μεῖζον / οὔτε τι βαιότερον πελέναι χρεόν ἐστι τῇ ἢ τῇ.

This is a much easier reading of the line than the currently fashionable one, 'of which (sc. mortals think) it is not necessary to name a unified form'.[15] The genitive plural with μίαν is much more likely to be partitive.

Another possibility that keeps τῶν as a partitive genitive is to take μίαν in the sense of ἑτέρην; it is wrong to name *one* of these forms, although the other is in order.[16] This possibility is now ruled out: it depends on the notion that light, for Parmenides, represents being and knowledge – in other words, on a wrong reading of B1.[17] It is true that the Peripatetic interpreters appear to associate light with being in Parmenides' philosophy;[18] this must be simply a mistake, based perhaps on Parmenides' choice of adjectives in B8.56–9, and on an interpretation of his 'theory of knowledge' in B16.[19]

Other interpretations of this ambiguous half-line have been tried out,[20] but we need not review them here.

The symbolism of the House of Night in B1 suggests that the error of mortals must lie in failing to see that the duality of Night and Day is 'really' a unity. 'They adjudged them contrary in form and assigned marks apart from each other: on the one hand flaming fire, very rare and light, in every direction the same as itself but not the same as the other; and also that other, separate, the very opposite, blind night, a dense and heavy form' (8.55–9, trans. Guthrie). But in the House of Night, where the goddess reveals the truth to Parmenides, these two opposites meet, they are of the same kin, they are both at home.[21] B1 tells us not to read B8.56 as recommending the naming of light or fire, while forbidding the naming of night. It is compatible either with the interpretation I am supporting, that they are both wrongly named, or with the interpretation of Schwabl and Mansfeld, that mortals are wrong in not naming a unity of the two. I prefer the former on grounds of simplicity.

---

15 So Schwabl (1953), 50–4; Tarán (1965), 220; Mansfeld (1964), 126.
16 So Guthrie, II.50; Long (1963), 99; and Mourelatos (1970), 80–5.
17 This dependence is avoided by Long's version, according to which μίαν has the sense ἑτέρην, but the two forms are Being and Not-Being, rather than Fire and Night. This version is also to be rejected, I believe, but for different reasons.
18 Aristotle *Metaph.* 1.5.986 b 27ff; Alexander *ad loc.*
19 See Theophrastus on this: *De sensibus* 3.
20 For a review of them, see Long (1963), 98–9; Mansfeld (1964), 123–31; or Mourelatos (1970), 80–5.
21 To clear away a possible objection, there is plainly no difference between 'flaming, heavenly fire' in B8.56, and Day, or the Light of Day, in B1.10–11. Fire becomes Light in B9.1, in what is clearly intended to be the same doctrine as that of B8.56ff.

This interpretation is in line with the other references to naming in the fragments. At B8.38–9, I prefer the reading τῷ πάντ᾽ ὀνόμασται / ὅσσα βροτοὶ κατέθεντο πεποιθότες εἶναι ἀληθῆ ('it is this that has been called all those things that mortals have set up, believing them to be true').[22] The antecedent of τῷ is τὸ ἐόν, the subject of the infinitive ἔμεναι immediately preceding: Being 'has been called all the things that mortals have set up ... coming to be and perishing, being and not being, changing place and altering bright colour'. There is only one thing, Being, or what is; when mortals talk about any of the forms they have wrongly set up, they are really talking about Being.[23]

B9 also contains a reference to naming:

αὐτὰρ ἐπειδὴ πάντα φάος καὶ νὺξ ὀνόμασται
καὶ τὰ κατὰ σφετέρας δυνάμεις ἐπὶ τοῖσί τε καὶ τοῖς ...

This presumably contains *both* of the possible passive constructions, and should be translated: 'But once everything has been called light and night, and this and that set of things have been called everything appropriate to *their* powers ... '[24] The point of adding the second line to the first might be this: the first line by itself might indicate that every individual thing in the universe 'is called' both light and night, whereas in fact there are some things (for example, the fiery 'wreaths' of Parmenides' astronomical system) which have the properties only of one of the two.

Once this 'calling' has been done, the fragment continues:

πᾶν πλέον ἐστὶν ὁμοῦ φάεος καὶ νυκτὸς ἀφάντου,
ἴσων ἀμφοτέρων, ἐπεὶ οὐδετέρῳ μέτα μηδέν.

'The whole is full of light and obscure night together, both equal, since neither has a portion[25] that is nothing.' Once mortals have set up the opposite forms, light and

---

[22] The manuscripts vary between ὄνομα (οὔνομα) ἔσται, which is the reading preferred by D–K and many others, ὀνόμασται and οὐνόμασται. The D–K text must be translated 'Therefore all things will be a [mere] name ....' The reading ὀνόμασται was defended in 1958 by Leonard Woodbury, and has been adopted by Mourelatos (1970), 180–91. Mourelatos' discussion is excellent. He uses the example, 'And God (A) called the light (B) Day (C).' Greek idiom with ὀνομάζειν allows the following constructions:
    (i) A (nominative) ὀνομάζει B (accusative) C (accus.); or
    (ii) A (nom.) ὀνομάζει ἐπὶ B (dative) C (accus.).
Turned into the passive these produce respectively:
    (i) B (nom.) ὀνομάζεται C (nom.) by A (agent construction); or
    (ii) C (nom.) ὀνομάζεται ἐπὶ B (dat.) by A.
Reading B8.38 in this way depends on the assumption that the simple dative τῷ may stand for ἐπὶ τῷ. I think this is reasonable, even though no exact parallels have been produced.

[23] There is a *prima facie* inconsistency in the inclusion of εἶναί τε καὶ οὐχί (line 40) in this list, because Being is not one of the things set up by mortals. Presumably they must be taken as a pair: the opposition between Being and Not-Being is something set up by mortals.

[24] 'Their powers' means the powers of light and night. Mansfeld (1964), 148–9, says that since it is reflexive it must refer to τοῖσί τε καὶ τοῖς, but there is at least one example in epic poetry of σφέτερος in an emphatic but not reflexive sense, viz. *Iliad* IX.327 (cf. also VI.500: ᾧ ἐνὶ οἴκῳ).

[25] I construe this on the analogy of Thucydides II.37: μέτεστι ... πᾶσι τὸ ἴσον; Plato, *Parm.* 163D; ᾧ δέ γε μηδὲν τούτου μέτεστιν.

night, and marked off different aspects of the universe as having the different powers, such as hot or cold, rare or dense, etc., that go with one or the other of these, then the whole universe is full of both together; and they must both be equal, since (so mortals wrongly imply) both light and night *are* in the full sense – neither of them, nor any part of them, is nothing.

I believe the logic of this fragment is something like this. Once we have set up *contrary* forms, for example, light and night, we cannot say 'there is light here and now' without entailing 'there is not night here and now'; and this last proposition is to assert a bit of not-being or 'nothing' of night. Mortals refuse to recognize this: they name their two forms as if they both *are* in the full sense, without any share of not-being. If they did recognize it, then they would see that they must give up their contrary forms, for reasons set out in B2, B3, and B6.

It may be appropriate to ask next: why did Parmenides choose as his contrary pair light and night, rather than the hot and the cold, the rare and the dense, or limit and unlimited? One might say that it does not matter: he clearly thought that light was characterized by one set of properties and night by their contraries, so that he might just as well have chosen a pair of these properties – say, the hot and the cold – as primary. He needed *contrary* forms for his logic to work, but he was free to choose among pairs of contraries – and chose light and night because they were the pair he had introduced already in B1. But there may be more to it than that.

Light and night, more than any other pair, suggest *temporal* alternation. If it is light, it is not night, and yet night will follow. If it is night, it is not light, and yet light will follow. Moreover, the world in the night is the same as the world in the light: we have a clear intuition of the continuity of the world through these alternating conditions. There could hardly be a more effective pair of contraries to symbolize Parmenides' message: temporal change, from one form now to its opposite later, is a deceitful notion. All is one.

THE HARD-HITTING REFUTATION AND THE SENSE OF ἔστι

'Judge by reason,' says Parmenides' goddess, 'the hard-hitting refutation that I have uttered. There still remains just one story of a way, that it *is*' (B7.5–8.1: κρῖναι δὲ λόγῳ πολύδηριν ἔλεγχον / ἐξ ἐμέθεν ῥηθέντα. μόνος δ' ἔτι μῦθος ὁδοῖο / λείπεται ὡς ἔστιν).

I want to argue the following points. The word ἔλεγχος means 'refutation', rather than 'proof', and this makes it even clearer that the remaining 'way' has been established by eliminating the alternatives. The fact that the refutation has been uttered before B8 begins justifies us in collecting between B2, where the first statement of alternatives is made, and B7–8 whatever refutations of alternatives we can find. That means B6. There we find an argument, of sorts, for the rejection of the way of not-being; the need for this rejection was asserted in B2. Hence we must trace the argument from B2 through to B6. This important point has been made before[26] and is usually taken for granted, but it seems worth defending again in view of Alexander Mourelatos' interpretation of B2 without B6. This is a mistake, I believe, that has important consequences.

First, ἔλεγχος. The meaning it had acquired by Socrates' time hardly needs to be emphasized. In Homer, the verb ἐλέγχειν means 'to disgrace', 'to put to shame'.[27] Mourelatos, who is more sensitive than most Eleatic commentators to nuances, sees this, and rejects the usual translation as 'proof': "Ἔλεγχος could not mean "proof" ... Strictly speaking, there are no "proofs" before B8.' But curiously he turns away from it and translates the word as 'challenge'. A 'very contentious challenge' is issued, and 'B8 provides the justification.'[28]

But the word λείπεται in B8.1 shows that something has been accomplished before B8 begins: there *remains* just one way, and that must be because the others have been refuted. There may have been no proof, but there has been a refutation.

The wording of B6 shows that two ways of inquiry are refuted: 'For I hold you back from this way of inquiry first, but after that from *this* one ...' (B6.3–4).[29] The second of the forbidden ways, described in B6.4–9, is clearly the way of mortal opinion. But what is the other way?

The two preceding lines of the fragment give no clear answer:

χρὴ τὸ λέγειν τε νοεῖν τ' ἐὸν ἔμμεναι. ἔστι γὰρ εἶναι,
μηδὲν δ' οὐκ ἔστιν. τά σ' ἐγὼ φράζεσθαι ἄνωγα.

The first line says something the goddess must agree with, and therefore it cannot describe the way to be rejected.[30] The sentence μηδὲν δ' οὐκ ἔστιν is ambiguous, but in all of its likely meanings it is something the goddess would not wish to reject. It is said by some[31] that the rejected way is to be understood as the contradictory of this sentence: the goddess says μηδὲν δ' οὐκ ἔστιν to contradict the way that says μηδὲν ἔστιν, and that is what line 3 refers to. But the simplest assumption is that ταύτης in 6.3 refers directly to the παναπευθέα ... ἀταρπόν of 2.6.[32] The goddess describes a way (2.5: ἡ δ' ὡς οὐκ ἔστιν ...), tells him that it is useless (2.6: τὴν δή τοι φράζω παναπευθέα ἔμμεν ἀταρπόν), explains why it is useless (2.7ff – the 'refutation' still to be analysed), tells him to think about the

---

[26] It is only recently that the point has been made clearly. It used to be said that Parmenides' *premiss* is ἔστι, and so there was no point in tracing an argument leading to the conclusion λείπεται ὡς ἔστι.

[27] P. Chantraine, *Dictionnaire étymologique de la langue grecque* (Paris, 1968), s.v. ἐλέγχω: 'ɪ) Chez Homère seulement (2 ex.) "faire honte de, mépriser"; 2) En Ionien-attique sens dialectique issu de l'usage des tribunaux "chercher à réfuter (par des questions notamment)"'.

[28] Mourelatos (1970), 91. Furth (1968) takes ἔλεγχος in the sense of 'refutation', and makes excellent use of it. I present supporting arguments in the next chapter.

[29] Since modern commentators are agreed on the supplement <εἴργω> to fill out the defective line 3, I shall not stop to defend it here.

[30] Tarán (1965) attempts to meet this by contending (pp. 59–60) that in line 3 the goddess is merely recommending that the Way of Being be set aside *temporarily*. This has not convinced anyone, so far as I know, and it is not likely to.

[31] E.g. by Guthrie II.22.

[32] Mourelatos (1970) agrees with this, without drawing out the implications (p. 77, n. 7).

moves involved in the refutation (6.2: τά σ᾽ ἐγὼ φράζεσθαι ἄνωγα), and sums up before moving on (6.3–4: πρώτης γὰρ ... αὐτὰρ ἔπειτ᾽ ἀπὸ τῆς ...). Let us obey the injunction to think about the refutation. The moves are mostly marked by the word γάρ. The explicit moves are these:

(1) B2.5–6 The way 'it is not, etc.' is useless.
(2) B2.7 οὔτε γὰρ ἂν γνοίης τό γε μὴ ἐὸν / οὔτε φράσαις.
(3) B3 τὸ γὰρ αὐτὸ νοεῖν ἔστιν τε καὶ εἶναι.
(4) B6.1 χρὴ τὸ λέγειν τε νοεῖν τ᾽ ἐὸν ἔμμεναι.
(3) B6.1 ἔστι γὰρ εἶναι (same move as B3).
(5) B6.2 μηδὲν δ᾽ οὐκ ἔστιν.

My argument now depends on several assumptions, many of them controversial; to attempt to defend all of them here would take too much space. I assume, with most editors, that B3 belongs here,[33] and I assume that it is to be translated: 'For the same thing is for knowing and for being.'[34] That is to say, all that is for knowing is for being; the expression 'is for knowing' means 'can be known' and 'is for being' means 'can be'.[35]

If it is possible to say of something τοῦτο ἔστι νοεῖν, 'this is for knowing', I assume that it may be referred to as τὸ νοεῖν ἐόν, 'what is for knowing'.[36] It is referred to in this way in B6.1, with the addition of another infinitive: τὸ λέγειν τε νοεῖν τ᾽ ἐόν.[37] Under this description Parmenides says it *must* be, because it *can* be (B3), and it is not nothing.[38]

If this is correct, it appears that Parmenides moves from 'it can be' to 'it must be' with the help of the unexpressed disjunction 'either it is, or it is nothing'.

Mourelatos makes the very interesting new suggestion that the ground on which Parmenides asserts (2) 'you cannot know what is not' is 'the vagueness of What-is-not'.[39] With this weapon in his armoury he is able to defend the view that the ἔστι of the way of Truth is to be construed as a proposition-form '— is —' or 'φx'. The first rejected way, described in B5, is then '— is not —' or ' ~ φx', and it is rejected

---

[33] For an argument, see Hölscher (1969), 80–1.

[34] Zeller's interpretation, defended by Hölscher (1968) and others. Νοεῖν is probably better translated as 'knowing' than as 'thinking'; see, e.g., Kahn (1969), n. 4.

[35] The objection that νοεῖν has to be translated passively and εἶναι actively (Mansfeld (1964), 63–4) is not cogent. The infinitive is functioning as a verbal noun, and at that level distinctions between active and passive disappear: the same noun may have a subjective or objective genitive – in English too 'the love of God' may mean that God loves or is loved.

[36] Hölscher (1968), 99, cites τὸ μὴ γενέσθαι δυνατόν (Simonides IV.13D) and ἐκβῆναι οὐκ ὄν (Demosthenes L.22). But one should not think too exclusively of the impersonal ἔστι or ἔξεστι of classical Greek: closer parallels are Homer, *Iliad* IX.688: εἰσὶ καὶ οἴδε τάδ᾽ εἰπέμεν; Aeschylus *Persae* 419: θάλασσα δ᾽ οὐκέτ᾽ ἦν ἰδεῖν (would there be anything odd about a participial derivative – θαλάσσης οὐκέτ᾽ οὔσης ἰδεῖν?).

[37] Kahn (1969), n. 26, says this interpretation is grammatically impossible, and 'in any case incompatible with the normal meaning of νοεῖν in early Greek'. I disagree with the first point; the second seems to be relevant only to translations using the expression 'what can be *thought*'.

[38] Or perhaps 'nothing cannot be' – and therefore, from (3), what can be known cannot be nothing. So Owen (1960), 94.

[39] Mourelatos (1970), ch. 3, heading.

because it is a way that leads to no definite goal. 'If we consider a journey to "what is really not-F" ... clearly this is a journey that could never be brought to completion. For we have no criterion for recognizing the goal (B2.7: οὔτε γνοίης) if we should chance to come upon it.'[40] 'Where do I go if I am told to go to "not-Ithaca"? Where do I go if I set my bearings on the "non-Cimmerians"? It is fated to be a journey of πλάνη, of regress and wandering.'[41]

Against this, attractive though it is, there is a direct objection to be brought from the text of Parmenides. He appears to insist on the equivalence of μὴ ἐόν and μηδέν, and to use this equivalence in his refutation. But μηδέν cannot plausibly be taken to mean 'nothing determinate', at least in the opening moves of the argument. If one of the first premises of the argument uses μηδέν, then since it must be one that would be accepted as self-evident by his hearers, μηδέν must be used in an obvious sense. Elsewhere in the fragments μηδέν and οὐδέν appear to have their natural meaning. The mortals εἰδότες οὐδέν of 6.4 are surely men who know nothing, not men who know 'the so-and-so which really is not such-and-such' or the 'such-and-such that so-and-so really is not'[42] – i.e. a negative answer or set of answers to a 'What is x?' question. Similarly οὐδέν in 8.36, μηδέν in 9.4,[43] both μηδέν and οὐδέν in Zeno B1–2 and Melissus B1, B4, B7(3) and (7), B8(3) and (5) – all these seem to work in the normal way.

This argument depends on an uncomfortable number of assumptions about the meaning of B6.1–2, but I believe the point can be reinforced by a look at B8.6–10. This is the first positive *use* Parmenides makes of the point he has been arguing for – that only the way ὡς ἔστι is viable. What he takes over from the earlier argument into B8 is just the rejection of the way ὡς οὐκ ἔστι and the rejection of the way of mortal opinion on the ground that it confuses ἔστι and οὐκ ἔστι. To show that what-is is ἀγένητον, he now uses the result of his earlier argument. 'I will not allow you to say or to think [that what-is grows] out of what-is-not. For it is neither speakable nor thinkable that it is not. Besides, what requirement could have compelled it, later or earlier, having started from nothing, to grow?' But we know, according to Mourelatos, that 'it is neither speakable nor thinkable that it is not' because 'what is not' is *vague*;[44] what we are to reject is 'the view that an unqualified, unrestricted proposition of the form "is really not-F" can ever feature as the last statement (or one of the last) in cosmological inquiry'.[45] That is plausible: but we are now considering the use of τὸ μὴ ἐόν in the *first* stages of cosmological inquiry. What ground have we been given so far, in Mourelatos' view, for rejecting a cosmogony like Anaximander's, in which what-is grows out of what is not bounded? True, we must not say: 'What-is is really (is constituted by,

[40] *Ibid.* p. 76.
[41] *Ibid.* p. 78.
[42] Mourelatos' explication of τὸ μὴ ἐόν, on p. 75. It is somewhat unfair to quote these cumbersome formulae out of their context. I do not mean to make them appear absurd. They are precise and helpful as Mourelatos uses them.
[43] 'Nothingness'; Mourelatos (1970), 85.
[44] *Ibid.* ch. 3, *passim.*
[45] *Ibid.* p. 79.

36

is in its essence) not bounded.' That, however, is something Anaximander need not say. The growth of what-is out of something vague into something balanced and finite seems to be just what he had in mind.

But Parmenides uses not only the expression ἐκ μὴ ἐόντος here, but also ἐκ μηδενός, and they seem to be equivalent. I take this to be another indication that the 'is not' in B8.7 cannot be read as ' ∼ φx'.

Is it possible, however, that μὴ ἐόν in B8.7 is equivalent to 'what does not exist' or 'what is not the case', and yet that the negative route rejected in B2 and 6.1–3 is the route '— is not —'? Is it possible that Parmenides thought his rejection of the route '— is not —' licensed the rejection, a fortiori, of '— does not exist'? This does not seem likely. In the first place, there is no trace of such a move in the fragments. Secondly, if the rejection of '— does not exist' is the premiss needed to get the argument of B8 started, it is uneconomical to interpret B2.5–6 as a different premiss from which the necessary one is silently inferred.

We must, then, retain the older view that ἔστι and οὐκ ἔστι in Parmenides' 'routes' have some existential force. But this statement needs a certain amount of explanation. It has recently been pointed out that we ought to speak of a sense of the Greek verb 'to be' in which the existential and the copulative senses are 'fused'.[46] The subject of this ἔστι may be the name or description of a thing or of a state of affairs: we may translate ταῦτα ἔστι as 'these things exist' or 'these things are the case'. Statements in which the ἔστι is copulative may be rephrased in Greek with an existential ἔστι; 'this is white' may be 'there is white here'; 'Simmias is tall' may be 'there is tallness in Simmias'.[47] This is all true, and important for understanding Parmenides. My point against Mourelatos is that the argument depends on the *fusion* of the senses, and to detach the copulative sense from the fusion, by representing Parmenides' ἔστι as '— is —' or 'φx', is to destroy the argument.[48]

---

[46] By Kahn (1966) and Furth (1968). Owen (1960), 94, n. 1, already had the main point.

[47] Furth (1968), 123–4, puts it very clearly.

[48] [Later: Mourelatos clarifies his position in 'Determinacy and Indeterminacy, Being and Non-Being in the Fragments of Parmenides', in *New Essays on Plato and the Pre-Socratics*, ed. Roger A. Shiner and John King-Farlow, *Canadian Journal of Philosophy*, suppl. vol. 2 (1976), 45–60.]

4

TRUTH AS WHAT SURVIVES
THE *ELENCHOS*

[1987]

Dedicated to G. B. Kerferd

My starting-point in this paper is a couple of lines from Parmenides' poem. There is some reason to claim that they are the most remarkable lines in that astonishing document:

> Judge by *logos* the hard-hitting refutation (ἔλεγχος)
> that I have uttered. Only one single account of a way
> is left: that it is.

(B7.5–8.2)

The paradox of Parmenides is presented in the strongest outline here. It is a goddess who speaks these lines, revealing the Way of Truth to the initiate. Instead of standing on authority or using the persuasive power of religious ritual, she tells him to take away her message and subject it to criticism: judge by *logos*. Moreover, the revelation itself takes the form of a criticism: what she first offers Parmenides on his arrival, when he has passed through the gates of which Justice holds the key, is described as an ἔλεγχος. This is the aspect of Parmenides' vision that I want to elaborate on this occasion. I am aiming to do two things: to improve the case for thinking that ἔλεγχος does indeed mean 'refutation' here, rather than 'proof';[1] and to see what this tells us about the underlying conception of truth.

What seems to me of interest in the context of an inquiry into the Greek conception of truth is the idea presented here by Parmenides that the truth is that which is left unrefuted: λείπεται ὡς ἔστιν, 'it remains that it *is*'. Parmenides offers some alternative Ways of Inquiry, as he designates them, and he presents arguments to persuade us to reject all of them but one. That one is described first as 'the Way of Persuasion, for she attends upon Truth', and then later as 'my trustworthy *logos* and thought concerning Truth'. It is usually referred to nowadays simply as 'the Way of Truth'. Parmenides gives us no direct argument in favour of adopting this Way of Inquiry, but only the indirect one of showing what is wrong with the alternatives. So after the other ways have been closed by the hard-hitting *elenchos*, 'only one single account of a Way is left'. And this is the

---

[1] I made a brief case for this thesis in chapter 3 above, first published in 1973. I was stimulated to think more about it by James Lesher's article (1984). The present chapter owes much to him.

Way of Truth. This seems to me interesting enough to warrant a look at the use and assessment of *elenchos* in other Greek authors in the early period.

Stripped to its essentials, Parmenides' argument takes the following form:

Either *p*, or *q*, or both *p* and *q*.
But not *q*.
And if not *q*, then not both *p* and *q*.
Hence 'it remains' that *p*.

The refutation mentioned in the lines with which I began is the argument that is introduced to refute *q*. It is not necessary for my present purpose to discuss what that argument is – and that is fortunate, because its structure is extremely obscure owing to the high degree of compression in Parmenides' exposition here or perhaps because of the fragmentary nature of what survives. Jonathan Barnes recently made a brave attempt to sort out the argument, and distinguished twenty-eight steps in it – these all being contained in less than half that number of Greek hexameters.[2] We will take some such analysis as read, and move on to look at the occurrences of ἔλεγχος and its cognates in earlier and contemporary literature.

These words first come to our notice in the context of the shame-culture of the *Iliad* and *Odyssey*.[3] At the funeral games in *Iliad* XXIII, Nestor gives long-winded advice to his son Antilochus on how to avoid crashing his chariot against the turning-post – 'a crash would be a joy to others but a shame (ἐλεγχείη) to you' (XXIII.342). Antilochus, during the race, passes on a similar thought to his horses – think of the shame if you get beaten by Agamemnon's horse Aithe, a mere mare, too (XXIII.408). In *Odyssey* XXI, Eurymachus despairs because he cannot string the bow: 'a matter of shame', he says, 'for those in the future to learn about (ἐλεγχείη δὲ καὶ ἐσσομένοισι πυθέσθαι: XXI.255)'. But Odysseus strings the bow and shoots through the rings, and says to Telemachus: 'So the stranger in the halls does not shame you (ἐλέγχει): I did not miss (XXI.424)'.

The concept involved in ἐλέγχειν in Homer is plainly a moral one, if it is granted that there is anything at all in Homer that counts as morality. Ἐλεγχείη is contrasted with the good reputation that comes from success. The word does not yet mean 'refute'. In *Iliad* IX.522, the verb has μῦθον as its object, but the phrase cannot mean 'refute the story'. The context is this: Phoenix appeals to Achilles to respect and yield to the prayers of the small embassy of Greek leaders that has come to his tent: τῶν μὴ σύ γε μῦθον ἐλέγξῃς, he says, μηδὲ πόδας. Do not bring shame on their words or their feet, by making their efforts unsuccessful.

As we would expect, this use of ἐλέγχειν survives in Pindar. In the victory ode for Aristomenes of Aegina (*Pythian* VIII) he tells the young man he brings no

---

[2] Barnes (1977), I.174–5
[3] The verb ἐλέγχειν retains its form through archaic and classical Greek, but the archaic feminine noun ἐλεγχείη and the neuter ἔλεγχος give way to the masculine form.

shame (οὐ κατελέγχεις) on his two uncles who were also panhellenic victors. There are other examples in Pindar of ἔλεγχος, ἐλέγχειν, and κατελέγχειν in this sense (*Nemean* III.15; *Pythian* XI.49; *Isthmian* III.14 and VIII.65).

Even in very early literature, however, we can see some traces of a more specialized use, which brings us closer to Parmenides. There is a line in Hesiod's *Works and Days* (714): σὲ δὲ μή τι νόον κατελεγχέτω εἶδος, 'let not your outward appearance bring dishonour to your mind'. The context is a piece of advice against picking up friends here, there, and everywhere: an over-friendly external manner should not be permitted to bring shame on your better judgement. What is noteworthy is that the cause of the dishonour is a certain kind of falsity. What is to be avoided is a mismatch between thought and manner, such that one *belies* the other. There is a similar occurrence of κατελέγχειν in Pindar (*Olympian* VIII.19): 'He was beautiful to look at', Pindar says of the boy Alcimedon of Aegina, 'and he did not disgrace his beauty by his deed.' The disgrace would consist of a mismatch between ἔργον and εἶδος: the translators use 'belie' to translate the verb here.

In both of these examples it is to be observed that both the subject and the object of the verb are things: νόος and εἶδος in Hesiod, ἔργον and εἶδος in Pindar. One thing is compared to another and puts it to shame by the comparison because it is good and admirable and the other is now seen to be defective in some way. And in each case the deficiency is a matter of being deceptive or concealing. If the boy had lost his wrestling-match, his deed would have shown that his physical beauty was only an appearance, something superficial that hides the truth. We can follow this line down to a rather absurd example in the Hippocratic treatise *On fractures*. The subject is fractures of the thigh-bone and how to deal with them: the surgeon must stretch them vigorously, and hold them apart.

One should extend very strongly and without deviation, leaving no deficiency, for the disgrace and harm (αἰσχύνη and βλάβη) are great if the result is a shortened thigh. The arm, indeed, when shortened, may be concealed and the fault is not great, but the leg when shortened will leave the patient lame and the sound leg being longer by comparison exposes (ἐλέγχει) the defect; so that if a patient is going to have unskilful treatment it is better that both his legs should be broken than one of them, for then at least he will be in equilibrium (ἰσόρροπος).

(*On fractures* XIX)

Notice that we have a mention of shame even here (and it is the patient's shame that is in question, not the doctor's), and that the deficiency in the short leg that is shown up lies in its not being a leg in its natural and true (as we might say) condition. If it could be concealed, as a short arm can, it would be able to get away with it; as it is, the deficiency is shown up, exposed.

This part of the semantic field of ἔλεγχος and ἐλέγχειν leads naturally into the area of testing for genuineness, where these words occur with some frequency in early fifth-century literature. Pindar complains that there is a big risk involved for the poet in telling stories in new ways:

40

Many things have been said in many ways.
But to think out new things, and give them to the touchstone for testing (ἐς ἔλεγχον)
That's where the danger lies: tales (λόγοι) are prize morsels for the envious.

(*Nemean* VIII.20)

The touchstone tests gold because only real gold will leave a yellow streak when it is rubbed on the stone. In Pindar's metaphor it is tales that are tested, or his versions of the myths and his praise of the victors, and the test is their reception by the audience:

Men pray for gold, others for unlimited land.
But I – may I be laid in my grave
having pleased my people, by praising what should be praised,
and casting blame on villains.

(*Nemean* VIII.38–9)

The quality of his tales that Pindar expects to survive the ἔλεγχος is a matter of values. Correct moral judgement will bring him fame: his poems will be admired if they praise and blame the right things. We are still very much involved with morality, with goodness and badness rather than truth – or perhaps one might say with truth interpreted as goodness.

There is a somewhat similar use of ἐλέγχειν in a fragment from Pindar's rival Bacchylides:

The Lydian stone discloses gold:
but the poet's art (σοφία) and all-powerful truth (παγκρατής ἀλάθεια)
evince (ἐλέγχει) the *aretê* of men.

(fragment 14.4)

The meaning is expressed more directly in other lines of Bacchylides, as Jebb points out:[4]

If uttered with truth by mortals [i.e. poets]
the glory – even when a man is dead –
survives in what the far-famed Muses delight in.

σὺν δ' ἀλαθείᾳ βροτῶν
κάλλιστον, εἴπερ καὶ θάνῃ τις
λείπεται Μουσᾶν ἀγακλειτᾶν ἄθυρμα.

(fragment 9.85)

Truth is what survives the ἔλεγχος: more exactly, truth is the quality that enables a man's *aretê* to survive the ἔλεγχος. We shall return to this theme shortly. But first we must follow the traces that lead from the sphere of morality to the true and the false.

The boundaries are unclear. In Herodotus IV.18 priests examine (ἐλέγχειν) a suspect to find out whether he has committed perjury. Perjury consists both in

---

[4] Sir Richard C. Jebb, *Bacchylides* (Cambridge, 1905), p. 415.

saying something that is false and in doing something immoral. In Thucydides (1.131), Pausanias, under suspicion of treachery with the barbarians, offers himself for examination (ἐλέγχειν). Both his truthfulness and his moral character are involved. But one soon finds examples that relate solely to testing for truth: most of the one dozen instances of ἔλεγχος in Sophocles fall into this category – as for example when Orestes says: 'This is he: don't examine me (μή μ' ἔλεγχε) with more *logoi*' (*Electra* 1353).

Sometimes, as in the examples I have used most recently, ἐλέγχειν is used in a neutral sense, with the meaning 'examine', 'test', 'inquire into'; it does not necessarily mean to *convict* someone of untruthfulness or wickedness. But we must remember that in its earliest attested uses it is not neutral: it involves shame, disgrace, dishonour. Κακ' ἐλέγχεα is a powerful epic formula of abuse: foul, shameful creatures. So it is natural that when the word moves out of the range of moral evaluation towards that of truth and falsity, it regularly means, not just to examine, but to examine and find wanting, to show up, to falsify, to refute. Since this is the usage I have claimed for Parmenides, it had better be illustrated a little more fully.

Early examples nearly always have persons as objects, rather than statements. In Herodotus there are six occurrences of ἔλεγχος and its cognates, and they all have persons as objects. The crew of Arion's ship planned to rob and kill him on his return journey to Corinth, but he jumped overboard and was rescued by the dolphin (1.24). The crew returned to Corinth, and said they had left Arion alive and well at Tarentum. Arion himself then appeared, 'and they, being refuted, could not go on denying' Arion's story (οὐκ ἔχειν ἐλεγχομένους ἀρνέεσθαι).

Harpagas claimed to have obeyed the King and put the King's dangerous grandchild to death, but he gave the baby to a herdsman instead (1.117). Confronted later with the herdsman, 'he did not turn to a false way (ἐπὶ ψευδέα ὁδόν), so that he might not be caught out being refuted (ἐλεγχόμενος)'.

In Herodotus 11.115, Proteus asked Paris how he got possession of Helen. 'He shilly-shallied and did not speak the truth (πλανωμένου ἐν τῷ λόγῳ καὶ οὐ λέγοντος τὴν ἀληθείην)' but was refuted (ἤλεγχον) by some runaway servants.

A particularly interesting passage occurs in Herodotus' account of various theories about the flooding of the Nile (11.21ff). Some suggest that it is caused by melting snow, but Herodotus rejects this theory: winds blow hot here, rain is unknown, the natives are black, kites and swallows and cranes winter in this region – but if there were snow, none of this would have been the case, as necessity ἐλέγχει. It would be natural to translate this into English 'as necessity proves' – that is to say, as this cogent argument proves. This would give ἐλέγχειν a positive meaning. But that is not in accordance with Greek idiom, I think. What is proved here is a negation: the proposition that these things would not have been the case. The proof of this is treated as the refutation of the affirmative equivalent.

But Herodotus goes on to mention another theory, that the flooding of the Nile is due to the river Ocean (11.21–3). 'The one who spoke about Ocean', he says, 'having taken the story into the realm of the obscure (ἐς ἀφανές), admits no ἔλεγχος.' This is fascinating, as the introduction of the idea of falsifiability as a criterion for demarcating scientific theories from others, in the manner of Sir Karl Popper.[5] At first sight it may seem to tell against my notion that we find in Parmenides a theory of truth as what is unfalsified; Herodotus does not believe that the theory of Ocean is true, just because it admits no ἔλεγχος. But in fact Herodotus is not claiming that the Ocean theory is unfalsified, but that it is unfalsifiable, which is a very different thing. This is the only instance that I have found in fifth-century literature and earlier of the ἔλεγχος root used to convey the idea of unfalsifiability.

There are three occurrences in Thucydides (out of a total of eight) in which there is a clear connection with the notion of false belief and false statement. The first (vi.86.1) is like those we have looked at in Herodotus, where the object is a person: if someone does not believe this, says the speaker, the fact itself refutes him. The other two have statements as the object of the ἔλεγχος, and thus provide a close parallel to the way the word is used by Parmenides. Both occur in the exchange of recriminations between Plataeans and Thebans before the Spartans. The Plataeans first (iii.53.3): 'to give true answers to your questions is against our interests, but false answers get refuted (τὰ ψευδῆ ἔλεγχον ἔχει – perhaps "can be refuted", "admit refutation")'. The second (iii.61.1) is the answer of the Thebans. 'Now we must defend ourselves against the first [set of claims, namely charges against the Thebans], and make an ἔλεγχος of the others [namely, what the Plataeans said in praise of themselves], so that having heard both sides you may make judgement of the truth.' Ἔλεγχος here might be an examination, but it is clearly a critical examination. The Thebans are proposing to say positive things about themselves in response to the Plataeans' charges, and to offer a refutation of the Plataeans' own claims.

To conclude this survey of the Presocratic use of ἔλεγχος in non-philosophical texts, I shall draw attention to the compound verb ἐξελέγχειν. First comes an uninteresting use in Pindar, where it seems to mean 'count' or 'reckon up'. Impossible, he says (*Nemean* x.45), to count the thousands of bronze prizes, 'for it were a work of longer leisure to number them' (Sandys' translation). Notice that there is no negative sense here: it means to reckon up and get the right answer. There is no negative sense either in a much more striking passage of *Olympian* x, relating the story of the foundation of the Olympic Games. Pindar describes how Heracles dedicated a precinct to his father Zeus, by the river Alphaeus. He goes on:

> In this first founding ceremony
> the Fates stood near at hand,
> and Time who alone establishes (ἐξελέγχει)
> the real Truth (ἀλάθειαν ἐτήτυμον).
> Time passing onward declared the plain story,
> how Heracles ...

> (*Olympian* x.52–5)

5 Popper (1959).

Time establishes the real truth, presumably by revealing which of the competing versions of the founding of Olympia commands most men's belief. The sense of ἐξελέγχειν here seems to be to winnow out the falsehood so as to leave the real truth visible. This is very similar to the cluster of ideas we found in Bacchylides. Time, allied to the skill of the poet, performs an ἔλεγχος, and the truth is what survives.

The same set of conditions is found in another passage of Thucydides (III.64), in the same speech of the Thebans at the trial of the Plataeans, from which I quoted earlier. 'The former virtues that you allege, you now show to be not proper to your character: the real bent of your nature has been at length damningly proved [this is Crawley's translation of ἐξηλέγχθη ἐς τὸ ἀληθές]: when the Athenians took the path of injustice you followed them.' There was an earlier pretence, but the passing of time refuted this, and so brought out into the open the hard core of surviving truth.

It is possible that the same idea is to be found in Heraclitus (B125a): 'let not wealth desert you, Ephesians, so that you get shown up as being wicked (ἐξελέγχοισθε πονηρευόμενοι)', he says, according to Tzetzes; but many editors regard this fragment as spurious.[6]

What emerges, then, from this survey of ἐλέγχειν and its cognates? I think it establishes clearly enough that the interpretation of Parmenides' strategy advanced earlier in this paper is not an impossible one. It is perfectly thinkable that he uses ἔλεγχος to mean refutation: this can be inferred from its use in the sense of 'test' in the lyric poets, together with its negative implications in the Homeric examples, and its undoubted use in this sense in Herodotus, who is not all that much later than Parmenides. From claiming that it is not impossible we move to the view that it is positively plausible when we examine the framework of argument in which it is used. 'I hold you back, first, from this Way of Inquiry', says Parmenides' goddess (B6.3–4), referring to the Way that says 'it is not', and secondly from the following one, which turns out to be a Way that says 'it is and is not'. She gives reasons for rejecting, for holding him back from, these two Ways, then speaks the words with which I began:

> Judge by *logos* the hard-hitting refutation
> that I have uttered. Only one single account of a Way
> is left: that it is.

(B7.5–8.2)

There is no positive reasoning to support the claims of this remaining Way: its only recommendation is that its rivals have been refuted.

As I have analysed Parmenides' reasoning, it looks suspiciously like a form of argument that was consciously recognized and labelled much later. In Stoic logic, the fifth 'undemonstrated argument' takes the following form:

---

[6] It is accepted as genuine by Diels–Kranz, by Marcovich (1967), and by Bollack and Wismann (1972). It is rejected by Kirk (1954), 150–1 (following Wilamowitz and Bywater), and by Kahn (1979), 289 with n. 436.

> Either the first or the second.
> But not the first.
> Therefore, the second.

As in Parmenides, the first premiss is a disjunction, the second is the denial of one of the disjuncts, and the conclusion is the assertion of the other. The fact that it is a Stoic pattern might be used to undermine the claim that it appears in Parmenides. But it need not be thought conclusive, or even very persuasive, in that role. There is often a long interval of time separating the intuitive use of a mode of reasoning and its logical analysis. There were syllogisms long before Aristotle catalogued them, and there were reasonings that fall into the Stoic schemata long before the Stoics formalized and labelled them.

To those brought up on the idea that truth is a property of propositions, it has sometimes seemed surprising that Greek thinkers describe things or states of affairs as being true, as well as beliefs or judgements or statements. The approach to the idea of truth through the concept of ἔλεγχος shows clearly enough how this comes about. The touchstone distinguishes true gold from its deceptive rivals: only the real thing stands the test. There seems to be no difference in logic between the way in which false gold is found out by the touchstone, and the way in which a false theory about the flooding of the Nile is found out in Herodotus by the test of the perceptible evidence. So both the thing and the theory can be found to be true or false.

A brief word may be added, in conclusion, about the great user of ἔλεγχος, Socrates.[7] What is the nature of that which survives, after he has used it to eliminate the deceptive appearances? He scrutinizes the beliefs of men in his search for the truth about virtue, and refutes them when they are shown to be inconsistent with other deeply held beliefs. His procedure was the main route by which Plato arrived at his theory of εἴδη. At the end of the educational road, Plato says (*Rep.* 533A3), the philosopher contemplates οὐδ' εἰκόνα ... ἀλλ' αὐτὸ τὸ ἀληθές, not an image but the true thing itself.

Plato's Forms collect many of the qualities that we have been looking at in the context of ἔλεγχος and its cognates. They are the survivors. False and deceptive 'unreal' impostors are shown up for what they are by Socratic ἔλεγχος, and that which is left unrefuted (λείπεται) is αὐτὸ τὸ ἀληθές: the Form itself.

Moreover, it is not only that the Form is the survivor in the logical sense. Like the reputation of the man celebrated by the epinician poet quoted above, the Form survives the ἔλεγχος of Time: it is eternal.

When we think of the moral contexts in which we first found the idea of ἔλεγχος, in Homer, it becomes less surprising that Plato invests the Forms with some kind of value. The Forms are not propositions, nor definitions, nor are they just universal concepts, or predicates. They are beings that stand in some kind of moral hierarchy, with the Form of the Good at the top: they represent not merely the natural kinds of the physical world arranged in a tree-like structure, but also an

---

[7] A new account of Socrates' use of ἔλεγχος has just been published by Vlastos (1983).

expression of the value inherent in the cosmic order. They have, so to speak, an *aretê* that enables them to survive the ἔλεγχος. Plato's Socrates in the *Parmenides* (130C–D) backs away from the idea that there should be Forms of such things as mud and hair: they are too undignified, unheroic.

Such are the qualities that survive the ἔλεγχος in Plato's philosophy, being embodied in the εἴδη. There is moral value in them, eternity and unchangeability, absence of contradiction and deceptiveness – and, of course, truth. As Socrates sums it up in the *Gorgias* (473B11): τὸ ἀληθὲς οὐδέποτε ἐλέγχεται, what is true is never refuted.

5

ANAXAGORAS IN RESPONSE TO PARMENIDES

[1976]

INTRODUCTION

What reason is there to suppose that those who did know Parmenides' poem necessarily thought that he had raised a real problem which they must try to deal with? Empedocles, perhaps also Anaxagoras, knew the poem, but they pursue a very different kind of philosophy from Zeno and Melissus: why, then, must we suppose that they are seeking an alternative answer to the problem posed by Parmenides, and that their ultimate material elements are to be seen as modifications of the Eleatic ἓν ἐόν?

These rhetorical questions, taken from M. L. West's book, *Early Greek Philosophy and the Orient*,[1] make a useful starting-point for this inquiry. They are, of course, what the grammar books call 'repudiating questions': the answer hoped for is 'no reason'. The argument with which Mr West goes on to support his negative implication is not likely to convince many students of the Presocratics. He determinedly makes light of Parmenides' chains of argument, apparently on the ground that 'these were not the actual stages of Parmenides' thinking' – as if Parmenides ought to have been writing his intellectual autobiography instead of a philosophical argument. Misunderstanding Parmenides, he makes it harder for himself to understand the post-Parmenideans. No long discussion, therefore, is needed just to defend the conventional account of this stretch of history against Mr West.

Although the conventional views which Mr West attacks[2] seem to me to be right on the whole, nevertheless it is worth pressing some questions about the nature of the pluralists' response to Parmenides. Which of Parmenides' positions did they accept and which did they reject? Do their surviving fragments show that they argued against the rejected positions, or that they merely ignored Parmenides' arguments? Did Anaxagoras and Empedocles take the same course in this respect or did they differ? If so, how, and why? This paper is a result of taking another look at Anaxagoras and Empedocles with these questions in mind. Its conclusion is that Anaxagoras, like Empedocles, certainly thought that Parmenides had raised a

[1] West (1971b), 219.
[2] West singles out Guthrie, II.1, and Kirk and Raven (1957), 368f.

47

real problem which he must try to deal with, but that his method of dealing with it was perhaps more radically different from that of Empedocles than is usually supposed.[3] Not all of these questions can be dealt with here; the focus of the present essay is Anaxagoras.

Simplicius says:

In the first book of his *Physics*, Anaxagoras plainly declares that coming-to-be and perishing are coming together and separating. This is what he writes: 'Coming-to-be (γίνεσθαι) and perishing (ἀπόλλυσθαι) are customarily believed in incorrectly by the Greeks, since nothing comes-to-be or perishes, but rather it is mingled together out of the things that are, and is separated again. Thus they would be correct to call coming-to-be "being mingled together (συμμίσγεσθαι)" and perishing "being separated (διακρίνεσθαι)".'[4]

A very similar statement is preserved among the fragments of Empedocles:

When they [sc. the four roots – earth, water, air and fire] are mingled together to form a man ... then men speak of coming-to-be, and when they are separated, then they speak of ill-fated death. They are right to call them so, and I follow the custom in so speaking.[5]

The text of this fragment is very uncertain; but editors are in general agreement about the sense of the quoted portion, except for the last line. As the manuscripts have it, it is metrically deficient; and one way of remedying this is to put in a negative, thus making Empedocles say the same as Anaxagoras: ordinary men are *not* right to speak of coming-to-be and perishing.

Did they say the same thing or not? It is impossible to be sure, but it is striking that in the preserved fragments of Anaxagoras there are no occurrences of these censured terms, whereas Empedocles has no scruple in using them.[6] It seems likely, therefore, that Empedocles held it to be *right* to speak of coming-to-be and perishing, even though they are to be *explained* as 'mingling together' and 'separating'. The argument of this paper does not at all hang on the interpretation of this line, but it turns out that there is some aptness about this result.

Other fragments confirm that Empedocles wants to approach the concepts of coming-to-be and perishing with much caution:

> Something else I will tell you: there is growth (φύσις) of *no one*
> of all mortal things, nor end in baneful death;

---

[3] Which wrote first, Anaxagoras or Empedocles? This paper remains neutral on the question. For an extensive discussion of the arguments, see O'Brien (1968), which concludes that Empedocles wrote later than Anaxagoras, and was influenced by him.

[4] Simplicius, *Physics* 163.18 = Anaxagoras B17. I do not think there is any need to defend the testimony of Simplicius again against the attack on it in Gershenson and Greenberg (1964). See for example Kerferd (1969), 490, n. 3. The fact that Simplicius' quotations from Anaxagoras' book take different forms in different places does not entail that he did not know the book at first hand. This can be proved by looking at his quotations from the *Timaeus*, which he certainly knew: compare the quotations from *Tim.* 51E6–52D1 in his *Physics* 224.30ff, 539.14ff, and 43.15ff. A few details vary, but he gets the sense right.

[5] Plutarch, *Adv. Coloten* 1113A–B = D–K 31B.9.

[6] Empedocles B17.3–4, 11, 35; 21.14; 26.4 and 10 all use some form of γίνεσθαι in a positive exposition of his own theory. Anaxagoras uses them only to reject them, as in B10.

but only mingling, and separation of things mingled,
is the case; and 'growth' is men's name for these.

(B8)

Childish fools – they have no deep-minded thoughts –
who claim that there is a coming-to-be of what formerly was not,
or that something dies and perishes utterly.

(B11)

From what in no way *is*, no coming-to-be is possible
and that what *is* should perish is unmanageable, unheard of;
it will always be *there* – wherever you may shove it!

(B12)

What caused such suspicion of the concepts of coming-to-be and perishing? The only argument against them surviving from an earlier time is that of Parmenides B8.1–21, which reaches the conclusion: 'Hence coming-to-be (γένεσις) is extinguished, and perishing (ὄλεθρος) is unintelligible.' There is no trace in the fragments of Anaxagoras and Empedocles of an original argument to this effect. But there is confirmation that it was a conceptual difficulty about coming-to-be *out of what is not* that persuaded all three of them. About Parmenides, there can be no doubt.[7] Anaxagoras B3 makes the same sharp contrast between what *is* and what *is not*; Empedocles B11 and 12 appear to be manipulating the same point.

But what are the two of them making of this point?

One of the fragments of Anaxagoras, on which most interpretations are built, is B10, from a scholium to the text of Gregory of Nazianzus: 'How, he says, could hair come-to-be out of not hair, and flesh out of not flesh?' Another 'repudiating question': he means that it could not. But if this is rightly taken to be a key to his thought, it surely means that he was taking the Parmenidean conclusion, 'nothing comes-to-be out of what is not', in a very strong sense – 'nothing comes-to-be out of what *it* is not'.

We can see the point simply enough when we compare Anaxagoras with Empedocles on the growth of bones. Empedocles says:

Earth, glad to do it, in its broad-breasted melting-pots
received two parts of bright Nestis [sc. water] out of eight,
and four of Hephaestus [sc. fire]; and they *came-to-be* white bones,
marvellously fitted together by the adhesives of Harmonia.

(B96)

Anaxagoras' view, as reported by Lucretius, is in line with the question about hair and flesh just quoted: 'Bones are born from diminutive, tiny *bones*' (*De rerum natura* 1.835–6). Empedocles accounted for the growth of bone by maintaining that it comes-to-be out of certain quantities of the four elements. There is no coming-

---

[7] I have attempted to set out my ideas of Parmenides' argument in chapter 3, and will not repeat that discussion here. There may be doubt about what Parmenides meant by 'what is not', but not that this was the crucial difficulty for him.

to-be in an absolute sense – out of nothing, or out of what *in no way* is – because the portions of these elements that make up our bone have always been what they are. Anaxagoras, much more rigorous, said that bone does not come-to-be at all: what is now bone has always been *bone*; all change is a matter of redistribution.

We must now explore the lengths to which he carried this idea.

A DIFFICULTY IN THE CONVENTIONAL ACCOUNT OF ANAXAGORAS

That there is a big difference between Anaxagoras and Empedocles has of course been a commonplace of history since the time of Aristotle.

There is a clear opposition between the followers of Anaxagoras and those of Empedocles: Empedocles says that earth, water, air, and fire are four elements and are *simple*, rather than flesh, bone, and similar homoiomerous bodies; the Anaxagoreans say that these [sc. the homoiomerous bodies like flesh and bone] are simple, and are elements.[8]

The conventional account of the difference between them is quantitative: Empedocles held that the elements are four, Anaxagoras that they are very numerous – flesh, bone, blood, hair, skin, etc, perhaps bark, leaf, etc, and iron, stone, silver ... For Anaxagoras, as Guthrie puts it, 'all the infinite number of natural substances ... must be equally real'.[9] Or as Vlastos puts it:

No Ionian had ever said that earth had been 'in' the original matrix. Empedocles had said just that, precisely because he had endowed earth with Parmenidean being. Anaxagoras takes a long step *in the same direction* [my italics]. He holds that earth, air, aether, as well as hair, flesh, and every other substance are 'in' the primitive mixture, for they all have Parmenidean being.[10]

Or Cherniss:

To Empedocles, ... [Anaxagoras] objected that there is no reason for singling out earth, air, fire, and water as the only bodies of which the Eleatic law of identity need be asserted. Hair and flesh have characteristics of their own and, if nothing comes into being, hair and flesh must preserve their identity eternally. To paraphrase Anaxagoras' objection, he saw that Empedocles was coming perilously close to a derivation of new characteristics from quantitative differences, and this to his mind was inadmissible on the basis of Eleatic logic.[11]

Thus Empedocles erred in thinking he could comply with Eleatic logic, as set out in Parmenides B8, by positing four 'beings' that are eternally, uninterruptedly, unchangeably and perfectly what they are. Anaxagoras proposed to correct the error by claiming that not just four but *all* the 'natural substances' satisfy this description.

But there is a major defect in this hypothesis, which appears to have gone

[8] Aristotle, *GC* 1.1.314 a 24–9. The following portion of this text is discussed below, n. 16.
[9] Guthrie II.272.
[10] Vlastos (1950), 327.
[11] Cherniss (1964), 400.

unnoticed in the literature. The expression 'all the natural substances' has an all-embracing look; but in fact it is being used in a highly selective sense, in which blood, bone, leaf, and silver are natural substances, but men, horses, and trees are not. *Empedocles'* physical theory was certainly concerned with explaining the birth and death of *organisms* – 'bushes, and water-housed fishes, and mountain-laired beasts, and wing-borne sea-birds'.[12] How are we to suppose that Anaxagoras thought he had done better than Empedocles? In Empedocles' theory, given quantities of earth, water, air, and fire come-to-be a 'water-housed fish'. In the strict sense, nothing comes-to-be, because the earth, water, air, and fire in the fish remain what they are. But we may say that the fish comes-to-be, so long as we remember the correct analysis. We are asked to suppose that Anaxagoras criticized this theory on the ground that new characters have emerged, in the skin, bones, and flesh of the fish, that *were not* in the four elements. He proposed to correct this by giving eternal being to the skin, bone, and flesh. But what can he say about the *fish?*[13] Presumably he must say just what Empedocles would say about the skin, bones, and flesh – that they do not strictly come-to-be, since they are reducible to given quantities of eternal elements. Unless we can find a reason why Anaxagoras should be content to allow *organisms* to lack 'Parmenidean being', while at the same time carefully elevating their *tissues* to that status, he appears merely to have postponed his problem, not to have solved it.

NUTRITION AND THE HOMOIOMEROUS BODIES

No one doubts that Anaxagoras did make the tissues such as bone, hair, or flesh into 'elementary' substances in some sense; so it may be useful to look carefully at the role played by this proposition in his physical theory.

There is no mention of any of the tissues in those fragments of Anaxagoras that are usually claimed as his own words (the B fragments in Diels–Kranz), except in the sentence (B10, quoted on p. 49) taken from the scholium to Gregory.[14] This in itself is striking enough: it suggests that Simplicius, the main source for our fragments, although he knew that Anaxagoras was said to have made elements of the tissues, could not find verbatim evidence to illustrate it. Perhaps the emphasis on the tissues – an emphasis that goes back as far as Aristotle – is overdone.

In fact, this emphasis is mainly due to the contrast that was drawn by Aristotle, as we have seen, between Empedocles and Anaxagoras. He looks at their theories through the frame of his own four-tiered analysis of physical bodies. At the base

---

[12] B20. Empedocles rather revels in ornately described examples of the 'myriad tribes of mortal things, made in every kind of form, a wonder to behold' (B35.16–17), and there are several others in the fragments.

[13] Brentlinger (1972) writes: 'Mixtures are not fundamental, since they may come-to-be and cease-to-be. A cat, for instance, is a mixture, hence not an entity the coming-to-be of which is the coming-to-be of any *thing*. Similarly for all perceptible things' (p. 65). But what justification is there for saying that a cat is not a thing?

[14] Moreover, the use of the word φησι by no means guarantees that these are Anaxagoras' own words. See Schofield (1975) for a cautious analysis of this fragment.

are the four 'simple bodies', earth, water, air, and fire, which happen to be the same as the four Empedoclean 'Roots'; they are 'simple' in that they are not correctly described as being 'made of' anything else as components. Next come what Aristotle calls 'the homoiomerous bodies' (so I translate the neuter plural adjective – τὰ ὁμοιομερῆ), which are made of the simple bodies as components, although they have characters of their own that are not in the components. They are called 'homoiomerous' – 'made of like parts' – to distinguish them from the third tier, parts such as a face or a hand. Aristotle explains the meaning of his term 'the homoiomerous bodies' in one of the passages in which he talks about Anaxagoras (*GC* I.1.314 a 17): 'He makes the homoiomerous bodies elements – I mean bone, flesh, marrow, and those others whose parts *have the same name as the whole*.' A part of bone is still called 'bone', but a part of a face is not called 'face'. (We must remember this criterion, because in some of the secondary evidence about Anaxagoras a different criterion is used.)[15] The fourth tier, to complete the list, is of course the whole organic compound, such as a bird or a bush or a man.

The point that Aristotle makes is simply that Empedocles agrees with him in distinguishing the first two tiers, whereas Anaxagoras puts the homoiomerous bodies into the first tier, making them into non-composite bodies, and at the same time, so Aristotle claims, denies the status of simple, elementary bodies to earth, water, air, and fire.[16]

It is easy enough to understand, in the case of Empedocles, how his 'elements' were supposed to function in a theory of perceptible change. Just as the painter mixes together four colours and produces with them the forms of 'trees, men, women, beasts, birds, and water-nurtured fish', so earth, water, air, and fire are mixed together to produce the 'mortal things' of the visible world (B23). The compounds are mortal, but the elements are immortal: they remain through the birth, life, and death of the mortal things that are made of them.

We must now discuss the question, how Anaxagoras, having made the homoiomerous tissues into 'elements', put them to use in his theory of change.[17]

Nothing comes-to-be from what it is not.[18] If something new appears, it has

---

[15] There is a sort of catalogue of homoiomerous bodies in *Meteor.* IV.10.388 a 13–20. 'By homoiomerous bodies I mean, for example, metallic bodies – bronze, gold, silver, tin, iron, stone, etc., and whatever comes from these by being separated out from them – and animal and vegetable tissues, such as flesh, bone, sinew, skin, intestine, hair, fibre, blood-vessels, from which in turn the anhomoiomerous parts are composed, such as face, hand, foot, etc.; and in plants wood, bark, leaf, root, and the like.'

[16] It is misleading of Aristotle to *contrast* the homoiomerous tissues with earth, water, air, and fire in Anaxagoras' theory (*De caelo* 302 b 1; *GC* 314 a 28). Certainly anything that we *perceive* as earth, water, air, or fire contains a portion of everything and so is a mixture; but the same is true of anything we *perceive* as bone, blood, or flesh. Unless I have misunderstood Anaxagoras' theory fundamentally, the four Empedoclean 'Roots' must be ingredients in the original mixture and have the same status as the homoiomerous tissues. See Vlastos (1950), 329ff, for more on this.

[17] In general I am in agreement with the account given by Guthrie II.279–94. In some respects, I differ with Kerferd's version (1969), and since that is more recent, and reprinted in an influential collection, I shall offer some arguments against some portions of it.

[18] Aristotle, *Physics* I.4.187 a 28 (D–K 59A.52), etc. For the translation of ἐκ τοῦ μὴ ὄντος, see above, p. 49.

merely been 'separated out' from an environment that formerly concealed it; if it grows, it is by the addition of similar material that likewise was formerly concealed.[19] The key concepts are what we may call the Principle of Latency, borrowing the term from a phrase Lucretius used in describing Anaxagoras' theory (*quaedam latitandi copia*), and the Principle of Predominance.[20] The whole cosmos, and every part of the cosmos, however small, is a mixture; there is no region of the cosmos where *any* identifiable substance is isolated – indeed (the strongest possible assertion), there is no region of the cosmos from which any substance is *absent*: 'everything has a share of everything'.[21] But different regions of the cosmos, at least in its present state, differ from each other in the proportions of their ingredients, and only the predominant ingredients are perceptible.[22]

There is good evidence that these ideas were applied to the explanation of nutrition and growth. Here is part of the report of Aëtius, probably reproducing in the main what was written by Theophrastus:

[Anaxagoras] thought it was quite unintelligible how a thing could come into being out of what it is not or perish into what it is not.[23] Now, we take food that is simple and of one form – bread, water – and out of it grow hair, vein, artery, flesh, nerves, bone, etc. Since this is what happens, we have to agree that in the food we take are all the things that there are, and everything grows from things that are. In that food there are parts productive of blood, nerves, bones, etc.[24] – theoretical parts, because we must not refer everything to the perception that bread and water produce these things, but there are in them parts that are to be distinguished in theory.[25]

The same text of Aëtius continues with a statement that has caused much trouble: 'So, from the fact that in the food the parts (μέρη) are like (ὅμοια) the substances generated, he called them "homoiomeries" (feminine plural noun, ὁμοιομέρειαι) and declared that they are the principles of the things that *are*.'

The term 'homoiomeries' here apparently means the parts, latent in a sub-

---

[19] 'Separating out' (ἀποκρίνεσθαι) in B2, 4a, 4b, 6, 7, 9, 12, 13, 16; for more on this, see below, n. 64. For growth, see Aëtius 1.3.5 (D–K 59A.46) or Lucretius, *De rerum natura* 1.834–42 (D–K 59A.44).

[20] Lucretius 1.875. For the principle of Predominance, see B12 *ad fin.*: 'Each thing is and was, most evidently, those things of which there is most in it.' See n. 61, below.

[21] B1, B6, B8. Aristotle, *Physics* 203 a 23–4.

[22] No doubt the proportions should not be thought of as measured by weight or volume or any such precise parameters, but rather by some vague, intuitive measure such as 'strength', as in 'strong coffee'.

[23] Aëtius 1.3.5 = D–K 59A.46. Again, it is necessary to translate τὸ μὴ ὄν as 'what *it* is not', rather than as 'what is not' or 'the non-existent'. There is no question, in the case of nutrition, of something coming into existence out of *nothing*, since food is obviously an existent thing.

[24] 'Parts productive of' (μόρια γεννητικά) is ambiguous, in that it might mean 'parts of character *a*, *b*, *c*, etc. capable of changing into things of character *x*, *y*, *z*, etc.' It certainly does not mean that. This is clear both from a sentence later in Aëtius, 'the parts in the food are like what is produced', and also from a similar account in Simplicius, *Physics* 460.17–19: 'hence he supposed that in food – in water, if trees feed on water – there is wood, bark, leaves, and fruit'.

[25] I.e. the tissues nourished by the food are *latent* in the food. The expression λόγῳ θεωρητὰ μόρια may indicate an Epicurean source for this part of Aëtius' report; so Lanza (1966), 78, and Schofield (1975).

stance, that may go to build up an apparently different substance – for example, the parts of *hair* in a piece of *meat* which nourish the *hair* of the eater.[26] Lucretius uses the same word 'homoiomery' in a slightly different way, to refer to the abstract principle according to which a substance is produced by the addition of like parts.[27]

It has long ago, and often, been pointed out that the fragments of Anaxagoras contain no instance of the word ὁμοιομερῆ or its relatives, that the concept is explained in Plato's *Protag.* 329D–E in a way that suggests that it is new there, and that although Aristotle uses the adjective ὁμοιομερής as a technical term in his own philosophy, as we have said, the abstract noun ὁμοιομέρεια first occurs in Epicurus. I am convinced[28] that it was Aristotle's statement, often repeated, that Anaxagoras made 'the homoiomerous bodies' (in Aristotle's sense) into elements that gave rise to the widespread but mistaken later tradition that Anaxagoras himself used the term ὁμοιομερῆ or ὁμοιομέρεια for his elements, thus claiming that a thing is an element if and only if it is homoiomerous, in some sense. Since this position is already well set out in the literature, there is no point in defending it again here; but it may be useful to pause to ask whether there is any sense in which Anaxagoras *could* have accepted a 'principle of homoiomereity' into his physical theory.

A recent article attributes this thesis to Anaxagoras: 'Things are made of parts which are like one another and are also like the whole. These parts are the elements out of which all things are made, and are what Aristotle calls *homoiomerê* ... This may be called the principle of Homoiomereity.'[29] But Anaxagoras cannot possibly have held a principle of just this form. In the first place, he must (everyone must) recognize some intuitive difference between homoiomerous and non-homoiomerous things: neither a man nor a tree is made of parts that are like each other and like the whole. Secondly, the expression 'made of' is ambiguous. The passage from Aëtius, and other evidence, shows that in Anaxagoras' theory flesh is *made of* parts of flesh, in the sense that it is *increased* or *replenished* only by the addition of parts of flesh. But the same text shows that flesh is *not* made of parts of flesh in the sense that if you divide it up you inevitably get *only* parts of flesh. For the same flesh may be eaten, and then it adds not only to the *flesh* of the eater, but also to his hair, bones, skin, etc – and all these, we know, were parts of the flesh that was eaten. Of course, flesh *may* be divided up into parts that are flesh (as ground beef – *Anglice*, mince): but whereas that is not essential to Anaxagoras' theory of change, it *is* essential that the flesh contains latent parts of all the other substances, which may in some circumstances cease to be latent. Everything is a mixture with the same

---

[26] Simplicius, *Physics* 167.12 uses the word with the same reference, but he takes it to mean that each of these latent 'parts' is itself divisible into parts like itself – i.e. he uses the Aristotelian criterion for ὁμοιομέρη described above.

[27] Lucretius 1.834–42: *ossa videlicet e pauxillis atque minutis/ossibus ... gigni.*

[28] The arguments are compiled by Bailey (1928, pp. 551–6), Peck (1931), Mathewson (1958), and Guthrie II.282–3.

[29] Kerferd (1969), 491.

54

ingredients; so everything is homoiomerous in a trivial sense. But that does not help to pick out the elements in Anaxagoras' theory.

GENESIS AND THE SEEDS

It was convenient to discuss nutrition first, because the role of the homoiomerous tissues in nutrition is described fairly fully by our sources. But the actual surviving fragments of Anaxagoras are more concerned with the origin of the cosmos and its parts.

'All things were together,' he begins (B1); and the question at once arises: what does he mean by 'things' (χρήματα)? We have a sort of list in B4b:[30]

Before these things were separated off,[31] when all things were together,[32] no colour was evident; for the mingling together of all things (χρήματα) prevented it – of the wet and the dry and the hot and the cold and the bright and the dark, much earth being in there also, and seeds infinite in number, in no way like each other, for of the others no one is at all like the other. These things being so, we must believe that all things were there in the whole.

We have three kinds of thing mentioned here as ingredients of the original mixture: the traditional 'opposites',[33] earth,[34] and seeds. There is no mention of the homoiomerous tissues, but we need not doubt that they were included. Apart from Aristotle's testimony that they were 'elements', their inclusion follows from other theses attested in the fragments: 'in everything there is a portion of everything' (B6), and '[a thing] could not be separated, nor come-to-be in isolation; but as in the beginning, so now, all things together' (B6). Since all things *now* include the tissues as ingredients, they must have been included 'in the beginning'.

What did Anaxagoras mean by 'seeds', and what role did they play in his theory? *Quot homines, tot sententiae:*[35] there are some very elaborate theories. I think he meant it, not as a technical term of his theory for some kind of particle, but in its normal sense. The same word σπέρμα does duty in Greek for the seed of both vegetables and animals. I believe that in B4b Anaxagoras claims that the primitive mixture contained not only all the opposites, and earth, but also the seeds of all plants and animals. Where else, indeed, could they have come from, if nothing comes-to-be? We must look again at the evidence to test this idea.

First, the reasoning in B4b: '... seeds infinite in number, in no way like each

---

30 For this division of what D–K prints as one fragment, see Fränkel (1955), 284ff.
31 If 4b is separated from 4a, we have no clear reference for ταῦτα. In one of his citations (*Physics* 156.4) Simplicius leaves the pronoun out; so its reference may well be quite vague, the whole content of the phrase being repeated in the next phrase, 'when all things were together'.
32 Notice that 'all things' is the neuter plural adjective πάντα here, instead of πάντα χρήματα in B1: an indication that the word χρήματα is not a technical term that picks out one class of things from others in Anaxagoras' theory.
33 For which see Anaximander, D–K 31.A.9–10.
34 See n. 16.
35 A sampling of views, all somewhat different: Cornford (1930), 286; Vlastos (1950), 323–9; Raven (1954), 130–1; Guthrie II. 298–300. For the right view, but a rather peculiar reason for it ('nothing important is involved'), see Peck (1931), 114–18.

other, for of the other [things] no one is at all like the other'. He means that all the differences there are must be *original*: if the no–coming-to–be rule is applied strictly, there are no emergent characteristics; all the present differences – between species, sub-species, varieties, perhaps even individuals – must have been latent in the original mixture. 'The other things' in the text of the fragment means the things other than the seeds: namely, everything that grows from the seeds. We can see that *they* are infinitely different: therefore, there were infinitely different seeds in the original mixture.[36]

There is only one other mention of the seeds in the fragments:

These things being so, it is right to think that there are, in all the things that are being put together, many things, of all kinds, and seeds of all things – [seeds] having forms and colours and savours of every kind. And [sc. these things being so, it is right to think that] men were compounded and the other living creatures that have soul; and that by the men cities were settled, and farms established, as is the case with us, and that they have a sun and moon and the rest, as is the case with us, and that the earth grows much of every variety for them, of which they collect what is useful into their dwelling and make use of it. This, then, is my doctrine about the separation: that the separation would take place not only with us, but anywhere else.

(B4a)

I take it that the general sense of the fragment is this. Given that there was an original mixture containing all the substances of the natural world and seeds of all things, and given that Mind started a process of 'separating out' as described in B12, then 'these things being so' it is only reasonable to expect the formation of a cosmos such as we see around us ('as is the case with us').[37] So far as the seeds are concerned, the fragment suggests that, since they were present in the original mixture, they will be present in 'the things being put together' (perhaps the cosmic masses – the earth, sea, air – that are separated out of the mixture in the early stages): and since the mixture also contains everything needed to make them grow, they will accumulate the necessary bone, blood, flesh, etc to grow into 'men and the other living creatures that have soul'.[38]

---

[36] Compare Hippocrates, *De victu* 1.4: 'These things being so, they [sc. the opposites, mixed together] separate off from each other many and various forms of seeds and living creatures in no way like each other in appearance or power.' The verbal echoes of 4b are strong enough to make it certain that the author knew Anaxagoras; and he links seeds at once with living creatures. For a commentary on the passage, see Joly (1960), 21–4.

[37] For the interpretation of this fragment, see Fränkel (1955), 284ff. I think Fränkel's interpretation survives the objection reportedly (see Furley and Allen (1975), 379, n. 28) raised by G. E. L. Owen, that the indicative χρῶνται in D–K 11.34.14 rules it out. This indicative, according to the objection, makes it impossible to understand the infinitives as potential. But Fränkel's interpretation, as he himself seems to suggest (p. 281), does not depend on the infinitives being potential. The whole construction is dependent on the opening phrase: τούτων οὕτως ἐχόντων, χρὴ δοκεῖν. The general sense is this: granted that the initial conditions are as we have described them, it is right to suppose (i.e. it is only what one would have expected) that ... 'men were composed ... and there are cities built by the men ... just as we see around us (ὥσπερ παρ' ἡμῖν)'. The potential optative in the last sentence follows quite naturally: given the initial conditions, the same *would happen* anywhere. There is no commitment to 'other worlds' here.

[38] Curiously, there is no coherent information on Anaxagoras' idea of soul.

We have the testimony of Theophrastus[39] that Anaxagoras asserted that the air contains the seeds (σπέρματα) of all things and that they are brought down by rainwater and so generate plants. Another witness[40] extends the same theory to 'animals' (perhaps maggots?). These presumably would be the examples cited by Anaxagoras to make more plausible his theory of seeds lying latent where they might not be suspected.[41]

But what of his view of regular reproduction? There is a passage of Aristotle's *De generatione animalium* that attributes to people whom he does not name a theory that is entirely in tune with Anaxagoras' thinking as I understand it. It comes from a passage where he gives the views of 'some of the φυσιόλογοι' (among whom he often classes Anaxagoras) on the causes of resemblances between parents and offspring.[42]

There are some who say that the semen (γονή), though a unity, is a sort of 'seed-aggregate' (πανσπερμία) of many things – as if someone were to blend many juices into one liquid, and then take some of it, and could not take always an equal amount of each one [sc. of the juices], but sometimes took more of one, sometimes more of another, and sometimes took some of one, and none of another[43] – and this happens with the semen, which is a multiple mixture. The offspring is like in appearance to that one of its parents from whom most enters into its composition.[44]

The scholium on Gregory of Nazianzus, which we will now quote in full (B10), fills in some details in a plausible way, although he is not a friendly witness:

Anaxagoras discovered the ancient dogma that nothing comes-to-be out of nothing and abolished coming-to-be, introducing separation (διάκρισις) instead of coming-to-be. He

---

[39] *HP* III.1.4, and *CP* 1.5.2, cited in D–K 59A.117.

[40] Irenaeus II.14.2 (D–K 59A.113).

[41] Contrast this analysis with one that takes a different view of the seeds. Cornford (1930) wrote as follows: 'Whence came the first composite germs, before there were existing plants and animals to reproduce their kind? The germs of plants were washed down with the rainwater out of the air, which contains 'Seeds' of all kinds – that is to say, particles of every homoiomerous substance. The germs of animals came from the higher and warmer region of the aether ... So much we are told; but not how the first germs were originally formed. We may conjecture that in the Air or Aether (each of which contains Seeds of all kinds) some particles of plant or animal tissue cohered in a sort of molecule (p. 181).' He mentions in n. 2 (p. 315) that he will use the word 'germ' to avoid confusion with Anaxagoras' use of σπέρμα but does not mention that his 'germ' translates Theophrastus' σπέρμα. The notion that Anaxagoras used the word σπέρματα to mean particles of elementary substance comes originally from Aristotle *De caelo* 302 b 1: 'Anaxagoras says that the homoiomerous bodies are elements ..., whereas air and fire are mixtures of these and all other seeds. For each of these two is an aggregate of all the homoiomerous bodies in invisible form.' In *GC* 314 a 18ff, he says that earth, air, fire, and water are composite, 'for they are a seed-aggregate (πανσπερμία) of these [sc. of the homoiomerous bodies]'. I do not think these two texts are a good enough foundation for a theory that the seeds in Anaxagoras' theory were particles of elementary substances. (See also n. 16, above.)
     Although I think Anaxagoras wanted to include whole organisms among the 'things that are', I do not imagine that he would promote artifacts, like the cities and farms mentioned in B4a, to the same status, or feel any difficulty about leaving them out.

[42] *GA* IV.3.769 a 7ff. The quoted passage begins at line 28.

[43] Anaxagoras' theory would deny this last possibility: everything is in everything.

[44] This passage was said, rather tentatively, to be about the theory of Plato, *Tim.* 73B–C by Cherniss (1935), 284, n. 243, on the ground that Plato there calls the marrow a πανσπερμία. This seems quite unlikely. It is claimed for Anaxagoras by Kember (1973), 11–12. See also next note.

put forward the nonsensical idea that all things are separated out as they grow. For in the same seed (γονή) there are hairs, nails, veins, arteries, nerves, and bones; they are imperceptible because of their fineness, but as they grow, they are gradually separated out. 'For how', he says, 'could hair come-to-be out of not hair, and flesh out of not flesh?' He said the same about colours, as well as bodies – that there is black in white and white in black. He laid down the same doctrine about weights, declaring that the light is mixed with the heavy and vice versa. All of which is false. How *can* opposites co-exist with their opposites?[45]

Anaxagoras' theory of reproduction is treated at length by Erna Lesky (1950, esp. pp. 51–6). She puts him in the chapter 'Die Rechts-Links Theorie' [sc. of sex-determination]. This is a little misleading, because it suggests that he is *not* relevant to the next chapter 'Die Pangenesislehre' [sc. the doctrine that the seed is drawn from all the tissues of the body], a doctrine that she attributes to the Atomists. But there is no inconsistency between the two theories, and the evidence suggests that Anaxagoras held both.

How does the intake of food and drink build tissues that appear to have a different character from what is eaten and drunk? They contain small quantities of the tissues, latent in them, and these are 'separated out' in digestion. How does the seed grow into an adult that appears different from itself? It contains, latent within it, small quantities of all the parts of the adult body, and these are 'separated out' as nutrition adds to them. How do any of the differentiated stuffs and creatures grow from the primitive mixture, which was apparently homogeneous? It contained, in latent form, everything that would later be separated out in the course of the 'whirl' imparted by Mind.

This is a theory that tries, in the most literal-minded way, to show how Parmenides' premiss that 'what is not' is not to be spoken of, and his argument against coming-to-be, can be accepted, without making the variety and change of the perceptible world mere illusion. The theory depends entirely on the Principles of Latency and Predominance: that in anything in the world there are things too small, relatively to other things, to be perceived, and that a thing is perceived as being just those things which predominate in it.

ANAXAGORAS AND ZENO

It is very commonly said by those who write about Anaxagoras that his theory was influenced by Zeno. I think this is wrong, and propose to present three arguments against it.

---

[45] This evidence gets a little confirmation, on the subject of seeds, from a passage in Censorinus (5.2ff = A107 in Lanza (1966), but not in D–K), which lists Anaxagoras among those who hold that *non medullis modo, verum etiam et adipe multaque carne mares exhauriri* ('that males [sc. through the emission of seed] are depleted not only in marrow, but also in fat and much flesh').

About the rest of Anaxagoras' theory of reproduction there is no certainty, because the evidence is confused. There is a contradiction between Aristotle *GA* 763 b 30ff where Anaxagoras is included among those who believe that only males emit seed, and Censorinus 5.4 and 6.8. On this problem, see Kember (1973).

The first point is purely chronological: there is no good external evidence for thinking that Anaxagoras wrote later than Zeno. The second point is that there is nothing in the wording or the content of Anaxagoras' philosophy that cannot be reasonably explained without the hypothesis that he was answering Zeno. The third is that what is often said to be a response to Zeno would be nothing but an *ignoratio elenchi*.

There is no need to do more than sketch the chronological arguments.[46] The best evidence for Zeno's date comes from Plato, who says he was about twenty-five years younger than Parmenides; and the dramatic setting of the *Parmenides* has Parmenides about sixty-five, Zeno nearly forty, and Socrates very young – perhaps about 450 B.C.[47] Others mention a *floruit* between 468 and 453.[48] Plato mentions that Zeno wrote his book when he was very young. So it seems likely that the book was written between about 470 and 450.

According to the famous 'autobiography' of Socrates in the *Phaedo*, when he was young he was very much interested in natural philosophy but was disappointed with its result until he heard someone reading from a book by Anaxagoras which said that Mind organized everything in the world. The implication is that Socrates did not hear Anaxagoras in person. Anaxagoras is said to have come from Clazomenae to Athens at the time of Xerxes' invasion (480) when he was twenty – but he is also said to have begun to philosophize in Athens under the archonship of Kallias (456). These dates can be brought into harmony, as many editors do, by the device of emending 'Kallias' to 'Kalliades'. The latter was archon in 480.

Guthrie[49] includes among the things that 'may be said with confidence' that Anaxagoras' book was finished later than 467, the year of the fall of the meteorite at Aegospotami. There is a long tradition associating Anaxagoras with this event, it is true – but the tradition says that he *predicted* it. The likeliest interpretation of that legend is that it arose from Anaxagoras' famous theory that the sun, moon, and stars are all stones: if there are heavy stones in the sky, perhaps they will fall one day. Guthrie says 'the theory was suggested or appeared to be confirmed by the fall of a stone apparently from heaven'.[50] It hardly needs arguing that empirical evidence is not a necessary precondition for Presocratic theories. And the story of the prediction is explained much better if Anaxagoras' book preceded the meteorite.[51]

The later chronology of Anaxagoras' life is extremely confused.[52] I do not think there is any firm evidence that would tend to force us to abandon the thesis that his book was written before 467. If so, then the chronological arguments suggest that Zeno probably wrote *after* Anaxagoras.

[46] Because the evidence is such that however meticulously one examines it, it will never yield a conclusive case.
[47] *Parm.* 127 A–C.
[48] D–K A.1–3.
[49] II.266.
[50] II.303.
[51] He wrote only one: Diogenes Laertius I.16.
[52] See Davison (1953).

There are two fragments of Anaxagoras that are said to constitute a reply to Zeno:[53]

For of the small there is no least but always a lesser (for what *is* cannot not be) – but also of the large there is also a larger. And it is equal to the small in πλῆθος, but with respect to itself each thing is both great and small.

(B3)

These things having been thus separated out, it is right to understand that all things are neither less nor more (since it is not possible that there be more than *all*), but all things are equal always.

(B5)

To take the second first: the allegation is that it is a deliberate echo of Zeno B3: 'If there are many, it must be that they are as many as they are and neither more nor less than themselves.' Zeno's proposition, in its context, is one half of an antinomy that aims to prove, from the premiss 'there are many', *both* 'they are finite' *and* 'they are infinite'. From this contradiction, Zeno wants to deduce that the premiss 'there are many' is false. Anaxagoras has no argument against this: the most he could be doing is contradicting Zeno by saying that 'being neither more nor less than themselves' does not entail being finite. But the word 'always' shows that he is making quite a different point, that the total of things does not change *in time*.[54] As I have shown earlier in this paper, this proposition is needed as part of Anaxagoras' answer to Parmenides, and there is no need whatever to erect a Zenonian target for him to fire at.

On the contrary, Zeno's argument in B3 might well be aimed at Anaxagoras. The latter shows no sign of noticing that if things are as many as they are (which is entailed by 'all things are equal always') then they are finite. So he asserts both 'all things are equal' and 'all things are infinite'. Zeno could be looking for a contradiction in this.[55]

The first of Anaxagoras' fragments quoted above, B3, is said to be connected with the Zenonian argument against plurality contained in B1–2.[56] The conclusion of the antinomy in this argument is: 'Thus if there are many, they must be both large and small – small so as to have no size, large so as to be infinite.'

To take the second arm first: Zeno argues that anything having size must be divisible into parts having size; 'to say this once is to say it always', therefore anything having size must have an infinite number of parts having size, and therefore it must be infinitely large. So far as I can see, there is nothing in Anaxagoras that answers this argument.

---

[53] See especially Raven (1954) and in Kirk and Raven (1957), 370–1, Guthrie II.289ff, Calogero (1967), 256ff. For some excellent critical comments on this position, see Jöhrens (1939), 78–80, and Strang (1963), 366–7.
[54] This was pointed out by Strang (1963), 377, n. 13.
[55] But it is not necessary to think that Zeno had Anaxagoras in mind as a specific target. He was systematically looking for contradictions to be derived from 'there are many', and it is not necessary to think that all the types of pluralism that he attacked were actually asserted by anyone.
[56] On this, see Strang (1963), 366–7.

As to the first arm: Zeno argues that each of the alleged 'many' must have no size, because otherwise it will be divisible and so not be a 'one'. Again, there appears to be nothing in Anaxagoras that takes note of this.

What Anaxagoras says can be wholly explained as part of his defence of his Principles of Latency and Predominance. A change from A to B is possible, in his view, only if B is latent in A. So if A is so small that it contains nothing latent in it, it cannot change. Since he apparently wanted to set no limits to change,[57] he had to maintain that there is nothing so small that it can contain nothing latent in it – that is, 'there is no least, but always a lesser'. Without this assumption, the 'portions' of everything that are in everything could be eliminated simply by taking smaller and smaller pieces, so that 'what is' would vanish into not-being.

The theory of change depends on the proportions of the ingredients of a thing: the possibility of change depends on there being a relatively large and a relatively small. Any limits on the large and the small would limit the possibility of change. Hence for any given size, there must be a 'larger', if latent things can be of any size and can cease to be latent.

When he says the large is 'equal to the small in πλῆθος', he probably means that both the large and the small contain an equal number of ingredients – namely, all that there are. The same is said in B6: 'There are equal portions, in number, of the large and the small.'

The last clause of B3, 'with respect to itself, each thing is both great and small', is a little puzzling. He has just been talking about *comparative* sizes – small and smaller, large and larger. One might expect him to say that with respect to itself each thing is neither large nor small. I suspect that what he means is that without comparisons a thing is whatever you like to call it – large or small. Large and small are entirely relative terms.[58]

Anaxagoras' theory of infinite divisibility – 'of the small there is no least but always a lesser' (B3) – is then a deduction from three propositions in his response to Parmenides:

(1)   There is no coming-to-be or perishing.
(2)   Nevertheless, a thing perceived as A can change into a thing perceived as B.
(3)   This is possible only if B is latent in A.

There is no reason to think that he was unable to work this out without a nudge from Zeno. On the contrary, if he did work it out after reading Zeno, then he either either stupidly misunderstood or shamelessly ignored Zeno's point. For Zeno introduced the infinite divisibility of 'what is' *only* to show that it leads to ridiculous and unacceptable consequences. If it is infinitely divisible into an infinite number of ultimate units, then it is impossible to give a non-contradictory account

---

[57] Simplicius, *Physics* 460.12: Anaxagoras saw 'that everything comes into being out of everything, if not immediately, then serially (air from fire, water from air, earth from water, stone from earth, fire from stone again) ...'

[58] This conclusion is the same as Calogero's (1967, pp. 261ff), but I differ from him about many details.

of these units (B1–2). If it is infinitely divisible without any ultimate units, then you can never traverse it or give any non-contradictory accounts of its limits (the Dichotomy and the Achilles).[59] The Atomists and Aristotle tried to deal with this powerful attack on divisibility; not Anaxagoras. If Zeno had argued *only* that infinite divisibility entails infinitely numerous parts with finite size, then we might believe that Anaxagoras' 'of the small there is no least but always a lesser' was a reply to him. But Zeno had already forestalled this alleged reply.

ANAXAGORAS COMPARED WITH PLATO

The late Arthur Peck called his 1931 article 'Anaxagoras: Predication as a Problem in Physics'. In fact, one can read his article without realizing why he chose that title, because he did not make the point explicitly. But it is a penetrating title, in that it starts us on the right road to understanding Anaxagoras. It may also point the way to a strange and little-noticed correlation in the history of Greek philosophy: that between Anaxagoras' theory of matter and Plato's theory of Forms, at least in its early appearances.[60]

'Predication' is no doubt too precise a term; it belongs to a later period in the history of grammar. Anaxagoras was concerned simply to show how the things of the perceptible world could reasonably be described as having different characters at different times or in different circumstances, without supposing that any 'things that are' (ἐόντα χρήματα) have come-to-be or perished. He aimed to do it by showing how an eternally static quantity ('all things are nothing less nor more ... but all equal for ever': B5) of things that *are* can alter the appearances by changing their predominance in different regions. We may observe now that this theory entails that the words we use to describe the physical world are systematically ambiguous. When we say of a portion of the perceptible world (a) 'this is a piece of gold', we mean (b) 'this is a piece of matter in which gold is the predominant ingredient'. In (a), the gold is the perceptible matter; in (b), 'gold' means just what gold is.[61]

Of course, a thing may have different characters at the same time: it may be, for example, dark, red, hot, and meat; that is to say, it has a predominant share in all these items. To make this work at all, there must be some intuitive notion of the

---

[59] For this interpretation of Zeno, see Owen (1957–8) and Furley (1967b), 69–70. Jöhrens (1939, p. 79) adds that Anaxagoras' thesis of infinitely many parts in finite things is contradicted by Zeno's argument (B1) that infinitely many parts entail infinite size.

[60] Brentlinger is one who does examine it, in his very interesting and important article (1972).

[61] It is an important element in Strang (1963) to bring out clearly this necessary implication of Anaxagoras' theory. Anaxagoras himself may not have been conscious of the ambiguity, since it does not obtrude itself in particular contexts. In the fragments he says only that the preponderant ingredients of a thing determine what that thing is 'most evidently'. The Derveni papyrus, which recalls many Anaxagorean ideas, says 'each thing *is called* (κέκληται) from what predominates' (see Burkert (1970), 445). Theophrastus *ap.* Simplicius, *Physics* 27.7 uses the phrase 'each thing is characterized according to what predominates'.

sorting of properties – into pairs of opposites, for example. Dark predominates over *light*, not over sweet, and so on. But there seems to be no trace in Anaxagoras of any theory of categories: the 'opposites' such as hot and cold are apparently treated as 'things that are' in the original mixture, along with earth and seeds (B4b).[62] I believe that he meant to be equally indifferent to categorial priorities in dealing with what Aristotle called substances. If my argument is right, man and horse and oak were present in the original mixture in the form of seeds, imperceptibly small; we say 'a man has come-to-be' when the seed grows, by addition of like parts, so that the ingredient 'man' comes to be predominant; but no man has come-to-be out of what is not man (out of flesh and bone, for instance). The mechanism creaks here a little. The homoiomerous bodies grow by the addition of parts that have the same name – bone by the addition of bone. Man grows not by the addition of *man*, but by the addition of flesh, bone, blood, etc. Anaxagoras does not explain the relation between man and flesh, bone, blood, etc., any more than he explains the relation between any of these and bright, dark, hot, cold, etc.

The analogies with the Platonic theory of Forms are sufficiently obvious, and need not be set out at great length. Both theories explain change in the physical world by introducing entities that are themselves eternally unchanging – with the crucial difference that the early theory makes these entities material, the later immaterial. In both, these entities can be described as 'just what [*x*] is' – 'the hot itself', 'gold itself', 'man himself'; physical objects merely 'have a share' of these entities. Again, there is the difference: the 'share' in Anaxagoras' theory is a physical quantity (the word he uses is μοῖρα) that is present in the object as an ingredient; Plato uses the same language of 'sharing', 'participating', 'presence in', but whatever this relation is in his theory, it is not physical mixture.

Both theories have the feature that the objects of the physical world are called after whatever Forms (if we may make Anaxagoras a present of this term for convenience) they partake in. Thus they both function as explanations of predication. Anaxagoras' explanation is a very simple *causal* one: *x* is F, because of the predominant quantity of F in *x*. This may help to explain a feature of Plato's theory that has often been found puzzling: the insistence that Forms are αἰτίαι (*Phaedo* 100Bff) – the word notoriously has a wider meaning than 'cause' in English. 'It seems to me that if anything is beautiful besides the beautiful itself, it is beautiful because of nothing at all other than that it participates in the beautiful; and the same goes for all of them. Do you assent to an αἰτία of that kind?' Anaxagoras' theory could not cope with predicates like 'beautiful', and that is one reason why Plato transformed the simple physical theory into something quite different;[63]

---

[62] There has been much discussion about the status of the opposites, but there is no need to repeat it. I agree with Guthrie II.285: 'there was no difference in the mode of their being between the opposites ... and other substances like flesh and gold'.

[63] See Brentlinger (1972) for an account of some of the deficiencies that Plato found in Anaxagoras' theory.

but the new theory must still explain the αἰτία of objects in the physical world having the properties that are predicated of them.

In both theories, the beings that are 'just what [x] is' are inaccessible to sense-perception. In Anaxagorean theory, they are inaccessible because no one of them can ever be found in isolation: in the physical world, everything is a mixture. Plato made the Forms imperceptible in principle, in that they have a different mode of being from perceptible things. In both theories, it is held that these beings are accessible to Mind. Νοητά commonly designates the Forms in Plato: Anaxagoras says '[Mind] has all judgement about everything ... and the things that were being mingled together and separated out and sorted from each other, Mind knew them all' (B12).

It is the difference between the two theories that is particularly striking when we consider the actual mechanism of growth and development. What we may call the forms in Anaxagoras attain perceptible status by being partially 'separated out'[64] from each other. The transcendent Forms of Plato's theory, as well as being qualitatively invariable, undergo no movement of any kind: they are the models or paradigms that somehow (the vague term cannot be avoided) guide change.

Neither of the two theories (to speak only of Plato's earlier dialogues) arranges the Forms in which particulars may partake into categorial hierarchies. If something is hot, it has a share of the hot itself; if it is fire, it has a share of fire itself. Plato begins to move away from such simplicities in *Phaedo* 103cff, when he laboriously points out that the predicate 'fire' is always accompanied by the predicate 'hot', and 'snow' always by 'cold'. His stress on this point may well be due to consciousness that his theory was better able to handle it than Anaxagoras'.

To Plato, the problem did eventually present itself clearly as a problem about predication: if we predicate the same thing of a number of particulars, what is that thing that they all have in common? It does not seem to me that this 'one over many' question was one that concerned Anaxagoras much, although his account of matter and its properties could account for it, within limits.

But this is not the place to pursue this topic further. What I have been concerned to stress is this. Anaxagoras lies on a path in the field of natural philosophy that leads from Parmenides to Plato – especially the Plato of the *Phaedo* and *Republic*. It is a path lined with a vast population of 'things that are' (ἐόντα χρήματα, ὄντως ὄντα), showing a huge range of real differentiae. Empedocles took a different path – the one also taken later by the Atomists – through metaphysical territory populated sparsely with just a few primary beings – the four 'Roots' and their irreducible properties, or the shape, size, weight, and motion of the atoms. It is perhaps pointless to ask whether Anaxagoras or

---

[64] Anaxagoras' word for this separating, ἀποκρίνεσθαι, is a medical term, used of the *secretion* of substances by the organs of the body. It is used of the secretion of semen, which may well be a significant paradigm for Anaxagoras. The 'separation' in his theory is never complete, as we have seen: there is always 'a share of everything in everything'.

Empedocles was the more 'advanced', since they chose different routes. But my picture of Anaxagoras is of a kind of Ajax among the Presocratics, unable to appreciate the advantages of modern, more flexible ways, and heroically[65] adhering to the strictest interpretation of the Parmenidean code.

[65] I owe the word to an incredulous comment by Montgomery Furth, on the occasion when I presented an earlier version of this paper to a 'Workshop on the Eleatics' at the University of Alberta in 1974. I am grateful to other participants in that meeting also. A second version of the paper was discussed at a meeting of the Society for Ancient Greek Philosophy in Washington in 1975, where it received some useful criticism from Nicholas White, Richard McKirahan, and others. I am particularly grateful to Malcolm Schofield, David Sider, and George Kerferd for written comments on one or other version of the paper.

6

ANTIPHON'S CASE AGAINST JUSTICE

[1981]

In this chapter, I shall argue that Antiphon in his fr. 44 (consisting of the famous papyrus fragments from Oxyrhynchus) criticizes and rejects justice on the ground that to be just is to damage or neglect one's own natural interest.[1] Antiphon's position is thus similar to that of Thrasymachus in Plato, *Republic* I, although Thrasymachus differs in making no explicit appeal to nature.[2] Callicles in Plato's *Gorgias*, on the other hand, although he commends the same kind of behaviour as Antiphon and Thrasymachus, differs radically from both of them in his treatment of the concept of justice.

What has most significantly delayed agreement about the interpretation of these three texts, I suggest, is a failure to keep in mind a feature of the semantics of words like 'just'. (To avoid inconvenient disagreements about labelling, I shall indicate the class in question simply by listing more examples: 'brave', 'wise', 'mean', 'cowardly', 'prudent', 'rash'.) These words in normal use have both a descriptive and a prescriptive force. They are *prescriptive* in that when we predicate them of a term denoting an action or type of action, we mean to *recommend* or *warn against* the subject. On the other hand they are not interchangeable in the sense that any recommending word can be substituted for any other, or any warning word substituted for any other. They are appropriate each to its own type of action, and thus they have a *descriptive* force. So the adjective 'brave', for instance, serves to commend an action, but at the same time classifies the action as being of a certain type. In this case, and others, the descriptive force may be quite vague, and the adjective may thus have a wide range of uses. But frontiers between the descriptive applications of commending adjectives, although vague, are certainly not non-existent. There are actions that one would commend as 'brave' but never describe as 'just'.

This simple point takes on particular importance when there is a *debate* about the commendability of some type of action, or a challenge to current morality. The

---

[1] By 'justice' I mean δικαιοσύνη or τὸ δίκαιον.

[2] Unlike many critics, I believe that Thrasymachus defends a single consistent position, until Socrates gets him to contradict himself at 350D.

challenger has a choice, in principle, between two ways of treating adjectives of this kind:

(i)   he can retain the descriptive force while questioning or rejecting or reversing the prescriptive value (e.g. he might say 'perhaps impartiality *is* just, but I'm against it – down with justice!');

(ii) he can retain the prescriptive value while proposing a change in the descriptive force (e.g. he might say 'true justice, which I will always uphold, is not impartiality but ...').

Callicles can be distinguished decisively from Antiphon and Thrasymachus on the basis of this choice: he takes the second option, whereas both Antiphon and Thrasymachus consistently take the first. Callicles' position is made clear in these few sentences:

Hence, by law and convention this is said to be unjust and immoral, to seek to get more than the many; and they call it 'unjust'; but in my view nature herself makes it plain that it is *just* for the better man to get more than the worse, and the more powerful than the less powerful.

(Gorgias 483c6–D2)

He wants to retain 'just' as a word of commendation, but proposes that it properly describes the vigorous and successful pursuit of self-interest, not self-abnegation in the interest of fair treatment for others.

Antiphon and Thrasymachus never describe the pursuit of self-interest as 'just', although they do claim, in the texts we have, that it is to be commended. They do not propose a new descriptive use of 'just', but rather that the traditional prescriptive value is wrong.

'You call one of the two [sc. justice and injustice] a virtue, and the other a vice?'
'Of course', [said Thrasymachus].
'That is, you call justice a virtue and injustice a vice?'
'Is that likely, my good man, since I say that injustice is profitable, and justice is not?'
'What then?'
'The opposite.'
'Do you call being just a vice?'
'No, but certainly high-minded foolishness.'
'And you call being unjust low-minded, then?'
'No, I call it good judgement.'

(Republic I, 348c5–D2, trans. Grube)

Thus Thrasymachus proposes to reverse the prescriptive value of these words 'just' and 'unjust'. Antiphon, in fragment B44, hardly goes so far as to reverse it, but at least annuls it. They both differ from Callicles about this.

Many scholars have found in the Antiphon fragment some positive theory of justice: that is to say, a theory in which justice is retained as a virtue to be commended, but with a changed content. I hope to rebut this idea, but I propose to make the attempt by offering an analysis of Antiphon's text, rather than a detailed criticism of my predecessors. This is not the first time that such an interpretation of Antiphon has been proposed: it was defended in a paper by G. B. Kerferd in 1959. My excuse for returning to the theme on this occasion is that writers since 1959 have not generally followed his lead.

So justice is to refrain from transgressing the laws and customs (νόμιμα) of the city in which one is a citizen.

So a man would be treating justice in the way that is best for himself (μάλιστα ξυμφερόντως) if in the presence of witnesses he held the laws in great respect, but when alone and without witnesses, the [claims] of nature; for the claims of the laws are imposed, whereas those of nature are necessary, and the claims of the laws are agreed, not natural growths, whereas the claims of nature are natural growths, not agreed.

So, one transgressing the laws and customs, if he escapes the notice of those who made the agreement, is rid of shame and penalty; if he does not escape notice, not. But if, contrary to what is possible, he attempts to force one of the things that grow naturally with nature, then the harm is no less if he escapes all men's notice, no greater if all see him. For he is damaged, not because of opinion, but because of truth.

(44A, col. 1–2)

The fragment begins in the middle of an argument, and there is no way of telling what point is being made by the connecting particle 'so' (οὖν) at the beginning. But we are presented, plainly enough, with a statement of the kind of action described by 'justice': it is the kind of action that is in conformity with the laws and customs of one's *polis*.

Some have found a problem in reconciling that statement with the next sentence – a problem that is, however, easily and legitimately removed by the translation 'would be treating justice', rather than 'would be using justice', for χρῷτ' ἂν δικαιοσύνῃ. If justice is refraining from illegality, how would a man be 'using' justice when in the absence of witnesses he ignored the laws? There is some temptation to suppose Antiphon to mean that he would then be using a *different* justice – a natural justice, after the style of Callicles. But the temptation vanishes with the translation 'would be *treating* justice'; preferring nature to law *is* a way of treating justice, still construing justice as in the opening sentence. And this is indisputably a reasonable way of interpreting the Greek verb χρᾶσθαι. So there is no justification for finding a hint of 'natural' justice in this paragraph. The distinction set up here is not between *justice* as obeying the law and *justice* as following nature, but rather between justice, always construed as obedience to the law, and respect for the claims of nature.

The contrast between opinion and truth in the last clause makes one think at once of the Eleatics. Antiphon's book, from which these fragments come, was called 'on Truth'; and I think J. S. Morrison (1963) may be right in arguing that its main concern is with natural and conventional divisions of τὰ ὄντα and the names attached to them. However, it is not necessary to introduce any specifically Eleatic notions in order to understand this clause, in which 'opinion' and 'truth' can be interpreted without any burden of theory: a lawbreaker is punished if he is *believed* by other men to be a lawbreaker, whereas one who flouts nature suffers for it just because it is *true* that he flouts nature.

The next sentences of the papyrus claim that there is not merely a distinction but actually an opposition between justice, still interpreted as observance of the law and customs of the city, and nature:

It is for all these reasons³ that we are making our investigation, because most of the things that are just, according to the law, are laid down in a manner hostile to nature.

For it has been laid down legally what the eyes must see and not see, what the ears must hear and not hear, what the tongue must say and not say, what the hands must do and not do, where the feet must go and not go, what the mind must want and not want. Now, these are in no way more likeable to nature or more akin – what the law averts men from, or what it turns them to.⁴

On the other hand, to nature belong life and death; and life for men is from whatever is good for them, death from whatever is not good for them. But the things laid down as good for you by the law are fetters on nature, whereas those laid down by nature are free.

Now, in right reason it is not the case that whatever is painful benefits nature more than whatever is pleasing. So the painful would not be *better for you*, either, as compared with pleasant. For whatever is in truth good for you should not be harmful but should help.

(2.23–4.22)

In the first paragraph of this, as in the last quotation, justice has a single reference, to observing the law. Antiphon is quite clear what justice is, and he is against it. He is not proposing a different justice, but opposing justice to nature. He is, in fact, consistently taking the first option of the two we distinguished above on p. 67.

But it is time to say something about the other word of commendation repeatedly used by Antiphon in our fragment: the verb ξυμφέρειν. I have translated this throughout with the expression 'good for you' or some variant of it, choosing the phrase deliberately because of its medical connotations in English. The Greek verb was much used in Greek medical texts, and Antiphon's relation with the medical writers in this respect was commented on by Heinimann (1965, pp. 128ff, especially n. 10); there is no need to repeat what he wrote, but a couple of examples may serve as a reminder of how the term is used:

---

³ Reading ἔστιν δὲ πάντων [δὲ] ἕνεκα τούτων with K. Schmidt. See the apparatus in Diels–Kranz.
⁴ I have translated ἤ in line 24 as 'or', rather than 'than', in spite of the fact that since the whole clause is negative one would normally expect οὔτε rather than ἤ. Although it seems a tolerable usage, I have not yet found an exact parallel to this. If therefore the translation 'than' must be preferred, there is no escaping the conclusion that the logic is bizarre: Antiphon would be saying that what the law forbids is no *more* likeable to nature than what it enjoins. But why should anyone suppose it to be *more* likeable? What he needs to show is that it is no *less* likeable.

The sweetest, lightest, and most sparkling waters are good for those whose digestive organs are hard and easily heated.

(Airs, waters, places VII.86, trans. Jones)

But if the weather be northerly and dry, with no rain either during the Dog Star or at Arcturus, it is particularly good for those who have a phlegmatic or humid nature, and for women; but it is very hostile to the bilious.

(ibid. x.84)

In the Antiphon papyrus we are told first that it is 'best for' a man to observe the law in the presence of witnesses, but to respect nature in the absence of witnesses (44A, col. 1). Most of the content of justice is 'hostile to nature' (col. 2.26–30) – and 'hostile to' is the contrary of 'good for' in *Airs, waters, places,* just quoted. 'Life for men is from whatever is good for them, death from whatever is not good for them' (col. 3.28–32). In all these contexts, what is good for you is plainly *commended* by Antiphon: he is not, in other words, treating ξυμφέρειν in the same way as δικαιοσύνη, but allowing it to retain its prescriptive value.

Obviously, it is possible to use a commending word, retaining its commendatory value, in such a way that the writer does not himself subscribe to the commendation (e.g. in 'what *you* say is just', 'the Roman idea of generosity'). This is what Antiphon does in col. 4.1–6: 'But the things laid down as good for you by the law are fetters on nature ...' We have already been told that 'most of the things that are just, according to the law, are laid down in a manner hostile to nature' (col. 2.26–30). Antiphon contrasts the claims of law and those of nature, and allies himself with nature. It is at this point that Saunders begins to go astray, I think, in his 1978 article. He translates col. 4.1–15, 'as to advantageous things (τὰ δὲ ξυμφέροντα), those laid down by the law ...', as if there were some class of advantageous ('good for you') things, adopted by Antiphon as objectively determined, some of them picked out by the laws and some by nature: and he uses this to establish the next step in his argument, 'it is to be noted (1) that the laws confer some advantage ...' But the Greek text does not warrant this. There are two classes of things in question, one 'laid down as good for you by the laws', the other 'laid down as good for you by nature'.[5] The former are said to be 'fetters on nature', and there is no hint of an implication that Antiphon believes them to be good for you at all.

Antiphon continues to use 'just' in the following section of the papyrus for what is commanded by law and custom; and there is still no trace of any *natural* justice. There is a break in the papyrus, so that the subject of the next preserved sentences is not exactly clear; but the actions described are connected with 'legal justice' (τὸ ἐκ νόμου δίκαιον) in col. 6.6. Three examples of types of behaviour are given

---

[5] The point of the participle κείμενα, which is to be understood in the second phrase, of course, as well as in the first, is that these things are *established as* good for you, either by law or by nature. Saunders understands him to mean that they are good for you, and some are prescribed by law and some by nature. A different participle, such as ἐπιταττόμενα, would be needed to make that point.

(col. 5): people who defend themselves only after they have suffered wrong, people who are kind to their unkind parents, and people who allow others to seize an advantage over them by swearing an oath. These are not examples of behaviour required by the law: they go beyond that, as Kerferd (1959) pointed out. But they are surely examples of conventionally approved behaviour. We are now told that they are hostile to nature, and unnecessarily painful:

> Of these things mentioned, you would find many hostile to nature, and there is in them more pain, less being possible, and less pleasure, more being possible, and suffering harm, not suffering being possible.
>
> Now, if to those promoting such courses help came from the laws, and to those not promoting but opposing them, loss, then obedience to the laws would be not disadvantageous. As things are, however, to those who promote such courses legal justice is not strong enough to give help. For it first allows the sufferer to suffer and the doer to do, and did not at the time prevent the sufferer from suffering and the doer from doing, and when it is a matter of redress, there is nothing special for the sufferer as opposed to the doer, since he must persuade those who will bring about redress that he has suffered, and be able to (induce them?) to punish. These same things are open to the doer to deny ...
>
> (5.13–6.33)

Legal justice is both powerless to prevent its followers from suffering, and unable always to set the balance right when suffering has taken place. The expression 'legal justice' may suggest, by its similarity to 'what is laid down by the law as good for you' in 4.1–5, that δίκαιον, like ξυμφέρον, is being used in the second of the two ways I distinguished, so that its prescriptive value is always positive and hence the valuer must be specified. But there is no trace, in fact, of a contrasting *natural* justice. The epithet 'legal' (ἐκ νόμου) is strictly redundant.

We shall return to this passage, and to the previous one, for information about Antiphon's criteria for deciding what is recommended by nature for men; but first, we will pursue the concept of justice to the end of the papyrus.

There is no direct evidence on the subject of justice in fragment 44B, which we shall return to later. Fragment 44C,[6] on the other hand, is about nothing else. The word δίκαιον appears in the first preserved line, but unfortunately without enough of the context to make reliable sense of it. The text continues:

> ... giving evidence among each other – true evidence – is customarily believed to be just, and useful no less for the concerns of men.
>
> Now the man who does this will *not* be just, *if it is just not to treat someone unjustly whenever one is not treated unjustly oneself* (A). For it is necessary that he who gives evidence, even if he gives true evidence, nevertheless treats another unjustly in a way ...
>
> (1.3–19)

---

[6] A different but plainly related papyrus, labelled C by editors subsequent to Diels–Kranz. It begins on p. 353 of D–K II.

The translation is clumsy because of the need to preserve the same word for δικ-
whenever it appears. The statement that a witness commits an injustice to
someone when he tells the truth about him sounds more paradoxical than the
Greek; we might all agree (except Socrates, I suppose) that such a witness *damages*
him, and in another context that might be an acceptable translation of ἀδικεῖ.
Antiphon's 'in a way' (πως) shows that he is sensitive to the paradox.

Fragment 44C continues with some development of the idea that the witness
treats the accused unjustly, and is himself treated unjustly by the accused or his
family when they try to take vengeance on him for his testimony (I think it is not
necessary to go through this in detail), and then goes on:

And indeed these are evidently not small injustices, neither what he himself receives nor
what he commits. For it is not possible that *these* are just, and also *to do no injustice and
himself not be unjustly treated* (B). On the contrary, it must be that either the one set of them
is just, or that both are unjust. Evidently, too, to be a juryman or a judge or an arbitrator,
however it may be concluded, is not just. For to help one side is to injure the other ...

(12.12–32)

Now, our interpretation of Antiphon's position in these fragments depends
crucially on how we take the two clauses emphasized in the last two quotations and
labelled (A) and (B). The first of these is made a little more obscure by the fact that
the conjunction is unreadable. Only the last letter is certain, according to the
editors; Wilamowitz restores ἐπείπερ, Hunt καὶ γάρ, Diels εἴπερ or ὥσπερ.
Some think it makes a difference to the status of the clause which of these is
chosen; I agree with Guthrie (III.110, n. 2) that it does not. On the other hand,
there is still room for disagreement about what is being said.

Bignone (1938) believed that in (B) we have 'la vera definizione proposta da
Antifonte'. Havelock claimed that in (B) 'he exposes a basic premiss of his moral
philosophy' (1957, p. 260), and he went on to call Antiphon, mainly on the
strength of this, 'a utopian thinker, devoted to a kind of Golden Rule of
nonaggression' (p. 267). Moulton speaks of (B) as being 'far more likely [than
A] to represent Antiphon's ideal concept of justice: mutual non-aggression'
(1973, p. 348). Guthrie seems to attribute to Antiphon the view that 'Complete
freedom from wrong-doing, either as doer or sufferer, is the ideal, but it is not in
anyone's power to ensure that no other man wrongs him, so that the best
practical expression of justice is never to take the initiative in wrong-doing'
(III.112). All of these are bent on finding in Antiphon a positive theory of justice as
a virtue.

Kerferd was surely right, however, when he wrote:

We have here a further ideal of justice – not to wrong another when not oneself wronged.
And it is presented as inconsistent with an earlier ideal, that embodied in certain kinds
of action usually regarded as just (?ranked as just by the laws). The conclusion is drawn
that either one of the two ideals is correct or neither is correct, but they cannot both be
correct.

(1959, pp. 30–1)

Exactly so. We have been told earlier that justice is hostile to nature, that it imposes fetters on nature, and that it is too weak to help its followers and protect them from harm. Now we hear another criticism – that it is *inconsistent*.

It is disappointing that Kerferd's analysis of this fragment, which is clearly right, has not been adopted by some of the later writers, and it therefore seems worthwhile to try to muster some reinforcements. In the first place, then, we should take note of the elegantly precise logic that Antiphon uses. We have here, he argues, a notion of justice that requires a man (1) to give true testimony against someone involved in a court case, if he happens to have been a witness; and (2) to do no 'injustice' (i.e. harm) to anyone and to suffer no injustice from anyone. Antiphon points out that (1) and (2) cannot *both* be just; (1) might be just, or (2) might be just, or (1) and (2) might both be unjust. Now, why would Antiphon put it in this form, if he wished to assert that in fact (2) is certainly just, but (1) is not?

Secondly, let us consider what is to be attributed to Antiphon, if we take it that either B alone, or A with B, represents Antiphon's real view of justice – not now a justice that he is criticizing and rejecting, but a justice that he wishes to recommend. How are we to reconcile this with his earlier criticism of justice as imposing fetters on nature? Either we must suppose (1) that there is a difference between the justice that he recommends and that which he criticizes; or (2) that what we took to be a criticism was not a criticism after all, or not much of one, and that Antiphon is in favour of fettering nature. (1) is plainly the more promising of these courses, and it is the one generally followed.

But (1) will not do, either. It consists of driving a wedge between legal justice, on the one hand, and the formula 'neither to do nor to suffer wrong' on the other. But it is impossible to carry this through. The phrase itself has 'legal overtones', as Moulton notes (1973, p. 349, n. 44): it is used in arranging a truce or inter-state agreement. Glaucon, in the *Republic*, uses this very formula in setting out the Social Contract theory of the origin of *laws*:

... it seems advantageous to them to make a contract neither to do nor to suffer wrong; and this is the origin of the establishment of laws and contracts among themselves, and hence they name what the law commands, 'lawful' and 'just'; and this (they say) is the origin and essence of justice.

(II, 359A)

Apart from this and other testimony that the formula was in fact commonly associated in Greece with *legal* justice, what other form of justice could it possibly represent? Havelock seems to envisage, tentatively, a kind of utopianism in which 'man is naturally benign and seeks to express himself in amicable fellowship' (1957, p. 262) – but he has to admit that it 'remains implicit rather than explicit'. I prefer to say that there is no evidence of it at all.

The clauses labelled A and B, then, cannot represent Antiphon's own idea of a *virtue* called 'justice'. They must be understood as simply another aspect of justice treated exactly as in fragment 44A. One aspect of justice as commonly understood consists in obeying the laws, another in neither doing nor suffering wrong. But the former turns out to require conduct forbidden by the latter; hence justice as commonly understood is a contradictory notion.[7]

Antiphon's moral position, however, is not entirely negative. To find out the kind of conduct that he appears to argue for, we must first return to the second column of the first fragment of papyrus (see above, p. 71). The law, says Antiphon, lays down what you may see and not see, although so far as nature is concerned there is no difference between what is allowed and what is forbidden.

On the other hand, to nature belong life and death; and life for men is from whatever is good for them, death from whatever is not good for them. But the things laid down as good for you by the laws are fetters on nature, whereas those laid down by nature are free.

Now in right reason it is not the case that whatever is painful benefits nature more than whatever is pleasing. So the painful would not be *better for you*, either, as compared with the pleasant. For whatever is in truth good for you should not be harmful, but should help.

(col. 3.25–4.22; see above, p. 69)

It is important, at least on my view of the argument, not to follow Morrison (*ap.* Sprague, 1972) and Guthrie (III.109, n. 1) in taking the ἀπὸ in 3.30 in a partitive sense, so as to give the meaning 'Life for men is among the things that are good for them', instead of 'Life for men is from whatever is good for them.' That would make the statement about life and death into a casual aside, with no real point in the argument. But in fact it is crucial to the argument. Antiphon contrasts the law, which sets up categories between which there is no real difference, with nature, in which there is this one utterly real and undeniable difference: life and death. The fundamental premises of his case are an explicit one, that life and death are facts of nature, and two unspoken ones, that they are opposed to each other, and that everyone prefers life to death. The next step, which is demolished by Guthrie's reading, is that life is maintained by preferring what is 'good for you'. The unspoken conclusion of this part of the argument is that every reasonable man will prefer what is good for him. Antiphon then goes on to a further characterization of what is good for you: the pleasant is more likely to be good for you than the painful. This connection between what is good for you and the maintenance of life becomes more plausible when we reflect on the common use of the term ξυμφέρειν in the medical writers (see above, p. 69).

Antiphon's conception of what is laid down by nature is developed a little in 44B, which we have so far omitted from consideration.

---

[7] Professor Amelie Rorty has suggested to me that Antiphon's argument might be read as a hypothetical one: we might read him not as *asserting* that justice is obeying the law but as drawing consequences from this as a hypothesis. The arguments might then be set out like this:

I If (A) justice is to obey the laws,
   and (B) justice is recommended,
   then (C) we are recommended to do what is not good for us.
II If (A) justice is to obey the laws,
   and (D) justice is neither to damage nor be damaged,
   then (E) it is just that a witness both damage and not damage the accused.

[Those of nearer neighbours, we understand and respect;] but those of [?] far dwellers we neither understand nor respect. But in this we have become as barbarians to each other. For by nature we are all born alike, barbarians and Greeks. It is possible to see that whatever belongs to the things of nature is both necessary for all men and able to be provided for all equally (?).

And in all these things, neither is one of us marked off as barbarian, nor one as Greek, for we all breathe into the air by the mouth and nostrils, and all ... and we shed tears when pained, and we receive sounds with our hearing, and we see by eye with our vision, and we work with our hands, and we walk with our feet ...[8]

(POx 3647)

Damage to the papyrus prevents one from being certain of the argument at some points, especially at the beginning. There is no difference in nature between Greek and Barbarian, because they share the same natural needs and satisfactions – so much seems reasonably clear. But the exact meaning of the unusual verb βεβαρβαρώμεθα is more difficult. At first sight it might seem to mean that we have become like barbarians by virtue of the piece of behaviour just described in the previous lines – through parochialism, if this restoration of the damaged text is accepted. But that means, I suppose, that wrong behaviour has made us like barbarians – whereas right behaviour would make us like Greeks: precisely the distinction that the next sentence demolishes. So perhaps we should understand the sense to be simply that we have *all* become equally barbarians with respect to each other, and the previous sentence should be restored in some different way.

This fragment is elevated beyond its proper status by Bignone (1938), who speaks of 'a feeling of brotherhood embracing all mankind', and sees a considerable contrast between the sentiment expressed here and that of the previous fragment. In fact, there is no reason why they could not be quite consistent. What we have here is another instance of the unreality of a distinction made by law and custom, as opposed to nature. The attitude to differences of birth shown here is indeed at odds with that shown in *Airs, waters, places*, where the point is precisely that we all breathe a different air and hence have different natural constitutions. But it does not seem to me, as it did to Bignone, to be different from that of the first fragment – or that of Callicles; or at least, not necessarily so. The legal and conventional distinction between Greek and foreigner has no basis in the facts of nature, Antiphon argues, and without inconsistency he can argue at the same time that we are all – Greek and barbarian alike – well advised to go after what is good for us.

Antiphon stands, I think at the very beginning of the tendency to seek for guidance for human behaviour in nature, and he has not advanced far in sophistication. He takes *life* to be the single fundamental value: he dismisses as irrelevant, or as

---

[8] [Later note: I have now followed the readings and conjectures of the editor of the new papyrus, POx 3647: see *The Oxyrhynchus Papyri*, vol. LII, ed. Helen M. Cockle (The British Academy, 1984), pp. 1–5.]

'fetters on nature', whatever makes no contribution to survival; and he associates survival with 'what is good for you', and that again with pleasure. There are the beginnings of utilitarianism here, but only the beginnings.

The function of the argument is surely criticism. Saunders writes: 'It is *a priori* unlikely that Antiphon wished to decry all laws or rules or customs or conventions of all kinds whatsoever: both in theory and practice, such extreme anarchism is difficult to maintain, and there is no evidence that Antiphon was attracted to it' (1978, p. 227). And he makes a brave shot at constructing a positive philosophy *of law* for Antiphon. But he has to work extremely hard to get any support for this idea from the text itself; and I fear that it is an effort in the wrong direction. The spirit of the argument is not unlike that of Parmenides' Way of Truth, of Zeno's antinomies; and one would look in vain in the fragments of Zeno, for example, for an account of how one *can* cross the stadium, after all, even though it is undeniably 'difficult to maintain' that no one can cross a stadium.

Perhaps Kerferd failed to convince everyone of this thesis in 1959 because he expressed it in a way that is liable to misunderstanding. 'It will be argued', he wrote, 'that the papyrus fragments throughout are discussing the views of others and that Antiphon's own views only appear incidentally, if at all.' It would be clearer to say that Antiphon *is* giving us his own view of justice – the virtue as it is commonly understood – and his view of it is a critical one. We may all agree that we have reason to do what is good for us: but justice is *not* good for us, as his argument shows. So what reason have we to pursue justice? It is an excellent question that he asks, and it took Plato nine books of the *Republic* to answer it.

7

ARISTOTLE AND THE ATOMISTS ON MOTION IN A VOID

[1976]

INTRODUCTION

This chapter is part of an attempt to study the controversy between the Greek Atomists and their opponents. The Atomists are Leucippus and Democritus (their individual contributions cannot be separately identified from the available evidence), Epicurus and his Greek followers, and Lucretius. Among their opponents I include Plato, Aristotle and his Peripatetic followers, and the Stoics.

The controversy was systematic and fundamental. The two groups took opposed positions on all these problems: Is the universe infinite or finite? Are there many worlds or only one? Is our world a mortal compound, having a beginning and an end in time, or is it everlasting? Have living species or natural kinds in general developed out of simpler states of matter, or are they eternal? Is matter atomic or continuous?[1] Is there void or not? Is all change reducible to the rearrangement of changeless elements or not? Are we to seek only for mechanistic explanations or for teleological ones?

The task is to analyse and evaluate the arguments set out by each side in support of its position, in the hope of contributing to an understanding of the post-classical history of the controversy. But there is a snag. In all the ancient polemical texts that bear on these questions, only Aristotle habitually identifies his opponents and systematically criticizes their arguments. At the opposite extreme, Epicurus, it appears, took a perverse delight in presenting his philosophy as something new, without antecedents. Lucretius was more generous, at least to those whom he could regard as the grandfathers of atomism, such as Empedocles; but he too preferred to identify his opponents as *quidam* or *stolidi*. So the interpreter of the Epicureans has to work hard to identify the targets of their polemics – and he can make mistakes in this work. If he looks everywhere for anti-Aristotelian polemic, he may find it where it does not exist; for no one quite knows how much of Aristotle Epicurus had at his finger-tips. On the other hand, it may be argued that this does not matter very much in the long run. What we have to do is to put

---

[1] Individuals who in general qualify as opponents of the Atomists sometimes differ from the others on particular points, as Plato does on this one.

ourselves in the position of someone like Cicero or Atticus, who could read both the Atomists and their opponents and assess the claims of each on their argumentative merits. For such an assessment, if a particular Epicurean argument *can* be turned against Aristotle, it may not matter much whether it was framed with that intention or not.

Within this general field, this chapter takes as its topic part of the controversy about motion. The Atomists held that atoms move in the void, and indeed that this is the only kind of change that there is. Their opponents denied the existence of void space (except that the Stoics allowed it outside the cosmos), and held that all locomotion is a matter of swimming through a medium. The first idea, of motion in the void, is the main subject of this paper; the alternative will feature only in passing.

DEMOCRITUS' THEORY OF MOTION

In the present context, the creation of the notion of void need not detain us long. Melissus, supporting Parmenides, argued that since the void is nothing, and a thing moving needs the void to move into, there can be no motion.[2] The Atomists turned the argument around: if there were no void, there would be no motion; but there is motion; therefore, there is void.[3] The void is thus introduced into the theory in order to allow for the motion of atoms: it is a necessary condition of motion. Aristotle sometimes writes as though he were criticizing a theory in which void is a sufficient condition of motion also;[4] but we shall see later exactly what the target of his criticism is.

The sources establish clearly enough certain properties of Democritean atoms. Their constituent material is qualitatively uniform: they differ from each other only in shape and size. Since the material is uniform, greater size in an atom entails greater weight – but how Democritus thought of weight is problematic, as we shall see. Atoms are not liable to any kind of change, except change of place or position. So it seems clear *a priori* that the only possible form of interaction between atoms is collision, and the only differences between interactions are those brought about by differences in the shape, size, and weight of the colliding atoms, and differences in the direction and speed of their motion before colliding. *A priori*, there appears to be no room in the theory for any kind of attraction or action at a distance.

What the atomic theory is required to explain is the whole of the natural world and our knowledge of it; and one of the problems to which it is applied is how this or any other cosmos is formed in the first place. We would expect *a priori*, before looking directly at the relevant evidence, that the Atomists would attempt to form a theory of motion that would account not only for the observed changes in the

---

[2] Melissus B7.7.
[3] Leucippus A7 = Aristotle, *GC* I.8.325 a 23ff.
[4] E.g. *Physics* IV.8.214 b 14ff.

natural world but also, without any additional *ad hoc* assumptions, for the formation of the world itself.

The evidence confirms our expectations, but with a good deal of ambiguity; the source materials are severely at odds with each other about some of the details. The thoughts on the subject that follow are by no means comprehensive, and focus as narrowly as possible on the question that most irritated Aristotle – the question of natural motion, to use Aristotle's own phrase.

Ancient Atomism was a steady-state theory, not a big-bang theory. The matter that composes the universe is constant in quantity and quality and is always distributed through void space in more or less the same density. The motion of atoms had no beginning; no atom ever moved for the first time. A cosmos begins to take shape when a number of atoms at random, by some unexplained mechanism, happen to distinguish themselves from all others by joining together in a vortex (δίνη), the first result of which is that the component atoms begin to be sorted like to like.[5]

Some historians have apparently thought of this sorting process as presupposing a form of attraction between atoms of similar size and shape. There is some evidence that suggests this. Democritus describes examples of the sorting process: birds of a feather flock together, pebbles of similar size and shape are grouped together by the action of waves on a beach, grains are sorted by size and shape by the motion of a sieve, 'as if the likeness in these had some [force] of attracting things'.[6] It is likely, however, that the examples (including the birds) are meant to illustrate that there are instances of natural sorting without the action of a discriminating mind, and that the last clause, which is almost certainly added by someone other than Democritus in any case, is meant in a strictly figurative sense – it is *as if* there were an attraction.[7] There are also statements about Democritus that say he held that only like can act on like;[8] but these are either parts of his argument for the uniform quality of all atoms, or they are about the qualities of compounds. The evidence, in fact, does not support the view that there is any irreducible law in Democritus' dynamics that gives special properties to atoms of similar size and shape. The sorting of like with like, so far as we can judge, happens because similar atoms are similarly affected by the same causes.

The cosmic vortex was evidently conceived on models familiar in ordinary life – whirlpools and eddies in water, tornadoes, or twisters of one sort or another in air. The essential element in these models is that objects caught in them are mechanically sorted, to some extent, into kinds. The actual dynamics of vortices are complex:[9] the one extended text that describes the early Atomists' use of this model, obscure though it is, makes it clear that in their theory the vortex has the

---

[5] Diogenes Laertius IX.31–2 = D–K 67A.I.
[6] Democritus fragment 164.
[7] This is the view, for example, of Kirk and Raven (1957) and Mueller (1965).
[8] D–K 68A.38 (Simplicius); A.63 (Aristotle).
[9] I am indebted to Ferguson (1971); and Tigner (1974). The vortex is discussed in more detail in chapter 8.

effect of bringing larger and heavier objects to the centre, where they tend to lose their rotatory motion, and sending smaller and lighter objects away from the centre.[10]

Now, where does the concept of weight fit into this theory? The evidence is contradictory: 'Democritus said [that the elements have] two properties, size and shape, but Epicurus added a third to these – namely weight.'[11] 'Democritus says the primary bodies do not have weight, but move in the infinite through collisions with each other.'[12] Against this, we have the testimony of Aristotle: 'Democritus says each of the indivisible [bodies] is heavier the bigger it is';[13] and of Theophrastus: 'Democritus distinguishes heavy and light by size: for he says that if each one [i.e. uncompounded body] when separated according to shape differs in weight, it differs in size.'[14]

Faced with this contradiction, modern interpreters have propounded a clever solution. So long as atoms are not involved in a cosmic vortex they are weightless, and collision is the only factor that explains their motion.[15] The vortex, however, drives *larger* atoms to the centre, and this tendency to move toward the centre is what 'weight' means.[16] This cake can be had and eaten.

But in spite of the general agreement about this solution, it seems to me very dubious. It breaks down on an ambiguity that has plagued both ancient and modern commentators – the ambiguity of 'centre'. Let us agree that the vortex produced a tendency in some bodies to move toward the centre; this sounds just like what 'weight' means in the familiar Aristotelian cosmology: a tendency to move toward the centre *point* of the cosmic *sphere*. But this cannot be what Democritus meant, for two reasons. First, a vortex turns about an axis; the centre of a vortex is a line, not a point, and although it may account for the motion of bodies towards the central axis, it does not yield an explanation of why bodies should congregate at the midpoint of the central axis, at least unless some extra assumptions are made. Second, the Aristotelian view of weight as a tendency to move toward the midpoint of the cosmic sphere entails that the earth itself is spherical, as he argues himself.[17] But Democritus believed the earth to be flat and shaped like a drum.[18] The vortex that originally shaped the cosmos still continues, and is seen in the movements of the heavenly bodies. It is true that the axis of the continuing vortex no longer coincides with the vertical, because a tilt is supposed to have entered the system (to account for the rising and setting of some heavenly

<hr>

[10] Diogenes Laertius IX.30ff. = D–K 67A.1.
[11] Aëtius 1.3.18 in D–K, 68A.47.
[12] Aëtius 1.12.6, *ibid.*
[13] *GC* 1.8.326 a 9. This translation is disputed by Cherniss (1935), 97, n. 412, but comparison with *De caelo* IV.2.308 b 9 seems to me to prove it correct.
[14] Theophrastus, *De sensibus* 61, according to the text and interpretation of McDiarmid (1960).
[15] In some versions of this interpretation, atoms are allowed to have weight at all times, but weight is construed as a power of resistance, not as a tendency to move in any direction.
[16] Burnet (1945), 343–5; Bailey (1928), 83; Kirk in Kirk and Raven (1957), 415f; Guthrie II.400–4; Alfieri (1953), 88ff.
[17] *De caelo* II.14.
[18] Aëtius III.10.5. = D–K 68A.94.

bodies). But even with its axis tilted in relation to the earth's surface, the vortex seems totally inadequate to explain weight – that is to say, to explain why a piece of rock dropped from a height in Abdera falls on a line perpendicular to a stationary, flat earth.

If the vertical fall of heavy bodies on the earth's surface cannot be explained by the vortex, and cannot be explained by the attraction of like to like, then we seem to be forced back on the interpretation that weight, meaning a tendency to fall vertically, is a primary, irreducible property of the atoms.[19] The direction that we call vertical will be a datum of the system: the earth must take the shape it has *because* atoms fall in that direction. In this respect, although not in others, Democritus' theory of motion will be the same as the Epicurean theory.[20]

But what then are we to make of Aristotle's repeated complaints that Democritus did not define *natural* motion and had no theory of absolute weight?[21] The question cannot be answered until we have examined Aristotle's criticisms of motion in the void.

ARISTOTLE'S CRITICISM OF THE CONCEPT OF VOID

Aristotle directly criticized the Atomists for their theory of motion on two grounds: that they could explain neither the speed nor the direction of motion of bodies moving in the void. These two lines of criticism will be explored on pp. 83–90. First we must review briefly the grounds on which Aristotle argued that there can be no such thing as void space.

He regards the question as being dependent on the concept of *place*. A void, if there could be such a thing, would be an empty place. In fact, his own idea of what place is makes it impossible that there could be an empty one.

We need the concept of place, he says, for two reasons: (1) we want to talk about displacement (ἀντιμετάστασις): this pot is full of water, but when I pour the water out, it becomes full of air. Air has taken the *place* of water; (2) we want to talk about natural place, i.e. the destination, the resting-place, of bodies with respect to their natural motion. A useful concept of place will be one that helps us to do these two things without confusion.[22]

Working mainly from the first criterion, Aristotle argues that place must be the inner surface of the containing body: the place of the water in the pot is the inner surface of the walls of the pot.

He considers and rejects another possible definition of place: according to this, place would not be the surface of the containing body but the interval (διάστημα) defined by that surface.[23] If we analyse a case of displacement into its component

---

[19] We had better call it a property of the atoms, not of the infinite void. By calling the void 'what is not', the Atomists must have meant to deny it all positive properties.

[20] This is a return to the interpretation of Zeller (1879).

[21] *De caelo* III.2.300 b 11; 1.7.274 b 30.

[22] *Physics* IV.1.

[23] *Ibid.* IV.4.211 b 15–29.

parts using the Aristotelian definition, we have three items: the body that first occupies the place, the body that displaces it, and the container. If we analyse it using the alternative definition of place as interval, we have four items: the first body, the second body, the container, and the place. Now Aristotle intends to go on, as he does in book IV.7, to show that we could have an empty place only if we adopt this alternative definition of place as interval; and so his refutation of the concept of void is just his argument against the alternative definition of place. How, then, does he argue against it?

His first move amounts to saying that we do not need this fourth item in the analysis of displacement: 'It is thought that there is an interval as something distinct from the changing body. But this is not so: one or other of the changing bodies capable of being in contact replaces the outgoing body.'[24] Simplicius fills out the details in his commentary: think of a wineskin full of wine; the place of the wine is the inner surface of the wineskin. Empty the wine out, and either air replaces it, or the skin simply collapses, in which case there is no place left to think about.[25] He quotes Galen: 'But let us suppose that when the water is emptied out of the pot, no other body flows in: then the interval between the inner surfaces remains as a distinct entity (κεχωρισμένον).'[26] But this, says Simplicius, is just an ἄλογος ὑπόθεσις. If there is nothing to take the place of the departing water, then it will not leave – as is proved by clepsydras.

In this argument, then, Aristotle observes that we do not need a place that is not the place of either the first body or the second body in order to account for displacement, because in our experience of displacements there never is such a distinct entity. And so he concludes that place is not the interval between the inner surfaces of the container, but is just those surfaces themselves. Then he goes on to say that since void means an empty place, there cannot be a void at all, because there cannot be an empty place, by his definition.

So what looks at first sight like an *a priori* argument based on an analysis of place turns out to be an *a posteriori* argument that begs the question raised by the Atomists' theory. If this were the only argument of Aristotle's against the interval concept of place, his opponents had only to point this out. But in fact he had more arguments against it.[27] They are, however, very obscure, at least in the received text, and it would be impossible to attempt an analysis of them here without taking too much space. They appear to depend on certain difficulties that arise in the interval theory of place when you consider either the parts of the contained substance taken as divisible *ad infinitum*, or the parts of something moving in a complex of moved containers. Perhaps all we need say about them in the present context is this: in so far as they depend on infinite divisibility, they would not worry the Atomists, who denied infinite divisibility; in so far as they depend on puzzles about moved containers, Aristotle's own theory was no better off. In any

[24] *Ibid.* IV.4.211 b 18–19.
[25] Simplicius, *Physics* 573.2–27.
[26] The reference is not known.
[27] *Physics* IV.4.211 b 20–9.

82

case they apparently failed to convince even his own supporters, such as Strato and Simplicius.[28]

On this score, then, the Atomists had little to trouble them.

ARGUMENTS ABOUT SPEED OF MOTION IN A VOID

Aristotle's first objection under this heading[29] grows straightforwardly out of his assumption that the time taken by a given object to traverse a stretch of the continuum under constant conditions varies in proportion to the resistance offered by the medium: the thinner, the shorter.

A body A moves through a thick medium B in a relatively long time C, and through a thin medium D of the same length in time E; and the times C and E are to each other as the media B and D are to each other in thickness.

$$C : E : : B : D$$

Now suppose, as the Atomists do, that there exists a void stretch Z of the same length as B and D, and that the body A would take some time to traverse it, say H. Then there is a ratio between this time and time E, and by the proportion already established we can show that there is a very thin medium (not void) L that bears the same relation to medium D that H bears to E.

$$E : H : : D : L$$

And according to our assumptions, body A will get through medium L in time H. But our statement of the Atomists' postulate held that body A gets through a *void* stretch in that time. It cannot take the same time to get through a void and a medium, however thin; and hence the Atomists' postulate is wrong.

This argument proceeds by taking the nature of the moving body as a constant and varying the thickness of the medium. Aristotle goes on to generate an argument of the same kind by assuming a constant medium and varying the nature of the moving body.[30] Bodies that have a greater force (ῥοπή) of weight or lightness get through the same distance in a shorter time (sc. than bodies that are less heavy or less light). But this is because the bodies that have more ῥοπή cleave the medium more quickly. In a void all bodies would move with the same speed, which is impossible.[31]

The Epicurean Atomists accepted that in a void there can be no explanation of why things move at different speeds, and asserted that all atoms moving in the void move at the same speed.[32] That assumption was also necessary if they were to

---

[28] Strato, fragment 55 (Wehrli), with Gottschalk's appendix 2 (1965), 169; Simplicius, *Physics* 577.24ff.
[29] *Physics* IV.8.215 a 24–216 a 11.
[30] *Ibid.* IV.8.216 a 11–21.
[31] Aristotle is thinking about his own theory of natural motions, of course, in which lightness is not defined as the absence of weight, but as a tendency to move upward.
[32] Epicurus, *Letter* I.61–2; Lucretius, *De rerum natura* II.225–39.

meet another of Aristotle's arguments, about the motion of indivisible magnitudes; but we will leave that aspect aside now.[33]

They refused, rightly, to accept Aristotle's proportion sums, which entailed that a medium of zero resistance takes no time to traverse, and instead they said that the speed of atoms through the void is a natural limit. It is not infinite, but simply faster than any other speed.[34]

Atoms are never stationary, and never slow down, even when they are involved in compounds; but they do change direction when they collide. So the speed of motion of a compound may vary from nil, when all the component atoms are simply colliding with each other within the same volume, to atomic speed, when all the component atoms are moving in the same direction and not colliding with anything.[35] At the level of compounds, therefore, the Epicureans would agree with Aristotle that a thing goes faster if the resistance is less or its weight is more; but as the medium gets thinner, the speed approaches the fixed atomic speed, not infinity.

I have not observed any *arguments* in Epicurean texts that directly attack Aristotle's proposition that speed varies inversely with the thickness of the medium. The Epicurean position appears to be to show that the phenomena *can* be explained consistently on the assumption that speed has a natural limit. They did, however, directly attack the Aristotelian theory of motion as swimming through a medium;[36] but an examination of that argument would be out of place here.

ARGUMENTS ABOUT THE DIRECTION OF MOTION IN A VOID

To understand Aristotle's criticisms of the Atomists under this heading, it is necessary to recall some points about his own theory of natural motion.

He marks out certain instances of motion as natural – the motion of earth and water toward the centre of the universe and of fire and air away from the centre, and the motions of living beings – and he defines nature as an inherent source of motion and rest.[37] This is by no means the end of the matter, however. It would be, if he thought of nature as some kind of immanent force or power. The author of the pseudo-Aristotelian *De mundo* seems to have had some such idea, in that he ascribes the operations of nature to the power (δύναμις) of a cosmic deity who presides over the cosmos using his δύναμις as an executive civil service, just as the king of Persia presides over his empire from his palace in Ecbatana.[38] Presumably no further explanation is needed then; heavy things fall, light things rise, because they are interfused with this δύναμις. We can describe in more detail, but no more

[33] *Physics* VI.1–2. I have discussed this at length: Furley (1967b), 111–29.
[34] 'As fast as thought': Epicurus, *Letter* I.61. 'Faster than lightning': Lucretius VI.325–47.
[35] Epicurus, *Letter* I.62. For more defence of this interpretation, see Furley (1967b), 121–5.
[36] Lucretius I.370ff.
[37] *Physics* II.1.192 b 21.
[38] *De mundo* 6.397 b 9ff.

causal explanation is called for. Something similar is true of Stoic cosmology, in which all things are permeated with a divine πνεῦμα, an agent that distributes active properties throughout the cosmos. In both cases we can add teleological explanations for this and that feature: the divine δύναμις or πνεῦμα acts in such and such a way, rather than somehow else, because the first is better. But nothing is lacking from the causal explanation.

It is reasonably certain, however, that Aristotle did not content himself with a concept of nature of this kind. In his most explicit discussion of the problem[39] he distinguishes between living creatures, which can correctly be said to move naturally and to move themselves, and the simple bodies, which move naturally but do not move themselves.

These are what might raise the problem: what are they moved by? I mean, the light and the heavy. They are moved to places opposite to their own by force, but to their own place (the light up, the heavy down) by nature. And yet it is not clear even so by what they are moved, as it is when they are moved contrary to nature. For it is impossible that they are moved by themselves, since that is a property of life and peculiar to living things, and they would in that case also be able to stop themselves.[40]

Are they moved by nothing? That would contradict the proposition that stands at the beginning of *Physics* VII: 'everything that is moved is moved by something'.

In the face of this, many commentators have taken the view that the mover that causes the natural motion of the simple bodies is their natural place, which exercises an attraction on them, as the Unmoved Mover does on the sphere of the stars. But this is contradicted by his statement that place is not a cause in any of the four categories of cause,[41] and it appears to be inconsistent with his analysis of natural motion in *Physics* VIII.4.

That analysis appears to evade the problem, rather than to solve it.[42] A body that is actually heavy is potentially light; the change from heavy to light is caused, as such changes are in Aristotle's theory, by the action of something that is already actually light. Once it has become light, it will move to its natural place *unless prevented*. That is to say, no further direct cause is to be sought for its motion.

It is important to notice, however, that even if we reject natural place as a *cause* of natural motion, it is still a necessary condition. Aristotle gives a causal account of how a body changes from heavy to light or vice versa, but he *defines* 'heavy' and 'light' in terms of natural place: 'The question is asked, "why do light things and heavy things move to their own place?" The reason is that their nature is to go somewhere: that is what it is to be light and heavy – the former is defined by "up" and the latter by "down".'[43]

[39] *Physics* VIII.4.
[40] *Ibid.* 255 a 1–7.
[41] *Ibid.* IV.1.209 a 20. This statement occurs in the context of a possible ἀπορία. Aristotle ought, I think, to qualify it; see below, n. 46.
[42] *Ibid.* VIII.4.255 a 24ff.
[43] *Ibid.* 255 b 13–16.

We must now recall that place for Aristotle is not a part of geometrical space defined by some system of co-ordinates but the inner surface of the containing body. So we can define the place of the whole homogeneous body of cosmic fire, for example, as the inner surface of the aetherial sphere of the moon on one side and the outer surface of the sphere of air on the other side. An individual portion of fire, however, has a place of its own only if it is surrounded by something non-homogeneous with itself. We can say, then, that it is only if a portion of one of the simple bodies is surrounded by a different body that its lightness or heaviness is manifested in motion. To be light is to be at rest in the natural place of the light body and to move upward, if not prevented, from any other place.

Let us compare the naturally falling body with a projectile. The thrower imposes a motion on the projectile, the projectile moves the air, and the air keeps the projectile going.[44] Aristotle once remarks that natural motion can be *assisted* in the same way: for example, if you throw a stone downward, the air 'blows helpfully on' the natural motion.[45] Now, the fact that it is just in this situation, in which a heavy body is *thrown* downward, that air is mentioned as contributing to the motion shows that, in the free fall of a stone, air does not function in the same way. The medium is not a sustaining cause of natural motion in the way that it is a sustaining cause of forced motion. It is nevertheless a necessary part of the explanation of natural motion, in that natural motion involves place in its essence, and there is no place if there is no containing body.[46]

With all this behind us, let us come back to Democritus' theory of motion and Aristotle's criticisms of it. In *Physics* IV.8, before the criticisms on the subject of speed of motion that we have examined in the last section (pp. 83–4), Aristotle has several criticisms that bear on the problem of direction of motion. He first argues that the void cannot explain any motion, and then goes on to argue that, so far from explaining motion, it actually makes motion impossible. The point of the first argument is repeated in the second; so we can look directly at that.

'If they say that void is necessary if there is to be motion, examination shows the opposite to be the case: if there is void, then nothing can move at all.'[47] First, just as some say the earth is at rest because it is in equipoise, so things must be at rest in the void, because there is no difference (sc. of place) in the void. Second, the idea of forced motion logically presupposes that of natural motion: but there can be no natural motion in the void and in the infinite, since there is no up, down, or centre in the infinite, and no difference between up and down in the void, which is

---

44 *Ibid.* VIII.10.267 a 2ff.

45 *De caelo* III.2.301 b 29. The verb is συνεπουρίζω. Simplicius has one of his engagingly erratic moments: he notes that it probably comes from οὔριος, which is used of favourable winds, but adds that perhaps the metaphor comes from lions, 'which are said to goad themselves into motion by lashing themselves with their own tails (οὐρά)' (597.1–5).

46 Hence I think Aristotle should modify his statement in *Physics* IV.1.209 a 20 (above, n. 41). He says there that place is not a cause in any of the four categories. It is, however, a factor in the formal cause, the λόγος or εἶδος, of the primary bodies.

47 *Physics* IV.8.214 b 28ff.

equivalent to 'nothing'.[48] Furthermore, there can be no motion of a projectile in a void. A projectile continues to move after losing contact with the thrower either by antiperistasis[49] or because the air that is pushed pushes with a stronger motion than the projectile's natural motion.[50] This cannot happen in a void. Moreover, no one could explain why a thing moved in a void should ever stop. 'For why should it stop *here* rather than *here*? So it must either rest or continue to move *ad infinitum*, unless something more powerful impedes it.'[51] Again, the idea is that a thing moves into the void because it yields; but in a void everything is all alike, so that it will move in every direction.

The sentences translated verbatim above sound like an early statement of a principle of inertia.[52] But that is only one point in Aristotle's argument. What he is saying in the whole passage is that in a void there is no reason why a moving object should stop *here* rather than *here*, but also there is no reason why it should move in this direction rather than that, or why it should go on moving at all rather than come to a baffled halt.

Void cannot be a place, in Aristotle's view, and consequently has no power (δύναμις), as place has.[53] We ought to try to see what he means without any presuppositions about inertia at all. He thinks that even the natural fall of a stone depends on its being all the time in a place. Suppose now that a stone is falling high up in the air, and between the inner surface of the sphere of air and the outer surface of the sphere of water and earth there is (*per impossibile*) a void interval.[54] It is consistent with Aristotle's doctrine, I think, that the stone should not carry over the interval in a straight line with some kind of inertial motion; its motion should rather become completely random.

If Aristotle had thought of nature as an immanent force of some kind, we should expect him to explain why this force could not account for a falling stone's continuing motion through a void. If he had thought of the natural place of an object as exercising an attraction on the object, we should expect him to explain why that attraction could not be exercised through a void interval. If he had thought of a projectile as having in it some kind of impetus imparted by the thrower, we should have expected an explanation of why the impetus could not carry over a void interval. In fact, however, his criticisms of the void under our present heading can be reduced to two: forced motion needs a mover always in contact with the thing that is moved, and obviously the void cannot provide one;

---

[48] Note that the infinity of the Atomists' void is mentioned here. Guthrie, criticizing the view of Democritus' theory that I am defending, says (II.401): 'Neither here [sc. *De caelo* 275 b 29ff] nor anywhere else does [Aristotle] criticize the atoms for the absurdity of moving downwards in an ἄπειρον.' Not so.

[49] Perhaps Plato's explanation, *Tim.* 59A.

[50] Aristotle's explanation, *Physics* 266 b 27–267 a 12.

[51] *Ibid.* 215 a 20–2.

[52] See Grant (1964).

[53] 'Void is that in which nothing is heavy or light' (*Physics* IV.1.214 a 2).

[54] Buridan's argument; see Grant (1964), 278.

natural motion depends on the properties of weight and lightness, they depend on place, and the void is no place.

Whatever can be said about motion in the void can also be said about rest, if we use Aristotle's premises. Forced rest, as he calls it,[55] needs something to explain why the thing that is at rest does not move with its natural motion, and void cannot provide that. Natural rest occurs only in natural place; and there is no place in a void.

Is Aristotle's criticism of Democritus consistent with the explanation of the Atomists' theory of motion that has been put forward in pp. 78–81?

When Leucippus and Democritus say that the primary bodies always move in the void and the infinite, they ought to say with what motion, and what is their natural motion. For if the elements move each other by force, still each of them must have some natural motion too, which the forced motion is contrasted with; and the primary movement cannot move by force, but only by nature; otherwise there will be an infinite regress, if there is to be no first thing that imparts motion naturally but always a prior thing itself moved by force.[56]

Could Aristotle have written this if he had been aware that Democritus believed atoms to have a natural tendency to fall downward? We shall have to assume that the burden of his objection is that the Atomists did not distinguish motion brought about by weight in the void from motion brought about by collisions. They said that both kinds of motion had been going on, naturally, from infinite time. There was no state of the atoms when no collision took place, nor was there ever a time when any atoms collided for the first time. From all eternity, atoms moved in the void in a jostling crowd.[57]

They say that the nature of the atoms is single – as if each were a separate piece of (say) gold. But in that case, as we say, they must have a single motion; for a single clod and the whole earth go to the same place, and so do the whole of fire and a spark.[58]

Would Aristotle say this if he knew that all atoms have a tendency to fall downward because of their weight? In the context it appears that his meaning may be just that the Atomists, lacking the idea of absolute lightness, have no good explanation of upward motion. Some atoms must move upward, in their cosmology; but if there are only differences between more and less heavy things, then there can be no explanation, according to Aristotle's view, of any natural upward motion. He concludes: 'Necessarily then neither do all things have weight, nor do they all have lightness, but some have one, some the other.' We might find some confirmation of this interpretation in a casual remark he makes elsewhere,

---

[55] *De caelo* III.2.300 a 29. See also p. 101.
[56] *Ibid.* 300 b 9–16.
[57] Cf. the fragment of Aristotle's book *On Democritus* (= D–K 68a.37), where the verb στασιάζειν ('to quarrel with each other') is applied to atoms in the void.
[58] *De caelo* I.7.275 b 32.

that earlier philosophers did not explain what is heavy and what is light, but only what is relatively heavy and relatively light *among things that have weight*.[59]

Is Aristotle's complaint that the Atomists assign no cause for motion[60] compatible with his knowing that they said atoms have a tendency to fall downward due to their weight? Both passages where this complaint is made occur in the context of a discussion of *first* causes of motion. It is quite clear that, whatever account we may give of Aristotle's own theory of weight and lightness, these two properties do not satisfy his criteria for a first cause: his own theory of the natural motions of the simple bodies does not preclude the need for an Unmoved Prime Mover, and it seems reasonable enough therefore that he should not say anything about the Atomists' notion of weight here.

Epicurus defended and revised the Atomist theory of motion by introducing something like the concept of a vector.[61] In the infinite, obviously, there is no 'highest' or 'lowest' point. But he rejected Aristotle's assumption that two extremes are needed to define a movement and claimed that it is enough to specify a point, a direction, and a sense. Take the point on the earth's surface 'wherever we stand', the direction as vertical, and the sense either up or down. In both senses, the vertical line can be prolonged to infinity, and 'down' is the direction of motion of atoms due to their weight.

In so far as it was acceptable, the introduction of this concept into Epicurean physics served to disarm all of Aristotle's objections to motion in a void that were based on his notion of place. A body moving through the void is no longer a body fatally deprived of a place and therefore deprived of direction and sense. There is no reason to think it will not continue to move in the same direction through the void until something causes a change, since the void offers no resistance.

Epicurus counter-attacked the Aristotelian theory by pointing out that one and the same line prolonged in the same direction is both up and down in his system: if you produce the vertical line downward until it passes through the centre of the Aristotelian cosmos, downward changes to upward at that point. Why should the geometrical centre of the cosmic sphere have such an effect? Perhaps it was partly to answer this counter-attack that the Stoics modified Aristotle's theory, substituting the centre of the *earth* for the centre of the cosmos as the focus of natural motions.[62]

I have been attempting to revive an old view of Democritus' theory of motion according to which the differences between Democritus and Epicurus are smaller than most interpreters allow them to be. These differences, however, still exist. We have already noted in the previous section (pp. 83–4) that Epicurus was persuaded by Aristotle's arguments that there can be no explanation for different

---

[59] *Ibid.* IV.1.308 a 11.
[60] *Metaphysics* 1.4.985 b 19; *Physics* VIII.1.252 a 32.
[61] *Letter* 1.60. I am indebted to Konstan (1972).
[62] The two centres coincide, in Stoic cosmology, but it is by virtue of its being the centre of the earth that this point is the focus of natural motions.

speeds of atoms in the void. He may also have been influenced by Aristotle's complaints that the early Atomists failed to distinguish the natural motion of atoms from motions caused by collisions. He was left with the proposition that the natural motion of all atoms is to fall downward in parallel straight lines at constant speed, and hence the explanation of the occurrence of collisions – that faster atoms catch up with slower ones – that was available to Democritus was closed to him. To deal with this problem, he introduced the notorious swerve.[63]

This Epicurean theory has been much criticized since antiquity on two grounds. The first is that the swerve is a completely arbitrary assumption, 'a piece of childish fiction', as Cicero called it.[64] It *is* arbitrary, and can be defended only on the ground that it is the most economical hypothesis that will save the appearances. The second line of criticism is that it is impossible to specify an 'up' or 'down' in an infinite void. This is, however, no more difficult, as far as I can see, than the idea of the existence of infinitely numerous atoms having shape, size, and solidity. These properties of the atoms are inferred from sense-experiences; and it is an argument of just the same kind that established the downward direction of motion of the atoms.

There is a feature of the Atomists' theory of motion that is much more vulnerable to criticism, and it is surprising that so little attention is drawn to it. It is simply that the theory depends on the proposition that the earth is flat. The direction up–down is a datum of the system. We know what the direction is by observation – that is, by taking the vertical from 'wherever we stand', as Epicurus says. All perpendiculars to the earth's surface must be parallel, if the theory is to work. If these perpendiculars are not parallel, the theory is faced with one of three equally fatal consequences: either the downward fall of the atoms focuses on a single point, as in Aristotle's cosmology, and in that case *our* cosmos gets back the uniquely privileged position that the Atomists wanted to deny it; or there is no single focus but a random assortment of directions, and in that case the theory is left with no coherent explanation of weight; or the motion of atoms in the cosmos must be different from that of atoms at large, and the theory cannot explain either that difference itself or our knowledge of the different conditions outside our cosmos.

So the plausibility of Atomism as an alternative to Aristotelianism hinges in part on this question: was it reasonable to believe that the earth is flat? What arguments were used to defend the sphericity of the earth *before* Epicurus, and was it reasonable to reject them? But that is another subject.

[63] Lucretius II.216–50.
[64] Cicero, *Fin.* I.19.

8

WEIGHT AND MOTION IN DEMOCRITUS' THEORY

A discussion of D. O'Brien, *Theories of Weight in the Ancient World*,
vol. I: 'Democritus'[1]

[1983]

From the earliest recorded times, Greeks measured weight by using balances. The Mycenean Linear B tablets use an ideogram representing a balance for the standard unit of weight (the symbol now conventionally labelled L).[2] The balance is referred to as a well-known device in the Homeric poems, under the name σταθμός or τάλαντα, the latter being used mainly in metaphors.[3] The metaphorical use of τάλαντον occurs in Theognis.[4] The σταθμός is referred to in Herodotus, Aristophanes, and Hippocrates; under the label ζυγόν, which is properly the beam of the balance, it is mentioned by Aeschylus.[5] When one side of the balance weighs more than the other, whatever is on the heavier side is said to ῥέπειν, sometimes to ἕλκειν. Aristophanes gives us a relatively full expression: τοῦ ταλάντου τὸ ῥέπον κάτω βαδίζει τὸ δὲ κενὸν πρὸς τὸν Δία ('the preponderant side of the balance goes downwards, the empty side goes to Heaven').[6]

The heavier side goes downwards, the lighter side goes upwards. That is the obvious, well-known, unmistakeable generalization of an experience familiar to every Greek who ever took part in commerce or housekeeping, from Mycenean times onwards.

Conceptual problems will arise concerning the definition of 'downwards'. It is intuitively obvious, and can be proved by the use of the plumb-line, which is also an ancient tool,[7] that the line of fall is perpendicular to the earth's surface; but

---

[1] D. O'Brien, *Theories of Weight in the Ancient World*, vol. I: 'Democritus, Weight and Size' (1981).
[2] See Michael Ventris and John Chadwick, *Documents in Mycenean Greek*, 2nd edn. (Cambridge University Press, 1973), 55.
[3] *Iliad* XII.434: the battle is evenly balanced, as when a careful housewife evens up two lots of wool in a balance (σταθμός). *Iliad* VIII.69, XXII.209 (τάλαντα).
[4] Theognis 157.
[5] Herodotus II.65; Aristophanes, *Frogs* 1365, 1407; Hippocrates, *Anc. Med.* 9; Aeschylus, *Supplices* 822.
[6] Fragment 488.4.
[7] The word is κανών, but this word is also used to denote a chalked string used to mark a straight line, then other straight edges, and finally everything taken as standard. I am grateful to my colleague Glenn W. Most for showing me his discussion of Pindar's use of the word σταθμή (*Pythian* II.90), and related uses of the word κανών, in his PhD dissertation, *Pindar's Truth: Occasional Unity in the Greek Epinician* (Tübingen 1980), 707–35.

what that means with reference to a larger frame will of course depend on what one takes to be the shape of the earth's surface. That was controversial in classical times. It could be agreed by all that all lines of fall were perpendicular to the surface (πρὸς ὁμοίας γωνίας: Aristotle, *De caelo* 11.14.296 b 20: that is, the angles between the line of fall and lines on the surface radiating from the point of impact are all equal);[8] what was controversial was whether or not all lines of fall, with different points of impact, are parallel to each other. For those who believed in a flat earth, all lines of fall must be parallel; for Aristotle and others who supposed the earth to be a sphere, lines of fall must meet at the centre of the sphere. This problem can be shelved so long as we rest content to define 'downwards' with reference to the earth's surface. Flat-earthers and sphericists can agree that the balance shows the heavier moving downwards, the lighter upwards.

In the first volume in what he plans to be a series of four on *Theories of Weight in the Ancient World*, Denis O'Brien proposes a new solution of the difficult philological problems that have bedevilled efforts to understand what Democritus said about the weight of atoms.[9]

It is only the supposedly inviolable force of the entailment between weight and movement that leads to the supposition *either* that the atoms have weight and therefore move downwards *or* that the atoms do not fall and are therefore weightless.

The radical alternative will be to abandon the entailment of weight and movement. This will at once enable us to embrace the only two conclusions for which there is sufficient, and satisfactory, evidence.

1. The precosmic atoms of Democritus do have weight.
2. They do not move only downwards.

(p. 175)

A formidable paradox! Weight is *measured* by its tendency to move the balance downwards: yet we are asked to abandon the entailment of weight and movement. How, then, does the balance do its work?

Later in the book O'Brien writes:

An otherwise sensible scholar (with the limitations as well as the advantages implied in that description) writes recently, when he comes to the question that has been the subject of this essay: 'We may here pause to consider what weight means: it means a tendency to move consistently in a certain direction, what we call "downwards", and a resistance to "upward" movement' (Kirk, *Presocratic Philosophers*, 415).

If only the writer of these words *had* paused to think. And if only, in pausing, he had taken time to reflect not on what weight 'means', as though meanings existed in themselves,

---

[8] See Guthrie (1953), *De caelo*, 244, n. *b*. He quotes Stocks (note in the Oxford translation of *De cael.* ad loc), who gives the explanation that I follow. Guthrie proposes that it more naturally means that the angles made by one falling body with the earth are similar to those made by another, and compares a second occurrence of the phrase at 297 b 19: πρὸς ὁμοίας γωνίας ἀλλ᾽ οὐ παρ᾽ ἄλληλα. Guthrie is wrong, I think: the proof that the lines of fall meet at the centre of the sphere depends on their being vertical to the tangent to the earth's surface, not on their falling at the same angle as each other.

[9] See above, n. 1.

nor even on what weight 'means' for us, but on what weight might have meant for those first philosophers of Greece, whose ways of thinking are related to, but are remote from, our own.

(pp. 363–4)

These hard words invite a response of the same kind. If only O'Brien had paused to seek for evidence of the earliest Greek views on weight, and reflected on their implications, before working out a hypothetical view designed primarily to reconcile the conflicting evidence of Aristotle and the Doxographers about Democritus. At least he might then have realized that he owed the reader of his book some answers to a number of pressing questions. *Why* did Democritus suppose that weight does not entail downward motion, if he did? What did he expect to gain from his theory of weight? What did he hope to explain by its means? And how did he reconcile his theory with the observed fact that on the surface of the earth the heavier pan of the balance always falls? It is astonishing that in a book of some 400 pages these questions are hardly raised, let alone answered.[10]

However, all is not lost. O'Brien's book has great merits, and up to a point it will be very useful for further study of the subject. Most of our evidence about Democritus' theory of weight is found in Aristotle and in writers who accepted his concepts and theories. The problem is a notorious one: how are we to discern the Democritean picture through the Aristotelian stained glass? With immense patience, meticulous attention to detail, and scrupulous philological exactness O'Brien examines the evidence and attempts this task. The method is right, so far as it goes.

The main target of O'Brien's polemic is what he calls 'the current compromise' (chapter 6 and elsewhere). Aristotle reports: 'Democritus says that each of the indivisibles is heavier according to its comparatively larger (size?)' (βαρύτερον κατὰ τὴν ὑπεροχήν: *GC* 1.8.326 a 8). This is not unambiguous, but O'Brien (chapter 2) and I agree on its meaning: atoms have weight, and their weight is proportional to their size. This is confirmed by *De caelo* IV, where he writes:

Those who say (that the primary, atomic units are) solids [as opposed to Platonists who suppose they are planes] may legitimately claim that the larger of them is heavier (τὸ μεῖζον εἶναι βαρύτερον αὐτῶν).

(*De caelo* IV.2.309 a 1–2)

Again I agree with O'Brien (chapter 3), against Cherniss and others who claim that it is about compounds, that this attributes weight to atoms, in proportion to their size.[11]

But Aëtius (1.12.6 = D–K 68A.47) explicitly denies that Democritus allowed his

[10] This is over-simplified. O'Brien does consider the last problem: what he fails to discuss adequately in it is how the suggested solution (the δίνη) was supposed to work, and why Democritus put himself to the necessity of having to solve this problem in the first place.
[11] Cherniss (1935), 211, n. 253; Guthrie II.403, n. 2.

atoms to have weight, and even (1.3.18; D–K *ibid.*) contrasts Democritus with Epicurus on this point. Hence 'the current compromise', which holds that atoms were taken to have weight *within* a cosmos, and to be weightless in the external void. O'Brien traces the emergence of the compromise from Zeller, who did not adopt it, through Liepmann, Brieger, and Dyroff, to Burnet, Guthrie, Kirk, and others (chapter 13, section 1 'Modern Scholarship: the Progress of Error').[12]

I agree with O'Brien that the current compromise is wrong, and in two articles that appeared too late to be noticed, except briefly, in this book, I began an effort to throw doubt on it.[13] I agree that the way to attack it is to show that the preponderance of evidence tells against Aëtius, and to find reasons why Aëtius might have been misled. There is no difficulty about the first. As to the second, we can show that Aëtius and others were misled about the possible existence of a Democritean atom of vast size, probably by misunderstanding the implication of an Epicurean criticism;[14] we can guess that he was similarly misled about the weight of atoms, mainly by misunderstanding the implication of an Aristotelian criticism – namely, the criticism that Democritus did not specify what is the natural motion of atoms (all this is set out in O'Brien, chapter 10). This is correct, I believe, and O'Brien's slow, millimetric examination of the evidence should suffice to convict the compromisers.

But what next? O'Brien seems to me to be left, in the end, in a position that is remarkably close to 'the current compromise'. When we pare away from Aristotle's evidence the obfuscating films of his own presuppositions, we are left with the thesis that Democritus' atoms have weight in proportion to their size. Since Aristotle and others deny that Democritus recognized a natural motion of the atoms, it must follow, O'Brien argues, that the weight of an atom does not entail downward motion. Weight must be 'expressed' in some other way: probably in force of impact, and in speed rather than direction of motion (chapters 11 and 12).

But the fact is that near the earth's surface weight expresses itself in motion, and in motion in a determinate direction. I have been complaining that O'Brien takes little notice of this fact, but of course he cannot deny it or ignore it completely. For one thing, the doxographical sources tell us that the size, and therefore the weight, of atoms was significant in the formation of the cosmos out of the δίνη.[15] And Democritus (although O'Brien does not mention this) was one of the many Presocratics who were concerned to give an explanation of why the earth remains where it is in the cosmos – that is to say, why it does not *fall*, as pieces of earth

---

[12] Zeller (1879); Liepmann (1886); Brieger (1884); Dyroff (1899); Burnet (1892); Guthrie 11.403, n. 2; Kirk and Raven (1957).

[13] See chapters 1 and 7 of this volume.

[14] I argued this in a paragraph in Furley (1967b), 96. The same argument, now grown to sixteen pages, can be found in O'Brien's book (pp. 282–98). It still seems convincing.

[15] For example, Diogenes Laertius IX.32 (D–K 67A.1); Aëtius 1.4.2 (D–K 67A.24). See O'Brien, pp. 372–4 on these. Also Simplicius, *De caelo* 530.30f. The point is hardly in doubt, although descriptions in the sources vary: μείζονα καὶ βαρύτατα in Aëtius; τὰ λοιπὰ after τὰ λεπτὰ have departed in Diogenes; τὴν γῆν in Simplicius.

do.[16] O'Brien concedes, then, that there is a difference between the effects of weight within the cosmic δίνη and outside it:

> Within the cosmos, the weight of atoms is expressed by the distribution of larger and smaller, or heavier and lighter, atoms in a δίνη, and as an element in the definition of lightness in terms of void.
>
> (p. 346)

In speaking of 'distribution', O'Brien is evidently thinking of the arrangement of the parts of the cosmos, according to the common fifth-century world picture – earth and water concentrated together at the centre, with air and whatever it is that makes up the heavens above and around them. But this distribution entails some motions, at least during the cosmogonical process:

> Movement towards a specific place has its footing in the theory of Democritus. Large atoms, and dense agglomerations of atoms, when they are drawn into a cosmos, will move towards the centre, while small atoms, and rarefied agglomerations of atoms, are squeezed out, and forced towards the circumference, or beyond.
>
> (p. 382)

This does not mention weight, but only size and density. But we know that the weight of an atom is directly proportional to its size; and the weight of a compound, as O'Brien has shown earlier, is dependent on the proportion of atomic material to void in its composition. It is conceivable that O'Brien would wish to maintain that it is only size and density, and not weight, that may be counted as causal factors in the move towards the centre, and thus to remain in a position to affirm that weight never entails movement in any specific direction. But there are many indications that this is not the path he would want to take; and it is in any case extremely implausible.

His position, then, amounts to this: weight is a property of the Democritean atom at all times; when the atom is at large in the void, weight is not expressed in a tendency to move in any particular direction, but 'probably' in force of impact and speed of motion. When the atom is caught in a δίνη, then its weight may be expressed as a tendency to move in a particular direction. This is to be contrasted with 'the current compromise', according to which the atom has *no* weight when at large in the void, and *therefore* moves in no particular direction, whereas when caught in a δίνη it gains weight and therefore moves towards the centre.

The weakness of both 'the current compromise' and O'Brien's proposal is that they give the vortex the job of causing heavy bodies to move vertically downwards towards the earth's surface. But the vortex is ill suited to this role in fact, and there is good evidence that in the fifth century B.C. the role that was given to the vortex is inconsistent with that of a cause of downward motion.

In fact, gravity is one of the factors that determine the behaviour of bodies

---

[16] See Aristotle, *De caelo* II.13.294 b 13.

caught in a vortex.[17] In a whirlwind or 'twister', it is the lighter or less dense bodies that are lifted most violently and carried to a greater distance, while the heavier and denser objects remain on the ground, sometimes collected together at the centre of the whirl. In a liquid vortex, floating objects behave differently from sinkers, but the fact that they float – that is, remain *above* the liquid – is plainly independent of their being caught in a vortex.

The point that tells most forcefully against the two-valued theory of the 'current compromise' and O'Brien's substitute for it is that the vortex is introduced by fifth-century thinkers in order to explain why certain heavy bodies do *not* fall downwards. This is well attested for Anaxagoras and Empedocles, although some of the details are unclear. The evidence is worth a closer look.

Anaxagoras says that the surrounding aether is fiery in substance, and by the force (εὐτονία) of its rotation it lifted rocks up from the earth, inflamed them, and thus made them into stars.

(Aëtius II.13.3 = D–K 59A.71)

The sun and moon and all the stars [according to Anaxagoras] are burning stones that were caught up by the rotation of the aether.

(Hippolytus, *Ref.* I.8.6 = D–K 59A.42)

Each one of the stars [Anaxagoras claimed] is not in its natural place: although stony and heavy, they shine because of the friction and cleaving of the aether, and they are pulled by force in the grip of the whirl and tension of the rotation – just as in the first place they were kept from falling to earth at the time when cold and heavy things were being separated from the whole.

(Plutarch, *Lysander* 12 = D–K 59A.12)

There appear to be two somewhat different accounts of the origin of the stars in these quotations. Hippolytus and Aëtius describe the stars being lifted up from the earth by the force of the rotation, whereas Plutarch has them somehow up aloft already and prevented from falling to earth at the time when other heavy things were being separated out from the general mass. For our purposes the difference is not significant: what matters is that all agree on the role of the δίνη in keeping the stars high in the sky. Without the δίνη they would be expected to fall, because they are heavy.

In Empedocles' system it is not only the stars that are kept aloft by the rotation of the δίνη but the earth itself. The authority is Aristotle:

[We have shown, in book I, that the body of which the heaven is composed moves eternally, without effort, with a circular motion.] There is no need, therefore, to suppose, as the ancient myth did, that it owes its security to an Atlas; those who made up that story seem to share the supposition of those of more modern times, in that they treated the upper bodies as having weight and being like earth, and therefore gave them the support in their myth of

---

[17] Two very helpful articles on the δίνη are Ferguson (1971); and Tigner (1974). I am also indebted to unpublished work by Professor Tigner.

an ensouled Necessity. So we must not think in this way, nor say, as Empedocles does, that the heavenly bodies are still preserved after all this time because they acquire from the rotation a swifter motion than their own natural impulse.

(Aristotle, *De caelo* II.1.284 a 18–24)

So all who posit a beginning of the cosmos say that the earth came together at the centre. They then seek the reason why it remains in place, and some do so in the way we have described, saying that its flatness and its size are the reason, while others do so in the manner of Empedocles, saying that the circular and excessively swift motion of the sky prevents the motion of the earth – like the water in a ladle (κύαθος), which for the same reason when the ladle is swung around in a circle often does not move when it comes to be underneath the bronze, although it is its nature to move.

(*ibid* II.13.295 a 13–22)

Empedocles, then, like Anaxagoras, thought that the stars are naturally heavy, and would naturally fall down unless they were kept in their lofty orbits by the force of the δίνη. His theory of why the earth stays where it is differs from Anaxagoras, who was among those who invoked the flatness of the earth as the explanation of this. Somehow, Empedocles supposed that the δίνη could be given this explanatory role as well. The simile mentioned by Aristotle gives a picture that is clear enough: if you fill the cup of a long-handled ladle and swing it round in a vertical circle by the hook at the end of the handle, the contents of the cup are kept in place by centrifugal force. The problem is to understand how this picture can be applied to the stationary position of the earth. Some suppose that Aristotle has mistaken the object of the explanation: Empedocles was not speaking about the position of the earth, but of the stars or other objects above the earth.[18] A recent alternative explanation accepts that the ladle simile may have been applied by Empedocles to the explanation of the heavenly bodies, but goes on to suggest a way in which he might nevertheless have used the δίνη to explain the position of the earth 'aloft', after the analogy of a flat dish raised from the bottom of a kitchen sink by swirling the water vigorously in the sink.[19] But again the details are less important for our purposes than the clear conclusion from this evidence that Empedocles, like Anaxagoras, used the δίνη to explain why it is that certain heavy bodies, which we might expect to fall, do *not* fall.

It would be very surprising if Democritus tried to use the same model of the δίνη to explain why heavy bodies *do* fall. What connection could possibly be suggested between the daily orbiting of the sun, moon, and stars – acknowledged to be the visible remnant of the original cosmic δίνη – and the fall of a jar knocked off its shelf or the return of an arrow shot vertically upwards? This is an objection that is as old as Aristotle's *De caelo*:

It is absurd, too, not to perceive that, while the whirling motion (δίνησις) may have been responsible for the original coming together of the parts of the earth at the centre, the

---

[18] Cherniss (1935), 204, n. 234. Compare Guthrie's note, II.198, n. 1.
[19] Tigner (1974).

question remains, why *now* do all heavy bodies move to earth? For the whirl surely does not come near to us. Why, again, does fire move upwards? Not, surely, because of the whirl. But if fire is naturally such as to move in a certain direction, clearly the same may be supposed to hold of the earth. Again, it cannot be the whirl which determines the heavy and the light. Rather that movement caused the pre-existent heavy and light things to go to the middle and stay on the surface respectively. Thus, before ever the whirl began, heavy and light existed; and what can have been the ground of their distinction, or the manner and direction of their natural movements? If the infinite exists, there cannot be an 'up' and 'down' in it, and it is by these that heavy and light are determined.

(Aristotle, *De caelo* II.13.295 a 32 – b 9; trans. Stocks, slightly adapted)

It might be claimed (although it is not claimed by O'Brien, and I have not observed such a claim anywhere else) that this passage provides evidence that the δίνη was in fact used by someone to explain why heavy things fall downwards. Why else, it might be asked, would Aristotle argue against it? But there is nothing in this suggestion. It is reasonably certain that Aristotle is here raising a general and theoretical objection against those, like Empedocles (who is the subject of the preceding lines), who fail to recognize *natural* motions and to distinguish them from forced motions. The translation given above accurately captures the nuance of Aristotle's point in the opening sentence: it was absurd of Empedocles and those who followed his line not to observe that they had a *question* to answer, about the fall of heavy things towards the earth (ἄτοπον δὲ καὶ τὸ μὴ συννοεῖν ὅτι πρότερον μὲν ... νῦν δὲ διὰ τίν' αἰτίαν ...;). It is not suggested that any of them thought of the question but then gave a wrong answer to it: Aristotle himself suggests the answer that they might have given, and then dismisses it. If some philosopher as well known as Democritus had already answered the question in this way, we might have expected Aristotle himself, or Simplicius in his comment on the passage, to mention the fact. Neither of them does so, and the argument from silence has some force in this instance because this chapter of Aristotle is full of such citations.

All this seems to me to constitute rather strong evidence that Democritus did not claim that the δίνη is the cause of the vertical fall of heavy bodies near the earth's surface. Is there any direct evidence that tells the other way?

One of the properties attributed to the δίνη by Presocratic philosophers is that of drawing heavy bodies 'to the centre'.[20] This dangerously suggestive phrase may well be the source of much of the error about Democritus' theory. In the world view that was given its definitive form by Aristotle, and adopted by the majority of natural philosophers in antiquity after him, weight is defined as a tendency to move 'towards the centre' – towards the centre of the universe, in Aristotle's own system, towards the centre of the cosmic body according to the Stoics.[21] If the

[20] Aristotle, *De caelo* II.13.295 a 10: 'So if the earth now stays where it is by force, so also did it come together at the centre, moved by the rotation; for all of them mention this explanation, from what happens in liquids and concerning the air.'
[21] For the Stoic view – a very important modification of Aristotle's cosmology – see Plutarch, *SR* 1054E.

δίνη, then, produces a tendency in certain bodies to move 'towards the centre', is this not equivalent to saying that it produces weight? Of course not, in a system like Democritus' in which the earth is flat.[22] But virtually all of our evidence about the use of the δίνη is transmitted by writers who subscribe to a centrifocal cosmology, and the question of what centre is referred to is easily ignored.

The idea that larger and heavier objects are drawn towards the centre of a δίνη was presumably derived from observation. The easiest way to demonstrate the tendency is to spread a number of objects that sink at the bottom of a jar full of water, swirl the water for a while, and see how the objects collect at the centre. They collect at the bottom of the axis of the rotation – at the bottom, because of their density, and at the axis because of the dynamics of the swirl. Much of the effect depends on friction between the objects and the bottom of the vessel and between the objects themselves; and this in particular explains the sorting action of the δίνη. Larger and heavier objects collect at the centre at the bottom and remain there; lighter and smaller objects, with less surface friction, may be lifted by the swirl and separated from the larger and heavier ones. As we have already mentioned, a large, flat object, even if it is relatively heavy, may be lifted and held in suspense by the swirl: it sinks when the water is at rest.

The important point to notice is that whatever centripetal force is produced by the δίνη is towards the central axis. The δίνη could not and was never intended to produce anything like the centrifocal dynamics of the Aristotelian cosmos, all determined by the central *point* of a sphere.[23] The centrifocal cosmology gets its first clear mention in Plato's *Phaedo* 108E: Socrates says he has been 'persuaded by someone' anonymous that this is the right picture of the earth and its relation to the cosmos.[24] Its origins are obscure; but no one will want to suggest that Socrates – or Plato – learnt it from Democritus. The Atomists and others of the Presocratics are reported to have believed that the cosmos as a whole is a sphere, and that the earth is at the centre of it.[25] But Democritus still believed the earth to be flat, so that lines drawn vertical to the earth's surface (lines of fall) must necessarily be parallel to each other and not centrifocal. He still thought it necessary to explain that the earth is prevented from falling by the support of the

---

[22] Aëtius III.10.5 (D–K 68A.94).

[23] The difficulties in using the dynamics of a vortex in the explanation of gravity are well illustrated by the theory of Christian Huygens. He proposed an arrangement of vortices of a subtle material moving around the earth, not on a single axis but circling the earth in all directions. This was to remove the objection to the cylindrical vortices of Descartes, that they could at best explain gravity towards the axis. See his *Discours de la Cause de la Pesanteur, Oeuvres Complètes*, vol. XXI; H. J. M. Bos, s.v. Huygens, *Dictionary of Scientific Biography* (Scribner 1972), esp. p. 610; A. E. Bell, *Christian Huygens and the Development of Science in the Seventeenth Century* (Arnold, 1947), 161–4.

[24] The passage of the *Phaedo* is generally thought to reproduce a theory that is to be attributed as a whole to Anaximander, because of Aristotle's mention of Anaximander in this connection at *De caelo* II.13.295 b 10–25. I believe Aristotle attributes much less than the whole theory to Anaximander. (See above, chapter 2.)

[25] Aëtius II.2 (D–K 67A.22). Aëtius III.10. Aristotle, *De caelo* II.13.293 a 17–18. It is of course our cosmos, not the universe as a whole, that Democritus held to be spherical.

air underneath it.[26] His cosmos, even if it was spherical, had a top and a bottom, vertically above our heads and vertically below our feet respectively.

The interpretation for which I am arguing, against both 'the current compromise' and the O'Brien amendment, goes back to Zeller (1879). Why was it ever abandoned? Plainly I must seek to meet the objections that were raised against it. To keep this article to manageable size it will be necessary to be brief: the opposition to Zeller is set out fully in Brieger (1884) and the course of scholarly controversy before and after this is reviewed by O'Brien (pp. 346–64, and in his bibliography, pp. 385–401). I shall confine myself to the core of the matter: the passages in which Aristotle blames the Atomists for neglecting to state either the cause of the original motion of atoms or what kind of motion it is. Brieger (pp. 9–11) lists *Metaph.* XII.6.1071 b 32; *Physics* VIII.1.252 a 34; *GA* II.6.742 b 17; *De caelo* III.2.300 b 8.

The first three of these make what is essentially the same point: the Atomists claimed that motion is eternal, and therefore refused to give an explanation of it. In the first book of the *Metaphysics* (985 b 20), Aristotle objects that they 'lazily dismissed' the question; elsewhere he suggests that they had an argument for dismissing it:

The necessity that belongs to the cause is not well expressed by those who say that it *always* happens thus and suppose that this is their cause – like Democritus of Abdera – because there is no origin (ἀρχή) of the 'always' and the infinite, and the cause is an origin, and the 'always' is infinite: so to ask for a cause of things like this, he says, is to enquire for an origin of the infinite.

(*GA* II.6.742 b 17–24)

The passage from *Metaph.* I just referred to gives a context for these objections of Aristotle: he is contrasting the Atomists with Anaxagoras, 'who seemed like a sober man' (984 b 17) and Empedocles (985 a 4 – 985 b 3). Their contribution, as opposed to the Milesian Monists and the Atomists, was to introduce a cause of motion – Anaxagoras' Mind, Empedocles' Love and Strife. What Aristotle misses in the Atomists' theory here is not something like weight or lightness, but something like the movers of the heavenly spheres in his own system. He himself attributes weight and lightness to the four sublunary elements and circular motion to the matter of the heavens, and he claims that the motions of the cosmos are eternal, but he still seeks for an 'origin' or first cause of motion that transcends the properties of physical matter.[27] If the Atomists claimed that the atoms moved eternally and moved because of weight, that claim would go nowhere towards

---

[26] Aristotle is our authority for this: see *De caelo* II.13.294 b 13–14. Aëtius (III.15.7) says that Parmenides and Democritus believed the earth to remain where it is because there is no reason for it to move in one direction rather than any other. Aristotle is quite definite about it, however, and it seems we must either think that Aëtius was mistaken about Democritus, or read his statement in some fashion that does not contradict Aristotle.

[27] I have tried to give some account of the cause of the natural motions of elementary bodies in Aristotle's system in chapter 7.

satisfying Aristotle's demand here. So this criticism cannot be used as evidence that they made no such claim.

More damaging is the criticism that they had no theory of *natural* motion:

Hence Leucippus and Democritus, who say the primary bodies always move in the void and the infinite, have got to say what motion they have, and what their natural motion is. For if one of the elements is moved by another by force, they must each have a natural motion to contrast with the forced; and the first mover must move not by force but by nature. For there will be an infinite regress if there is to be no first mover that is natural, but each prior mover is to produce motion by being moved by force.

(*De caelo* III.1.300 b 8–16)

There is no doubt that the Atomists never claimed that *once upon a time* all the atoms moved in one way, and *then* there was an interruption that caused collisions among them. Such a thesis is never in question. They held that the atoms have been jostling among themselves – στασιάζειν is the word used by Aristotle (quoted by Simplicius, *De caelo*, 295.9, from Aristotle's lost *On Democritus*) – from all eternity. The question concerns the components of this jostling motion: can we analyse it into a forced component, due to blows, and a natural component, due to weight? Aristotle says no.

Just this failure to distinguish two components is evidently a major theme in Aristotle's criticism. The Atomists held that the atoms moved hither and thither in the void for all time, and a part of the explanation of the particular motion of an individual atom at any time is the set of collisions that it has most recently experienced. This, in Aristotle's terms, is *forced* motion, and he demands to know the *natural* motion with which this is contrasted. But the Atomists did not say, it seems, that it is contrasted with anything: they merely said that it has always happened so, and they did not inquire into the unreal hypothetical question, how would the atoms behave if it were not so? The Epicureans, by contrast, did put this hypothetical question, perhaps because it was forced on them by Aristotle.[28] All this is compatible with the view that the early Atomists believed weight to be a component in the explanation of the motion of atoms in the void. O'Brien holds that this component takes the form of resistance to the force of a colliding atom: I am arguing that it takes the form of a tendency to move downwards.

Other elements in Aristotle's criticism come again from his own theory of natural motion. First is the point that the Atomists are committed to the existence of not more than one kind of substance. Since the natural motion of bodies depends, in his view, upon the kind of substance they have, it follows necessarily that all bodies must have a single natural motion. Hence the Atomists are incapable of producing an adequate theory of natural motion – that means, one that will account for both the natural fall of heavy bodies and the natural rise of light ones. This line of criticism is followed especially in *De caelo* I.7.275 b 29 – 276 a 14, and also in Theophrastus, *De sensibus* 71. These passages neither assert nor deny that the atoms have a tendency to move downwards because of their weight.

---

[28] See Lucretius, *De rerum natura* II.221–4.

The point is simply to insist that, having only one kind of substance, they can have only one kind of natural motion. Aristotle puts the question of the weight of atoms on one side. In the last sentence he entertains the possibility that they might all have lightness (κουφότης) instead of weight (βάρος), although he asserts elsewhere that they all have weight (an atom is βαρύτερον in proportion to its size: GC 1.8.326 a 9, quoted above).

A similar point is made in De caelo III.5.304 a 1–7, where Aristotle claims that the Atomists (they are not named, but the description fits), like Anaximenes, cannot make a definite distinction between fire and air and water and earth because their elements differ only in size: different sizes bear proportional relations to each other and so something will be (say) air just because of the proportion its constituents bear to other bodies. Hence the theory cannot accommodate the absolute distinction between the heavy elements and the light elements. Aristotle might have mentioned in either of these passages that Democritus attributed weight to all atoms and downward motion to weight (if Democritus did, and Aristotle knew he did), but there was no necessity for him to mention it, and neither passage implies its denial.

Aristotle finds another reason why the Atomists cannot produce a theory of natural motion in their thesis that atoms move in a void. In his own view, no proper account of motion in a void can be given: there can be no rational way of determining either the speed or the direction or the duration of a motion through the void.[29]

How can there be any natural motion if there is no difference in the void and the infinite? For being infinite it can have no up or down or middle, and being void it can have no difference between its up and down.

(Physics IV.8.215 a 6–9)

This passage is preceded by some sentences using the same language as the section of De caelo III.2 that we quote on p. 100: so there is a presumption that there, too, Aristotle has in mind the objection drawn from 'the void and the infinite'.

The balance of the evidence suggests, then, that we are not obliged to attribute to Democritus the paradoxical and unmotivated thesis offered to him by O'Brien as a means of saving the doxographical phenomena. We may continue to believe, as Zeller did, that Democritean atoms have weight, meaning a tendency to fall downwards, and this removes the necessity of finding another explanation for the fall of heavy bodies to earth. Democritus did not call this a natural motion, because he thought all the jostling motions of the atoms were equally original, eternal, and natural. Aristotle criticized him for not producing any account of natural motion because he believed the void, and the sameness of substance of the atoms, made it impossible for him to produce any such account.

[29] See Physics IV.4, and pp. 83–90, above.

9

ARISTOTLE AND THE
ATOMISTS ON INFINITY

[1969]

Aristotle and the Atomists agreed that time is infinitely extended. Aristotle maintained that it is also infinitely divisible; of the Atomists, the Epicureans at least appear to have denied that it is infinitely divisible. As regards spatial magnitude, the Atomists denied that it is infinitely divisible and asserted that it is infinitely extended; Aristotle reversed this position.

The purpose of the present essay is to review some of the arguments used by the two sides in the defence of their positions: first, the arguments of the Atomists of Abdera, so far as they can be recovered; then the counter-arguments of Aristotle; finally the attempts made by the Epicureans to rebut Aristotle.

TIME

Since the problem of the divisibility of time is chiefly a problem in Epicureanism, we shall not consider it here. Most interpreters of Epicureanism agree that its tenets include the finite divisibility of time; but the texts are difficult, and agreement is not universal. Some have said that Leucippus and Democritus also held a theory that time is composed of indivisibles; but there is no convincing evidence to show this, and the fact that Aristotle does not attribute such a theory to them tells heavily against it.

Democritus is said by Aristotle (*Physics* VIII.1.251 b 15) to have asserted that time had no beginning, and to have used this proposition to show that not everything came into being. Simplicius (*Physics* 1153.22) comments that Democritus treated it as self-evident (ἐναργές) that time had no beginning. No Democritean arguments are reported. Aristotle provided arguments, but since this was the one proposition in this field that was agreed between the Atomists and Aristotle, there is no need to repeat the arguments here.

THE DEBATE ABOUT INFINITE DIVISIBILITY

I have written at greater length about this problem elsewhere. I shall not set out the whole story here, but single out a few points for special emphasis.[1]

[1] See Furley (1967b) and Mau (1954). I am generally in agreement with Mau.

We are concerned with *arguments*. The deplorable habit of compiling doxographies has left us very short of Presocratic arguments, but Aristotle fortunately decided to give us Democritus' argument for 'indivisible magnitudes', in *GC* 1.2.316 a 13ff. There is some doubt about the authenticity of the argument: some have found it too Aristotelian in expression to be attributed to Democritus. I believe that we do well to regard it as essentially the work of Democritus: it is the kind of argument that we should expect *a priori*, if the Atomists were engaged, as Aristotle says, in combat with the Eleatics; there is no counter-evidence which cannot be explained away; and Aristotle compliments Democritus on the character of the argument itself.

The argument tries to establish the thesis of indivisible magnitudes by proving its contradictory false. The contradictory is that magnitude is divisible everywhere. If it is divisible everywhere, what will be the end products of such a division? They cannot be parts with magnitude, because such parts would be further divisible, *ex hypothesi*. Nor can they be parts without magnitude, because such parts could not be added up to make a whole with magnitude. There is no viable third way. Hence magnitude is not divisible everywhere: i.e. there are indivisible magnitudes.

What does 'magnitude' mean in this argument? Physical matter? Anything extended in space? Or the continuum of geometry? The first answer is right, because in the context, περὶ γενέσεως καὶ φθορᾶς τῶν φύσει γινομένων καὶ φθειρομένων, only physical matter is relevant. But this should not be taken, as it sometimes is, to settle the question about the nature of Democritean atomism. If we grant that the indivisible magnitudes which the argument aims to establish are in fact atoms, we still have to ask whether their indivisibility is just unsplittability, or whether they are also 'partless' – i.e. such that no parts can be distinguished in them even in theory. There are difficulties in either answer; but the balance is heavily in favour of atoms that are also partless. To say this, however, is not to say either that Democritus believed the void to be made of indivisible parts, or that he was a geometrical or mathematical atomist. The Atomists of Abdera still distinguished between atoms and void as between τὸ ὄν and τὸ μὴ ὄν, and they may well have supposed that arguments applicable to τὸ ὄν are not necessarily transferable to τὸ μὴ ὄν. I have not found any evidence to show that Democritus regarded space as atomic, and such evidence as there is about his geometry is confused.

Aristotle answers the Atomists' argument with his own theory of the physical continuum which is potentially but not actually divisible to infinity. Like its rival, this too is about physical matter but about theoretical divisibility. That is to say, the distinction between potential and actual does not correspond with a distinction between theoretical and physical. Aristotle does not say that the physical continuum is theoretically divisible to infinity, but in practice not. He says that it is, even theoretically, only potentially and not actually divisible to infinity. Even theoretically, any finite number of cuts may be made, but there are always more to be made. The *process* of dividing goes on to infinity.

Thus Aristotle never says that a finite physical continuum consists of infinitely numerous parts. His theory dispenses with the possibility of talking of the *sum* of an infinite series. This is a detail that has some importance in the later history of this problem. What Aristotle says is that the process of dividing up a continuum is one that has no end; and he adds that the converse process of adding is one that has no end. For example, a given line A can be divided so as to give *a* and a remainder, and that remainder divided in the same ratio so as to give *a*| and a remainder, and so on to *a*||, *a*|||, etc. However long this process is continued, there will always be a remainder. Conversely, the sum *a* + *a*| + *a*|| + *a*||| ... is one that *never* reaches the dimension of the original line A, so that the line A does not consist of parts like *a*, *a*|, *a*||.

A finite continuum in Aristotle's theory does not consist of an infinite set of parts. What would Aristotle say about such an infinite set? There is no doubt about what his followers Eudemus and Simplicius said. On many occasions Simplicius repeats that an infinite set of quantities makes an infinite quantity, and he quotes Eudemus as being in agreement.[2] Simplicius does not appear to notice any inconsistency between this proposition and Aristotle's statement about the kind of 'infinite by addition' that is the converse of the infinite by division – namely, that one can continue adding finite fractions of a whole magnitude in the same proportion without exhausting the whole (*Physics* III.6.206 b 7). Indeed, Simplicius obviously supposes that what he is saying is wholly consistent with Aristotle's theory; so much can be proved from his comment on *Physics* III.6.206 a 18. Aristotle observes that the infinite exists potentially, and then adds that it does not exist potentially in the same sense as the bronze is potentially a statue: the bronze is potentially a statue because it will be a statue in actuality, but we are not to say that there will be an infinite in actuality. Simplicius comments on this (492.14ff):

Εἰπὼν δυνάμει εἶναι τὸ ἄπειρον ἐν τῇ τῶν μεγεθῶν διαιρέσει κατὰ τὸ ἐπ' ἄπειρον, ἐπειδὴ καὶ τὸ δυνάμει πᾶν ἐκβῆναι δεῖ ποτε εἰς ἐνέργειαν, εἰ μὴ μάτην εἴη, ἐὰν δὲ γένηται ἐνεργείᾳ ἄπειρα διαιρήματα μεγέθη ἔχοντα, καὶ μέγεθος ἄπειρον ἂν γένοιτο (τὸ γὰρ ἐξ ἀπείρων τῷ πλήθει μεγεθῶν ἄπειρον ἔσται μέγεθος, ὡς εἴρηται πολλάκις), ἀποδέδεικται δὲ διὰ πολλῶν μὴ ὂν ἄπειρον μέγεθος, καὶ ταύτην λύων τὴν ἔνστασιν καὶ τὴν φύσιν τοῦ ἀπείρου παραδεικνὺς ἐναργέστερον, φησὶν ὅτι διχῇ διαιρεῖται τὸ δυνάμει κατὰ τὴν τοῦ ἐνεργείᾳ διαίρεσιν.

Here Simplicius is assuming that the magnitudes produced by the infinite division of a continuum, *if all actualized simultaneously*, would add up to an infinitely large total.

Aristotle himself remarks about Anaxagoras and Democritus (*Physics* III.4.203 a 19ff) that they both made their elements infinite in number and thus posited the infinite as 'continuous by contact'. He means that they assert what he believes to

[2] Simplicius, *Physics* 460.2–4: τὰ γὰρ ἄπειρα τῷ πλήθει μεγέθη ἐνεργείᾳ ὄντα καὶ τῇ ἀφῇ συνεχιζόμενα ἄπειρον ποιεῖ καὶ τὸ μέγεθος, ὡς εἴρηται πρότερον. Eudemus, quoted by Simplicius, *Physics* 459.25–6: τὸ κατὰ πλῆθος ὁμοειδὲς ἄπειρα λέγειν οὐδὲν διαφέρει ἢ κατὰ τὸ μέγεθος ἄπειρον. Cf. also Simplicius, *Physics* 453–67 *passim*, and 1046.19.

be impossible, an actually existing physical object that is infinitely large. He appears to attribute this thesis to them on the ground that it is entailed by their assertion of infinitely *numerous* στοιχεῖα, and he does not distinguish between Anaxagoras, who believed in infinite divisibility, and Democritus, who did not. Thus in this context Aristotle himself seems to be overlooking the possibility of the infinite by addition that is merely the converse of the infinite by division.

Thus Aristotle's theory of potentiality leaves some residual puzzles. He insists that a finite continuum is potentially divisible to infinity, with the proviso that the potentiality can never be wholly actualized at any one time. He says that in traversing a line one actualizes a point by stopping at it, not by merely passing over it, so that to traverse the whole of a finite line is not to actualize an infinite number of points in it. What then would he say about an *actual* infinite set of magnitudes? That it cannot exist. That is what he also says about an actual infinite magnitude. Did Eudemus and Simplicius believe that the two are equivalent? If so, would Aristotle have agreed with them, or corrected them?

Aristotle sought to answer the Atomists' assertion of indivisible magnitudes by showing that the Eleatic divisibility puzzles could be solved differently. Thus he tried to show that Atomism was unnecessary. But he also tried to prove it false, in *Physics* VI, with his demonstrations that nothing continuous can be composed of indivisible or partless units (chapter 1), that magnitude, time, and motion must all be composed of indivisibles if one of them is and that this leads to many paradoxes (chapters 1–2), and that no account can be given of the motion of a partless body (chapter 10).

The Epicureans sought to answer this case point by point. Perhaps the most obscure part of their answer concerns Aristotle's own theory of the continuum as potentially divisible to infinity. It is clear that they rejected it, and substituted their own theory of *minimae partes*.[3] But there is no mention of potentiality in the texts, and we have to guess at their attitude to it.

Epicurus writes (*Letter* 1.56):

One must not suppose that in the limited body there are infinitely numerous parts, even parts of any size you like. Therefore we must not only do away with division into smaller and smaller parts to infinity, so that we may not make everything weak and in our conceptions of the totals be compelled to grind away things that exist and let them go to waste into the non-existent, but also we must not suppose that in finite bodies you continue to infinity in passing from one part to another, even if the parts get smaller and smaller. For when someone once says that there are infinite parts in something, however small they may be, it is impossible to see how this can still be finite in size; for obviously the infinite parts must be of *some* size, and whatever size they may happen to be, the size [sc. of the total] would be infinite.

---

[3] For a different account, see Vlastos (1965b). According to Vlastos, the Epicurean theory did not maintain that there are theoretically indivisible magnitudes, either of space or of matter, but only that the volumes of all atoms are integral multiples of a common unit, the *minima pars*. If this were true, the Epicurean theory would have no connection with Aristotle's continuum. But I am not convinced by Vlastos' arguments. For the text used here and the translation see Furley (1967b), 8ff.

Here Epicurus agrees with Eudemus and Simplicius in thinking that if a whole contains an infinite number of parts, each having some size however small, then the whole is infinite in size. There is perhaps some importance in the rather careful connection that Epicurus makes here with his theory of knowledge. The infinite divisibility of τὰ ὄντα, he says, would mean that 'in our conceptions' (ἐν ταῖς περιλήψεσι) we should have to grind them away into τὸ μὴ ὄν. Similarly, we cannot 'see' (οὔτε ... ἔστι νοῆσαι) how infinitely numerous parts can add up to less than infinity. He goes on to point out that there is a minimum perceptible quantity that gives us a standard for the measurement of perceptible things, and argues by analogy that there must be a minimum theoretical (τῇ διὰ λόγου θεωρίᾳ: § 59) quantity that gives us a standard for the measurement of theoretical bodies (atoms). If we contrast the Aristotelian with the Atomist theory of knowledge, we can see how Aristotle's idea of the abstraction of whole forms from concrete objects by sense-perception or mind can accommodate the potentiality of infinite divisibility, whereas the Atomists' idea of the building-up of images through actual atomic εἴδωλα cannot. For Aristotle, the unit (so to speak) is the whole form; for the Atomists, the unit is the fundamental part, and without fundamental parts the whole system would collapse. One might add that the concept of potentiality belongs to the Aristotelian physics of continuous change and development, and is basically alien to the Atomists' world of unchanging elements.

There is an argument in Lucretius that bears on this subject. Unless there is a minimum, he says (*De rerum naturae* 1.615–27), then the smallest thing in the world and the whole world will both consist of infinite parts, and there will be no difference between them. 'Since true reason rejects this and says that the mind cannot believe it', there must be minimum, partless units. (This is a passage that has been said to be directed against the Stoics; but since a similar argument is reported in the pseudo-Aristotelian *On indivisible lines*, it need not have anything to do with the Stoics.) It may be thought to offer some confirmation of the belief that the Epicureans rejected the potentiality of infinite divisibility because they thought that ultimate, irreducible units were necessary for measurement, i.e. for knowledge of size.

Aristotle's argument that indivisible, partless units cannot make a continuous quantity was answered rather curiously by Epicurus. Aristotle argued (*Physics* VI.I.231 a 28) that whatever is partless cannot have an extremity, since there can be no distinction in this case between the extremity and that of which it is the extremity; and hence, since according to Aristotle's definition two things are continuous if they have unified extremities (συνεχῆ μὲν ὧν τὰ ἔσχατα ἕν), and in contact if their extremities are together (ἁπτόμενα δ' ὧν ἅμα), it follows that partless units can neither be continuous with each other nor in contact with each other. Epicurus could perhaps have replied with a distinction between a part and an extremity – i.e. between a product of dividing a whole, and a limit. This would have enabled him to say that his ultimate parts could not be further subdivided into smaller *parts*, but nevertheless had edges; and thus he could have given an account, in Aristotelian terms, of a continuum composed of such parts (though it would, of course, have landed him in other kinds of trouble). Instead of doing this, however, he accepted the Aristotelian concept of a partless unit as not having extremities but *being* an extremity.[4] And he answered Aristotle's objection to a continuum composed of such partless units by asserting that there must be some other way in which they make up a continuum, not dealt with by Aristotle. He argues from the minimum perceptible quantity (*Letter* 1.58). Like larger perceptible quantities, it is a *quantity*, and yet no parts can be distinguished within it (ἔχον μέν τινα κοινότητα τῶν μεταβατῶν, διάληψιν δὲ μερῶν οὐκ ἔχον). Such parts are arranged in succession (ἑξῆς) and they do not coincide or touch part to part (οὐκ ἐν τῷ αὐτῷ, οὐδὲ μέρεσι μερῶν ἁπτόμενα), but measure out dimensions by retaining their own individuality (ἐν τῇ ἰδιότητι τῇ ἑαυτῶν τὰ μεγέθη καταμετροῦντα). The same thing happens on a smaller scale, he says, with the minimum in the atom.

The Epicureans accepted Aristotle's demonstration that magnitude, time, and motion must all be composed of indivisibles, if one of them is. They were therefore obliged to fall in with his claim (*Physics* VI.2) that there can be no difference in the speed of motion of atoms (*Letter* 1.61). It should be observed that the denial of differences of speed holds not only for atoms falling freely through the void, as is sometimes suggested, but of atoms moving in any way whatever (οὔθ' ἡ ἄνω οὔθ' ἡ εἰς τὸ πλάγιον διὰ τῶν κρούσεων φορά, οὔθ' ἡ κάτω διὰ τῶν ἰδίων βαρῶν). This must be so, if Aristotle's arguments are accepted.

The Epicureans also accepted Aristotle's argument that a partless unit cannot move by itself. They amended the Democritean theory, in which the atom itself was the partless unit, by positing atoms that consisted of a plurality of partless units, and they laid stress on the proviso that the partless units were incapable of motion by themselves (*Letter* 1.59; Lucretius 1.611–12).[5]

In this case, however, it appears that the Epicureans were over-insured. Aristotle's arguments against the motion of an indivisible (*Physics* VI.10.240 b 17 – 241 a 26) are all met just as well by the Epicurean account of the arrangement of indivisible parts in succession and by their theory of indivisible units of motion. Why then did they make this amendment to the theory of Democritus? Perhaps the answer is that Aristotle's arguments about motion had forced them to consider not merely the dimensions of atoms but also the dimensions of the spaces successively occupied by a moving atom. It follows from these arguments that all the indivisible units of magnitude must be equal; hence partless *atoms* would have to be all of equal size – and all the Atomists believed that differences of size were necessary to explain the phenomena.

---

[4] Epicurus agrees with Plato, *Parm.* 137D: εἰ μηδὲν ἔχει μέρος, οὔτ' ἂν ἀρχὴν οὔτε τελευτὴν οὔτε μέτρον ἔχοι· μέρη γὰρ ἂν ἤδη αὐτοῦ τὰ τοιαῦτα εἴη.

[5] Perhaps this is the origin of Alexander's otherwise inexplicable assertion that the theoretical parts of (Democritean!) atoms have no weight (*Metaph.* 36.26–7).

THE DEBATE ABOUT THE INFINITELY LARGE

The early Atomists held that the void is infinite in extent, that atoms are infinitely numerous, and that the variation in atomic shapes is infinite. There is no doubt that they asserted these three propositions, but as usual the reasoning with which they defended them is hard to extract from the Doxographers. We will take the three in reverse order, and try to discover the original reasoning, Aristotle's criticisms, and the Epicurean answers.

INFINITE VARIETY OF ATOMIC SHAPES

We are often told that Leucippus and Democritus asserted both (a) that the atoms are infinitely numerous and (b) that the number of their different shapes is infinite (Aristotle, *De caelo* III.4.303 a 4ff, etc.). Simplicius (*Physics* 28.8–11) says that Leucippus held these two propositions: διὰ τὸ μηδὲν μᾶλλον τοιοῦτον ἢ τοιοῦτον εἶναι καὶ γένεσιν καὶ μεταβολὴν ἀδιάλειπτον ἐν τοῖς οὖσι θεωρῶν. The former is given as a reason for (b) above, and attributed to Democritus as well as Leucippus, a few lines below (28.25). Simplicius adds a little more (28.22–4): Leucippus and Democritus made atomic shapes account for the nature of compounds, and hence 'the first principles being infinite, they claimed reasonably enough that they would explain all the qualities and substances, and what makes a thing, and how; and so they say that it is only for those who make the elements infinite that all things happen κατὰ λόγον'.

The argument διὰ τὸ μηδὲν μᾶλλον τοιοῦτον ἢ τοιοῦτον εἶναι is clearly meant to establish the conclusion that there is no limit to the number of different atomic shapes. Since atomic shapes were one of the two ingredients in their explanation of sensible qualities and compounds (the other being the distribution of the atoms in the void), it was natural that they should claim that they had the apparatus for explaining *every* sensible quality. In fact, Epicurus thought they had been extravagant:[6] the varieties of sensible qualities are not infinite, and therefore the varieties of atomic shapes need not be infinite. This was convenient, because the Epicurean theory of minimal parts entailed that within the limits of a given maximum size only a finite variety of shapes was possible; and Epicurus wished to deny that atoms ever reach perceptible size. (In my opinion, Democritus probably agreed with Epicurus about this last proposition.) Epicurus' modification of Democritean theory (namely, the substitution of finite for infinite variety of atomic shapes) may possibly have been due to Aristotelian criticism. Aristotle criticizes theories that use an infinite number of elements in *De caelo* III.4, and one of his criticisms, which is clearly meant to apply to Democritus as well as Anaxagoras, is that an infinite variety of elements is incompatible with the finite range of sensible phenomena (302 b 32 and 303 a 18). However, this argument, though interesting

---

[6] See *Letter* 1.42–3, 55–6 and Lucretius, *De rerum natura* III.478–521.

in itself and for its ramifications, does not directly concern our theme of the infinitely large.[7]

INFINITE VOID

We are not concerned now with the reasons why the Atomists asserted the existence of void, nor with Aristotle's reasons for denying it, but only with the debate about its infinity.

Some clues to the early Atomists' position are to be found in a famous passage of the *Physics*, where Aristotle lists five reasons that have led people to believe in 'the infinite' (III.4.203 b 15–30). He mentions no names, and the attribution to Democritus must be judged in each case on its merits. People have been persuaded, he says, (A) because of the infinity of time and (B) the infinite divisibility of magnitudes; (C) because they suppose that genesis can be kept up only if there is an infinite store to draw on; (D) because a thing can be limited only if there is something beyond it; and (E) because one can always imagine something further in the number series, in geometrical magnitudes, or even outside the cosmos.

It will be useful to consider the last of these five arguments first. Simplicius, in his comment on it (467.26ff), says that Eudemus attributed the following argument to Archytas: if one stood on the outer edge of the universe, could one stretch out one's hand into the region beyond, or not? It is absurd to imagine that one could not, and so it appears that there must be something – either body or place – outside the cosmos.[8] Lucretius (1.968–79) argues similarly: if you could throw a javelin outwards from the boundary of the universe, there must be a space into which it is thrown; if not, there must be something outside to prevent its being thrown. In either case, there must be something outside the universe. The case for thinking that Democritus used something like this argument rests on its use by his fellow-Atomist Lucretius and by his contemporary Archytas, and on Aristotle's mention of the void in his development of the argument.

Aristotle criticizes the argument, in the form in which he gives it, in *Physics* III.8.208 a 14–19: because we can *imagine* something beyond any given limit, it does not follow that there *is* something beyond; it is easy to imagine any one of us increased in size *ad infinitum*, but the sizes of people are matters of fact that are not affected by our imagination. This criticism, however, does not really touch the problem at all. The problem is not that one *can* imagine something beyond any given limit but that one *cannot help* imagining it. Simplicius found himself still worried by Archytas' difficulty (*Physics* 407.35: μήποτε δὲ οὗτος ὁ λόγος καὶ πρὸς ἡμᾶς ἀπορήσει δριμέως τοὺς λέγοντας μηδὲν εἶναι ἔξω τοῦ οὐρανοῦ κ.τ.λ.); Sir David Ross agreed with him (1936, p. 53).

Aristotle's argument (D), however, has a strong resemblance to (E), and must be

[7] See further Mugler (1953); Luria (1964).
[8] The further developments of this argument are discussed below.

considered at the same time: people are led to believe in the infinite τῷ τὸ πεπερασμένον ἀεὶ πρός τι περαίνειν, ὥστε ἀνάγκη μηδὲν εἶναι πέρας, εἰ ἀεὶ περαίνειν ἀνάγκη ἕτερον πρὸς ἕτερον. This is really a more precise version of (E) as it applies to spatial extension: the reason why we can always think of something beyond any given limit, or more precisely why we *cannot help* so thinking, is that the notion of limit itself seems to entail a distinction between one side of the limit and the other. This notion of limit appears to be as old as Melissus (see Aristotle *GC* 1.8.325 a 15: τὸ γὰρ πέρας περαίνειν ἂν πρὸς τὸ κενόν), and it is Epicurus' chief argument for the infinity of the universe (*Letter* 1.41: τὸ πᾶν ἄπειρόν ἐστι· τὸ γὰρ πεπερασμένον ἄκρον ἔχει· τὸ δὲ ἄκρον παρ' ἕτερόν τι θεωρεῖται. See Lucretius 1.960: *extremum porro nullius posse videtur esse, nisi ultra sit quod finiat*).

Aristotle attempts to dispose of this argument in *Physics* III.8.208 a 10–14. There is a distinction between contact and limit: contact, certainly, is a relation between two things, and is an accident of things that are limited; limit, however, is not a relation of this kind. Small wonder that the Epicureans refused to accept this, for Aristotle does nothing to make the idea more palatable. Mondolfo has suggested (1956, pp. 467–8) that Aristotle's own definitions of body, surface, etc. imply that a limit is always πρός τι. Certainly Aristotle acknowledges that the instant of time is always a μεσότης (*Physics* VIII.1.251 b 20); it is hard to see why the spatial limit should not fall under the same rule, and indeed Aristotle himself seems to say as much in *Metaph.* III.5.1002 a 18: φαίνεται ταῦτα πάντα [sc. planes, lines, and points] διαιρέσεις ὄντα τοῦ σώματος.

It is necessary to pause further here in order to consider Aristotle's position. Why did he believe that both time and motion are without ultimate limits, whereas space has ultimate limits? Wieland (1962, pp. 314ff) has pointed out that the type of infinite sequence that Aristotle objects to is that of 'eines unendlichen Bedingungszusammenhangs'. This is indeed helpful in understanding Aristotle's application of the principle ἀνάγκη στῆναι, but it does not help us to understand his objection to infinite spatial extension, which is not a 'Bedingungszusammenhang'. The assertion that motion is without ultimate limits suggests that space must likewise be without ultimate limits, but of course Aristotle avoids this conclusion by using the idea of *circular* motion. The origin of his objection to infinite spatial extension seems to be his conviction that a vacuum cannot exist. The order of demonstration is this. He first tries to show that there is no void: to establish this he uses his own definition of place (*Physics* IV.7.214 a 16–26), and his own theory of motion of the elements (IV.8), at the same time showing that the observations used by his opponents to establish the existence of the void can be explained otherwise (IV.7.214 a 26 – b 11, IV.9). Hence, if there is to be something infinitely large, it can only be body; and so he devotes himself to proving that there cannot be an infinite body (*Physics* III.4–5; *De caelo* I.5–7).

The task that faced the Epicureans, therefore, in their controversy with Aristotle, was a relatively simple one. Aristotle's arguments against the *existence* of void would not disturb them so long as they could avoid being trapped by his definition of place, and could substitute a theory of motion that overcame those of his objections which were drawn from this source. Having done this, they argued for the infinity of the void by rehabilitating the old argument from the nature of limit, ignoring Aristotle's unconvincing attempt to refute it.

INFINITE 'BODY'

Aristotle's argument C in his list of the sources of men's belief in the infinite is τῷ οὕτως ἂν μόνως μὴ ὑπολείπειν γένεσιν καὶ φθοράν, εἰ ἄπειρον εἴη ὅθεν ἀφαιρεῖται τὸ γινόμενον. This has often been attributed to Anaximander, but without any good reasons. Simplicius assigns it to Democritus.

At first sight, it seems an irrelevant argument for the Atomists to use. The main point of the Atomists' programme, if the usual account of it, based on Aristotle, is correct, was to show how change could be explained as the rearrangement of unchanging, permanent elements. It would appear at first sight that they could fulfil this programme with a constant, finite stock of unchanging elements – as Empedocles had done before. This is indeed the ground on which Aristotle dismisses the argument (III.8.208 a 9–11: ἐνδέχεται γὰρ τὴν θατέρου φθορὰν θατέρου εἶναι γένεσιν, πεπερασμένου ὄντος τοῦ παντός). But we may suspect that there is more to it than that. *Prima facie*, Aristotle's criticism is a good one. So it will be interesting to see what the Epicureans make of it.

Epicurus argues for the infinity of body from the infinity of the whole universe, which he has already established by the argument from the nature of limit (*Letter* 1.41–2): if the void were infinite and body were finite, then the body would be dispersed at large and the atoms would not collide with each other. Lucretius (1.1014–20 – there is a lacuna, but the sense is sure enough) makes the same point in more concrete terms: the things of this cosmos (sea, earth, stars, etc) could never have come to be or persisted, if matter could disperse for ever into the great void. Diogenes of Oenoanda too: πῶς ἀπογεννήσωσι τὰ πράγματα χωρὶς ἀλλήλων [sc. αἱ ἄτομοι φύσεις]; ὥστ' οὐκ ἂν ἦν οὐδ' ὅδε ὁ κόσμος. εἰ γὰρ ἦσαν πεπερασμένοι, συνελθεῖν οὐκ ἠ[δύναντ' ἄν] (fragment 20, col. 2). This is clearly a version of the argument mentioned by Aristotle.

This is a perfectly sound argument on Atomist principles, and the Epicureans were justified in over-ruling Aristotle's refutation. If Democritus did make use of the argument, he may well, like Epicurus, have made it follow from the infinity of the void. Aristotle would no doubt feel free to ignore this qualification, since he had his reasons for rejecting the void, and he was not much concerned with history here.

We must also consider the difficult passage that Aristotle adds on to his argument (E). We have so far considered only the main statement of what he calls the chief reason for believing in the infinite: the fact that one can always go on in the imagination persuades people to believe in the infinity of number, of mathematical magnitudes and of τὸ ἔξω τοῦ οὐρανοῦ. He goes on (203 b 25): (E1) ἀπείρου δ' ὄντος τοῦ ἔξω, καὶ σῶμα ἄπειρον δοκεῖ εἶναι καὶ κόσμοι· τί γὰρ μᾶλλον τοῦ κενοῦ ἐνταῦθα ἢ ἐνταῦθα; ὥστε εἴπερ μοναχοῦ, καὶ πανταχοῦ εἶναι τὸν ὄγκον. (ε2) ἅμα δ' εἰ καὶ ἔστι κενὸν καὶ τόπος ἄπειρος, καὶ σῶμα εἶναι ἀναγκαῖον· ἐνδέχεσθαι γὰρ ἢ εἶναι οὐδὲν διαφέρει ἐν τοῖς ἀιδίοις. Whose reasoning is this? Simplicius' note on the passage refers ε 1 to Democritus, and although apparently it is not more than a guess (ὡς ἐδόκει λέγειν Δημόκριτος: 467.16), it is a very plausible guess. 'Infinite worlds' are a well-attested feature of the Atomists' world picture. The Epicureans do not appear to use precisely the argument reported by Aristotle, though they do use the principle τί μᾶλλον τοῦ κενοῦ ἐνταῦθα ἢ ἐνταῦθα in their attack on the Aristotelian theory of elementary motions (Lucretius I.1052–82). The conclusion stated by Aristotle καὶ πανταχοῦ εἶναι τὸν ὄγκον means of course that the density of body in the universe should be everywhere and always about the same (as in modern 'steady state' cosmologies), not that the void should be everywhere *full* of body. Aristotle makes no direct comment on the argument.

ε 2 looks at first sight to be based on the Aristotelian theory of place and the Aristotelian theory of potentiality and actuality. But this is not wholly true. Simplicius explicates the last proposition, ἐνδέχεσθαι ἢ εἶναι οὐδὲν διαφέρει ἐν τοῖς ἀιδίοις, without reference to Aristotle's theory of eternal being that has no potentiality for change. The point is simply this, he says: eternal things will realize all their possibilities in the course of time, since if something is not realized, then it was never a possibility; the same is not true of perishable things, because they may perish before all their possibilities are realized. This could well be a Democritean argument; at least there is nothing too advanced in it, and (as we shall see in the next paragraph) something similar was used by the Epicureans. The point about place is more dubious. There is no reason to believe that Democritus defined the void as τόπος δυνάμενος δέξασθαι σῶμα, as Simplicius puts it in his explication;[9] and in any case a finite stock of atoms could occupy all possible places in succession, given infinite time.[10]

The proposition that all the possibilities will be realized by eternal atoms in infinite time is used in a most interesting context by the Epicureans. The best text is Lucretius v.422ff:

> sed quia multa modis multis primordia rerum
> ex infinito iam tempore percita plagis
> ponderibusque suis consuerunt concita ferri
> omnimodisque coire atque omnia pertemptare,
> quaecumque inter se possent congressa creare ...

---

[9] Though Aristotle too says κενὸν δ' εἶναί φασιν (anonymous) ἐν ᾧ μὴ ἐνυπάρχει σῶμα, δυνατὸν δ' ἐστὶ γενέσθαι (*De caelo* I.9.279 a 14).

[10] Ross's note on ε 2 says 'the argument is an abbreviated form of one ascribed by Eudemus to Archytas'. But this is a mistake, I think. The quotation from *Eudemus* may run all the way in Simplicius, *Physics* from 467.26 to 35, as Diels' punctuation suggests. But the quotation from *Archytas* is only from 26: ἐν τῷ ἐσχάτῳ ... to 27: ἢ οὔ, as in D–K 47A.24. The rest is probably Eudemus' commentary on Archytas' argument.

This argument plays a vital role in the Epicurean attack on Aristotelian teleology: it helps to rehabilitate Empedocles' theory of the survival of the fittest against such attacks as Aristotle's in *Physics* II.8. But that is a topic to be pursued in chapter 10.

Aristotle's direct attacks on the notion of infinite body do not affect the Atomists. Most of his arguments are based on his own theory of elements, and in particular his theory of the motions of elements and natural place, and since the Atomists were not committed to these theories such arguments can be omitted. This applies to all the arguments of *De caelo* I.5–7, and all those of *Physics* III.5, from 204 b 10 to the end. The beginning of *Physics* III.5 deals with a self-subsistent infinite ἀρχή, which is not quantitative at all. We are left with a single argument at III.5.204 b 5–7: εἰ γάρ ἐστι σώματος λόγος τὸ ἐπιπέδῳ ὡρισμένον, οὐκ ἂν εἴη σῶμα ἄπειρον, οὔτε νοητὸν οὔτε αἰσθητόν. This of course has no direct relevance to the Atomists' theory of an infinite plurality of finite bodies.

IO

THE RAINFALL EXAMPLE IN
PHYSICS II.8

[1986]

Dedicated to David M. Balme[1]

There is a little-noticed disagreement among commentators about Aristotle's first argument for the teleology of nature in *Physics* II.8. Since the point is by no means trivial, although small, it seems worth examining it again.

The point of disagreement is the role played in his argument by the example of rainfall:

There is a difficulty: what prevents nature from acting not for the sake of something nor because it is better, but as Zeus makes rain, not in order to make the grain grow but of necessity, because what is drawn up must be cooled and what is cooled must turn to water and fall, and the growth of the grain is the outcome of this.

(198 b 16–21)

There are two schools of thought about this example: one takes the statement about rainfall to be Aristotle's own example of a non-teleological process – that is to say, an example of a process that Aristotle himself takes to be non-teleological;[2] the other takes it to be part of the opponents' argument for a wholly mechanistic account of nature – that is to say, an instance, which Aristotle gives to the opponents as being especially plausible, of the kind of process that is universal in nature according to their view.[3] In this chapter, I shall argue that the latter view is correct, and that in *Physics* II.8 Aristotle *rejects* the non-teleological account of regular rainfall along with the rest of the non-teleological world view.

The chief importance of this controversy is that the first interpretation would allow us to claim that Aristotle uses teleological explanations only in accounting for the presence, growth, and functioning of the parts of organisms and the motions of

---

[1] It is a pleasure to be able to dedicate this essay to David Balme, who guided my first steps into the field of Greek philosophy, and whose articles, especially 'Greek Science and Mechanism' (1939), have served as a model to me as to many others in the field.

[2] Ross (1936), 42–3; Charlton (1970), 120–6; Balme (1965); Nussbaum (1978), 94 and 322; Gotthelf (1976), 246–9.

[3] Simplicius, *Physics* 374.18ff; Aquinas, *De physico auditu* 2.12; Mansion (1946), 252, n. 2; Sorabji (1980), 147, n. 85; Cooper (1982), 216–18 with n. 12.

animals (with the rather awkward addition, since the evidence is too explicit to hide or explain away, of the movements of the heavenly bodies). The second, at first sight at least, seems to imply a much wider application of teleology – perhaps embracing all the workings of the whole natural world. The first interpretation is popular because it allows Aristotle to be defended against criticisms like those of Bacon in the *Advancement of Learning* (Wright 1900, pp. 264–5): he could plead Not Guilty to the charge of bringing theology and metaphysics into the study of nature (if he wanted to). On the minimal version of this interpretation, his teleology is hardly a mode of explanation at all, but rather a heuristic device for exploring the relation of the parts of organisms to the whole (see Wieland (1962), 275–6). But we must take a closer look at the text.

On first reading the passage, one finds no signs that Aristotle presents the rainfall example as an inadequate explanation of the phenomena. He does not write 'What prevents nature from acting invariably as *these people say* Zeus makes rain, not in order to make the grain grow ...?' He uses plain, unadorned indicatives: 'What prevents nature from acting ... as Zeus makes rain, not in order to make the grain grow ...' I must first argue that the text can, without distortion, be read as equivalent to the former.

The whole discussion begins with the brisk phrase ἔχει δ' ἀπορίαν ('there is a difficulty'); it ends rather more elaborately: ὁ μὲν οὖν λόγος, ᾧ ἄν τις ἀπορήσειεν, οὗτος, καὶ εἴ τις ἄλλος τοιοῦτός ἐστιν ('So this is the argument, and perhaps others of the same kind, with which one might pose the difficulty' (198 b 32)). If Aristotle had begun with the latter phrase, it could hardly be doubted that the whole of the argument, including the example, might well be in the phrasing of the poser of the problem. If he is stating an opponent's ἀπορία, not reasoning with himself, there is nothing surprising if the subordinate clauses as well as the main clause belong to the opponent. The same thing occurs elsewhere in the course of the argument: 'What prevents the parts in nature too from being like this? ... Where everything came about just as if it happened for the sake of something, the organism survived, having accidentally been put together in a well adapted way.' In this case there is no doubt that he is quoting an adversary, not merely for the question but also for the example, since he goes on to mention Empedocles and his account of zoogony.

But it is not merely that the text *can* be read in this way: there are also positive reasons for preferring such a reading. Why should Aristotle present his own mechanistic account of rainfall, if that were truly what he was doing, using the anomalous phrase 'Zeus makes rain'? It is good Homeric Greek, but it is not used elsewhere by Aristotle. The choice of phrase here would be explained by the assumption that he is calling to mind a commonplace bit of polemic from Presocratic *physiologia* – the same polemic that Aristophanes made fun of in the *Clouds*.

Moreover, our text even contains an *argument* for the non-teleological interpretation of rainfall. After the sentence quoted in my second paragraph, Aristotle continues: 'Similarly if someone's grain perishes on the threshing floor, it doesn't rain in order that it may perish, but that is an outcome of the rain.' There is no need to argue for something that is common to both sides of the controversy; so if Aristotle agreed with the opponents that all rainfall is wholly mechanistic, the sentence about the destruction of the grain would be redundant.

But the most convincing reason for thinking that Aristotle himself rejects the wholly mechanistic explanation of winter rainfall is that the contrary supposition makes nonsense, or something close to that, of the following lines:

These things (ταῦτα), then, and everything that is by nature, happen as they do either always or for the most part, but of the things that are by luck (ἀπὸ τύχης) or by chance (ἀπὸ ταὐτομάτου) none does so. For it does not appear to be by luck or coincidence (ἀπὸ συμπτώματος) that it rains often in the winter, but rather that it does in summer, nor that it is hot in summer, but rather that it is in winter. So if it appears that these things seem to be either by coincidence or for the sake of something, and if these things cannot be by coincidence or chance, they must be for the sake of something. But all such things are by nature, as even those who advance these views would agree. Hence, things that come about by nature and are by nature have the property of being for the sake of something.

(198 b 34 – 199 a 8)

At first sight this passage seems to settle the matter. Aristotle offers only two alternatives: coincidence, or for the sake of something. But rainfall in the winter, being regular, cannot be coincidental, and must therefore be for the sake of something. But if Aristotle suggests a teleological explanation of winter rainfall here, we can hardly suppose that he joins the mechanists in denying it in the previous paragraph.

However, the question is not so easily decided. Many commentators find a teleological explanation of rainfall so far out of line with their interpretation of Aristotle's teleology that they have sought for a reading of the second paragraph consistent with the mechanistic reading of the first. The most careful such reading that I have found is the one defended by W. Charlton (1970, pp. 120–3), and it deserves close examination.

The major obstacle in Charlton's way is the apparent implication in the second paragraph that with regard to *everything* that happens by nature the case is either one of coincidence or 'for the sake of something'. The crucial element in his strategy is to limit the application of the phrase 'everything that happens by nature' so as to exclude rainfall from its scope.

Now some limitation on the range of this phrase in the argument is inevitable. It is plain from the earlier chapters of *Physics* 11 that the disjunction, 'either by chance, luck, coincidence, or for the sake of something', is not meant to apply to everything that happens in nature. The range is limited to what may be called 'end-like outcomes'. If, for example, a number of pine trees are self-seeded and grow in some haphazard fashion with no identifiable pattern, we shall not inquire whether they grew thus by luck or for the sake of something. It is only if we recognize some structure, some pattern or organization, some good in a very general sense, that we ask this question. Aristotle insists on this when he classes chance and luck, rather misleadingly, *within* the group labelled 'for the sake of something' in chapters 5 and 6.

This limitation, however, is obviously not sufficient for the purpose. The growth of plants brought about by suitable rainfall is certainly a case of an 'end-like outcome', and indeed functions precisely in that role in the argument.

Charlton finds the necessary limitation by claiming that Aristotle here refers to only one of the two subclasses of 'things that happen by nature'. There are (A) 'things which are due to nature in the sense of matter' (Charlton (1970), 120), and (B) 'the parts of living things (198 b 23, 28) and, in general, the class marked out in 196 b 17–22 as such as might be due to nature [sc. in the sense of form ...]' (1970, p. 123). Charlton's argument is that our passage (198 b 16–21) uses an instance from (A) to illustrate what is meant by a mechanistic process; but the inference 'if regular, then for the sake of something' applies only to (B). Winter rainfall, although regular, does not constitute a counter-example because it belongs to (A). At the beginning of the second quotation above (198 b 34 – 199 a 8), then, the words 'these things, and everything that is by nature' mean only subclass (B) of the things that happen by nature.

It is worth repeating that some such limitation as this is necessary, if the mechanistic interpretation of winter rainfall is not to be a fatal counter-example that ruins the argument. There is no way out by denying that the sequence of rainfall followed by growth of crops is regular, or by denying that it is natural, or by denying that it is an 'end-like' result. The only course is to exclude it from consideration by fiat or by definition.

Is there any indication in the text, then, that Aristotle silently restricts the range of 'these things' in 198 b 34, so as to exclude such things as rainfall? Quite the contrary. Admittedly the immediate antecedent to which ταῦτα most naturally attaches itself in the preceding paragraph is the parts of animal bodies. But Aristotle says 'these things' happen either always or for the most part, and immediately quotes the example – and it plainly is an *example* – of winter rainfall and summer heat.[4] These cannot be matters of chance or coincidence, says Aristotle. But what does it matter that they are not coincidences, if they are excluded, as Charlton claims, from the class of things to which the disjunction 'either coincidence, or for the sake of something' applies? To put it more forcefully, it would be a fatal weakening of Aristotle's argument if he even suggested, at this point, that the disjunction 'either coincidence or for the sake of something' is not exclusive, that there is sometimes a third possibility. It would be

---

[4] Allan Gotthelf points out to me that 'immediately' is over-stated, since the assertion and the example are separated by the words τῶν δ' ἀπὸ τύχης καὶ τοῦ αὐτομάτου οὐδέν. He himself defends the interpretation of ταῦτα as referring to the parts of animal bodies, the rainfall example being quoted *only* to illustrate a generic point about chance: we do *not* call regular winter rainfall a matter of chance. But if we are not then to be thrown back on to Aristotle's alternative, 'for the sake of something', rainfall must be shown to be outside the class of events to which he applies the disjunction. If there is any way out in this direction, it must be that rainfall is due to nature in the sense of matter, as opposed to form. This is Charlton's view again, and I think it is open to the objections I have stated above.

necessary at least to explain what class of cases admitted a third possibility and what class did not, and why the relevant cases belonged to the latter; and there is of course no trace of this explanation.

The conclusion seems inescapable that when Aristotle says of the suggested *aporia* 'it is impossible that this should be the true view', he means both that the mechanistic interpretation of winter rainfall is inadequate, and that it is wrong to interpret all other natural processes on that inadequate model.

But is it conceivable that Aristotle should be content with the mechanistic explanation of chancy summer rainfall, while denying its adequacy in the case of winter rainfall? There is no doubt, of course, that Aristotle accepts the mechanistic interpretation as at least part of the truth; he states it often enough in his own voice (*Meteor.* I.11.347 b 12ff; *De somno* 3.457 b 31ff; *PA* II, 7.653 a 2ff; *APo* II.12.96 a 2ff). He states it without any hint of the caveat: 'Of course, in the case of regular winter rainfall this is only part of the explanation.' However, in the *De somno* passage clearly, and less clearly in *PA* II.7, he uses his mechanistic account of rainfall to illustrate a function of the brain that he evidently regards as being 'for the sake of something'. This is just one instance among many that might be quoted in support of the claim that Aristotle saw no difficulty in combining the two kinds of explanation. The process is explained mechanistically; and *it appears* that the explanation is complete. But it regularly produces a useful outcome; so we must say the process is for the sake of the outcome, and the outcome is a part of the explanation of the process, or perhaps a kind of explanation of it.

It may be objected that immediately before the passage we have been discussing, at the end of *Physics* II.7, Aristotle makes a remark that might be interpreted in such a way as to rule out in advance the result we have reached.

Since nature is for the sake of something, the natural philosopher is to know this [sc. nature]; and he is to state the cause in all ways: i.e. that A necessarily comes from B ..., and if B is to come-to-be, then ..., and that *this* is the essence, and that it is better thus, not in an unqualified way but with regard to the substance of each thing.

(198 b 4–9, slightly abridged)

It is sometimes claimed that the last line of this limits the application of teleology to biological species ('with regard to the substance of each thing') and to the contribution made by each of the parts to the good of the whole organism. But it makes good sense if taken in a more general way, as just demanding something more specific than a reference to a universal 'good'. Rainfall contributes to the good of plant life quite specifically enough to satisfy this criterion. What Aristotle is disparaging is surely (as Wagner notes (1967, p. 476)) the unfocused kind of teleology found in Socrates' speech in the *Phaedo*:

I thought that if this is the case, Mind in setting all things in order orders each thing in whatever way is *best*. So if one wishes to find out the explanation of anything – how it comes-to-be or perishes or just is – one must find out this about it, namely, how it is *best* for it to be or act or be acted upon. As a result of this reasoning, I thought that concerning each and every object of inquiry a man should look for nothing but what is most excellent and best.

(97C–D)

It is not enough, Aristotle objects, to claim that something is best: we must say what it is best *for*.[5]

---

[5] The conclusion this paper comes to raises many problems; some of them are discussed now by John Cooper (1982). He points out that in the rainfall example the end of the process is still the 'good' of biological species: Aristotle is not committed by it alone to a cosmic teleology that refers to the good of the whole world.

This chapter was completed before I read Sarah Waterlow, *Nature, Change and Agency in Aristotle's Physics.* In an exceptionally clear and interesting treatment of the problems of *Physics* ii.8, she does not quite commit herself on the issue discussed here, but seems inclined towards the view I have taken. See Waterlow (1982), 80, n. 29.

II

SELF-MOVERS[1]

[1978]

Aristotle sometimes calls animals self-movers. We must try to determine what exactly he means by this. In particular, we must look at this thesis in the light of certain passages in the *Physics* that appear to deny that there can be self-movers. Is this apparent anomaly to be explained genetically? Are we to believe that Aristotle criticized and rejected his earlier thesis that animals are self-movers? Or is his position as a whole consistent? How then are we to explain away the apparent anomaly?

To anyone who reads *Physics* II a little incautiously it might appear that since nature is declared to be an internal source of change and rest (ἀρχὴ κινήσεως καὶ στάσεως: 1.192 b 13–33), anything that has a nature must be a self-mover.[2] For what else is a self-mover but a thing that has *in itself* a source of change and rest? Thus all the things specified at the beginning of *Physics* II.1 would be self-movers: living things and their parts, plants, and the simple bodies, earth, water, air, and fire.

But this turns out, of course, to be too generous. We are told explicitly in *Physics* VIII.4. 255 a 5–10 that the bodies that move by nature up or down cannot be said to move themselves. Three reasons are given: (a) to move itself is a 'life property' (ζωτικόν) and confined to things that have souls; (b) if they moved themselves, they would be able to stop themselves, and if it is 'in its own power' for fire to move upward, it must likewise be in its power to move downward; (c) nothing that is homogeneous and continuous can move itself.

Clearly, then, things with souls have an ἀρχὴ κινήσεως καὶ στάσεως in themselves in a stronger sense than lifeless natural bodies. The refinement, according to *Physics* VIII, is a difference in the voice of the verb: the natural bodies,

[1] During the preparation of this chapter I had the opportunity of studying the manuscripts of two books not yet published at that time: Nussbaum (1978) and Hartman (1977). The problem investigated in this chapter is one that has interested me for a long time; but the manner of treating it here is much influenced by these two works. I am also indebted to their authors for comments on an earlier draft.

I am especially indebted to Prof. D. J. Allan, Dr Malcolm Schofield, and Dr Richard Sorabji for their comments, which have greatly assisted me in revising the paper for publication.
[2] For a review of this subject, especially in its relations with Plato and the Presocratics, see Solmsen (1960), 92–102.

as opposed to things with souls, have a source not of causing movement or of acting (κινεῖν, ποιεῖν) but of being acted on (πάσχειν). In fact, this gives too little to the natural bodies in Aristotle's theory. He should at least stress that they have an internal source of being acted on *in a fully determinate way*. But we do not need to pursue that subject here, and we can also leave aside the difficult question of what is the *active* mover of the natural bodies when they move according to their nature – a question to which Aristotle offers no wholly satisfactory answer.

In chapter 5 of *Physics* VIII Aristotle starts from the proposition that we can distinguish chains of movers, such that A is moved by B, which is moved by C, and so on. He produces a number of arguments to show that such a series cannot be infinite: it must be stopped – or rather started – by something that is not moved by another but by itself: 'If everything that is moved is moved by something, but the first mover, although moved, is not moved by another, it must be that it is moved by itself' (256 a 19–21).

Initially, Aristotle considers only the possibility that such a series is started by a self-mover, not the alternative that it is started by an unmoved mover. It is something of a surprise that he next (256 b 3ff) produces an argument from which he says 'these same conclusions will follow', but from which he draws a conclusion in the form of a disjunction: 'So either the first thing that is moved will be moved by something at rest, or it will move itself' (257 a 26–7).

The reason why Aristotle can regard this disjunctive conclusion as the same as the other is clear from its context in chapters 4 and 5, in which the concept of a self-mover is analysed. As a whole, a thing may be said to move itself; but within the whole it must always be possible to distinguish a mover and a moved. This is argued *a priori*, on the ground that one and the same thing cannot simultaneously be active and passive, or in a state of actuality and potentiality, in the same respect. The conclusion is expressed in these words:

Well, it is clear that the whole moves itself not by virtue of having some part such as to move itself; it moves itself as a whole, moving and being moved by virtue of part of it moving and part of it being moved. It does not move as a whole, and it is not moved as a whole: A moves, and only B is moved.

(258 a 22–7)

This conclusion is quite general: for *any* self-mover we can distinguish a part (or aspect – the article with the genitive is as non-committal as possible) that moves without itself being moved, and a part that is moved.

The same analysis is applied explicitly to living creatures in chapter 4 (254 b 14–33). There is no doubt, says Aristotle, that there *is* a distinction in this case between the mover and the moved, but it is not obvious how to draw the distinction. 'For it seems that as in boats and things that are not naturally constituted, so in living beings also there is something that causes movement distinct from what is moved, and thus the whole animal moves itself.' At first sight this explanatory sentence appears to support the statement that there *is* a distinction rather than the nearer statement that there is some difficulty about how to draw it. But Simplicius' interpretation probably gets the right nuance (*Physics* 1208.30 ff). It is obvious, he says, that a living being is moved by its soul, but it is not clear how this is to be distinguished from that which it moves – whether it is altogether distinct in nature and place or in some other way. The movement of a living being looks like that of a boat or a chariot, in which the cause of motion is the helmsman and the driver (not, incidentally, the oarsmen or the horses); and these both have a distinct spatial individuality and their own nature. But, he implies, there is doubt about whether the soul is such an individual. Simplicius probably has an eye on *De anima* II.1.413 a 8, where Aristotle writes: 'On the other hand, it is still unclear whether the soul is the ἐντελέχεια of the body as a boatman is of a boat.'[3]

There is a qualification to be added to the conclusion that a self-mover includes an unmoved mover. What Aristotle has shown is that the first mover in a series must cause motion in some way other than *by* being moved itself. The first mover may be moved incidentally. This is true, of course, of living beings, which are moved by their souls and in turn carry their souls about with them (259 b 16–20).

Aristotle now faces the suggestion that if animals can initiate motion by themselves from a state of rest, without being moved by anything outside themselves, perhaps the whole cosmos might have initiated motion in itself in this way. He attempts to rebut this argument by showing that, after all, animals do *not* start moving from a state of rest without any external cause.

There are two passages where this point is made: (A) *Physics* VIII.2.253 a 11–21 and (B) *Physics* VIII.6.259 b 1–16. Aristotle seems to think of A as an outline sketch, the detail of which is to be filled in by B (see 253 a 20–1). But in fact each passage contains some details omitted from the other. There is some significance both in the differences and in Aristotle's attitude to them; so we shall have to look at them in detail. I number the points in A; B can be divided into three sections, in the middle one of which I number the correspondences with A.

A

But this [sc. that animals move from a state of rest, having been moved by nothing external to them] is false. [i] We always see one of the connatural parts of the animal in a state of motion, and [ii] it is not the animal itself that is the cause of the motion of this, but perhaps (ἴσως) its environment. [iii] In using this expression, that a thing moves itself, we speak not

[3] This very controversial sentence is also discussed by Lefèvre (1978), 22–4. Although it is not strictly relevant to my argument, it may be worth mentioning one or two points on which I differ from him.

(a) Grammatically, this sentence beginning ἔτι δὲ ἄδηλον ... is co-ordinate with a 4: ὅτι μὲν οὖ ... οὐκ ἄδηλον ... It is neither a new beginning, as M. Lefèvre thinks, nor co-ordinate with a 6: οὐ μὴν ἀλλὰ ... (On this point see Easterling (1966).)

(b) The boatman–boat analogy is not inconsistent with the ἐντελέχεια theory of soul. The problem raised in this sentence is whether the activity that constitutes soul is *localized* (in the heart, although Aristotle does not mention the heart here); that is what is still unclear. That Aristotle would not have thought localization in itself to be inconsistent with the ἐντελέχεια theory (as Sir David Ross thought, among others) may perhaps be shown by considering the analogies with which he introduces the ἐντελέχεια theory – the analogies of the axe and the eye (412 b 10ff). The 'soul' of these is the ἐντελέχεια of the whole, but in both cases it is localized – the chopping power of the axe in its edge, and the seeing power of the eye in its pupil, or wherever it may be.

of every [kind of] motion but only of locomotion. [iv] So nothing prevents – perhaps rather it is necessary – that many motions come about in the body because of the environment, and some of these move the mind (διάνοια) or desire (ὄρεξις), and the latter then moves the whole animal – [v] as happens in sleep, for when there is no perceptive motion present, but there is *some* motion, animals wake up again.

B

[a] We see that there plainly are things that move themselves, such as the class of things with souls, and animals; and these suggested that it may be possible for motion[4] to arise in something from total non-existence, since we see this happening to them (being immobile at some time, they are then put into motion, as it seems).

[b] Well, we must note this, [iii] that they move themselves with *one* motion, and this not strictly; for the cause is not in themselves, but [i] there are other natural motions in animals, [ii] which they do not have because of themselves – for example, growth, decay, respiration, which are motions undergone by every animal while it is at rest and not moved with its own motion. The cause of this is the environment, and many of the things that enter [the animal], such as food; for [v] while it is being digested they sleep, and while it is being distributed they wake up and move themselves, the first cause being outside themselves.

[c] Hence they are not always being moved continuously by themselves. For the mover is another, which is itself moved and in change with respect to every self-mover.[5]

We shall return to discuss these two passages shortly. Before doing so it may be as well to look around elsewhere in *Physics* VIII to see the extent of the disharmony in Aristotle's attitude to self-movers.

Aristotle does not *reject* the concept of self-movers in *Physics* VIII. Chapters 4 and 5 are sometimes regarded as amounting to the rejection of the concept. Chapter 4 contains the sentence 'It is clear, then, that none of these moves itself' (255 b 29), which has been taken as a general rejection of *all* self-movers.[6] But it is not. The reference of the pronoun is to inanimate natural bodies only – 'the light and the heavy' (255 b 14–15). Nothing is said or implied about animals. Nor does the *analysis* of self-movers into a moved part and a moving part imply that there is no such thing as a self-mover. It is evidently quite legitimate, in Aristotle's view in these chapters, to call the whole a self-mover, provided that the moving part is itself unmoved, except accidentally.

But passages A and B seem to deny that proviso and hence, taken together with chapters 4–5, to reject the possibility of self-movers. Yet Aristotle clearly does not want such a conclusion. Even at the end of B he continues to speak of self-movers ('the cause of its moving itself by itself': 259 b 17). Even in his final argument for the existence of an eternal unmoved mover he continues to allow the possibility of non-eternal unmoved movers, and although he does not say so, commentators

---

[4] Motion in general, not *a* motion.

[5] For analysis of these two passages, see especially Solmsen (1971). I am not wholly convinced, however, either that these passages attack particularly the Platonic notion of a self-moving soul or that passage B interrupts the 'triumphant progress of the thought' in the rest of ch. 6.

[6] For example by Seeck (1965), 151; and Guthrie (1953), xxix. Guthrie interprets the cross-reference at *De caelo* 311 a 12 in the same sense.

124

generally take him to mean animal souls (258 b 12, 20, 32). The *De motu animalium* summarizes the position reached in the *Physics* thus: 'Now, that the ἀρχή of other motions is that which moves itself, and that the ἀρχή of this is the unmoved, and that the first mover must necessarily be unmoved, has been determined previously' (698 a 7–9). Self-movers here are still allowed the role of ἀρχή for other movements: he still has in mind the distinction between inanimate natural bodies, which have an ἀρχή of *being* moved, and animate beings, some of which have an ἀρχή of *causing* movement (*Physics* VIII.4.255 a 5–10). He has neither rejected this distinction nor provided different criteria for drawing it. In *Eudemian Ethics* II.6 and *Nicomachean Ethics* III.5 he insists that a man is the ἀρχή of his actions. There is a class of actions that are voluntary, and one of the criteria for picking them out is that the ἀρχή is *in* the agent himself (*NE* III.1.1111 a 22).

The tension in Aristotle's thinking about this subject is set up by a clash of motives. He clearly wants to preserve the commonsense intuition that the movements of animals, and especially the actions of human beings, are not brought about by external agents in the same way that the movements of inanimate beings are. Yet he sees a danger that *all* the movements in the cosmos might be thought explicable on this principle of the self-movement of autonomous parts, and so insists that even this self-movement presupposes some external changes that are independent of animal movements.

What is particularly striking about the argument of passages A and B is the way in which it assimilates intentional action to mere mechanical movements. What moves the animal is διάνοια or ὄρεξις, but what moves this is the physical metabolism that goes on all the time in the animals, and what moves this is in the first place food and so forth, which enters from the environment. This is a pattern of explanation that one might think suitable, perhaps, for the movements of the periodical cicada of the eastern United States (*magicicada septemdecim*), which lies dormant in the earth until it emerges, noisily, and with all its millions of congeners, every seventeen years (next in May 2004). It seems thoroughly inadequate for explaining the action of a man signing a contract or even of a bird building a nest.

Passage B does not even mention ὄρεξις. Passage A does (iv), but instead of treating it teleologically, as Aristotle does in *De anima* and *MA*, it reduces it to a simple mechanical response. Even food is not something the animal moves to get (an ὀρεκτόν), but only something that 'enters from the environment' and eventually causes the animal to move when it wakes up from its post-prandial sleep. The reason why Aristotle puts it this way is surely the nature of his argument. He has an *a priori* argument in *Physics* VIII.1 to show that both time and motion have no starting-point. Observation of animals suggests that they do function as starting-points for motion. All Aristotle needs to show is that their motions do not provide an example of a beginning of a motion in a system in which *no* motion took place before, and that they could not be explained at all on the assumption that no motion took place before. It does not matter to his argument *how* the previous motion is related to the alleged beginning of motion, so long as it is a necessary condition for it. So he uses the simplest possible mechanical model: A is pushed by B, B by C, and so on.

The same over-simplified model seems to be in his mind in *De anima* III.10. 'There is good reason for the view that these two are the causes of motion, ὄρεξις and practical intelligence; for the object of ὄρεξις causes motion, and because of this the intelligence causes motion, because its ἀρχή is the object of ὄρεξις' (433 a 17–20). The pronouns are slightly ambiguous; but presumably the sense is that the object in the external world that is desired stimulates the practical intelligence to search for means to get it and thus to put into practice the steps needed to get it.

'What causes motion would be one in form, the ὀρεκτικόν as such, but the first of all would be the ὀρεκτόν, since this moves without being moved, by being the object of thought or imagination (νοεῖν or φαντάζειν), although the causes of motion would be many in number [sc. because desires can oppose each other]' (433 b 10–13). Again, the unmoved mover of animals in this is the *object* of desire.

If we distinguish three items in a case of motion – (*a*) that which causes motion but not by virtue of being moved itself, (*b*) that which causes motion by virtue of being moved by (*a*), and (*c*) that which is moved by (*b*) without necessarily moving anything – then the role of (*a*) is played by the external object of ὄρεξις, that of (*b*) by the faculty of ὄρεξις in the soul, and that of (*c*) by the animal (433 b 13–18).[7] Here again the unmoved mover is not the soul or any 'part' of the animal but something external to it – the object of ὄρεξις, here identified with the πρακτὸν ἀγαθόν. At the end of this section Aristotle sums up: 'In general, then, as has been said, it is as appetitive (ὀρεκτικόν) that the animal is such as to move itself (ἑαυτοῦ κινητικόν)' (433 b 27–8). As in the *Physics*, we have both an account of an external mover and a claim that the animal is a self-mover.

The picture is not essentially different on this point in the *MA*: 'The first cause of motion is the object of ὄρεξις and of διάνοια' (700 b 23–4). 'ὄρεξις and the ὀρεκτικόν cause motion by being moved' (701 a 1). 'According to the account that states the cause of motion, ὄρεξις is the middle item, which causes motion by being moved' (703 a 4–5).

This over-simplified model produces at first sight a very blatant clash with *De anima* I.3–4, where it is explicitly denied that the soul is moved. The ὀρεκτικόν is certainly part of the soul or an aspect of it; in III.10 it is described, deliberately, emphatically, and repeatedly, as a *moved* mover; yet in these early chapters of the *De anima* Aristotle has claimed that the soul is not moved. In a justly famous passage (408 b 1–18) he argues that the habit of saying that the soul is pained, pleased, encouraged, terrified, or angered, and that it perceives and thinks, might suggest that it is moved; but this, he says, does not follow. It would be better – that is, less misleading – to say that the *man* is moved to pity, or to learn, or to think, *with* or *in* his soul (the simple dative): 'and this not in the sense that the motion is in the soul but in the sense that [sc. the motion proceeds] sometimes as far as the

---

[7] For more comments on this passage see Skemp (1978). I do not differ from his interpretation.

soul and at other times from it'. The cryptic last clause is explained briefly in the next sentence: 'Perception, from *these* [sc. objects in the perceptible world]; recollection, from *it* [sc. the soul] to the movements or cessations from movement in the sense organs'. We can ignore the second part of this; but what does the first suggest? Perceptible objects, it seems, cause the motion (cf. 417 b 19–21, 426 b 29–31), and the motion proceeds 'as far as' (μέχρι) the soul, which is not, however, moved by it.

In *De anima* II.5 Aristotle says something about the difficulty of finding the right language to describe the relation between the soul and the objects of perception. αἴσθησις consists in being moved and in πάσχειν (416 b 33). We first proceed on the assumption that being moved and πάσχειν are the same as ἐνεργεῖν (417 a 14–16). But we have to distinguish different senses of πάσχειν and ἐνεργεῖν. A man who is ignorant of letters πάσχει something when he learns his letters from a teacher. His ignorance is destroyed, and his potentiality for knowledge is actualized. But this degree of actualization is itself a potentiality for further actualization when the man actually has in mind the letter A. In this latter move the state of potentiality is not destroyed but preserved: hence we ought not to say that the man is changed (ἀλλοιοῦσθαι), or at least we ought to recognize a different kind of ἀλλοίωσις (417 b 2–16). So with αἴσθησις. To have an αἴσθησις is to pass from the first to the second state of actuality, and what causes the actualization is the object of perception.

So the soul is not *moved* by the objects in the external world in any of the senses enumerated in I.3 (φορά, ἀλλοίωσις, φθίσις, αὔξησις), except that it experiences this highly specialized form of ἀλλοίωσις.[8] Is this qualification sufficient to allow Aristotle to maintain his distinction between the movements of animals and the natural motions of inanimate bodies? It is certainly not sufficient in itself, because he uses the same pattern in his explanation of natural motion (*Physics* VIII.4.255 a 30 – b 13). In this case too we can distinguish two stages: the change from (say) water, which is potentially air, into air, through an external agency; and then the full actuality of the element in attaining its natural place. Here too Aristotle uses the simile of the man first learning, and then exercising, his skill. So if animals are self-movers but inanimate natural bodies are not, the difference in the explanation of their motions is not be found in this point.[9]

The problem comes into particularly sharp focus in the *Ethics*. In the *Physics* and the biological works, including *De anima*, Aristotle was concerned with fitting the movements of animals into certain general patterns of explanation. In the *Ethics* he has to find the distinguishing characteristics of a subset of animal movements – namely, human actions for which we hold the agent morally responsible. It now becomes crucial for him to decide whether a man is really a self-mover, and in what sense, and when. The notion that the object of desire is

---

[8] Aristotle nevertheless freely uses the term ἀλλοίωσις of sense-perception in *MA* (701 a 5, b 17–18) and elsewhere.
[9] This is explored further by Carteron (1923), 142ff.

what moves a man to action becomes a challenge to the whole concept of moral responsibility.[10]

Suppose someone says that pleasant and good objects are compulsive, since they exercise force upon us and are external to us. Then [1] everything would be compulsive on such a theory, since these are the objects for which everyone does everything. Moreover, [2] people who act because they are forced, involuntarily, do so with pain, whereas those who act because of anything pleasant and good do so with pleasure. But [3] it is absurd to blame external objects, rather than oneself as being too easily caught by such attractions, and to take the credit for one's good behaviour but blame pleasant objects for one's bad behaviour.

(*NE* III.1.1110 b 9–15)

The third point in this passage is the only one that gives an idea of *how* Aristotle proposes to rebut this challenge: the responsibility lies in the man's character and cannot be shifted to an external object of desire. 'A man is the source and originator of his actions as he is of his children' (1113 b 17). We cannot go back to ἀρχαί beyond those that are in us. Aristotle considers a possible objection: perhaps our feeble moral character is itself given to us by nature and is out of our control:

But perhaps he is the kind of man *not* to take care. No; people are themselves responsible for having become men of this kind, by living in a slack way. They are responsible for being unjust or over-indulgent, by cheating or by spending their lives drinking, and so on. In every field of action, actions of a certain kind make a corresponding kind of man. This is clear from the case of people who practise for any sort of contest or similar activity – they practise by continually repeating the action.

(*NE* III.5.1114 a 3ff)

He raises a similar kind of objection a little later, this time in a form more directly relevant to our present theme:

Suppose someone were to say that everybody desires what *appears* good (φαινόμενον ἀγαθόν) but is not master of the appearance (φαντασία) – the goal appears to each man in accordance with the kind of man he is. But [against this] if each of us *is* somehow responsible for his disposition, he will be somehow responsible for this appearance; otherwise no one is himself responsible for acting badly, but does these things through ignorance of the goal, believing that he will achieve what is best for himself by these means. And the desire for the goal is not a matter of choice, but it is necessary to be born with a natural faculty of sight, as it were, by which one will judge well and choose what is really and truly good; in that case, to be born well will be to have a good natural faculty of this kind ... Well, if this is true, how will virtue be any more voluntary than vice? To both alike, the good man and the bad man, the goal is presented and established by nature or however else it may be; and they both act in whatever way they do act by referring all the rest to this. So, whether the goal is presented to each man, in whatever form it may be presented, not by nature but with some dependence on the man himself, or the goal is natural but virtue is

---

[10] I have examined Aristotle's theory about this at greater length in Furley (1967b), part 2: 'Aristotle and Epicurus on Voluntary Action'.

128

voluntary because the good man performs the actions leading to the goal voluntarily, in either case vice must be no less voluntary than virtue.

(*NE* III.5.1114 a 31ff)

This passage suggests – admittedly in a very sketchy way – an important modification of the theory of desire set out in the *Physics*. In the latter, 'the object of desire' (ὀρεκτόν) was presented as if it were simply an object in the external world. But people desire things in the external world, and exert themselves to get them, *under certain descriptions*, and their actions cannot be explained without some notion of what each of their goals means *for them*. The ὀρεκτόν cannot be identified as such independently of the ὀρεκτικόν, and in this sense the ἀρχή of action produced by desire is 'inside' the agent.[11]

Does Aristotle recognize that the ὀρεκτόν, as the unmoved mover of human action, is always an intentional object? He does not say so explicitly. At first sight he appears to hedge his answer somewhat in the passage just quoted: 'whether the goal is presented ... not by nature but with some dependence on the man himself, or the goal is natural but virtue is voluntary because the good man performs the actions leading to the goal voluntarily ...' One might think that Aristotle meant to suggest here that the goal, being natural, moves a man to action in some way that does not involve how it appears to him, by the properties inherent in the nature of the external object that constitutes the goal. But clearly that is not what he meant. He was still thinking rather of the nature of the *agent*. The suggestion is just that one's *perception* of the goal may be in some sense natural – the same suggestion that has just been rejected in the preceding twelve lines. Probably he revives it again here to forestall a possible objection that *some* human goals do after all have a claim to be called natural – εὐδαιμονία itself, for example. Even in that case, he suggests, virtue and vice would be equally voluntary, because the subordinate goals depend on moral character, which is in our power.

The answer is given more clearly in *De anima* III.10. Aristotle begins the chapter by observing that there are apparently two causes of motion, either ὄρεξις or νοῦς, 'if one lays it down that φαντασία is a kind of νόησις' (the latter proviso is to take care of the case of animals that have no νοῦς). But these are not put

---

11 'Systems to whom action can be attributed have a special status, in that they are considered *loci* of responsibility, centres from which behaviour is directed. The notion "centre" seems very strongly rooted in our ordinary view of such systems, and it gives rise to a deep-seated and pervasive metaphor, that of the "inside". Beings who can act are thought of as having an inner core from which their overt action flows ... What is essential to this notion of an "inside", however, is the notion of consciousness in the sense of intentionality' (Charles Taylor, *The Explanation of Behaviour* (London, 1964), 57–8). Taylor quotes (pp. 68–9) Merleau-Ponty, *Structure du comportement* and *Phénoménologie de la perception*, for an extension of this notion to include the goals of non-human animals.

Stuart Hampshire explains Aristotle's position thus: 'The reason for an action has been given when the agent's conception of the end has been explained together with his calculation of the means to it. We then see the fusion of the thinking, which is an inhibited discussion of the desired end and the means to it, and the mere wanting. The reason for the action is a fusion of these two elements, because the representation to myself in words of an object desired modifies the direction, and sometimes the intensity, of the original, blind appetite' (*Thought and Action* (London, 1959), 167).

forward as alternative causes of motion, as it seems at first sight: ὄρεξις is always involved, whether or not νοῦς or φαντασία is involved. Aristotle continues: 'Now νοῦς is always right, but ὄρεξις and φαντασία are both right and wrong. Hence, although what causes motion is the ὀρεκτόν, this may be the good or the seeming good' (φαινόμενον ἀγαθόν: 433 a 26–9). Does this suggest that νοῦς is an alternative to φαντασία in this case and that either one or the other apprehends the object of desire? The same may be suggested by 433 b 12, where he says that the object of desire moves either by νοηθῆναι or by φαντασθῆναι. This would appear to be a consequence of Aristotle's regard for linguistic usage as a guide to the truth. When we are clear and in no doubt about something, we do not say 'it appears so' (φαίνεται: 428 a 14), and hence we do not want to say there is a φαντασία in this case.[12] But it is awkward to use two different terms for what is evidently the same faculty according to whether it gets something right or possibly wrong. At the end of the chapter, in his summary, Aristotle lets νοῦς drop out of the picture: 'In general, as has been said, an animal moves itself in that it is capable of ὄρεξις; and it is not capable of ὄρεξις without φαντασία. Every φαντασία is either rational (λογιστική) or perceptual (αἰσθητική). Animals other than man have a share of the latter too' (433 b 27–30). The discussion in *MA* repeats this point: 'The organic parts are put into a suitable condition by the πάθη, the πάθη by ὄρεξις, and ὄρεξις by φαντασία; the latter comes about either through νόησις or through αἴσθησις' (702 a 17–19).[13]

This line of thought will give Aristotle most of what he wants in order to defend his distinctions in *Physics* VIII and to make a consistent whole of the theses announced there. Animals are clearly distinguished from inanimate natural bodies in that although both require external things to explain their movements, only animals require external things perceived (or otherwise apprehended) as having significance *for them*. Note that this is not just a difference in the complexity of the response to a stimulus, but a difference in kind. Only a being with a soul can move in this way. An animal is correctly described as a self-mover, because when it moves, its soul moves its body, and the external cause of its motion (the ὀρεκτόν) is a cause of motion only because it is 'seen' as such by a faculty of the soul.[14] There must *be* an external object, however, and hence the movement of an animal does not provide an example of a totally autonomous beginning of motion (as noted earlier, Aristotle thought that if such an example could be produced, his cosmology would be in danger).[15]

The suggestion made in this paper is not that Aristotle was ready with an

---

[12] See Schofield (1978), 99–140.

[13] There is an excellent discussion of φαντασία and its role in action in Nussbaum (1978).

[14] There is no reason to think it is an internal *image* of the object that moves the animal, rather than the object itself, perceived in a particular way. Dr Nussbaum has discussed this fully (1978), and has persuaded me that some of what I wrote (Furley (1967b), part 2) about 'mental pictures' was at least too hasty.

[15] What about delusions, hallucinations, etc? Aristotle could reply that although animals may on occasion move in pursuit of a purely imaginary goal, these cases are parasitic on genuine cases. They would not pursue the imaginary goal unless there were similar goals in reality.

articulate theory of intentionality to defend his view of animals as self-movers. It is that he was sufficiently aware of the intentionality of objects of desire to want to retain the notion that animals move themselves, in spite of finding that they are moved by the objects of desire. I think therefore that the apparent inconsistencies in his texts on this subject are not to be explained genetically but rather as coming from two different approaches that he has not fully articulated. I think they could reasonably well have been made into a consistent theory that would have required him to do only a little rewriting.

Although he could plausibly retain the proposition that animals are self-movers, I am not sure that it would be worth struggling to retain the concept of the animal soul as *unmoved* mover. The point is that external objects are not in themselves sufficient causes for the voluntary movements of animals. But they do have some effect on the soul, and it would be obstinate of Aristotle to deny that the effect can be called a movement.

There is one conspicuous loose end in the theory that the ἀρχή of human actions is 'in' the agent. Aristotle maintains that people are moved to act by what appears desirable to them, that what appears desirable depends on their character, and that their character in turn depends on their actions and is *therefore* 'in their power'. His theory needs some explanation of these character-forming actions and of how it is that they are not caused by external pressures but proceed from an ἀρχή in the agent himself.

12

THE MECHANICS OF *METEOROLOGICA* IV: A PROLEGOMENON TO BIOLOGY

[1983]

INTRODUCTION

I take it that Dr Hammer-Jensen's thesis that the fourth book was written by Strato has been thoroughly refuted, particularly by Düring, Lee, and Gottschalk.[1] To state the case summarily: book IV is referred to in genuine Aristotelian treatises that were in all probability written before Strato was old enough to read, let alone write book IV;[2] the theory of pores contained in chapters 8 and 9 of book IV is not the same as the theory of microvoid attributed to Strato;[3] and the minor role of the final cause in book IV is explained by the author in chapter 12 in a manner incompatible with Strato's position.[4]

H. B. Gottschalk claimed that the book as it stands cannot be by Aristotle, because the theory of πόροι put forward in chapters 8 and 9 and apparently referred to also in chapter 3 is inconsistent with Aristotle's theory of matter as continuous, defended in *GC* I.8–9 and *Physics* IV.6ff.[5] He pointed to similar passages in Theophrastus' scientific treatises, and claimed that our book is a Theophrastean recension of a lost book of Aristotle's with two chapters, 8 and 9, of Theophrastus' own composition. This thesis was rejected in a brief note by Eichholz, and criticized in some detail by Pepe; but I shall start out with the assumption that it is still a competitor.[6]

I think the following chapter has some bearing on the question of authenticity, and at the end I shall try to draw some conclusions on that subject. But instead of confronting that question head on and comprehensively, I intend to concentrate on one particular aspect of the text – namely, its theory of motion. I shall examine the theory for its own sake, and compare it with other texts, both Aristotelian and

---

[1] Hammer-Jensen (1915); Düring (1944); Lee (1952); Gottschalk (1961).
[2] *PA* II.2.649 a 33; *GA* II.6.743 a 7.
[3] Strato fragments 54–67 Wehrli.
[4] Strato fragments 33–5 Wehrli, with Wehrli's notes *ad loc.*
[5] Gottschalk (1961). 'Physics 2.6ff' in both the English and the German versions of this paper is presumably a slip.
[6] Eichholz (1965); Pepe (1978).

others. But although I believe it has its own intrinsic interest, I have chosen the topic because it is also highly relevant to the issue of authenticity.

The subject of *Meteor.* IV, as set out at the beginning, is the operations (ἐργασίαι) of the hot and the cold, as active agents, and their effects on what they act on. *Meteor.* IV is in agreement with *GC* II.2 that the hot and the cold are the active agents, the moist and the dry passive:

(1)   For hot is what combines things of the same kind – sorting out, which is what fire is said to do, is in fact combining things of the same family, since it has the effect of removing what is alien – and cold is what collects and combines both things of the same kind and things of different kinds alike; moist is what is not bounded by a boundary of its own, being easily bounded, and dry is what is well bounded by its own boundary, being bounded with difficulty.

(*GC* II.2.239 b 24–32)[7]

The note by Joachim (1922) on this passage is instructive. He distinguishes two kinds of action that Aristotle attributes to the four primary opposites. (1) Hot and cold act on each other and dry and wet act on each other: 'each tends to assimilate its contrary to itself, and to be assimilated to it; and the result is the tempering of both qualities and their fusion into an intermediate quality' (p. 205). (2) To be distinguished from this is the action performed by the hot and cold on the dry and wet, described in the passage just quoted.

Meteor. IV is undeniably concerned with the second kind of action. One of the questions we must ask is whether this second kind is reducible to the first. In other words, do the hot and the cold perform their shaping and combining and solidifying operations, in *Meteor.* IV alone or in other Aristotelian texts, by heating and cooling, or have they some other powers beyond these? But we should consider the converse possibility too: are heating and cooling themselves reducible to different ways of collecting and combining? Are moistening and drying reducible to different ways of being collected and combined? If it turns out that collecting and combining are powers that are not reducible to heating and cooling, what is the nature of these powers? Do they necessarily involve locomotion, or may they be only changes in quality? If they involve locomotion, what is moved, and by what force?

This is one of the crucial issues for Aristotle in his controversy with the Atomists. In *GC* I.2 and *De caelo* III.8 he mounts a barrage of criticisms against their theory that generation and destruction can be reduced to combinations and separations of unchanging elements, that alteration (ἀλλοίωσις) can be reduced to 'order and position' (τάξει καὶ θέσει: *GC* 315 b 9), and that differences of quality can be reduced to differences of shape in the elements. So when we examine the theory of *Meteor.* IV about the generation of homoiomerous bodies and their qualitative differences, we must bear in mind the question of its consistency with Aristotle's attack on the Atomists. If the theory of *Meteor.* IV turned out

---

[7] To facilitate cross-references, I have numbered the quotations in this chapter.

to contain nothing but locomotions of substances, each with a single defining quality, all dependent on the availability of 'pores' of the right size, one would think it unlikely to be by the author of *De generatione et corruptione*.

Locomotion is, of course, prior to other forms of change in Aristotle's theory;[8] but that is not to say that other changes are reducible to locomotion. There is just one passage where he seems to come perilously close to saying just that, in an argument for the priority of locomotion:

(2)   Further, the ἀρχή of all affections is condensation and rarefaction: thus heavy and light, soft and hard, hot and cold, are considered to be (δοκοῦσι) forms of density and rarity. But condensation and rarefaction are just combination and separation, to which processes the coming-to-be and the passing-away of substances are ascribed (λέγεται). But things being combined and separated must necessarily change place.

(*Physics* VIII.7.260 b 7–13)

This is presented as if it were one of Aristotle's own arguments for the priority of locomotion: Simplicius apparently takes it at face value, followed by Ross, among the moderns. Philoponus, however, says firmly that the argument aims to show that on Presocratic premises, too, such as Anaxagoras' and Empedocles', locomotion is prior, and he points to the words δοκοῦσι and λέγεται to back up his claim.[9] This is probably right, although Aristotle does not make it easy to see that he does not subscribe to the premises of the argument himself.

NATURAL MOTIONS

The normal theory of natural motion, as presented in *De caelo*, seems to be preserved intact in *Meteor.* IV, without any explicit comment. It is simply taken for granted.

(3)   Olive oil ... is full of air; hence it floats on water, because air moves upwards.

(7.383 b 25)

But it is kept in the background to a rather remarkable extent. The key concepts of the theory – light and heavy, up and down – hardly occur in *Meteor.* IV: there is one unimportant occurrence of βαρύτερος at 3.381 a 5. There is one passage where commentators have found what would be an important use of the theory of natural motion:

(4)   It is possible, then, for such parts to come into being through heat and cold and *the motions caused by them*, since they are solidified by the hot and the cold – I mean homoiomerous parts like flesh, bone, hair, sinew, etc. All of these are differentiated as already described, by tension, ductility, fragmentability, hardness, softness, etc. They come into being through hot and cold and *their motions* when they [sc. the motions] are mingled. But the things composed of these – namely, the anhomo-

[8] See *Physics* VIII.7.260 a 27ff.
[9] Philoponus, *Physics* 840.5. So also Wagner (1967), note *ad loc.*

iomerous parts like head, hand, foot – no one would believe that they are composed thus. Bronze or silver may come-to-be because of cold and heat and *their motion*, but not a saw, or a cup, or a box. Here, however, there is art; there, nature or some other cause.

(12.390 b 2–14)

What exactly are the motions associated with cold and heat that produce bronze and silver, and by analogy also organic homoiomerous tissues? Düring, followed by Strohm, refers to the natural up-and-down motions of the four primary bodies.[10] It is not entirely clear why they invoke natural motions at this point, unless it is because of the mention of φύσις in the last sentence of the extract: ἀλλ' ἐνταῦθα μὲν τέχνη, ἐκεῖ δὲ φύσις ἢ ἄλλη τις αἰτία. If this is taken to refer to the antithesis between anhomoiomerous things like boxes and homoiomerous things like silver, we reach the conclusion that whereas τέχνη is the cause of boxes, φύσις or some other cause (what would that be?) is the cause of silver. Since silver is the analogue of flesh, bone, hair, sinew, etc, in Aristotle's comparison, φύσις would then be the cause of these. In other words, the hot and the cold, which produce the homoiomerous organic tissues, as we have been repeatedly told, would be doing so by virtue of 'natural motions'. And the only natural motions we know of are not qualitative changes but the up-and-down motions of earth, water, air, and fire.

If this were the reason for mentioning natural motions in this context, it would be mistaken. Although the phrase ἐνταῦθα μὲν ... ἐκεῖ δέ ... *could* refer to the antithesis between homoiomerous and anhomoiomerous, it seems plainly to refer instead to the antithesis between saws, cups, and boxes, and heads, hands, and feet. Alexander's comment, 'For man begets man by nature, and the horse begets the horse thus', shows that he was not thinking of any 'natural' production of silver and bronze.[11] It is only if the sentence is taken this way that the introductory particle ἀλλά has any force. Moreover, it would be grossly inconsistent with Aristotelian principles to set τέχνη against φύσις, making τέχνη the producer of highly organized things, in which the final cause is discernible, and φύσις the producer of less: the author of *Physics* II must certainly have been in his grave, and turning in it, when that was written, if it was written in that sense. Such a reading, however, is even inconsistent with *Meteor.* IV itself (3.381 b 4, 12.390 b 14), and it can be confidently dismissed. (Whether this passage is consistent with *GA* II.1 is another matter, which we shall return to on pp. 146ff.)

This passage in itself, then, does not tell us that the homoiomerous bodies are formed by the hot and the cold by virtue of the natural up-and-down motions of the elements. Alexander's comment seems hardly more likely to be right:

(5) He tells us what the motions originating from heat and cold are: tensility, tractility, comminuibility, hardness, softness, and the rest.

[10] Düring (1944); Strohm (1970).
[11] Alexander, *Meteor.* 226.23.

This is Coutant's translation:[12] the English nouns, derived from adjectives, do not properly represent the verbal nouns, in which there is notoriously an ambiguity between process and product. But heat does not produce τάσις in a body by exercising τάσις on it, as Alexander appears to suggest. Τάσις and the other nouns represent potentialities, or dispositional properties. Heat and cold produce bodies with these differentiating qualities by *solidifying* them in different ways. The motions referred to are just those motions that are involved in the processes of solidification.

The question at issue, then, is what these motions are. We shall find that they may include the natural motions of the elements, but they are a good deal more complex.

HOT AND COLD AS CAUSES OF MOTION

At first the author seems content with unanalysed verbs denoting either generation or destruction or qualitative change, with the addition of some συν-compounds denoting combination. All of these, of course, entail some changes of place, according to the doctrine of the priority of φορά in *Physics* VIII; but the locomotions, and their causes, are not as a rule discussed, or even mentioned.

There are some exceptions, however:

(6) Everything that decays becomes drier, and in the end is earth and dung; for as its own heat departs (ἐξιόντος) its natural moisture evaporates along with it, and there is nothing to draw moisture in (σπᾶν), because it is its own heat that brings it in by attraction (ἐπάγει ἕλκουσα).

(1.379 a 22–6)

We shall return later to the problem of attraction. For the moment, consider some more passages that involve the *departure* of heat and the *evaporation* of moisture:

(7) What is cooked on griddles is roasted: it is acted on by external heat, and it dries up the moisture [sc. the fat] in which it lies and absorbs it. What is boiled does the opposite: the moisture is taken out of it (ἐκκρίνεται) by the heat in the external moisture. Hence boiled things are drier than roasted (fried) things, because boiled things do not attract moisture to themselves. The external heat overpowers the internal; if the internal were overpowering, it would attract to itself.

(3.380 b 17–24)

The point here is that in roasted or fried things the internal heat is sealed in by the rapid cooking of the exterior surface, as described in the next extract. Internal heat then 'overpowers' (κρατεῖ) external heat, and therefore attracts moisture to itself. In boiling, which does not seal the exterior surface, the reverse happens. The sealing process is described in the account of roasting that follows: it is

[12] Coutant (1936).

actually moisture rather than heat that is described as being sealed in, but presumably the effect is the same:

(8)   Always what is nearer to the fire is dried up more quickly and therefore more thoroughly. So when the external pores contract, the moisture contained inside cannot be taken out (ἐκκρίνεσθαι) but is closed in when the pores shut.

(3.381 a 33 – b 3)

So far the extracts in this section have shown that moisture is acted on by heat. The next quotation describes how it is acted on by cold, in a rather paradoxically similar way:

(9)   Whatever is of water is not solidified by fire [6.383 a 7] ... But things made of both earth and water are solidified both by fire and by cold, and condensed (παχύνεται) by both, in some respects in the same way, in some respects differently: (a) by the hot driving out (ἐξάγοντος) the moist, since when the moist is vaporized the dry is condensed and concentrated, and (b) by the cold squeezing out (ἐκθλίβοντος) the hot, upon which the moist evaporates and moves out with it.

(6.383 a 13–19)

EVAPORATION OF MOISTURE BY HEAT

This is the simplest case of motion caused by the hot and cold, and needs little comment. What departs in evaporation is a body: it cannot escape if there are no pores open for its movement (passage 8). 'The moist' is here – and very often elsewhere in the Aristotelian corpus – no more than a synonym for the primary body usually called 'water'. According to the doctrine of *GC* II.3, water is cold and moist. So when it is acted on by heat to a sufficient extent, it loses the property 'cold' and becomes warm. But the moist and warm is 'air'. Having turned from water to air, it is no longer in its natural place, which it will at once seek if not prevented.

The local movement in cases of evaporation, then, may well be explained by the familiar Aristotelian doctrines of the interchange of the primary bodies and of natural place and motion. These doctrines are recalled in *Meteor.* I.9, when Aristotle introduces the idea of the 'moist exhalation', which he will use to explain many meteorological phenomena. There is nothing in *Meteor.* IV that seems to show different thinking on the subject.

We should observe, however, that heat is sometimes said to attract moisture (see passage 6). In the case of the sun 'drawing up' the moist exhalation from the earth, this may be no more than a short way of referring to the evaporation process we have just described. In artificial situations, however, like cooking, and perhaps in some of the biological processes to which *Meteor.* IV is primarily addressed, this explanation may not be plausible. We shall discuss later whether there are genuine, irreducible cases of attraction of moisture by heat.

137

SOLIDIFICATION CAUSED BY COLD

In passage 9, the cold 'squeezes out' the hot, which then evaporates the moist and takes that out with it. What exactly is this process of squeezing out (referred to also at 385 a 25)? Is it merely a metaphor for the natural tempering of the hot by the cold? A passage in *Meteor.* I suggests strongly that it is not a metaphor:

(10) Sometimes, then, the exhalation generates them [sc. shooting stars] when inflamed by the motion [sc. of the heavens]; sometimes, owing to the contraction of air because of the cold, the hot is squeezed out and ejected (ἐκθλίβεται καὶ ἐκκρίνεται) – hence their motion is more like throwing than flaming. [Sometimes these phenomena occur after the manner of a lamp being lit from another one held above it.] Some of them are projected by being squeezed out (διὰ τὸ ἐκθλίβεσθαι ῥιπτεῖται), like fruit-stones from the fingers, and are seen falling to the earth or into the sea, both by night and by day, from a clear sky. They are projected downwards because the contraction that propels them has a downward inclination. Hence thunderbolts fall downwards, although fire moves upwards by nature. For the origin of all these is not combustion but projection by squeezing out, since by nature the hot always moves upwards.

(*Meteor.* I.4.341 b 35 – 342 a 16)

The same theory is referred to, using some of the same terms, in *Meteor.* II.9.369 a 20–30 and b 5, and III.1.371 a 18.

The example of fruit-stones makes it plain enough what Aristotle means: cold causes some material to contract, the contraction puts pressure on something held in the contracting material, and that pressure forces it out. So we must look further into the mechanics of contraction.

First, some rather curious linguistic facts come to light. The verb πυκνόω and its noun πύκνωσις, standard words for contraction in *Physics* IV.7 and VIII.7, in *De caelo*, in *De generatione et corruptione*, and also in *Meteor.* I–III, do not occur in *Meteor.* IV at all. On the other hand, παχύνω and πάχυνσις are very common in *Meteor.* IV but do not occur even once in any of the previous list. In the five biological works (Z– in Bonitz's index), there are two instances of πυκνόω, ten of παχύνω. *Physics* IV uses πιλεῖσθαι as a variant for πυκνοῦσθαι, and this occurs also in *Meteor.* II and once in *De partibus animalium. Meteor.* IV uses the adjective πιλητός, but not the verb.

If παχύνω is a real synonym for πυκνόω, and does not denote a different idea, then we can find some measure of confirmation in these figures for the hypothesis of a distance between the main physical works of Aristotle (including *Meteor.* I–III) and *Meteor.* IV, and a closer approximation between *Meteor.* IV and the biological works. That it is indeed a synonym is shown by the following passage:

(11) Whatever is of water is not solidified by fire. It is dissolved by fire, and one and the same thing will not be the cause of opposite effects on the same thing in the same respect. Furthermore it is solidified by the departure of heat, so of course it will be dissolved by the entrance of heat. So it is solidified by the action of cold. Hence such

things are not condensed (οὐ παχύνεται) when solidified: condensation comes about when the moist departs and the dry packs together (συνισταμένου). Of moist things, only water is not condensed.

(6.383 a 7–13)

Only the departure of 'the moist' causes contraction; the departure of 'the hot' does not cause a loss of body unless moisture is evaporated along with it. (At 4.383 a 20, 'things that are soft but not moist are not condensed but solidified when the moist departs'. Here the moist is not a body but the quality of fluidity. This is exceptional.)

In passage 11, then, cold causes solidification without contraction; this is its action on water, i.e. in forming ice. In passage 9 (in fact the continuation of passage 11), cold squeezes out the hot, which takes the moisture out with it and thus causes contraction as well as solidification. The author does not explain why the moisture departs in this case but not in the other.

Exactly the same process of contraction is described, in almost the same terms, in *PA* II.4 (651 a 9) and *GA* V.3 (783 a 16): cold squeezes out the hot; the hot takes the moist with it in the form of vapour; the substance contracts and solidifies.

In this process, the contraction is caused by the departure of the moist, whereas in passage 10 the contraction *causes* the expulsion of the hot. There is no real inconsistency, however. The action of the cold on air is to condense it, turning it, ultimately, to water; the compounds of earth and water discussed in *Meteor.* IV cannot be condensed in the same way.

It is difficult to get a clear notion of the mechanics of the action of the cold from Aristotle. (He even contradicts himself about its nature: he asserts that it is the στέρησις of the hot, e.g. in *De caelo* II.3.286 a 25 and *GC* I.3.318 b 16, but denies this in *PA* II.2.649 a 17.) There is, however, a general consensus among Greek philosophers of nature that cold *repels* heat or fire. This forms part of the theory of *Phaedo* 103Cff. It is discussed again in *Tim.* 79E, where Plato accounts for it as a case of like-to-like attraction – the 'hotter' recedes from the cold because it seeks the company of its like. This explanation is not available to Aristotle, since he gave up Plato's like-to-like doctrine in favour of the idea of natural place.

If the cold surrounds the source of heat, its repelling force has the effect of concentrating or compressing the heat. This effect is frequently mentioned in Theophrastus' *De igne*. In § 14 he describes how cold can sometimes have the same effect as heat: it burns οὐ προηγουμένως ἀλλὰ κατὰ συμβεβηκός, ὅτι συστέλλει καὶ συνάγει τὸ θερμόν (cf. § 27 τὸ ψυχρὸν συνθλίβον ἰσχυρότερον ποιεῖ [sc. τὸ πῦρ]). In § 15 he explains that this effect is used when cold water is thrown on someone who has fainted, and adds that the heat thus concentrated cannot escape because the pores are blocked by the contraction caused by the cold; this suggests that in other cases the heat would be squeezed out. The same mechanism postulated by Aristotle in *PA* II.4 and *GA* V.3 (and in passage 11 from *Meteor.* IV) is invoked in *De igne* 17: in the Pontus region, bronze is alleged to break 'when frost and winter are intense, evidently because the contraction and concentration of the heat vaporizes the moisture, and the exit of the moisture causes the break.'

Aristotle himself quite frequently uses the idea that cold surrounds heat and concentrates and intensifies it (and heat similarly can concentrate cold). This is one sense in which he uses the term ἀντιπερίστασις and its corresponding verb – the other sense will be discussed shortly. Heat is concentrated by cold in *De somno* 3.457 b 2 and 458 a 27, cold by heat in *Meteor.* 1.12.348 b 6 and 16. Other instances are quoted in Lee's helpful note on the concepts involved, on 1.12.348 b 1. In *Meteor.* IV we have the following single instance of the verb in this sense:

(12)   Sometimes the cold is said actually to burn and to heat, not in the way that the hot does, but by collecting or surrounding the hot (συνάγειν ἢ ἀντιπεριιστάναι).

(5.382 b 8–10)

This is a mutual force of repulsion between the cold and the hot. It cannot be reduced to the qualitative action of these two powers on the primary bodies, producing a change from one element into another and so bringing natural up-and-down motions into play. It is an unexplained, unanalysed, and traditional assumption – one might claim that it goes back as far as Anaximander, and it appears to continue at least as far as Galen.[13] As we have seen, it is common to Aristotle's theoretical physical treatises and *Meteor.* IV.

HOW DO BODIES CONTRACT?

This is perhaps the appropriate place for a discussion of the controversial question of contraction in *Meteor.* IV.9–10, from the point of view of the contracted, rather than the contractor.

(13)   Compressibles (πιεστά) are those that are able to contract into themselves (εἰς αὐτὰ συνιέναι) when pressed, their surface yielding in depth without being divided and without the displacement of one part by another as water does. Pressure is the motion that comes by contact with a mover: impact comes from locomotion. Things are compressed that have pores empty of kindred body: compressibles are those that can contract into their own empty spaces, or into their own pores, since sometimes the pores into which they contract are not empty – e.g. a soaked sponge has full pores. In those cases the pores must be full of something softer than what is to contract on itself.

(9.386 a 29 – b 7)

This is ambiguously expressed: one does not know whether 'their own empty spaces, or their own pores' is a genuine disjunction, or only two alternative descriptions of the same thing; and one does not know whether the statement that the pores sometimes are not empty implies that sometimes they really are. If this were the microvoid theory adopted by Strato and Hero, then I think it would be

---

[13] See for instance Galen, *De usu respir.* 3 (Kühn IV.490).

very unlikely to be by Aristotle (or Theophrastus, for that matter).[14] But I doubt if it is that theory. The opening statement says the pores are 'empty of kindred body', and that is probably all that is meant throughout. The apparent disjunction marks only a hesitation about the term τὰ ἑαυτῶν κενά; and a soaked sponge has full pores by contrast with a dry one which has 'empty' pores.

Even so (and I believe H. B. Gottschalk is ready to settle for this weaker sense of 'empty'),[15] the passage seems hard to reconcile with Aristotle's sharp criticism of the pore-theory, especially in *Physics* IV.9 and *GC* I.8.

In *Physics* IV Aristotle's concern with the pore-theory is solely its use by his opponents in arguments for the existence of void space. There are two arguments, and it is helpful to keep them separate, since Aristotle's answers are different. The first (6.213 b 14–18) is that the observed facts of compression of some bodies demand the hypothesis of internal spaces, empty when the body is expanded, full when it is contracted. Aristotle's answer (7.214 a 32ff) is that the compression may be explained by supposing something inside is squeezed out like a fruit-stone (ἐκπυρηνίζειν). The second (9.216 b 22–30) is that if there is no void, there is no rare and dense, therefore no possibility of compression, therefore either there is no κίνησις at all, or the whole cosmos will bulge. Aristotle's response (9.217 a 26 – b 11) is that the same matter – continuous all the time – can exist in an expanded or contracted state, as when water changes to air or vice versa.

Now, so long as we accept that *Meteor.* IV's pore-theory does not include the existence of void, there is nothing that is inconsistent with *Physics* IV on this score. Aristotle is clearly not committed by his arguments in *Physics* IV to the thesis that *all* compression takes place through a qualitative variation in the density of continuous bodies: his own use of the fruit-stone model at 7.214 a 33 (and in *Meteor.* I.4) makes that quite clear. He never says or implies that predominantly solid ('earthy') things, or liquid things without any 'air' in them, can occupy a smaller volume when squeezed – and it is solid and liquid things that *Meteor.* IV is concerned with. In *Physics* IV he aims to show only that contraction does not entail void, and the author of *Meteor.* IV can agree with that.

PORES AND QUALITIES

It is not only to explain compression that *Meteor.* IV introduces pores, and H. B. Gottschalk claims that some of their other functions are inconsistent with Aristotle's position, especially in *GC* I.8–9.[16]

Eighteen πάθη of bodies are listed in *Meteor.* IV.8–9, and pores are involved in the explanation of the following seven of them: meltable (385 a 29); softenable by water (b 20–5); breakable and fragmentable (κατακτά, θραυστά: 386 a 9–17); compressible (386 a 30 – b 10); fissile (σχιστά: 387 a 2); combustible (387 a 18–

---

[14] See Strato fragments 54ff, Wehrli; and Gottschalk (1965), esp. 143–7 and appendix 2.
[15] Gottschalk (1961).
[16] Gottschalk (1961).

23). We have already looked at the explanation of compressibility. The first two in the above list involve nothing more than the mechanism used in compressibility: namely, channels that will allow the passage of moisture. Those which offer the most difficulty are the various species of breaking, and combustibility.

In *GC* 1.8.326 b 26–8, Aristotle claims that, since bodies are divisible through and through, pores are an absurd fiction – any body can be parted anywhere. This would appear to be in contradiction with *Meteor.* IV's theory that different forms of breaking are explained by the assumption of different arrays of pores. But I am at a loss to see how Aristotle could distinguish between three different kinds of breakableness in the terms set up in *GC* 1.8. 'The agent can make a channel for itself in the patient', says Joachim (1922) in explaining the *De generatione et corruptione* passage. But the point in *Meteor.* IV is precisely that differently constituted bodies break differently, not according to the agent but according to their own differences as patient. And that is obviously correct. Every woodworker knows that the same drill or chisel will split one species of wood but not another. As soon as Aristotle considered such points (i.e. when he moved from *a priori* polemics against Empedocles and the Atomists to constructive biology) he was bound to abandon the crude generality of the statement in *De generatione et corruptione*.

In *GC* 1.8.326 b 21–4, Aristotle argues that in any case of qualitative change πάθη must be distributed through the patient body itself somehow, and if the agent cannot act on the surface by contact with it, there is no reason to think it will do any better if it passes along pores inside the body. This would appear to demolish *Meteor.* IV's theory of combustible things: 'combustibles are things with pores that admit fire and with moisture in their longitudinal pores that is weaker than fire' (387 a 19–21). But the mention of moisture here suggests that we have another case similar to compressibility: that is to say, we are concerned not with the transmission of a πάθος like heat (as in *De generatione et corruptione*) but with the movement of a physical body.[17]

This raises a wider question: whether the treatment of qualities in general in *Meteor.* IV is compatible with Aristotle's view of them.

'The moist' inside a body cannot escape from it when the exterior pores are closed (passage 8, above). This will serve as a typical instance for the purpose of discussion: the quality involved is usually the moist, but the hot is sometimes treated similarly. The position of *Meteor.* IV in this respect is well discussed by H. Happ;[18] he describes the tradition of *konkretisierte* qualities beginning with the Presocratics and Hippocratic writers and continuing with Strato (a notable case) and Galen. He observes that it is especially in biology that the qualities tend to

---

[17] It is worth comparing *GA* II.6.743 a 1–17 (a passage already cited in n. 2 above as containing a reference to *Meteor.* IV). This passage concerns the formation of τὰ ὁμοιομερῆ by cooling and heating, out of the nourishment that percolates διὰ τῶν φλεβῶν καὶ τῶν ἐν ἑκάστοις πόρων. The harder kinds of ὁμοιομερῆ (like horns and hoofs) are made by a process of evaporation (ἐξατμίζοντος τοῦ ὑγροῦ μετὰ τοῦ θερμοῦ).
[18] Happ (1971), § 6, 13.

receive this treatment. F. Solmsen has written of 'the perhaps reluctant yet in any case unqualified recognition of "the hot" as a substance in our body' in Plato's *Timaeus* – reluctant, presumably, because there is a *prima facie* clash between this and the doctrine of geometrically shaped elementary particles.[19] 'Whatever philosophers had decided about them', Solmsen writes, 'the moist and dry, the cold and hot remained firmly entrenched in medical theory – there was nothing that could take their place.'

If there is a conceptual confusion in *Meteor.* IV about 'the moist' and other qualities, it is not peculiar to *Meteor.* IV and does not distinguish *Meteor.* IV from at least the biological treatises of the Aristotelian corpus. It is enough to quote a few instances:

(14) Ice and every solidified moisture are called dry in actuality and accidentally, being moist potentially and in themselves; earth and ash, etc., when *mixed with the moist* are actually and accidentally moist, but in themselves are potentially dry.

(*PA* II.3.649 b 12)

(15) Of blood, part is more watery, and so does not solidify; the earthy part solidifies when *the moist evaporates* off.

(*ibid.* II.4.650 b 16)

(16) The eye alone of the sense organs has its own body. It is moist and cold; and it is not, as the other parts are, pre-existent in its place in potentiality, then later coming to be in actuality, but *the purest of the moisture* (τῆς ὑγρότητος) around the brain is *taken off* (ἐκκρίνεται) *through the pores* that can be observed leading from the eyes to the membrane around the brain.

(*GA* II.6.744 a 5–11)

(17) Both the hot and the cold are hardeners, since *the moist is evaporated* off by both of them, by the hot in itself, by the cold accidentally, for it departs along with the hot.

(*GA* V.3.783 a 33)

H. B. Gottschalk claims (and it is the crucial element in his case against the authenticity of *Meteor.* IV) that the pore-theory is fundamentally inconsistent with Aristotle's conception of continuous magnitudes. 'Aristotle insisted that all material substances are continuous and homogeneous.'[20] But that is surely over-stated: continuous, certainly, but not necessarily homogeneous. Some are homogeneous through and through, like clean water: others are not, like earth, or like blood in passage 15. The doctrine of homoiomereity, as used by Aristotle, is a biological concept rather than a geometrical one. All biological tissue is, according to him, divisible *ad infinitum*, but not necessarily into parts always identical to each other in all of their qualities. Aristotle's discussion of blood in *PA* II.4 shows that in his view a substance may be continuous, and homoiomerous, and yet contain some parts that are solid (αἱ καλούμεναι ἶνες) and some that are liquid. Essentially the pore-theory of *Meteor.* IV requires nothing more radical than that.

---

[19] Solmsen (1960), 346.
[20] Gottschalk (1961), 68.

ATTRACTION

There is no mention of magnetic attraction in *Meteor*. IV. Perhaps one would not expect it, in view of the predominantly biological interest of the book.

The adjective ἑλκτός is used to denote one of the πάθη of bodies in chapters 8 and 9, but it has nothing to do with attraction. Lee translates it 'ductile', Strohm 'elastisch zu dehnen'.

There are a few cases of attraction, however, in the physics of *Meteor*. IV, marked by the use of the verbs ἕλκειν and σπᾶν:

(18) [Things that decay dry up.] For as their own heat leaves, the natural moisture evaporates along with it, and there is nothing to attract (σπᾶν) moisture; for it is their own heat that draws it in by attraction.

(1.379 a 23)

(19) Boiled things are drier than roasted, since boiled things do not attract (ἀνασπᾶν) moisture into themselves. For the external heat overpowers the internal; if the internal overpowered the external, it would have attracted to itself.

(3.380 b 22)

Both of these are instances of heat attracting moisture *into* something, as opposed to extracting moisture by evaporation. We have already looked at the mechanics of evaporation and treated it as a case of natural motion, following change of substance; but it should be noted here that it could also be treated as a case of attraction by heat.[21]

Plato explains a case of attraction by heat – or rather, explains it away – in *Tim*. 79E. He uses his theory of περίωσις to account for the operation of the medical cupping-glass (σικύα), as a part of a general polemic against ὁλκή. All alleged cases of attraction are to be analysed as resulting from circular thrusts; according to Plutarch, some of the air in the cupping-glass, on being heated, turns to fire and escapes through the bronze of the vessel; it then gives the external air a push, which is transmitted in an arc of a circle back to the body of the patient, thus thrusting the flesh up into the glass.[22]

The fact that Plato offers such an explanation in a polemical fashion shows that others postulated an unexplained force of attraction in the heat of the cupping-glass. This is confirmed by another polemic, in Hippocrates, *Anc. Med.* 22, where the author – an enemy of the hot and the cold – argues that the cupping-glass attracts because of its *shape*. In fact there is much direct evidence in the Hippocratic corpus of an unexplained attraction of moisture by heat.[23]

[21] See the discussion of the question by Carteron (1923), 56–70.
[22] *Platonic questions* 7, 1004Dff. See Cherniss's excellent notes on the passage (1976), 63–9.
[23] See *Flat.* 10 and 15–18; *Reg.* II.57–8, 62, 64; *Morb.* II.3, 11; *Carn.* VI.13. My research in the Hippocratic corpus for this chapter has been greatly helped by the use of a computer tape of the corpus provided by 'Projet Hippo', Laval University, Quebec, and I acknowledge this assistance with gratitude. The concept of attraction in these texts deserves a separate study. There is much evidence, but a preliminary look suggests that it is not consistent. There appears to be no significant use of ἀντιπερίστασις, on the other hand.

Apart from purely mechanical instances of ἕλκειν (= pulling or sucking), and those that can be reduced to substantial change and natural motion, there are rather few cases in Aristotle, but enough to show that *Meteor.* IV is not un-Aristotelian in attributing an unexplained attractive power to heat. Those that I have found (s.v. ἕλκειν, ἑλκύειν, σπᾶν) are concerned with the capacity of flesh to attract moisture (*PA* III.10.672 b 29, 11.673 b 8); this capacity is mentioned as an illustration of something else in *Meteor.* II.2.355 b 10, where the causal agent is said to be the inborn heat. Aristotle recognizes the existence of attraction, but does not elevate it to a principle of importance against his opponents, as Galen does in his polemic against Erasistratus, Asclepiades and others in *On natural faculties.*

’Αντιπερίστασις

The second sense of ἀντιπεριίστασθαι is found in *Meteor.* IV.4 at 382 a 11–14 (for the first sense, see above, pp. 140ff). It helps to distinguish the hard from the soft: the soft is what yields *without* ἀντιπερίστασις, that is, without displacing something else as it does so. Water yields, but it is not soft, in that an equal amount of air is displaced somewhere else when it yields.

This idea is used quite frequently in Aristotle,[24] and it becomes important in the physics of Theophrastus.[25] As Strohm observes,[26] the whole concept deserves a monograph: but since it plays only a very minor role in *Meteor.* IV, there is no need to say more here.

METEOROLOGICA IV AND THE BIOLOGICAL WORKS

The preceding sections of this paper seem to me to support the view that *Meteor.* IV may be a genuine work of Aristotle. They tend to confirm Düring's opinion of the treatise, then, but with some reservations.[27] The book is not well described as 'Aristotle's Chemical Treatise': that title suggests too strongly a connection with the basic physical sciences. Inorganic substances certainly enter into the picture, especially in chapters 10–11 – but even there Düring is wrong to give them the subtitle 'On inorganic homogeneous bodies'. A quick look through these chapters shows that like the rest of the book they are primarily concerned with organic tissues. The last paragraphs of *Meteor.* III, indeed, promise that something like a 'chemical treatise' is to follow: it would consist of a detailed discussion of the effects produced by exhalation when it is enclosed in the parts of the earth. But *Meteor.* IV is not the fulfilment of that promise.

Since it is primarily concerned with the formation of organic homoiomerous tissues, it must obviously be compared with other accounts of the same processes in Aristotle's biological works: that means *PA* II.1–3 and *GA* II.1–6.

---

[24] Lee (1952) gives a list of passages in his note on p. 82.
[25] See Steinmetz (1964), index s.v. Antiperistasis.
[26] Strohm (1970) 152, n. 27.11.
[27] Düring (1944).

PA II.1 draws attention explicitly to a feature of *Meteor.* IV that tends to differentiate it, as we have noticed, from *De generatione et corruptione*.²⁸ The first order of composition, says Aristotle, is out of the four elements – or better, out of the δυνάμεις, and especially hot, cold, dry, wet, which are the ὕλη of compound bodies (646 a 14–17). He mentions that he has discussed the importance of these four ἐν ἑτέροις; this is referred to *GC* II.2 and 8 by A. L. Peck,²⁹ but P. Louis is surely right to refer it 'surtout' to *Meteor.* IV, which is just where the elements are most clearly displaced by the δυνάμεις.³⁰

In *PA* II.2 (649 a 20) Aristotle has a brief note about the solidifying action of hot and cold on different kinds of matter – a subject that has been 'analysed more clearly elsewhere'. This clearly presupposes the discussion of solidification in *Meteor.* IV.5–6. Chapter 3 continues with the moist and the dry, then a general account of the 'cooking' of the food by innate heat. The theoretical discussions of cooking in *Meteor.* IV.2–3 and of the effects of the hot and the cold on the dry and the wet in *Meteor.* IV.4–7 seem to me to complement these chapters of *PA* II as if they were meant to do so.

Book II of *De generatione animalium* has a lengthy discussion of the formation of the different parts and tissues of the embryo. And here we have a theme that needs a more detailed look:

(20) Homoiomerous and organic³¹ parts grow simultaneously; and just as we should not say that fire alone makes an axe or any other tool, so we should not say it makes a hand or a foot. Just so too with flesh: for it too has a function. Hard, soft, viscous, brittle, and all other such characteristics of living parts – these could be produced by heat and cold; but not the *logos* by virtue of which this is flesh and that is bone. That is done by the motion that comes from the begetting parent, being in actuality what the material from which the offspring grows is potentially. As with things that are formed by art: the hot and the cold make the iron hard and soft, but a sword is made by the movement of the tools, which have the *logos* of the art.

(II.1.734 b 27–735 a 2)

This passage contradicts what is said about the homoiomerous tissues in *Meteor.* IV (passage 4 above). Yet the contradiction is one that can be explained away. It is precisely those qualities of hardness and softness, etc. of the homoiomerous tissues that *Meteor.* IV is concerned with. They are still said to be produced by the hot and the cold in *GA* II. It is understandable enough that *De generatione animalium* should claim that a cause of a different kind is needed for producing the *logos*, the precise ordering of qualities in each of the biological tissues. The spirit of the

²⁸ Above, p. 142.
²⁹ Peck (1937), 106, n. *c*.
³⁰ Louis (1956), 174.
³¹ τὰ ὁμοιομερῆ καὶ τὰ ὀργανικά. The English 'organic' is used here to represent the Aristotelian category of structured parts of the body as opposed to homoiomerous tissues (e.g. faces as opposed to flesh). Hitherto I have used it in its normal English sense, roughly biological as opposed to inanimate.

distinction in the two passages is of course the same, but the cut is made in a different place.

In the rest of these chapters of *De generatione animalium* we can find several passages that make use of the theories put forward in *Meteor.* IV. The discussion of the effects of heat and cold in semen in chapter 2 has as its background the different hardening and softening of different materials in *Meteor.* IV.6 (passages 11 and 9 above), and certain details are repeated, in different words, from *Meteor.* IV.[32] The uterus when hot draws in the semen, as a hot jar draws in water when dipped into water mouth downwards.[33] In chapter 6 we have an explicit reference to *Meteor.* IV, as mentioned on p. 132, n. 2: the homoiomerous tissues are formed by cooling and heating (in spite of the qualification made in passage 20), some being composed and solidified by cold, some by heat – a distinction described 'elsewhere', where there is also a discussion of what can be dissolved by moisture and fire, and what is insoluble in moisture and unmeltable by fire. This clearly refers to *Meteor.* IV.7–10, and the following brief discussion of the formation of flesh, nails, horns, hoofs, bills, shells, sinews, bones, and skin does in fact make use of the theory of solidification by heat and cold put forward in those chapters.[34]

In conclusion I return to some of the questions raised at the beginning of this chapter, on the relation between heating and cooling and 'combining' (σύγκρισις). We have examined various ways in which the homoiomerous bodies are said to be formed by solidification, and how solidification is brought about in various ways by heat and cold. The simplest action involved is the action of heat warming moisture, turning it to vapour, causing it to leave the body, and thus making the body more solid. Cold is said to act in a similar way. In addition, hot and cold have certain very ill-defined properties of attraction and repulsion, which also play a part in solidification.

The general thrust of this chapter is to suggest (or rather to confirm the suggestion put forward by others) that Aristotle saw no contradiction or inconsistency between his theory of potentiality and actuality and ἀλλοίωσις, on the one hand, and his 'locomotive' language and 'concretized' qualities of hot, cold, moist, dry in *Meteor.* IV on the other. The point can be illustrated once more by a passage of *De generatione animalium.* In the same chapters in which he makes use of the language and theories of *Meteor.* IV, as we have seen, he also enters into controversy with the φυσικοί on the subject of the growth of the parts of an embryo.

(21)   The principle of 'moving towards the like' invoked by some of the φυσικοί must not be taken to mean that the parts move in the sense of locomotion, but that they remain where they are, changing (ἀλλοιούμενα) in softness, hardness, colour, and the other

---

[32] Compare 735 b 35–7 with 389 a 22; 735 b 26 with 383 b 25.
[33] Compare 739 b 5ff with 379 a 23 (passage 18 above) and 380 b 22 (passage 19 above).
[34] Nor have I found anything inconsistent with *Meteor.* IV in the account in *De generatione animalium* of the formation of other homoiomerous substances such as shell (1.8.718 b 18) and semen (1.17ff).

differences of homoiomerous bodies, becoming actually what they were previously in potentiality.

$$(GA \text{ ii.5.741 b 10–15})$$

The manner in which these changes in the quality of the homoiomerous bodies are brought about is just what is described in *Meteor.* iv. Aristotle saw no inconsistency between the theories of *Meteor.* iv and his own polemical stance against the φυσικοί.

From the vantage point adopted in this chapter – and there are other valid ways of approaching the problem – *Meteor.* iv seems to me to have a genuine look. Moreover there is a sense in which it is even in the right place. It is not the book that was meant to follow immediately upon *Meteor.* iii; the concluding chapter of that book promised something different. But the introduction to *Meteorologica* announced that biology should follow meteorology. If *Meteor.* iv is Aristotle's prolegomenon to his biological works, then it is not out of place at the end of the *Meteorologica*.

13

STRATO'S THEORY OF THE VOID

[1985]

Dedicated to Paul Moraux

At the beginning of his *Corollary on place* (*Physics* 601.14–24), Simplicius classifies theories about place, as follows. First, there is a distinction between those who make place a corporeal thing and those who suppose it is incorporeal. Only Proclus falls into the first class. Of the latter, some think it is without extension, the rest think it is extended. The first group consists of Plato, who said place is the material substrate of bodies, and Damascius, who said it is that which completes the nature of bodies. The second group is further subdivided, into those who held place to be extended in two dimensions, 'as Aristotle and the whole Peripatos did', and those who gave it three dimensions. The latter can be subdivided again: on the one hand, there is the school of Democritus and Epicurus, who held that place is everywhere undifferentiated, and sometimes persists without any body in it, and on the other hand, 'the famous Platonists and Strato of Lampsacus', who said that place is an extended interval (διάστημα) that always contains body and is adapted to its particular occupant.

The word διάστημα recurs in the definition of place attributed to Strato by Stobaeus (fragment 55 W):[1]

τόπον δὲ εἶναι τὸ μεταξὺ διάστημα τοῦ περιέχοντος καὶ τοῦ περιεχομένου.

At first sight, this appears to mean that there is a gap between the exterior surface of any body described as being 'in a place' and the interior surface of the body that contains it, and that this gap is the place of the contained body. But this cannot be right, as Mr Gottschalk saw.[2] It must mean rather 'the interval in the middle of the container and the contained'. Alternatively, we may suppose with Mr Gottschalk that the words τῶν ἐσχάτων have fallen out of the text after the word διάστημα. In either case, the meaning would be that place, in Strato's theory, is a three–dimensional extension defined by the exterior surface of the contained body, or by the coincident interior surface of the containing body.

---

[1] In this chapter W refers to Wehrli (1969) and G to Gottschalk (1965). Frequent reference is also made to Gatzemeier (1979).

[2] G (1965), appendix 2, p. 169.

The language of Stobaeus' report, and the whole context of the discussion, is dominated by Aristotle's arguments. In *Physics* IV.4 Aristotle considers the idea that place is an interval extended in three dimensions, and gives reasons for rejecting it. Strato's view therefore puts him in opposition to Aristotle on this subject. But having rejected Aristotle's theory of place, he had to take up a new position with regard to the void, since Aristotle's argument against the existence of void space, in *Physics* IV.7, depends heavily on the conclusions of his earlier discussion of place. Strato wrote a book, *On the Void*, mentioned by Diogenes Laertius V.59, and there is enough fragmentary evidence surviving to suggest that he did indeed take a different position from Aristotle. The evidence is not altogether clear, and sometimes appears to be contradictory. It is the purpose of this article to try to arrive at a probable account of Strato's position.

The texts relevant to Strato's theory of the void can be grouped conveniently in five sections:

(1)   Simplicius states that Strato claimed that the void is a theoretical entity only, in practice always filled with a body (fragments 59 and 60 W).

(2)   Other texts in Simplicius inform us that Strato criticized at least some of the arguments for void attributed to the Atomists in Aristotle *Physics* IV.6–7 (fragments 61–3 W; see also fragment 32 W, from Cicero). There are some problems about the interpretations of these texts, which we shall return to shortly.

(3)   There are some brief citations in the Doxographers saying that in Strato's theory there is no void outside the cosmos, although it is *possible* for there to be a void inside it (fragments 54–5 W).

(4)   Simplicius attributes to Strato the *microvoid* theory, as I shall call it: that is, the theory that all or most material body contains imperceptibly small void interstices (fragment 65A W).

(5)   Finally there are texts that do not mention Strato by name, as the other four types do, but refer to theories mentioned in the first four: the main text in this class is the theoretical introduction to Hero's *Pneumatica* (fragments 56 W, 57 W, 64 W, 65 W, 66 W, 67 W, all contained in passage 1A, G). There is a passage of seven lines in Hero (fragment 65B W) which is almost word for word the same as the passage in Simplicius (fragment 65A W) that attributes the microvoid theory to Strato by name.

These texts do not immediately fall into a consistent pattern: there appears to be some contradiction between (1), the claim that the void is always in practice filled and (4), the theory of microvoid; and it is not clear how to take the idea of a potential void, in (3). Scholars have varied between what we might call maximalist and minimalist positions with regard to the texts. The maximalist position is that of Mr Gottschalk, and runs as follows. The microvoid theory attributed to Strato by Simplicius (4) is the foundation of Hero's pneumatics; Hero acknowledges that he is following certain others in this theory although he does not name them; this and other aspects of Hero's theory are found in Erasistratus, the third-century physiologist, who is known to have been associated with the Peripatos; Strato was the only Peripatetic of the right date and the right interests to father all this theory: large portions of Hero's introduction can therefore be regarded as drawn from Strato, either directly or after some reworking.

The minimalist position is that of Gatzemeier. Simplicius, according to him, misinterpreted Strato's theory of the potential void; Hero and Erasistratus were not working with Strato's doctrine at all. Strato's theory was that void space exists in potentiality, but is in fact always filled with something – and this applies equally to the microvoid, which is not an actual state but a certain capacity in some kinds of matter to open up channels (πόροι) through which other matter can penetrate.[3]

I believe it can be shown that Gottschalk's interpretation is closer to the truth than Gatzemeier's, although it may need to be modified somewhat. We must begin with the explicit statement of Simplicius that Strato held the microvoid theory (fragment 65A W). This is unfortunately unique, but it is quite definite, and it will take a strong argument to persuade us to reject it.

Strato of Lampsacus tries to show that the void exists interspersed in every body so that it is not continuous. He says that otherwise water and air and other bodies could not be penetrated by light or heat or any other corporeal power (δύναμις σωματική). How could the rays of the sun penetrate to the bottom of the jar? If the liquid had no pores in it, and the rays forced a way through, then full jars would overflow, and it would not be the case that some rays would be reflected upwards and others would go on downwards through the liquid. But I [sc. Simplicius] think it is easy to solve these problems on Peripatetic principles, according to which heat and other corporeal powers and light, being incorporeal, do not require the existence of a void interval ...

Opponents of the attribution of the microvoid to Strato, like Gatzemeier, cannot deny that Simplicius in the opening sentence does indeed make the attribution of an actual void, not merely a potential one, to Strato. The only escape is to suppose that Simplicius misinterpreted the conclusion Strato drew from his argument about penetration. Gatzemeier's grounds for denying an actual microvoid in Strato are the following:

(a)   that it is inconsistent with the texts numbered (1) above, stating that in Strato's view the void is always full of body;

(b)   that it is inconsistent with Strato's criticism of the Atomists' arguments for the existence of void;

(c)   that it is inconsistent with Strato's view of the continuity of body;

(d)   that his view of matter makes sense as a theory of *potential* void that is not inconsistent with any of these.

I think, however, that none of these grounds stands up to close examination.

(a) Gottschalk pointed out (p. 131) that the microvoid theory is not inconsistent

3 Gatzemeier, 94–7.

with the view (fragment 60 W) that the void is isometric with the cosmic body and is always filled with body, if the microvoid is conceived to be an integral part of bodies in their natural state. We use the same idiom, it might be added, when we speak of a cylinder 'full' of gas.

(b) This is more complicated, and as promised earlier we must shortly analyse the texts in more detail.

(c) It is important to distinguish clearly between Democritean Atomism and the microvoid theory. The microvoid theory is not an atomic theory; it is fully compatible with infinite divisibility, whether construed as a thesis about geometrical extension or as one about the structure of matter as such. The matter between the postulated void interstices can be just as divisible as Aristotle would have it. When Simplicius says (fragment 65A W, quoted above) that the void is 'interspersed in every body so that it is not continuous', he does not mean that the theory entails the Atomists' thesis that there is no such thing as continuous body, but only that stretches of continuous body are interrupted by void interstices. The following examples of water and air make this clear enough. Not being committed to any kind of atomic theory, Strato could quite consistently criticize the 'dreams' of Democritus, as our source Cicero puts it (fragment 32 W) – Democritus who 'hoped, not argued (non docentis sed optantis) ... that all things were put together out of rough and smooth and hooked and barbed bodies with void in between'.

(d) It seems to me that the argument from percolation (in fragment 65A W, quoted above) demands more than merely potential channels in the structure of penetrable matter. The example of the penetration of light through water is especially significant here. When the evidence is so scanty we must make the most of what we have: I suggest that we must pay particular attention to the fact that Strato pointed to the double phenomenon of reflection and penetration. If the surface of the water were all homogeneous, one would expect perhaps that either all of the light would be reflected or all of it would penetrate.

Gatzemeier claims that the argument from percolation points only to potentially void interstices in the water – misinterpreted by Simplicius as actually void. The notion of potentially void πόροι might be interpreted in two ways, but neither of them is satisfactory. In the first place, it might be the case that the water can be parted so as to make a channel at any point whatever in its continuous volume, just as a geometrical line can be divided at any point in its length. But this is open to the objection that there seems then to be no reason why the πόροι should not sometimes be large enough to be visible. Why should light or heat not make its way through water just as a diver does? Alternatively, it might be that potential πόροι exist only in certain places but not in others – this appears to be the version intended by Gatzemeier. But this is surely an incoherent idea. The potential πόροι, it is claimed, at times when they are not under pressure from light or heat or something of the kind, are filled – with water. But what is the difference between the water that fills the πόροι and the rest of the water? Why is one bit of water weak enough to yield a path for light or heat, another bit strong enough to reflect it? If it is not some characteristic of the water that makes the difference between penetration and reflection, then what is it that has this characteristic? There seems to be no suitable candidate. It will not help to suggest that the πόροι are filled with some less rigid substance (a suggestion considered by Aristotle, *Physics* IV.7.214 a 32), because for every penetrable substance it would be necessary to posit a thinner or more yielding substance to fill its pores. This will hardly do as an explanation of the penetrability of air. The solution must be that the water is porous, not merely divisible: i.e. that the pores are actual, not potential, and may sometimes be left empty.

We can see some of the point of the microvoid theory if we compare it with Aristotle on the propagation of light. Aristotle describes his view thus:

> Well, there is something transparent, and by this I mean that which is visible, but not visible in itself without qualification, but because of colour which belongs to something else. It is exemplified by air and water and many solids. They are not transparent *qua* water or air, but because there is a certain nature (φύσις) present both in them and in the eternal body up above. Light is the actuality of this – of the transparent as such ... Now we have said what the transparent is, and what light is, namely, neither fire nor any corporeal substance nor an emanation from any such ... but the presence of fire or some such in the transparent.
>
> (*De anima* II.7.418 b 4)

This serves to distinguish light from fire on the one hand, and from colour on the other; but it does so at the expense of introducing a totally unexplained entity called 'the transparent'. Aristotle tells us nothing more about it. It is not explained as the outcome of other properties of air, water, and other transparent bodies. The model he uses – the actualization of a potentiality – does not help us to understand the most essential property of light, that it is propagated in straight lines, as the microvoid theory does. Even if the potentiality/actuality model works well enough for the transmission of heat, its inadequacy for dealing with light could well be enough to explain Strato's preference for the microvoid.

The point of Strato's theory, and the need for actual rather than merely potential πόροι, can be seen in some of the pseudo-Aristotelian *Problemata physica* which were referred to Strato by H. Flashar, followed by Gottschalk.[4] XI.58 (fragment 8 G) is particularly clear. The problem is why light cannot penetrate solid bodies although sound can, and the answer is that light travels only in straight lines, and is therefore blocked 'by the fact that the πόροι are not opposite to each other' (διὰ τὸ μὴ κατ' ἀλλήλους εἶναι τοὺς πόρους). This explanation can hardly function, if the πόροι are taken to be nothing more than a potentiality that is only made actual by the passage of light through the body.

I conclude that we have rather strong evidence for attributing the microvoid theory to Strato, that there is no good ground for explaining it away as a mere potentiality, and that we can see the philosophical motivation for holding such a theory.

It is now time to study the rather more complex situation with regard to Strato's

---

[4] Flashar (1962): *Probl.* XI.33, 49, and 58; XXIII.8; XXV.9 and 22. Gottschalk, fragments 6–10, 12.

treatment of the arguments in favour of the existence of void mentioned by Aristotle in *Physics* IV.6 (item 2 in the list of Strato's fragments given on p. 150 above, and item (b) in the list of Gatzemeier's objections on p. 151).

Aristotle listed four arguments (213 b 2–29); from motion, compression, growth, and the alleged fact that a tub full of ash accepts the same quantity of water as the same tub empty. Simplicius says that Strato reduced (συνήγαγε) these four to two: motion and compression (Strato fragment 61 W). We may guess that Strato, like Aristotle (214 b 1–10), regarded these last two phenomena, growth and the waterlogged ash, not as being examples of the introduction of matter into an apparently full place, but as some kind of qualitative change.

Simplicius says that Strato added a third argument, not mentioned by Aristotle – an argument from magnetism (ὁλκή); then he goes on to say that Strato held it to be a bad argument, on the grounds that it is not clear whether there is any such thing as magnetic attraction at all, and if there is, it is not clear that 'the stone attracts the iron through the void and not through some other cause' (fragment 62 W).[5]

What, then, did Strato make of the arguments from motion and from compression? Aristotle claimed that the argument from motion was not cogent, because motion could occur in a continuously filled place by the exchange of places between the parts of the contained body, as in swirls in liquids (214 a 28–32). In his comment on this Simplicius points out a weakness in the objection, namely that it applies only to bodies rotating as a whole in the same place. He says Strato's example is therefore more suitable (προσφυέστερον) for making the point:

> If you drop a pebble into a vessel filled with water and invert the vessel, blocking the exit at the mouth, the pebble moves to the mouth of the vessel as water moves around into the place of the pebble. The same thing happens with swimmers, and fish, and so on.
>
> (fragment 63 W)

Although Simplicius does not explicitly say so, he appears to regard this as a demonstration by Strato that the argument from motion does not prove the existence of void. If Strato held, however, that water, like other transparent and penetrable substances, contains microvoid, his example is not good enough. It might be the case that the pebble can move in water *only* because the microvoid allows for some rearrangement of the material structure. The most the example can prove is that the pebble does not need a *perceptible* void space to move into. In other words, it fits into the context of a world that fills all of the void: the void is 'isometric with the cosmic body' (fragment 60 W): in such a world, motion can take place without causing a bulge in the external surface of the cosmos, as Aristotle had suggested as the consequence of allowing motion without either void or compression (*Physics* IV.9.217 a 10). The example of the pebble still has a point, then, even if the body that fills the cosmic space is itself porous, containing

[5] The argument about which Strato expressed scepticism might be that of Democritus: see D–K 68A.165 = Alexander, *Quaestiones* II.23.

microvoid. If this is correct, there is no inconsistency between Strato's use of this example and the microvoid theory. The example is used merely to show that motion does not require what was often referred to as a 'massed empty place' (κενὸς ἄθροος τόπος).

Aristotle's strategy in *Physics* IV, with regard to motion and the void, was first to show that the phenomenon of motion does not prove the existence of void, and then to claim that motion is in fact impossible in a void (*Physics* IV.8). Philoponus demolished this claim in his *Corollary on void*,[6] but we have no evidence that Strato anticipated him. It seems clear that the only innovation made by Strato with regard to the void was the theory of microvoid. He continued to accept Aristotle's picture of the world as filled with body, and he may well have continued to believe that natural motions could not be explained without this assumption. If so, we can understand why he should want to join Aristotle in his attacks on the Atomists' notion of void, including what was evidently their favourite supporting argument, from motion.

Compression, however, is a different matter. If the argument from compression proves anything about void, it is the existence of microvoid within the texture of compressible bodies that it proves. Strato may not have needed an argument from compression, if he regarded the argument from penetration as sufficient. But he can hardly have wanted to dismiss it in just the same way as the argument from motion. Fortunately there is no evidence in the surviving testimonia that he did dismiss it. As we have seen, Simplicius reports that he reduced Aristotle's four arguments to two, motion and compression, and then added magnetic attraction. We are told that he rejected the one from magnetism, and there is a strong case for saying he rejected the one from motion. Simplicius himself is for rejecting all three, and his arrangement of the material from Strato may suggest that Strato rejected all three. But he does not actually say anything that entails Strato's rejection of the compression argument.

It is worth going back over Aristotle's discussion of compression, in order to see what Strato's position might have been. At first he rejects the compression argument for void on the weak ground that when something is compressed it need not be squashed into previously existing empty spaces, but may have some matter squeezed out of it, imperceptibly, as it is compressed. Later in the same book (*Physics* IV.9) he offers a more detailed answer. Just as one and the same ὕλη can take on different qualities, such as hot and cold, without addition or subtraction of another ὕλη, so it can take on different degrees of density or rarity without subtraction or addition. But a different theory of compression is found in *Meteor.* IV. In chapters 8 and 9, we have a list of eighteen pairs of qualities of bodies, including the following:

Things can be squeezed (πιεστά) which have pores empty of their kindred material: those things are squeezable which can contract into their own void spaces, or else into their own pores, since sometimes they do not contract into pores that are empty – for example, a

[6] Philoponus, *Physics* 675–95.

155

soaked sponge has full pores. In those cases the pores must be full of something softer than what is to contract on itself.

$$(386 \text{ a } 29 - \text{b } 7)$$

Things are compressible (πιλητά), we are told (387 a 15–17), if in addition to being squeezable they remain in a contracted state after being squeezed and released.

There are those who think that *Meteor.* IV, or parts of it, cannot be by Aristotle, and the use of a theory of pores is the prime reason for doubting it, since Aristotle criticized the theory in an attack on Empedocles in *GC* I.8. My own view is that its affinities with the biological works show it to be genuine.[7]

But it is impossible to be sure exactly how and at what pace the theory of microvoid developed. At one extreme stands Aristotle, with his sweeping denunciations of all kinds of void in his theoretical physical treatises. At the other end is Hero of Alexandria, who wrote:

We should not suppose that among the things that exist is a certain void nature, in a mass, self-subsistent by itself, but rather that it exists scattered in small portions in air and liquid and other bodies.

(*Pneumatica* I, p. 6.11 Schmidt, printed as fragment 56 W)

Our problem is to decide how soon Hero's theory came into existence, and where to locate *Meteor.* IV and Strato in the story.

In this article I have tried to show that the argument from penetration, especially of light, tends to set up an actual microvoid, and therefore to put Strato in agreement with at least this much of Hero's position. The arguments of *Meteor.* IV, on the other hand, do not require an actual void at all, but only pores 'empty of kindred material', as the text quoted above has it. There is some ambiguity in this text, since at one point it seems to contrast 'pores' with 'void spaces'; but I think this may be explained as being two expressions for the same notion. If this is right, *Meteor.* IV represents a movement away from the theory of *Physics* IV and *De generatione et corruptione*, in the direction of the microvoid theory, but it does not yet go all the way.

One further topic should be explored a little before I try to summarize the position: the relation between the microvoid theory and the notion of πρὸς τὸ κενούμενον ἀκολουθία, or *horror vacui*. The principle states simply that whenever a body leaves its place, some other body must 'follow into that which is emptied'. When stated in this neutral way it is compatible with many physical theories; differences appear only when it is explained by reference to some other principle. So Plato explained breathing on this principle in the Timaeus (79A–80C), adding that it happens because of a 'circular thrust' (περίωσις): the body that moves sets others in motion, and so on until some body is moved into the place that would otherwise become empty. Aristotle was inclined to explain it by

---

[7] Gottschalk (1961) claims it for Theophrastus. It was defended by Düring (1944) and Lee (1952). I give my view in chapter 12.

referring to a principle of continuity of adjacent surfaces (*De caelo* IV.5.312 b 5ff).[8] Hero of Alexandria sometimes seems to suggest that it is the empty place itself that pulls the adjacent body in: he writes ἐπισπωμένου τοῦ κενοῦ τὴν σάρκα (p. 109.12 G), κενούμενος ὁ ἐντὸς τόπος ἐπισπᾶται τὴν παρακειμένην ὕλην (p. 112.7 G). But elsewhere he implies that it is just because there is nothing to prevent it that matter moves in to fill an empty place.

There is no direct evidence as to whether Strato made use of the principle of *horror vacui* in his physics, nor how he explained it if he did. Mr Gottschalk describes the principle as being a consequence of Strato's theory of matter (p. 146), but that is not self-evident. The theory of matter depends on the concept of the microvoid, whereas *horror vacui* is simply the view that there is no *massed* void; and the latter is equally true for Aristotle's theory of matter, which denies the microvoid. Indeed the microvoid theory might be thought to be an impediment to *horror vacui*, in the following way. If the small intervals in a body can be *reduced* in size when the body is compressed, why should they not be *increased* in size also, if the conditions demand it? The phenomena of suction are explained by the principle of *horror vacui*: if one sucks the air out of a tube dipped in water, the water is drawn up into the tube because otherwise there would be an empty space in the tube. But the believer in microvoid will be called on to explain why the microvoid in the air is not simply expanded indefinitely when the air is sucked, so that there is no need for the water to rise into the tube. It is plain that the microvoid theorist needs some extra assumption in order to make *horror vacui* work.

One context where the microvoid theory is bolstered with such an extra assumption is in the preface to Hero's *Pneumatica*, in a passage that both Wehrli and Gottschalk print as a fragment of Strato:

If the corpuscles of air are separated when some force is applied, and a larger empty place comes about unnaturally, they move to coalesce with each other again. For it is a property of bodies that their motion takes place swiftly through the void, since there is nothing to resist or collide (μηδενὸς ἀνθισταμένου μηδὲ ἀντικρούοντος), until the corpuscles impact (προσερείσῃ) one another.

(Hero, *Pneumatica* I, included in fragment 56 W)

The problem with this passage, not noted by Wehrli or Gottschalk, is that the extra assumption is a paraphrase of Epicurus:

Motion through the void, taking place in conditions of no resistance from colliding things (κατὰ μηδεμίαν ἀπάντησιν τῶν ἀντικοψάντων), accomplishes every conceivable distance in an inconceivable [i.e. inconceivably short] time.

(*Letter to Herodotus* 46)

In § 42 of the Letter Epicurus also uses ὑπερείδειν in a similar way to Hero's προσερείδειν in referring to atomic collisions. We will consider the significance of the Epicurean echo in a moment.

[8] See also Simplicius' very interesting comments on this passage: *De caelo* 723. 22–32.

If matter can be compressed by being crushed into its own void spaces, and if expanded matter returns to normal just because matter moves easily and quickly into the non-resistant void space, what prevents bodies from being always in a fully compressed state? Hero's answer, mentioned in this same passage (printed as fragment 56 by Wehrli) is that the 'proper tension' (εὐτονία) of bodies prevents it, 'as in the case of horn shavings and dry sponges'. This is a noun that is not found in the Aristotelian corpus; the adjective is used a few times, but not in this sense. The adjective appears once in Plato (Laws 815A8) in connection with human bodies dancing, the noun never. Neither adjective nor noun is listed in Usener's Glossarium Epicureum. As one would expect, the idea is clearly represented in Stoic literature, for example in Plutarch's report of the qualities of air and fire (SVF II.444 = De comm. not. 1085C).

It is reasonable to guess, then, that someone was borrowing elements for a theory of matter from both Stoic and Epicurean sources. Hero is more likely to be the borrower than Strato. This remains nothing better than a likelihood, but it seems to me enough to throw doubt on the value of Hero's Pneumatica as evidence for Strato's theory, except where there is confirmation from an independent source.

However, we have not yet considered one more source of evidence concerning the principle of horror vacui: Strato's contemporary, the physician Erasistratus, who was said explicitly in antiquity to have borrowed ideas, if not from Strato, at least from the Peripatos and from Strato's predecessor, Theophrastus.[9] Erasistratus undoubtedly made use of the principle of horror vacui. He used it in his explanations of appetite, digestion, the secretion of bile and urine, blood flow, and respiration.[10] He was also familiar with the microvoid theory of matter, although it is not clear whether he adopted it himself; what is clear, from Galen's report, is that he considered the relationship between horror vacui and microvoid. In one passage, Galen criticizes an Erasistratean theory of the composition of nerves. Perceptible nerves, the theory said, are composed of three kinds of tissue – vein, artery, and nerve – each imperceptibly small. In that case, Galen objects, the principle of horror vacui cannot be available for explaining what happens to these elements:

For it has power only in the case of perceptibles, not in the case of theoretical entities, as Erasistratus explicitly concedes – saying that he is not putting forward a theory about the kind of void that is dispersed in small portions in bodies, but about that which is clear, perceptible, massed, large, evident, or whatever else you want to call it. Erasistratus himself says that there cannot be a 'massed perceptible' void; the other names I have added, from my abundant store of words meaning the same thing, at least on the present topic.

(Galen, De nat. fac. II.6: Kühn II.99)

---

[9] See Galen, De nat. fac. II.4 (Kühn II.88) and An in arteriis 7 (Kühn IV.729). I have written on this topic elsewhere (see Furley and Wilkie (1984), 26–37).
[10] See Galen, Kühn II.104–5, II.63, II.77, IV.709, IV.473.

STRATO'S THEORY OF THE VOID

It is clear from this passage that Erasistratus expressed his principle of *horror vacui* in terms of ἄθροον κενόν, and dissociated this from διεσπαρμένον κενόν. Hero used the same terms. Whether precisely this distinction, in these terms, is to be attributed to Strato remains unconfirmed, but it seems likely.

It is important to notice that Strato's definition of 'place', mentioned at the beginning of this chapter, differentiated him sharply from Aristotle and made it much easier for him to set up the conceptual apparatus required for a theory of *horror vacui*. There is a difficulty, pointed out with some relish by Philoponus (*Physics* 571.9ff), in explaining this principle in Aristotelian terms: if an empty place is a *conceptual* impossibility, as Aristotle would have it, then there cannot be any *vacuum* to inspire *horror*. But if place is a three-dimensional διάστημα, as Strato believed, then there is no *conceptual* reason why there cannot be an empty place, and a physical reason must be sought (if one is not to become an Epicurean). The principle of *horror vacui* is such a reason, and so it might well have been a part of Strato's physics. What extra assumption he incorporated into his microvoid theory of matter, to guard against the difficulty we have noticed, remains unclear to me.

When we try to assess Strato's position in the history of cosmology, the most significant points are that he adopted the theory that place is a three-dimensional διάστημα, over-riding Aristotle's objections, and at the same time asserted that it is always filled with body. This means that we must regard him as a reforming Aristotelian, not as any kind of Atomist.[11]

It appears that he dropped or modified the Aristotelian system of unmoved movers, and developed the theory of nature as an internal mover found in *Physics* II (fragments 32–6). He dropped the fifth element and spoke of the heavens as 'fiery' (fragment 84). Perhaps because he had thereby removed the outer shell from the Aristotelian cosmos, he dropped the theory of natural upward motion and held that all the elements have a natural downward motion towards the centre (fragments 50–2). But these modifications left him opposed to the Atomists on most of the fundamentals. His universe was finite and geocentric; there is no trace of the infinitely extended, centreless space of Atomist theory, and as we have seen he did not subscribe to the idea that there must be space in which bodies move. His theory of matter was not atomistic: Sextus reports that he made both bodies and places divisible to infinity (fragment 82).[12] He retained the Aristotelian view that qualities such as heat and cold are irreducible principles (fragments 42–8). On space, matter, and motion, he was anti-Epicurean.

We shall never know whether Strato read Democritus or Epicurus. My own

---

[11] Diels' statement (1893/1969, p. 250) 'Straton stellte sich im Wesentlichen auf den Standpunkt der Abderiten' is a hasty judgement; Diels himself follows it with a whole list of items in which Strato adopted non-Atomist positions. In contrast, the most recent essay on the subject that I have seen concludes: 'Straton hat sich durchaus als Peripatetiker gefühlt' (Stückelberger (1984), 139).

[12] There is some confusion about Strato's view of the divisibility of time. See Sorabji's clarifying comments (1983), 377–9.

view is that there is nothing in the surviving reports of his opinions and arguments that requires us to think that he did. His modifications of Aristotelian cosmology may well be due to reflection on weaknesses in Aristotle's arguments rather than external influence. Criticism of Aristotle's physics had begun already with Theophrastus: but that is another story.

14

KNOWLEDGE OF ATOMS AND VOID IN EPICUREANISM

[1971]

There is an obvious paradox in the theories of the Atomists. They held that nothing exists but atoms and void, and that the atoms are imperceptibly small, and invariant in quality. The thinking part of a man is composed of these materials and no others; his thinking can only be a function of the motions of invariant atoms. Knowledge of the external world must be some kind of reaction between the atoms of the external world and the atoms of the thinking man; and the only reaction in the Atomist's theory is simply collision. That is to say, the connection between the thinking subject and the external world is nothing but touch: *tactus enim, tactus, pro divum numina sancta* as Lucretius strenuously insists (*De rerum natura* II.434). The Atomists are then ready to show how all our senses are really varieties of the sense of touch; each faculty of sense is stimulated by actual contact with suitable formations of atoms proceeding from the external world.

It is a picture which has a certain plausibility as a theory of sensation. And the Atomists liked to say that sensation is indeed the basis for all our contact with the external world. The paradox of course is this: if knowledge comes to us by means of sensation, how are we to explain the Atomist's knowledge of the basic propositions of his special theory: that the world consists of void, which is called 'the intangible', and atoms, which are said to be imperceptibly small? It is a question that arises with regard to the earlier Atomists and the post-Aristotelians; but this paper deals only with the latter.

One answer to the question has acquired authority during the last few decades of classical scholarship, and I want first to examine it. Its best known statement is in the work on Epicurus by Cyril Bailey.[1] According to Bailey, the Epicureans believed in a form of direct knowledge of the external world which by-passed sense-perception. It was a sort of focusing of the mind analogous to focusing the eyes, straining the ears, dilating the nostrils (and presumably doing whatever one does do to the tongue and the skin for the other two senses).

Bailey correctly drew attention[2] to a striking difference in what Epicurus said

---

[1] (1928), 265, 559–76.
[2] *Ibid.* pp. 264–5.

about the two classes of subjects which he grouped together under the heading *adela* (non-evident). Meteorology and the stars were one such class; Epicurus asserted that since we cannot get the close view and since many explanations of the same phenomenon are often equally in conformity with our observations, the philosopher must hold all these explanations to be equally true. To prefer one to the others, he said, would be to plunge into mythology.[3] And everybody knows that the Epicureans exhibited something like relish in offering multiple explanations for these things.[4]

However, the fundamental principles of the atomic theory, such as the statement that there exist atoms, that there is void, that there is no third sort of being, and so on – these are also *adela*, in that they are not accessible to direct sense-perception. But in this case, the Epicureans accepted no multiple explanations: just one theory was right, and one could accept it confidently.

What was the Epicurean's justification for this certainty? Bailey thought he had found the answer in the expression used by Epicurus with some frequency but without definition: ἐπιβολὴ τῆς διανοίας. I quote from Bailey:[5]

Thought – or reasoning – about the ultimate realities of the world is conducted by the comparison and combination of 'clear' concepts, each stage in the process being a new concept recognized as self-evident. These concepts are grasped by 'an act of apprehension on the part of the mind' (ἐπιβολὴ τῆς διανοίας) exactly similar to that by which the senses apprehend the 'clear vision' of the near object, or the mind the subtle images which penetrate to it.

This assertion was defended in a long appendix on ἐπιβολὴ τῆς διανοίας that Bailey put at the end of both of his books on Epicurus.

Striking use of Bailey's explanation was made by Cornford, in the second chapter of his *Principium Sapientiae*, where he attacks the verdict of some writers that Epicureanism was one of the most 'scientific' of ancient philosophical systems. Cornford says:

A system which professes to rest on the testimony of the infallible senses might be expected to put forward only a tentative hypothesis about the wholly imperceptible, and to recommend suspension of judgment ... But Epicurus' attitude is exactly the reverse of this sceptical caution: he is more dogmatic in this field than in either of the other two ... 'Atomism is not one among several possible theories of the universe, nor with regard to any of its details is there a hint that any other view than that expounded by Epicurus himself could be true' [Bailey (1928), 265]. Epicurus is content to assert roundly that his atomism is the only theory consistent with phenomena.[6]

A curious feature of this appreciation of Epicurus is the way in which it ignores some of the evidence, and distorts the rest. 'How did Epicurus suppose we come

[3] *Letter to Pythocles* 87.
[4] Many examples in *Pyth.* and Lucretius, *De rerum natura* VI.
[5] (1928), 265.
[6] (1952), 26.

by our knowledge of atoms and the void?' Bailey asks. But he does not look for the answer in the obvious place: namely, in the text in which Epicurus defends his basic propositions. Instead he seizes upon the obscure phrase ἐπιβολὴ τῆς διανοίας and manipulates the contexts[7] in which it appears until they seem to justify his theory of direct mental apprehension.

It must be conceded first that the notion of direct mental apprehension *does* play a part in Epicureanism. What I want to deny is only that it plays the supremely important part in the foundations of the atomic theory that Bailey has given to it.

There is enough textual evidence in Epicurus himself and Lucretius to show that the Epicureans held that certain εἴδωλα, of the same kind as the εἴδωλα which cause sense-perception, do not stimulate the senses, because they are too fine (λεπτός) but rather penetrate directly to the soul-atoms of the mind.[8] There they may produce a phantasia or image, which is similar to the images produced by sensation. The experiences which the Epicureans hoped to explain by this thesis were dream-visions, certain types of imagination (in the modern sense), and especially ideas about the gods.

The texts which serve as our evidence for *this* theory do not speak of the fundamental propositions about atoms and the void. It is my belief that this theory was strictly limited to the explanation of those experiences with which it is associated in the surviving texts.

The inflation of ἐπιβολὴ τῆς διανοίας into a kind of intuitive knowledge that includes knowledge of the fundamental propositions of Atomism can be punctured by the study of one text in particular. This text is in the right place: that is, it is no *obiter dictum*, but centrally placed in the *Letter to Herodotus* 50–1, in the passage that deals with our knowledge of the external world. To my mind all the editors misunderstand it.[9]

---

[7] E.g. the quotation at the top of Bailey (1928), 565, which is not 'extracted' but rewritten: note the substitution of τὰς for ἄλλας τινάς.

[8] *Letter to Herodotus* 49.8: εἰς τὴν ὄψιν ἢ τὴν διάνοιαν. *Letter* 51.2: καθ' ὕπνους γινομένων (on which see below). Lucretius IV.722–822.

[9] Bailey (1928, p. 563) treats sentence A as an instance of ἐπιβολὴ τῶν αἰσθητηρίων, ignoring διάνοια for the moment. 'This is exactly', he says, 'the idea of ἐπιμαρτύρησις which Epicurus has just been expounding in the preceding context.' We get first a mere passive sensation, but it is not until we have *looked* closely that we can be sure the image is clear; 'ἐπιβολή is required for the confirmation (or non-confirmation) of the δόξα founded on the original passive perception.'

It is not true, however, that Epicurus has been expounding the idea of ἐπιμαρτύρησις. He has been *using* the criterion of ἀντιμαρτύρησις in sections 48–9; but that is a very different thing. He has been saying that there is nothing in our sense-experience to contradict his statements about the εἴδωλα that they are incomparably fine textured, move as swiftly as thought, and so on. But there is *nothing* in the preceding context that warrants a distinction between the first passive sensation and the subsequent act of looking.

Bailey then argues (1928, pp. 564–5) that sentence C is about normal, reliable sense-perception. His method is to remain silent about the previous sentence, which is concerned with error, and to substitute a row of dots for ἢ καθ' ὕπνους γινομένων.

Arrighetti (1960) puts sentence B in square brackets. But this seems to be only because he has accepted the wrong interpretation of C.

A

καὶ ἣν ἂν λάβωμεν φαντασίαν ἐπιβλητικῶς τῇ διανοίᾳ ἢ τοῖς αἰσθητηρίοις εἴτε μορφῆς εἴτε συμβεβηκότων, μορφή ἐστιν αὕτη τοῦ στερεμνίου, γινομένη κατὰ τὸ ἑξῆς πύκνωμα ἢ ἐγκατάλειμμα τοῦ εἰδώλου.

Whatever image, of shape or of properties, we get by apprehension of the mind or the senses, this is the shape of the solid object, when it comes about because of the successive repetition of the εἴδωλον, or because of the remaining effect of the εἴδωλον.[10]

B

τὸ δὲ ψεῦδος καὶ τὸ διημαρτημένον ἐν τῷ προσδοξαζομένῳ ἀεί ἐστιν ...

But falsehood and error always lie in the addition made by *doxa* ...[11]

C

ἥ τε γὰρ ὁμοιότης τῶν φαντασμῶν οἱονεὶ εἰκόνι λαμβανομένων ἢ καθ᾽ ὕπνους γινομένων ἢ κατ᾽ ἄλλας τινὰς ἐπιβολὰς τῆς διανοίας ἢ τῶν λοιπῶν κριτηρίων οὐκ ἄν ποτε ὑπῆρχε τοῖς οὐσί τε καὶ ἀληθέσι προσαγορευομένοις, εἰ μὴ ἦν τινα καὶ ταῦτα πρὸς ἃ ἐπιβάλλομεν.

For there would have been no similarity between the appearances seen as if in a picture or occurring in dreams or in any of the other apprehensions (ἐπιβολαί) of the mind or of the other criteria, and things which really exist and are called true, unless these things that we apprehend really existed.[12]

D

τὸ δὲ διημαρτημένον οὐκ ἂν ὑπῆρχεν, εἰ μὴ ἐλαμβάνομεν καὶ ἄλλην τινὰ κίνησιν ἐν ἡμῖν αὐτοῖς συνημμένην μὲν τῇ φανταστικῇ ἐπιβολῇ διάληψιν δὲ ἔχουσαν· κατὰ δὲ ταύτην, ἐὰν μὲν μὴ ἐπιμαρτυρηθῇ ἢ ἀντιμαρτυρηθῇ, τὸ ψεῦδος γίνεται· ἐὰν δὲ ἐπιμαρτυρηθῇ ἢ μὴ ἀντιμαρτυρηθῇ, τὸ ἀληθές.

But the error would not have happened if we did not have a second motion, in ourselves, connected with the apprehension of the image, but different from it; in this motion, if there

---

[10] For the meaning of ἐγκατάλειμμα, see n. 14.

[11] The words which follow these in the text are disputed. They fill out the meaning of 'the addition made by δόξα' by referring to the concepts of confirmation and non-confirmation. None of the likely readings would alter the logic of the passage as a whole; the important point is that sentence A is about reliable sense-perception, sentence B is about error, and sentences C and D explain B.

[12] The MSS have πρὸς ἃ (or ὃ) βάλλομεν. Bailey reads τοιαῦτα προσβαλλόμενα with Usener. I have adopted the emendation of Schneider followed also by Arrighetti.

is no confirmation, or refutation, error arises, and if there is confirmation or no refutation, truth.[13]

Sentence A of this text is about reliable perception and mental apprehension. It might perhaps be thought that the word ἐπιβλητικός mentions the necessary and sufficient condition for reliable perception; but this need not be so. The conditions for reliable perception are mentioned in the clause beginning γινομένη. Mental images (φαντασίαι) are reliable when they are produced by the successive repetition of the εἴδωλον (that is, when a constant stream of εἴδωλα comes from the external object to the perceiver, as when one is directly looking at the object), or when they come about through what is left behind by the εἴδωλον (that is, the pattern left behind as a memory by previous sense-experience).[14] The word ἐπιβλητικός means no more than 'by the apprehensive process', the process by which the mind or the senses 'get hold of' something. This is confirmed by a fragment of the lost work of Epicurus, On nature, where the ἐπιβλητικὸς τρόπος is contrasted with 'proceeding from oneself alone' (XXIX.15.8)

Sentences B, C and D are all about illusion. This is the point missed by the editors, who believe that C is about reliable perception. The passage as a whole is telling us something essentially simple, and it runs like this:

Sentence A (following a description of the εἴδωλα and their reception by the perceiver): the image that results from the apprehension of εἴδωλα, when it comes from a succession of εἴδωλα, not just a random one, or when it corresponds to a memory image, reproduces the shape of the external object that produced the εἴδωλα.

Sentence B: error is not in the act of apprehension, but in a subsequent movement of the soul, called δόξα.

Sentence C: the misleading resemblance between dream-images and other illusory appearances[15] on the one hand and what is true and real on the other – the resemblance that leads into the error of supposing that the illusion is the truth – exists because illusory images, as well as reliable images, are produced by the

---

[13] The words τῇ φανταστικῇ ἐπιβολῇ are supplied here by all recent editors from 50.11–12, where they are probably misplaced.

[14] 'The remaining effect' (ἐγκατάλειμμα) is mysterious. There is no doubt that in Epicurean theory the εἴδωλα leave some mark on the soul-atoms – presumably some more or less durable pattern of motion. This is probably what ἐγκατάλειμμα refers to (although there have been other interpretations of it). It would take too much space to examine the possibilities fully. I believe Epicurus is thinking of the role of πρόληψις in his theory of knowledge. See further Bailey (1928), 245–7; Kleve (1963), 23–9; Furley (1967b), 202–8.

[15] There is much obscurity in 'the appearances seen as if in a picture (ἐν εἰκόνι)'. Centaurs, Scyllas, Cerberuses, as in Lucretius IV.732–3?

apprehension of real εἴδωλα (real εἴδωλα, we have to understand, but not in a steady succession).[16]

Sentence D: error occurs when such an image is wrongly assessed by δόξα – the 'second motion' (sc. of soul-atoms) 'in ourselves': it is treated as a clear image, resulting from a steady stream of εἴδωλα, when it is not.

Here, then, ἐπιβολὴ τῆς διανοίας occurs in the explanation of illusions of many kinds. This surely should have been enough to give Bailey pause. What kind of a concept is it that is *both* the explanation of illusory dreams and visions, *and* the guarantee of scientific truth? If this phrase is to mean 'an act of deliberate attention' is it not disconcerting to find it in an account of dreams?

At this point we can turn to the other approach to Epicurus' idea of his knowledge of the atomic theory: that is, the method of argument used to defend it. First, it may be worth saying that Bailey and Cornford were probably distracted from this approach by the notion, which seems to me mistaken, that we must look for the distinguishing characteristics of an empirical theory in the manner in which the theory is first reached, rather than in the manner in which it is defended. As against this, I agree with Popper, who wrote at the beginning of his *Logic of Scientific Discovery*: 'The question of how a new idea occurs to a man ... may be of great interest to empirical psychology; but it is irrelevant to the logical analysis of scientific knowledge.'[17]

The relevant section of the *Letter to Herodotus* is preceded by a methodological note: 'We must control all our investigation by the sensations and by the immediate apprehensions (ἐπιβολαί) either of the mind or the various other criteria, likewise by the immediate feelings, so that we can make inferences about that which is in suspense and about things which are unclear.'[18]

He continues at once: 'About things that are unclear, we must get the following points made and keep them in mind. First, that nothing comes to be out of that which does not exist; for everything would in that case be coming into being with no need of seeds.'

Notice the very simple method: he asserts his thesis, then makes its contradictory the protasis of a conditional statement, of which the apodosis is a proposition falsified by sense-perception. 'P. For, if not-P, then Q, which is observed to be false.'

---

[16] Note the similar argument in Lucretius IV.750–1:

> quatenus hoc simile est illi, quod mente videmus
> atque oculis, simili fieri ratione necessest.

And lines 757–9:

> nec ratione alia, cum somnus membra profudit,
> mens animi vigilat, nisi quod simulacra lacessunt
> haec eadem nostros animos quae cum vigilamus.

The occurrence of this in Lucretius is a strong confirmation that we are now interpreting C correctly.

[17] Popper (1959), 31.

[18] *Letter* 38.3–7. The text is disputed, but none of the variations proposed would affect the present discussion.

We have very nearly the same pattern repeated frequently, and especially in the argument for the existence of void, which became famous and much talked-about in antiquity – indeed it was famous before Epicurus used it at all, for it was used in the reverse direction by the Eleatics,[19] and was almost certainly borrowed from them by Leucippus and Democritus.[20]

First Epicurus notes that the existence of σώματα is confirmed by the direct evidence of the senses, 'which we must use for making inferences about what is unclear by reasoning (λογισμός)'. He goes on: 'If there did not exist that which we call void and space and untouchable nature, bodies would have nowhere to be or to move, as they are observed to move.'

The schema is this: 'Void exists: for if void did not exist, there would be no motion, which we observe to be false.'

A century or more after Epicurus, when *Stoic* logic was developed into a systematic study, this pattern of inference was formalized and grouped with other similar patterns. It is in fact the second of the undemonstrated arguments collected by Benson Mates (1961, p. 71): 'If the first, then the second. Not the second; therefore not the first,' with negative propositions substituted for the propositional variables.

The Stoics, with their new interest in logic and epistemology, attacked the Epicureans. Although the Epicureans were probably never much interested in logic as such, they evidently felt impelled to offer some sort of reply to Stoic criticism. We have evidence of their replies in the Epicurean work by Philodemus, called *On signs*, which partly survives in the form of badly mutilated papyrus fragments. It was published by Gomperz (1865) and there was a further study of it by Philippson (1909 and 1910), so there was no excuse for Bailey's total neglect of it in his books on Epicureanism; though of course he did not have the advantage of Professor De Lacy's edition of it. This book should at least be scrutinized for any evidence it may provide on the way the Epicureans thought about the epistemological basis of their theory. Like all the Herculaneum papyri that contain Epicurean material (at least, those so far unrolled and read), Philodemus' *On signs* has very limited value. What it does show is that a debate went on about the validity of inductive inference. The Stoics, it appears, wanted a logic of science based on the model of Aristotelian ἀπόδειξις, in which only necessary truths would be admitted. Hence they claimed that the implication, 'If there is motion, then there is void', was valid only if it was contradictory to deny the second and assert the first; i.e. only if void were somehow involved in the definition of motion. The Epicureans replied with an insistence that the inference is empirical, not analytic. 'We study all the things that move in our experience and we reckon up the accompanying conditions, without which we see nothing move; and we claim

---

[19] Melissus B7.7
[20] Leucippus A7 (Aristotle, *GC* 325 a 4).

that everything that moves, moves like these things, and so infer that there cannot be motion without void.'[21]

Now, these Epicurean arguments are no doubt naive and lacking in scientific precision. But they do not, as far as I can see, suggest that knowledge of the proposition, 'there is void', and of the other basic proposition of the atomic theory, was thought to depend upon some kind of direct mental perception called ἐπιβολὴ τῆς διανοίας. Of course, the Stoics had a point when they said that the arguments that moved from instances in our experience to instances outside our experience depend on the assumption that there are uniformities in nature. But this is clearly only a weakness if you demand analytic truth in the realm of empirical knowledge.

However, let us look at some Epicurean arguments of a different type, where the appeal to sense-perception is less obvious.

One example is the argument with which Epicurus supports his theory of τὸ ἐν τῇ ἀτόμῳ ἐλάχιστον, or *minimae partes*, as Lucretius calls them.[22] There are other ways of reading this argument, but if I am right about it, it includes the following: Suppose that an atom contains infinitely numerous parts, each of them having size: *it is impossible*, in that case, *to see* how it can still be finite in size, since the parts must all be of some size, and if they are infinitely numerous, the total must be infinitely large. Hence we must not suppose that the atom is infinitely divisible.

This argument contains the expression οὐκ ἔστι νοῆσαι, 'it cannot be thought', 'it is impossible to see'. Does this indicate some appeal to a kind of direct intuition? Are we perhaps supposed to make use of the ἐπιβολὴ τῆς διανοίας, and rely on its negative report: 'It is not possible to see how a finite body can have infinitely numerous parts'?

No. Epicurus continues at once with an appeal to sense-perception. There is a minimum visible quantity: one cannot – experience shows that one cannot – divide a *visible* area into infinitely numerous parts. We must believe that the sub-visible area, which is accessible only to the theorizing mind, follows the same pattern as the visible one.

It is interesting that there are two analogies in this argument, one of which is supposed to hold while the other is not. Epicurus uses the analogy between the visible and the intelligible: he regards this as valid. But we might suppose that there is likewise an analogy between the minimum and multiples of the minimum in the visible field, and conclude that because we can distinguish parts of something that is larger than the minimum we must be able to distinguish parts of

---

[21] De Lacy (1941), VIII.32–IX.3 (p. 42). Lucretius' way of handling this argument is interesting. In 1.370–97, he gives reasons for rejecting the proposition that there *can* be motion without void. The second seems the better argument: if two flat bodies are in contact, surface to surface, and are then separated suddenly, then if a void space is impossible the air must fill the newly created gap instantaneously.

[22] *Letter* 56–9. Lucretius 1.599–634. See Furley (1967b), 7–43, for a defence of the explanation given here.

the minimum itself, since it is the same kind of stuff. This analogy obviously has to be rejected. Epicurus goes on at once to reject another one: if we say the atom has parts, we might be tempted to think that it could be resolved into its parts like compound bodies in the sensible range: but this again is obviously false. The reason why the analogy can be seen to be invalid in both these cases is just that the conclusion yielded by the analogy has already been falsified by another argument. We know already that there is a minimum visible quantity, and that atoms are indissoluble.

This passage may perhaps throw some light on another part of the *Letter to Herodotus*: an obscure remark that Bailey used as the main prop to support his argument about ἐπιβολὴ τῆς διανοίας.[23]

The subject is this. Epicurus has just asserted that atoms moving in the void all move at the same speed, in whatever direction they are moving. Compound bodies, however, are seen to move at different speeds. How can this be? The answer is that though the compound appears to move all in a solid mass, it is in reality composed of atoms and void, and within its surfaces its component atoms *are* moving to and fro in all directions all at constant speed. The speed of motion of a compound body depends on the overall direction taken by its component atoms during a stretch of time. Now, suppose we have a compound moving from A to B, a distance of 1 metre, in one hundred seconds. Then all its component atoms have moved 1 metre in that direction in one hundred seconds. It is natural to suppose that each atom therefore moves 1 centimetre in that direction in one second, 1 millimetre in one-tenth of a second, and so on. But this would be false. If we take the smallest time-intervals, each atom may be moving in any direction whatever.

This is how Epicurus concludes the paragraph:

τὸ γὰρ προσδοξαζόμενον περὶ τοῦ ἀοράτου, ὡς ἄρα καὶ οἱ διὰ λόγου θεωρητοὶ χρόνοι τὸ συνεχὲς τῆς φορᾶς ἕξουσιν, οὐκ ἀληθές ἐστιν ἐπὶ τῶν τοιούτων· ἐπεὶ τό γε θεωρούμενον πᾶν ἢ κατ' ἐπιβολὴν λαμβανόμενον τῇ διανοίᾳ ἀληθές ἐστι.

The inference of δόξα about the invisible, namely that the time-intervals that can be examined [only] by means of theoretical reasoning will also retain that continuity of motion [sc. which is observed during perceptible time-intervals], is false in such cases as these; for everything that is studied or grasped by apprehension is true.[24]

Bailey seizes upon this statement because it appears to say that ἐπιβολὴ τῆς διανοίας is infallible. He makes the statement into an entirely general one by taking θεωρούμενον to mean 'that which is grasped by the senses when "looking" at the close view'; thus he makes it a general statement of the two sources of knowledge according to his view of Epicureanism: the close view, and the direct mental apprehension. But in fact θεωρούμενον must mean 'studied': the same root has occurred sixteen words before, precisely to distinguish what is studied theoretically from what is observed by the senses. Whatever this concluding

[23] *Letter* 62.
[24] I am grateful to Father T. J. Tracy, S.J., for some helpful comments on this passage.

sentence says, it is all about thought. However, it still appears to say that the processes of thought are infallible. The contribution of δόξα is false, since what is grasped by thought is true. 'Why is δόξα liable to produce false results, while the other (ἐπιβολή) can only give us what is true?' Bailey asks;[25] and he answers, 'with some hesitation', that it is because the mind moves by one ἐπιβολή after another, from one clear and distinct concept to another, each of these concepts being clear in the same technical sense as that in which the unimpeded view of a new object is clear.

I think the clue to understanding this cryptic sentence of Epicurus lies in the passage quoted above.[26] What we have in both passages is a contrast between the operation of δόξα, and the ἐπιβολή of the senses or the mind. The important thing is to realize the exact nature of the contrast. Bailey takes it to mean that δόξα goes wrong, whereas ἐπιβολή is always right. But we have seen in the earlier passage that ἐπιβολή is responsible for dreams and illusions, as well as for truth-telling apprehensions. The point of the contrast is that when we experience a mental image, it always pictures accurately the εἴδωλον or set of εἴδωλα that cause it. Error never arises because of a lack of correspondence between the mental picture and the atomic configuration that caused it. The possibility of error (and of being right, too, we ought to add) arises only at the second stage, when δόξα, a second movement of the mind, distinct from the ἐπιβολή, pronounces upon the relation between the mental picture and the external world.

Epicurus should not use the word ἀληθής of the primary impressions of the senses or the mind. It would be better to say they are neither true nor false. But it is quite clear that he does use ἀληθής in this sense, since he is quoted as saying that 'the illusions (φαντάσματα) of madmen and dream-visions are true'. The explanation is added: 'they are true because they move (the sufferer), and what does not exist does not cause movement'.[27]

So I suggest that Epicurus is not saying, as Bailey thought, that δόξα's inference from the seen to the unseen in this case is wrong, whereas the inference of ἐπιβολή to the unseen is always right: he is saying that it must be δόξα's inference to the unseen that is wrong in these cases, because the error never lies in the mental picture itself. He is not saying that direct mental apprehension infallibly tells the truth about the external world, but only that our mental images are not the level at which mistakes occur.

So, what are we left with?

An examination of all the evidence, of which the greater part has been discussed here, offers no ground for accepting Bailey's view of Epicurus.[28] Epicurus did not

---

[25] (1928), 569–70.
[26] *Letter* 50–1.
[27] Diogenes Laertius x.32. Rather than chiding Epicurus for misusing ἀληθής, I ought rather to say that the Greek word itself is not strictly equivalent to the English word 'true'. See the article by Heitsch (1962), and the bibliography cited there. There have been some interesting studies of Plato's use of ἀληθής – Rankin (1963); Benardete (1963); Vlastos (1965a), 1–19.
[28] Other relevant passages are *Letter* 35 and 38; *Kyriai doxai* 24; *On nature* XXIX.14–15.

claim to have some kind of direct insight that led to clear and distinct ideas about the structure of the world. He tried to present arguments for his basic propositions, based on the evidence of sense-perception. Admittedly, his arguments were extremely simple-minded, for the most part. But I do not see any fundamental inconsistency in his position. In particular, he is not liable to the charge laid against him by Cornford, that he dogmatically ruled out multiple explanations in his atomic theory, while accepting them in his meteorology. His method was to set up a pair of contradictories – either there is void or there is not, either matter is infinitely divisible or it is not – and then to present an argument for rejecting one of them.

15

VARIATIONS ON THEMES FROM EMPEDOCLES IN LUCRETIUS' PROEM

[1970]

Commenting on Lucretius *De rerum natura* 1.2–3 and 6–9, Munro wrote:

Thus early the poet calls attention to the three great divisions of the world, to which he as well as other writers before and after him so constantly revert that the thing passed into a common proverb: *mare terra caelum di vostram fidem*, says Plautus *Trin.* 1070. ... *ut nulla pars caelo mari terra, ut poetice loquar, praetermissa sit*, says Cicero *De finibus* 5, 9.

Similar remarks are to be found in the commentaries of Giussani (p. 11), Ernout and Robin (p. 5), Leonard and Smith (p. 199) and Cyril Bailey (p. 592).[1]

It has apparently not been observed that the picture of lines 2–3 is not simply repeated in lines 6–9. What Munro says is perfectly true of lines 2–3: *caeli subter labentia signa | quae mare navigerum, quae terras frugiferentis | concelebras*. But the picture is significantly changed in lines 6–9, where *two* propositions refer to *caelum*:

> te, dea, te fugiunt venti, te nubila caeli
> adventumque tuum, tibi suavis daedala tellus
> summittit flores, tibi rident aequora ponti
> placatumque nitet diffuso lumine caelum.

The picture in these lines is not the threefold division of the world common in poetic tradition, but the fourfold division that belongs to the tradition of natural philosophy. The cosmos consists of four great masses, distinguished by the character of the elements or substances that compose them. Traditionally they are earth, water, air, and fire. Most Greek philosophers of nature, including Plato, Aristotle, Epicurus, and the Stoics, agreed that our world consists approximately of layers, with earth at the bottom or centre, water above it, air above water, and fire above air (Aristotle added a fifth, but we need not consider it here).

Let us postpone consideration of the fourth of these lines of Lucretius for the moment. There can be no doubt about the identification of the three lower elements in lines 6–8. The first sentence is about the 'winds and clouds of the sky',

[1] Munro (1866), 332; Giussani (1896–8); Ernout and Robin (1925); Leonard and Smith (1965); Bailey (1947).

which are typical manifestations of the element 'air'. The second is about earth, and the third is about the sea. There is nothing ambiguous. Lucretius is offering a description of spring. He could have said that the clouds disperse and the snows melt; he could have substituted *imbres* for *venti*. Instead, he chooses to mention only the things that the tradition treats unambiguously as *air*. In the second sentence, he might have said only that the flowers bloom; instead he makes *earth* the subject. The 'laughter' of the sea is not an inevitable part of the picture of spring; he might have preferred to talk about trees budding, birds singing, cattle leaving their stalls, ploughmen leaving their fires, or about many other things, or about nothing else. Instead, he adds a third sentence that is about the sea and nothing but the sea.

Having observed the trio, air, earth, and sea, anyone versed in Greek philosophy of nature will expect some mention of the fourth. What is missing so far is something about the sun and the other heavenly bodies, the source of heat and light in the upper sky, above the winds and the clouds. So it is no surprise to find that the fourth line singles out this fourth division of the cosmos just as unambiguously and exclusively as the first three.

It may be objected that the fourth sentence is formally somewhat different from the other three, and therefore ought not to be considered as co-ordinate with them. There is triple anaphora in the first three sentences (lines 6–8), and the fourth is detached. The fourth does not mention the fourth in a list of elements, but simply returns to the subject of the first, the *caelum*; the description of the sky, shining and peaceful, leads up to the 'opening' of the face of spring in the next line (10), and thus to the renewal of growth and propagation of living species.

It is true that the fourth sentence is not exactly co-ordinate and parallel with the first three. Formally it serves as the climax of the four-line passage. The fact that this sentence is the only one of the four to fill one line exactly, and the restful spondaic rhythm with the long vowels of *placatum* and *diffuso lumine*, make it a little different from the other three. It is a kind of destination, towards which the others have been leading. But it achieves this effect not by repeating something, nor by summing up, but by moving on, in sense, to the remaining member of the fourfold division. There is nothing surprising or unusual in a structure in which the last member of a group receives emphasis by being treated somewhat differently in syntax.

It is not true that the fourth sentence simply repeats the first. The disappearance of the clouds may *cause* the light of the upper sky to shine on earth. But the clouds are not the same as the light. The sentence about the clouds differs from the sentence about the light in just this way, that according to the traditional fourfold division the former says something about *air* and the latter says something about *fire*.

It may be objected that if Lucretius had meant to distinguish clearly between air and fire he would not have mentioned *caelum* twice, and would have chosen a clearer expression for the fourth sentence. It is true that *caelum* is usually the upper sky, and especially the heavenly bodies. It is normally the equivalent of οὐρανός.[2] The things that belong to the region below the stars are technically called μετέωρα. But there is nothing very surprising about the expression *nubila caeli*, which Lucretius uses twice elsewhere. He can also say that clouds *cover* the sky (v.466). Obviously *caelum* is not a very precise expression, and it may include both of the upper two cosmic divisions. Lucretius divides the cosmos into two, *terra* and *caelum*, at v.245.

The upper element is usually thought of as fire, and its characteristic property as heat. But a reference to the upper element does not necessarily mention fire or heat. The basic distinction between the two upper elements in this fourfold division of the cosmos is between the heavenly bodies, which give light or heat or both, and the air, which merely transmits light and heat or else takes the form of winds and clouds that are obstacles to light and heat. Light is thus one of the essential characteristics of the upper element, and Lucretius was not running any risk of ambiguity when he chose to talk about the light of the sky.

Other expressions used by Lucretius to refer to the upper division of the cosmos, or to parts of it, are *largus ... liquidi fons luminis, aetherius sol* (v.281), *solis rota ... lumine largo altivolans* (v.432–3), *aether ignifer* (v.458 and elsewhere), and of course *ignis* and *aether* separately. He might have spoken in line 9 about any of these. But a clear mention of the light of the upper sky was sufficient for his purpose.

It may be objected that Lucretius would be merely confusing the issue by mentioning the four elements here, since he was about to present a poetic exposition of the atomic theory, which rejected the four elements. Indeed, the poem itself contains a detailed criticism of the theory of four elements, at 1.763–829.

But a distinction has to be made here. It is true, of course, that the Epicureans rejected the theory that the world is made of four irreducible elements, eternally endowed with the properties of earth, water, air, and fire. It is true too that they rejected the Aristotelian theory of the four primary bodies that exchange properties with each other. But they did not deny the existence of earth, water, air, and fire, nor did they deny that these four are in some way more basic than other substances. In particular, they were quite willing to accept the fourfold division of our cosmos into these four. In his long polemic against the idea that the cosmos is eternal, Lucretius goes through the four divisions one by one, to show that each of them is mortal: earth (v.251–60); water (261–72); air (273–80); fire (281–305). In his own cosmogony he describes how the four masses came to be in their present position (v.433–508).

> sic igitur terrae concreto corpore pondus
> constitit atque omnis mundi quasi limus in imum
> confluxit gravis et subsedit funditus ut faex;

---

[2] But see Empedocles B22.2.

inde mare inde aer inde aether ignifer ipse
corporibus liquidis sunt omnia pura relicta.

(495–9)

We may now consider the four lines 6–9 in relation to their context in the proem.

Lines 1–5 contain the address to Venus, mentioning what will turn out to be the poet's reason for addressing his prayer to her and not to some other fount of inspiration: she fills the sea and the earth with living creatures. Next, the four lines we have studied: spring is brought about by Venus' power over the four cosmic masses. Then as soon as the cosmos takes on its vernal aspect (*nam simul ac species patefactast verna diei*), the whole animal world, inspired by Venus, devotes itself joyously to propagating its kind (10–20).[3]

Lucretius then sums up his reasons for praying to Venus, and states his prayer. Since she alone thus governs the whole of nature (*rerum naturam sola gubernas*), and without her nothing is born into the realm of light and nothing happy or delightful comes to be, he asks her to be with him as he writes about nature (*de rerum natura*), for Memmius, whom she has always favoured (21–8).

He adds a second prayer, for peace *per maria ac terras*. Venus has the power to charm Mars, and thus to bring peace to mortals. If the Romans are not at peace, Lucretius cannot find the tranquillity to write, and Memmius must give his attention to the country's security.

In the long history of scholarly criticism, many different meanings have been perceived in this proem. For example, some have stressed the connection with Epicurean theory: Venus is 'the pleasure of the gods and men', and pleasure is of course the goal of life for an Epicurean. On the other hand, some have viewed the proem against a purely literary background, and have quoted examples of invocations to deities in other poems. Others have sought for the explanation of the proem in the Roman context: there is evidence for a cult of *Venus physica*, and there is evidence of a connection between the family of Memmius and the cult of Venus.[4]

The intention of this present argument is not to deny the force of these other observations; Lucretius' proem is not a simple or single-minded piece of work. There is no doubt whatever that its surface appearance – an invocation to an anthropomorphic goddess – is not all that we are to see in it. Its meaning is to be found by interpretation, and there is no good reason to think that one line of interpretation alone will yield the whole of its meaning. The present intention is to emphasize one line in the complex harmony.

The appeal to a divinity for inspiration, as it has often been said, is a *traditional* element in ancient poetry. That is to say, by beginning his poem in this way, Lucretius placed it in a succession; he placed himself in a certain relation to earlier writers. It is therefore worth asking some questions that have surprisingly not been

---

[3] I take it that *nam* ... is elliptical '[I address you,] for ...' This is common in prayers (e.g. Horace, *Odes*, III.11.1).

[4] See Bailey (1947), 589–91; Schilling (1954), 346–58.

pressed very hard by Lucretian scholars: *which* earlier writers does Lucretius claim as his predecessors, and what is the significance of his claim?

The poem is to be on nature, *de rerum natura*. He addresses the goddess of Love because her influence on the four cosmic masses and on the animal kingdom brings about the creation of new life. Since she alone has this power over nature, she can inspire him to create a poem about nature. Moreover she has power over the god of Strife, and thus can bring peace to the cosmos: and this power again is needed, if his mind is to have the peace necessary for creation.

There was one other poet who wrote a hexameter poem *On nature* in which the goddess of Love had power over the four cosmic masses and over all the processes of creation in nature, and over the god of Strife: Empedocles.

Luckily, it can be proved that there is nothing far-fetched or improbable about the suggestion that Lucretius claimed to be a follower of Empedocles. Empedocles' Περὶ φύσεως was well known from the time it was written until the time of Lucretius.[5] Theophrastus wrote a book about Empedocles.[6] Hermarchus, the third-century Epicurean, wrote twenty-two open letters about him.[7] More interestingly, a work called *Empedoclea* was written in Latin, by someone called Sallustius, at just the same time as Lucretius was writing his poem. This we know from one of Cicero's letters to his brother, written in 54 B.C., in which he mentions just two works: the *poemata* of Lucretius and the *Empedoclea* of Sallustius.[8] It is clear that there was interest in Empedocles in the Roman literary world at this time. Lucretius could count on some knowledge of him and his works.

His own attitude to Empedocles is described explicitly in the well-known lines of book I: Empedocles was wrong to say that all things are made of four irreducible elements – but nevertheless his discoveries were such that he seems like a god (712–33). Many instances have been pointed out in Lucretius' poem of imitation of lines of Empedocles;[9] and perhaps we should recognize more if more of Empedocles had survived.

It has never been doubted that Lucretius knew the works of Empedocles, either directly or from some intermediary source, and that he admired him. The point of this article is to prove something that has been doubted, that Lucretius wrote his proem so that comparison with Empedocles was inevitable, and also to suggest that by prefacing his poem thus Lucretius was claiming a particular position for it in the history of natural philosophy. We must therefore make some detailed comparisons between Empedocles and Lucretius, first of all on the subjects brought up in the first forty-three lines of *De rerum natura*.

On the subject of the four elements, the most instructive fragments of

---

[5] It is sometimes forgotten that the title *De rerum natura* is a translation of the Greek Περὶ φύσεως. The recent translation of Lucretius by Mr Rolfe Humphries (Indiana University Press, 1968), which has many virtues, is marred by its unfortunate title, *The Way Things Are*.
[6] Diogenes Laertius v.43.
[7] *Ibid*. x.25.
[8] Cicero, *Ad Quint. Frat.* II.9.3.
[9] See especially Jobst (1907), Kranz (1944), and Bollack (1959).

Empedocles are B21 and 22. In B21, the four elements are listed. Fire is represented by the sun, which is characterized as 'bright and hot'.[10] Air is described very obscurely, apparently as that which is passively 'bathed in the heat and bright ray' of the sun. Water is represented by 'rain, everywhere dark and cold'. Finally 'from earth are born whatever are rooted and solid'. In a briefer list in B22, the four appear as 'the shining one (ἠλέκτωρ), earth, sky (οὐρανός) and sea'. It is noteworthy that *air* here counts as sky (as in Lucretius I.6), and the fire of the upper sky is characterized by its brightness. It is also important that the four elements are identified not so much as *materials*, characterized by certain properties, but as distinct features of the cosmos, characterized not only by their properties but also by their position in the cosmos. Empedocles makes no distinction between these two roles. 'The shining one' and the sea and the sky of fragment 22 are also the ingredients of mortal compounds.

After listing the four elements or cosmic masses in B21, Empedocles continues: 'In Anger [i.e. Strife] all are diverse in form and separate, but they come together in Love and are desired by each other. For out of these [come] all things that were and are and will be: trees grew, and men and women, and water-nurtured fish ...' As in Lucretius' proem, the growth of plant and animal life is brought about by Love's work with the cosmic masses. Lucretius' use of this Empedoclean idea is very delicate. He cannot say, as Empedocles does, that living things grow from the *mixture* of these four elements, because that would commit him too precisely to the theory of the four elements, as the unchanging material out of which compounds are formed by mixture. Instead, he takes the four *only* as cosmic masses, in perfect conformity with Epicurean theory, and relates them to the creation of living things through the idea of the season of spring.

When we turn from the elements to the force or forces that move them, we find some difficulty in deciding what to say both about Empedocles and about Lucretius. At the present time, there is a fundamental disagreement among historians of Greek cosmology over the interpretation of Empedocles. According to one group, Empedocles' doctrine was that a period of cosmogony and zöogony brought about by the agency of Love was followed by a second period in which the same sorts of effect were brought about, in reverse order, by the agency of Strife.[11] This would mean, presumably, that the generation of life might just as well be ascribed to Strife as to Love, and it would then be rather arbitrary to find a similarity between Lucretius' proem and the theory of Empedocles. It seems to me, however, that at least so far as zöogony is concerned the balance of the evidence is heavily in favour of the second view, according to which there is only one kind of zöogony in Empedocles, that brought about by the agency of Love.[12]

---

[10] The MSS vary about the adjectives, but both properties are probably mentioned.

[11] For this view see Kirk and Raven (1957), Guthrie II, and O'Brien (1969). But O'Brien concedes (p. 183) that even in the periods of increasing Strife, Love may still be responsible for the creation of life.

[12] For this view, see Hölscher (1965), Solmsen (1965), and Bollack (1965). There is a useful summary of the position in Kahn (1968).

But what did Lucretius himself think about Venus and Mars? We must make some careful distinctions. There is no doubt that Lucretius' cosmology included a polarity of creation and destruction, of associative forces and repellent forces. Indeed, how could it be otherwise, since he wanted to say that mortal things disintegrate, and are replaced by others, in a more-or-less balanced cycle? But to say that he believed in such forces is not to say that he believed in some kind of transcendent Duality. We know what the moving forces are in the Epicurean system: they are the weight, the collisions, and the swerves of atoms. The effects of these forces depend on the shapes of the atoms involved. Sometimes collisions lead to the creation of a new compound, even of a new cosmos; sometimes they lead to destruction. It would be false to the spirit of Epicureanism to hypostasize these tendencies into a metaphysical Dualism.

When Lucretius describes the origin of animals, which Empedocles explicitly puts down as the work of Love, he does not mention Love or Venus at all; animals were born from mother Earth, but there are no sexual metaphors in the passage (v.783–820). Likewise in the passage where he warns the reader that the cosmos will disintegrate one day, he does not mention Strife (v.91–109).

His attitude to Venus, the goddess of sexual love, so reverent and significant in the first lines of the poem, becomes angry and contemptuous at the end of book IV.

It seems clear that although Lucretius used Empedocles' theory of the four elements and his two cosmic forces of Love and Strife as a means to signify his enrolment in the Empedoclean tradition, it was not just these features of Empedocles' philosophy that he admired and claimed to follow.

The natural philosophy of Epicurus was put forward as an alternative to the world picture of the Platonists and Aristotelians, later adopted with some modifications by the Stoics. One of the chief points of difference was that the Epicureans believed the cosmos to be a compound that grew and will perish, made of everlasting physical elements, whereas the alternative theory made the cosmos either itself eternal and ungenerated, or else the creation of a divine craftsman who worked according to an eternal pattern. As a matter of historical fact, Empedocles is the earliest philosopher who is known to have worked out a theory of the growth of the cosmos from unchanging physical elements. In this respect the Epicureans were certainly followers of Empedocles. Lucretius evidently saw this as a feature of primary importance in Epicureanism, because it is the first physical doctrine he mentions, immediately after the prayer to Venus:

> rerum primordia pandam
> unde omnis natura creet res auctet alatque
> quove eadem rursum natura perempta resolvat.

(1.55–7)

Lucretius had every reason to pay tribute to Empedocles as the inventor of elements, even though he could not accept the Empedoclean theory in detail.

It may be said that Empedocles' theory was different from Epicureanism in the crucial respect that his moving causes, Love and Strife, are gods, whereas the

Epicureans insisted above all that gods are not needed to explain the growth of the cosmos or any other physical process. But it is clear that this feature of the Empedoclean theory does not necessarily contain anything offensive to the Epicureans. Lucretius may well have thought that it can be completely demythologized. The moving force called 'Love' or 'Aphrodite' is simply a force that attracts unlike elements to each other, and 'Strife' or 'Eris' is a force of repulsion between unlike elements.[13] These are forces that are as natural as the weight, swerve, and collision of atoms. Lucretius himself, having written to Venus *rerum naturam sola gubernas* in I.21 can say *rerum primordia pandam | unde omnis natura creet res* in lines 55–6. He may well have thought that Aphrodite in Empedocles' poem was as little inconsistent with a theory of purely natural causes as Venus evidently was in his own.

The second fundamental point of difference between Epicureanism and its opponents was that the Epicureans rejected teleology. This statement needs no defence or elaboration here. What is relevant to the present argument is that Empedocles was sometimes regarded as the paradigm case of an anti-teleological philosopher of nature. Aristotle's classic defence of teleological explanation is in *Physics* II. He singles out Empedocles as the leading exponent of the wrong kind of philosophy of nature, and takes examples from the famous passage in Empedocles' Περὶ φύσεως in which he speaks of βουγενῆ ἀνδρόπρῳρα.[14] The point is that Empedocles explained the formation of living forms as a *random* natural process, in which only the successful forms survived. This is exactly contrary to Aristotle's own view of nature, according to which processes are *for the sake of* the resultant forms. Lucretius follows Empedocles particularly closely in the doctrine here criticized by Aristotle. His own account of the development of living forms includes translations of lines from the relevant part of Empedocles' Περὶ φύσεως.[15] There is thus every reason to think that he made a similar assessment to Aristotle's of Empedocles' position in the history of the conflict about teleology.

These two great points of difference – between a cosmos that grows naturally out of elementary bodies and a created or eternal cosmos, and between 'mechanical' and teleological explanation – together constitute the essential distinction between Epicureanism and its opponents. It is a distinction that marks off the succession of philosophers beginning with Empedocles and continuing with Anaxagoras, Leucippus, Democritus, and Epicurus, from the opposed tradition of Plato and Aristotle. Lucretius' *De rerum natura* is the last great document of the former tradition in antiquity, and it is entirely appropriate that its proem should pay tribute to the pioneering work of Empedocles.

If Lucretius felt that he owed much to Empedocles, did this feeling clash in any way with his reverence for Epicurus? This is a question which may throw new light on the later part of the proem, lines 62–101.

---

[13] Bollack (1965) and Kahn (1968) would say that Love attracts and Strife repels, without any stipulations about like and unlike. I am not yet convinced of this.

[14] Aristotle *Physics* II.7.198 b 29ff; Empedocles B61.

[15] Compare Empedocles B82 with Lucretius v.788ff; B57 with v.837–41.

After the very brief statement of his theme in lines 54–61, which we have already quoted, Lucretius changes to the past tense to describe a historic event:

> humana ante oculos foede cum vita iaceret
> in terris oppressa gravi sub religione
> quae caput a caeli regionibus ostendebat
> horribili super aspectu mortalibus instans,
> primum Graius homo mortalis tollere contra
> est oculos ausus primusque obsistere contra.

> (1.62–7)

This tribute has almost universally been assigned to Epicurus, although he is not mentioned by name. It is sufficiently similar in expression to the later passages that praise the work of Epicurus, III.1–17 and V.1–54; in these again Epicurus is not mentioned by name, but there can be no doubt that he is intended. Some strange features of 1.62–79, however, led one scholar, Ludwig Edelstein, to doubt whether Epicurus was meant at all. Epicurus was *not*, after all, the first *Graius homo* to seek to 'break open the tight bolts of nature's gates' (lines 70–1) and to fight against religion (78–9). Edelstein suggested instead that Lucretius did not mean any particular Greek, but the Presocratics in general; he was stressing that the inventor of natural philosophy was a *man*, not a god, and a *Greek*, not an oriental.

This suggestion was rightly rejected by subsequent editors. Nevertheless, Edelstein's doubts had a perfectly real foundation. There *is* something strange in what Lucretius attributes to Epicurus. As well as the historical anomaly already mentioned, we should note that the metaphor of the 'flight of the mind', common in ancient philosophy,[16] is particularly inappropriate to the atomic soul of Epicurean theory:

> ergo vivida vis animi pervicit, et extra
> processit longe flammantia moenia mundi
> atque omne immensum peragravit mente animoque.

> (1.72–4)

One of the most interesting occurrences of the 'flight of the mind' is in a fragment of Empedocles, which is commonly taken to be about Pythagoras:

> ἦν δέ τις ἐν κείνοισιν ἀνὴρ περιώσια εἰδώς,
> ὃς δὴ μήκιστον πραπίδων ἐκτήσατο πλοῦτον,
> παντοίων τε μάλιστα σοφῶν <τ'> ἐπιήρανος ἔργων·
> ὁππότε γὰρ πάσῃσιν ὀρέξαιτο πραπίδεσσιν,
> ῥεῖ' ὅ γε τῶν ὄντων πάντων λεύσσεσκεν ἕκαστον
> καί τε δεκ' ἀνθρώπων καί τ' εἴκοσιν αἰώνεσσιν.

> (B129)

Pythagoras when he 'strained with all his mind' (πραπίδες) was able to see the whole of reality, ranging over many generations. Epicurus, because of his *vivida vis*

---

[16] See Edelstein (1940), p. 81, n. 12, for some examples.

animi, traversed the whole universe; his range was in space, not in time. Both passages stress that there was a single human being, unique among his peers, who performed this feat at a particular time: ἦν δέ τις ἐν κείνοισιν; *primum Graius homo mortalis tollere contra / est oculos ausus.*

This fragment of Empedocles is from the *Purifications*. As he said in the opening line of this poem (B112), people followed him 'to hear a healing spell' (κλυεῖν εὐηκέα βάξιν). The evidence is too fragmentary to give any certainty about the 'diseases of all kinds' that were to be healed. But there is one very striking passage that clearly describes one aspect of the polluted life:

> μορφὴν δ' ἀλλάξαντα πατὴρ φίλον υἱὸν ἀείρας
> σφάζει ἐπευχόμενος μέγα νήπιος· οἱ δ' ἀπορεῦνται
> λισσόμενον θύοντες· ὁ δ' αὖ νήκουστος ὁμοκλέων
> σφάξας ἐν μεγάροισι κακὴν ἀλεγύνατο δαῖτα.

(B137.1–4)

This describes the ritual sacrifice of an animal – which may be identified with the sacrificer's son, because of the Pythagorean doctrine of transmigration. Empedocles' message is that animals must not be killed, if human life is to be pure.

Lucretius was not a believer in transmigration. But it is a remarkable fact that his first example of the pollution from which Epicurus rescued human life by his inquiry into nature is a human sacrifice: the sacrifice of Iphigeneia.[17] This is remarkable for many reasons: human sacrifice was *not* a feature of the religious practices of Epicurus' time, and was not in any way symbolic of the evils that he actually saw in the religion of the time. It is true that Ennius had treated the subject of Iphigeneia; but that does not seem a sufficient reason why Lucretius should put it in here. A much more likely explanation is that Lucretius was recalling this passage of Empedocles. The detailed similarities are quite numerous: both speak of a father sacrificing his child (which would indeed be an extraordinary coincidence, if it were coincidence); both describe the attendants who are embarrassed (οἱ δ' ἀπορεῦνται / λισσόμενον θύοντες· *hunc propter ferrum celare ministros / aspectuque suo lacrimas effundere civis*):[18] in both, the child knows and fears what is happening and adopts an attitude of prayer (λισσόμενον: *muta metu terram genibus summissa petebat*). The choice of the Iphigeneia story enables Lucretius both to place himself in the tradition of Greek epic verse, like Empedocles, and to repeat this theme from Empedocles without reference to the rejected theory of transmigration.

It may reasonably be suggested, then, that in lines 62–101 Lucretius continues to make use of Empedoclean themes. He uses them in a most interesting way. Empedocles wrote not only Περὶ φύσεως, which provided the model for the *De*

---

[17] Note how Lucretius makes the point about pollution by repeating '*foede*': *foede cum vita iaceret* (62); *aram ... turparunt sanguine foede* (85).
[18] There is some doubt about the reading. Guthrie (II.250, n. 1) follows Bergk and Bignone: οἱ δ' ἐπορεῦνται λισσόμενοι θύοντος. I follow Diels–Kranz. Their reading would receive some slight confirmation if my comparison were accepted as valid.

rerum natura, but also Καθαρμοί. The relation between his two poems is notoriously obscure.[19] Very little survives from the Καθαρμοί. Did Empedocles think of his own physical doctrines, set out in the Περὶ φύσεως, as a means to 'purification'? It seems unlikely. But it is true at least that he both wrote about nature and claimed to be a purifier of human life. Now Lucretius hints that Epicurus follows in this same tradition. He writes a tribute to Epicurus (*primum Graius homo*) that is deliberately ambiguous; in some respects it applies more exactly to Empedocles than to Epicurus.[20] He implies that, like Empedocles, Epicurus found human life in a polluted state – polluted by wrong ideas about the gods and their relation to the cosmos – and like Empedocles he showed the way in his writings to be rid of the pollution.

[19] See Kahn (1960b) for a recent treatment of the problem.

[20] The 'flight of the mind' passage in Empedocles is apparently about Pythagoras, not about himself. But this is hardly an objection to the comparison between Empedocles and Epicurus that I am attributing to Lucretius.

16

LUCRETIUS AND THE STOICS

[1966]

Lucretius' poem contains several attacks on rival theories. I believe that their target or targets have often been mistaken by the editors and commentators, who fairly constantly refer particular passages to the Stoics. Cyril Bailey (1947, p. 15) says: 'Above all, the beliefs of the Stoics ... are set aside, sometimes with argument, often merely with a contemptuous *delirum* or *desipere est*.' Elsewhere in Bailey's commentary we find many remarks like this: 'What is doubtless most in Lucretius' mind – the Stoics' (p. 782); 'There can be little doubt that he has now passed in mind ... to the Stoics' (p. 949). Similarly in Munro's commentary (1866): 'No doubt the zeal with which the Stoics maintained this doctrine added vehemence to Lucretius' denunciations' (p. 554); 'The whole of this reasoning is doubtless directed against the Stoics' (p. 577). And in Robin's commentary likewise: 'mais il s'agit sans doute des Stoiciens' (Ernout and Robin (1925), 1.225).

I am persuaded that the editors have been too quick to banish doubt about this matter. In this chapter I shall examine the passages that have been declared to be directed against the Stoics; I hope to show that some of them are certainly not, and most of them probably not, attacks on the Stoics, and that none of them is necessarily aimed at the Stoics. This may sound tiresomely destructive. It seems necessary to be destructive, however, since the assertions of the editors continue to exercise influence, and in the course of the investigation some more positive results may be achieved.

To identify the 'anti-Stoic' passages I have used the indices in Munro's edition and in the commentary of Ernout and Robin. Giussani's edition has no index; Bailey's index recognizes nothing between 'sterility' and 'style'. I have gone through the latter edition with as much care as my patience allowed, but there may be allegations which I have overlooked. I have also studied the text of Lucretius on my own account to see if there might be allusions to Stoic theories that the editors have missed.

1.449–482.   PROPERTIES AND ACCIDENTS

After establishing that there exist atoms and void, Lucretius asserts that there is no third thing to be discovered (430–48). Everything that you can name is a compound of atoms and void, or else a property or accident of these (a *coniunctum* or an *eventum*) (449–58). Thus time does not exist *per se*, independently of *things* that change in time (459–463). Thus also the argument that, because we can still speak of Helen raped (*Tyndaridem raptam ... esse*) or the Trojans defeated, and because that rape and that defeat cannot now be the accident of Helen and the Trojans since they are long since dead, therefore the rape and the defeat are *per se* entities, is quite invalid. For they are accidents of a certain quantity of atoms and void, which still exist (464–82).

'Doubtless he dwells at such length ... on this argument, because the stoics taught that all states, qualities, virtues, etc., were body' (Munro, p. 376). But this cannot be right. Lucretius is not protesting against the wrong inclusion of states, etc in the category of bodies, but against setting up a third category, other than bodies and void.

Bailey asserts only that the last two points are anti-Stoic ('combatting his natural opponents, the Stoics'). (1) The Stoics held that time is a *per se* entity, and Lucretius argued against them. This is false, for two reasons. First, the same point about time is made in the same context in Epicurus' *Letter to Herodotus* 72–3, and no one is likely to make a serious claim that the argument there is aimed at Zeno. Second, the Stoics did not hold that time is a *per se* entity, but defined it in much the same way as Lucretius did (cf. *SVF* 1.93: Ζήνων ἔφησε χρόνον εἶναι κινήσεως διάστημα. Also *SVF* 11.509–21). Bailey quotes a little snippet from Sextus to the effect that for the Stoics time was a καθ' αὑτό τι νοούμενον πρᾶγμα; but the context shows that this was an inference by Sextus, not a report (ἐξ οὗ δῆλον γίγνεται ὅτι ... δοξάζουσι: *SVF* 11.331).

(2) The second point supposed to be anti-Stoic is the point about the rape of Helen. Robin finds in this an attack on an alleged contradiction in Chrysippus' theory of time (for which see Plutarch, *De comm. not.* chapter 41), but does not explain at all clearly how he understands Lucretius' argument. The argument was correctly understood by Bailey, who realized that its target could not be as Robin had said, but found another Stoic target for it – a theory that events or occurrences had independent existence and were indeed bodies. He thought there was evidence that the Stoics held such a theory in some sentences in Seneca's *Epistulae* ('quod accidit alicui ... corpus est': CXVII.7). But this will not do. Seneca's purpose in the passage is to argue, against Stoic orthodoxy, that, since *sapientia* is a good, *sapere* must also be a good. This has nothing whatever to do with the independent existence of *res gestae*, which is Lucretius' target. No other evidence has been produced to show that the old Stoics believed in the independent existence of *res gestae*.

It is quite likely that the whole passage is not directed against any opponents. It may be that Lucretius, or his source, is dealing with possible objections to the

Epicurean theory of *coniuncta* and *eventa* that had not in fact been raised by any particular group of people. If a definite target must be suggested, however, it is Plato's Academy that comes to mind, since it was the Platonists who argued from the possibility of talking about past events to the existence of certain *per se* entities. According to Aristotle *Metaph.* 1.9.990 b 14, there was an argument for the existence of Ideas that had the technical name κατὰ τὸ νοεῖν τι φθαρέντος.

1.615–626. INFINITE DIVISIBILITY

Part of Lucretius' argument for the existence of *minimae partes* of atoms is as follows (I have commented on the whole argument more fully in Furley (1967b)). If there were no minimum, both the smallest and the largest bodies would consist of infinitely numerous parts. Hence the whole universe and the smallest parts of the universe would contain an equal number of parts. Lucretius held this to be unthinkable.

The Stoics were among those who believed in the infinite divisibility of matter, and according to Plutarch, *De comm. not.* 1079 A, they were apt to say that 'a man does not consist of more parts than his finger, nor the cosmos than the man'. But there were other possible targets for this polemic. Anaxagoras, who is to be attacked by name and at length 200 lines further on, said: 'Of the small there is no smallest, but always a smaller, since what exists cannot cease to exist; also there is always a larger than the large. And it [sc. the large] is equal to the small in number ...' (fragment 3). In *Physics* III.5.204 a 20ff, Aristotle argues that it is impossible that the infinite should exist as an actual being, for in that case any part of it you like to take will be infinite, and it is impossible for the same thing to be many infinities. The Epicureans may have adopted this argument from Aristotle and turned it against his own theory of infinite divisibility – for they were impatient with his careful distinction between potential and actual division. Again, the pseudo-Aristotelian *On indivisible lines* 968 a 2ff mentions an argument that is quite similar to these lines of Lucretius, and this treatise is usually thought to be concerned with debates that belong to a pre-Stoic age.

There is some slight reason for thinking that Chrysippus aimed to *answer* this Epicurean argument. For he pointed out explicitly that the theory of infinite divisibility does not entail that a finite thing consists of an infinite number of parts (*SVF* II.482), and it appears from the Plutarch passage quoted above that he avoided saying that two infinites are equal.

1.635–704. FIRE

Nearly 300 lines of book I are devoted to attacks on the theories of matter put forward by Presocratic philosophers. Heraclitus, Empedocles, and Anaxagoras are named. Lucretius expresses admiration for Empedocles, though he was wrong about the four elements; and he is fairly gentle with Anaxagoras. 'But the attack on Heraclitus', Bailey remarks (p. 709), 'is more vehement and bitter, doubtless because his theories had been adopted ... by Epicurus' rivals, the Stoics.' (As a matter of fact, the Empedoclean theory of four elements was adopted by the Stoics too; so this argument is not a strong one.)

Lucretius objects that a single element cannot generate such *varied* things as there are in the world. By supposing that fire varies in density, all you can get is weaker or stronger fire, if parts of fire retain the character of the whole; but in any case people who say this also deny the existence of void among things and therefore cannot explain variations in density at all (645–64). If on the other hand they say that fire is extinguished and thus changes its nature, then they fall foul of the argument set out earlier in Lucretius, book 1 (215ff), according to which the elements must persist through change since otherwise everything will in the end be reduced to nothing (665–74).

Now what reasons are there for thinking that this attack is directed not only against Heraclitus but also, and chiefly, against the Stoics? Only Heraclitus is named. However, Lucretius does frequently use the plural instead of the singular to refer to his opponents in this passage, and he says that Heraclitus was only the leader of the fire-men. But the plural certainly need not refer to the Stoics, since plural Heracliteans were well known in the doxographical tradition from Plato onwards. Bailey claims that rarefaction and condensation as the mode of transformation of fire is well attested for the Stoics, but badly attested for Heraclitus; the truth is not so simple.

There is good evidence that Heraclitus held this doctrine in the report of Theophrastus (*Physicorum opiniones* fragment 1; see Kirk (1954), 22ff). The Stoic position is more obscure. They certainly held that fire was in a sense the primary element and that it was transformed into the other elements by σύστασις and reconstituted by χύσις (*SVF* 11.413). It is perhaps significant, however, that they chose these words, rather than πύκνωσις and ἀραίωσις. Their meaning is more like solidification and liquefaction than condensation and rarefaction; changes of quality or state were explained by variation in the tension of the pervading *pneuma* (*SVF* 11.379 etc.), which might cause the parts of a substance to occupy a different volume but was not synonymous with such a process. But they did admit that when the world was changed into pure fire at the periodic conflagrations, a great expansion would take place; they admitted the existence of the void *outside* the cosmos to allow for this expansion (*SVF* 11.597, 609, 618, 619). Since they did not admit the existence of void *inside* the continuum of matter, and yet held that the continuum could expand, from an Atomist's viewpoint their theory was open to the objection brought forward by Lucretius.

Bailey maintains that Lucretius' objection cannot be directed against Heraclitus, because Heraclitus was too old (i.e. pre-Parmenides) to deny the existence of void in things. This is an argument that deserves some respect, but I think it can be answered. Lucretius treats the three Presocratic theories, of Heraclitus, Empedocles, and Anaxagoras, as rivals to Atomism. He sees them, I believe, as three variations on a single theme – the theme of continuity, the contradictory of atomism. Empedocles and Anaxagoras both denied the existence of void in the universe; Lucretius would naturally take Heraclitus, as a typical *monist*, to be denying it too. So he begins (635): 'Those who thought that fire is the material of all things, and the universe consists of fire alone [i.e. no void] are evidently far from the truth. Their leader was Heraclitus ...'

I conclude that the evidence does not show that this passage must be directed against the Stoics. The strongest reason for thinking that it is – the deliberate mention of the denial of void in the cosmos and the assertion that this is incompatible with condensation and rarefaction – turns out to be illusory, because Lucretius could well have criticized Heraclitus on this ground, and because the Stoic theory of the transformation of fire appears to have implied condensation and rarefaction only incidentally. It is important to add, too, that there is no trace here of the characteristic Stoic doctrines about fire – the distinction between creative and destructive fire, *ekpyrosis*, and the divine properties of fire.

1.782–802. THE FOUR ELEMENTS

Part of Lucretius' criticism of Empedocles' theory is directed against the idea that the four elements change into one another. Empedocles himself did not believe in such a change; so the editors have wondered whom Lucretius had in mind. 'It may be', Bailey writes, 'that there was some sect of the "four-element" thinkers who adopted this extreme form of the "transformationist" theory.' It is odd that Bailey did not think of mentioning Aristotle as being a member of such a 'sect', for he has surely at least as good a claim as 'Lucretius' usual opponents, the Stoics'.

1.1052–1113. GEOCENTRIC COSMOLOGY

After arguing that the universe is infinite, Lucretius continues with an attack on the geocentric cosmology.

> Illud in his rebus longe fuge credere, Memmi,
> in medium summae quod dicunt omnia niti.
>
> (1052–3)

There is some doubt about the construction of this sentence. Giussani (1896–8) took 'quod dicunt' to be dependent on 'in medium summae'; 'do not believe this, Memmius, that all things tend towards the centre of the whole universe, as people call it'. Ernout (Ernout and Robin, 1925) agrees with Giussani. Munro says that 'quod dicunt' is parenthetical and equal to 'id quod dicunt': 'do not believe this, that all things tend towards the centre, as they say'. Bailey says that 'quod dicunt' depends on 'illud' and governs the noun clause: 'do not believe what people say, namely that all things tend towards the centre'. Against Munro he quotes another instance where 'illud' is picked up by 'quod' in the next line; and he dismisses Giussani's interpretation without deigning to say why. But as a matter of fact the interpretation of Giussani and Ernout, taking 'quod dicunt' as modifying 'medium summae', is syntactically as reasonable as any other interpretation, and makes good sense; for Epicureans denied that there is such a thing as the *medium summae*. On balance I slightly prefer this interpretation.

It should be noticed first that the subject of 'dicunt' is not identified by Lucretius. None of the editors shows any doubt that the Stoics are meant. Lucretius continues:

> atque ideo mundi naturam stare sine ullis
> ictibus externis neque quoquam posse resolvi,
> summa atque ima quod in medium sint omnia nixa,
> ipsum si quicquam posse in se sistere credis,
> et quae pondera sunt sub terris omnia sursum
> nitier in terraque retro requiescere posta,
> ut per aquas quae nunc rerum simulacra videmus.

(1054–60)

In 1042ff he has explained the Epicurean theory that the world remains relatively stable because the material that would be lost to it through the expulsion of atoms by internal collisions is kept in its place by an infinite series of atoms colliding with the world from outside. So now he warns Memmius against believing that it can remain stable, *sine ullis ictibus externis*, for a different reason – that the *summa atque ima* all tend towards the middle. The Epicureans believed that the downward fall of atoms provided a datum in the infinite universe; so the *summa* here are the things at the top of the world, on our side of it, and the *ima* are things on the under-side. Lucretius continues by contrasting the paradox of the geocentric theory with the commonsense of Epicureanism. The geocentric theory asserts that the heavy body of the earth and the things on the earth remain where they are because they are mutually supporting; those on our side of the world are sustained by the opposite pressure of those on the other side. In that sense it says that 'a thing can stand on itself'. The Epicurean relies on observation that heavy things fall in just one direction – downwards; the geocentric theory says that heavy things rest upside-down on the under-side of the earth, like reflections in a lake. (I have followed Lachmann's punctuation of this section. Modern editors, except Martin, read it slightly differently.)

Next, Lucretius describes the ridiculous antipodes in more detail and advances his objections to this theory (1061–82); the text is mutilated, but there is not really much doubt about its contents. First, he objects that since the universe is infinite it cannot have a centre; second, that if it had a centre there would be no reason why anything should come to rest there, because heavy bodies go on falling through any space whatever, and it makes no difference to call one piece of space the middle; there is no place such that heavy bodies lose their weight when they arrive there, and there is no part of the void whose nature is to resist rather than to yield.

These objections are clearly framed from an Epicurean point of view. Lucretius has already proved that void exists (1.335ff) and that the universe is infinite (1.951ff); he simply uses these two propositions to criticize his opponents. There is certainly no reason to think that either of them was asserted by his opponents. But these objections make one 'thing clear about the rival theory: it depended on the notion of the centre of the universe as a whole, not some other centre.

Now comes a surprise. Lucretius continues with some more polemic against the geocentric theory, and now he points out that his opponents after all do not maintain that *all* bodies are centripetal:

> praeterea quoniam non omnia corpora fingunt
> in medium niti, sed terrarum atque liquoris,
> umorem ponti magnasque e montibus undas,
> et quasi terreno quae corpore contineantur;
> at contra tenuis exponunt aeris auras
> et calidos simul a medio differrier ignis ...
>
> (1083–8)

Earth and water are centripetal, air and fire are centrifugal. Strictly speaking, this is inconsistent with lines 1053 and 1056, which assert that *omnia niti in medium*. One might argue that the opponents aimed at in 1083ff are different from the omni-centripetalists aimed at in 1052ff; but no one will wish to choose that way out. The fact that the opponents are an anonymous third-person plural in line 1083, without any new specification, tells against it, and so does the conjunction *praeterea*. The use of the word *omnia* in 1053ff is easily explained. Lucretius was thinking there of the queer theory of the antipodes, and by *omnia* he meant not only the things on our side of the earth, but also things on the other side.

The text continues with two more features of the rival theory:

> atque ideo totum circum tremere aethera signis
> et solis flammam per caeli caerula pasci,
> quod calor a medio fugiens se ibi colligat omnis,
> nec prorsum arboribus summos frondescere ramos
> posse, nisi a terris paulatim cuique cibatum ...
>
> (1089–93)

At this point the text breaks off. MS *O* leaves a gap of eight lines, obviously corresponding to the eight mutilated lines 1068–75.

The two additional details are these. First the stars twinkle in the sky and the sun's flame is nourished because all the heat or fire that rises from the centre collects in the place of the stars and the sun; and second, some related point explains how the high branches of trees get enough nourishment from their roots in the earth.

What was in the lacuna? The *nisi*-clause beginning in 1093 lacks its verb, the *quoniam*-clause beginning in 1083 lacks its apodosis. The text continues with a *ne*-clause that lacks an antecedent main clause. This might be different from the apodosis of the *quoniam*-clause, or it might be identical with it. These elements must be supplied, but there is room for more as well. For our present purpose all that matters is this: the *ne*-clauses beginning in 1102 and continuing to 1110 cannot easily be construed in any other way than as consequences drawn by Lucretius from the theory of centrifugal air and fire, with the intention of refuting the theory. The logic of the whole passage might be this: Since our opponents assert (1) that air and fire are centrifugal, (2) that the stars and sun are kept going by centrifugal fire, (3) that trees grow upwards somehow because of centrifugal air and fire ... perhaps also (4), (5), etc in the lacuna – therefore, on these assumptions, there is a danger lest ...

> ne volucri ritu flammarum moenia mundi
> diffugiant subito magnum per inane soluta
> et ne cetera consimili ratione sequantur
> neve ruant caeli tonitralia templa superne
> terraque se pedibus raptim subducat et omnis
> inter permixtas rerum caelique ruinas
> corpora solventis abeat per inane profundum,
> temporis ut puncto nil exstet reliquiarum
> desertum praeter spatium et primordia caeca.
> nam quacumque prius de parti corpora desse
> constitues, haec rebus erit pars ianua leti,
> hac se turba foras dabit omnis materiai.

(1102–13)

A few lines earlier, as we saw, Lucretius applied some Epicurean ideas to the rival theory: the rival theory assumes that the centre of the universe has great significance, but on Epicurean principles there is no centre. Similarly in these last lines Lucretius' objection does not seek to punish an internal inconsistency in the rival theory, but to show that from it, together with some Epicurean principles, most disagreeable consequences would follow. The danger in the rival theory is that air and fire, being centrifugal, will disperse into the vast void. On Epicurean principles it would then follow that the whole world would disintegrate; for the Epicureans believed that the heavy earth remains stable because it is essentially unified with the rest of the cosmos. There is no direct evidence from the fragments of Epicurus for this view, but there is a strange and unpalatable passage in Lucretius v.534–63 that explains why the heavy earth does not crash through the bed of air and fire on which it rests. We can omit the weird dynamics for the present: all that matters is that Epicureans believed the world to remain as it is, suspended in space, because it is a single unity and because the weight of the earth is somehow modified by its unity with the lighter elements that surround it. The point is just this: if the air and fire are going to vanish outwards into the vast void, then the earth will start to collapse under our feet. It does not matter where the weakening begins; wherever it begins, the unity of the world is broken and it will rapidly disintegrate. The editors have been mistaken in their interpretation of this passage. It is true as they say that Lucretius ignores the opponents' tenet that earth and water are centripetal, so that on their theory there would be no danger of the earth and water following the air and fire away from the centre into the vast void. But Giussani, and Bailey (who offers a translation of Giussani without acknowledgement), is wrong when he says that the danger is not of the earth's precipitating itself downwards but of 'scivolandoci', slipping away, from under our feet in the form of atomic dust. Lucretius is not substituting mysteriously centrifugal earth for his opponents' centripetal earth: he is canvassing the peculiarly Epicurean fear of the earth's falling downwards through space.

We have now, if this analysis is correct, dissociated the rival theory from the Epicurean elements that Lucretius employs to criticize it. The rival theory asserted that there is a centre of the universe, and that our world is held together by the centripetal tendency of the elements earth and water, so that in the antipodes people walk as it were upside-down. The sun shines in turn on our side of the earth and on the antipodes. Fire and air are centrifugal, and this fact accounts for the stars' light and the sun's heat and the upward growth of trees.

Whose theory was this? Not the Stoics', in spite of what the editors say. Admittedly on this occasion they are able to quote evidence, some of it persuasive. Munro quotes Stobaeus' report of Zeno (*SVF* I.99):

All the parts of the cosmos have motion towards the centre of the cosmos, and especially the parts that have weight. The explanation is the same, both for the stationary position of the cosmos in the infinite void, and for that of the earth in the cosmos ... Not every body has weight; air and fire are weightless; but these also are somehow drawn towards the middle of the whole sphere of the cosmos, and they take up their position towards its circumference, since they are naturally centrifugal (ἀνώφοιτα) because of having no weight.

At first sight, this looks just like the target theory: earth and water are centripetal, air and fire are centrifugal, and the cosmos is held stable because of the equal balance all round. But if we look more closely, we can see that Zeno's theory in fact contains the *answer* to the Epicurean criticism. Zeno said, it seems, that *all* the elements are somehow 'drawn towards the centre', including air and fire. He did not say that air and fire have lightness (κουφότης) but only that they have no weight. This is surely the answer to the Epicurean criticism that if air and fire are positively light, there is nothing to prevent them vanishing outwards into the infinite void. Zeno answered that they are not positively light: they occupy the outer regions of the spherical cosmos because they have no weight, whereas the middle is occupied by elements that have weight; but they do not fly off into outer space because there is no reason why they should, and they are joined continuously with the rest of the cosmos.

The evidence for this Stoic theory is of course confused. Stobaeus reports, as we saw, that according to Zeno air and fire are naturally centrifugal. This is not strictly true: if Zeno's theory was as we have just described it, it said that air and fire are neither centripetal nor centrifugal. But the confusion is easily explained: air and fire *are* naturally centrifugal compared with earth and water, and the Doxographers, unconscious of the importance of the distinction, might well forget that they are centrifugal only in the presence of earth and water.

We must dwell a little longer on the evidence for the Stoic theory, because its interpretation is not generally agreed yet. There are some more scrappy assertions of the Doxographers in *SVF*; but the key passage is a longish section of Plutarch's *De Stoicorum repugnantiis*. Two chapters are relevant.

In chapter 42 he asserts that Chrysippus held two contradictory views about air: he held both that it is centrifugal and light, and that it is neither heavy nor light. The significant thing is that Plutarch can quote chapter and verse for the latter, but he has to work hard for the former. He deduces it in fact from two propositions of Chrysippus: that fire, being weightless (not light), is naturally centrifugal, and that air is akin to it. Chrysippus, then, did not say that air and fire are light: if he had said so Plutarch could have had his contradiction without working for it. Chrysippus said that air and fire are weightless, and are therefore centrifugal when in the presence of earth and water.

In chapter 44 Plutarch asserts that Chrysippus held both that all bodies tend towards the centre of space (a concept that Lucretius attacks in our passage), and that space, being infinite, has no centre (which Lucretius accepts). Again, the significant thing is that he can quote chapter and verse for the latter, but needs a subtle argument to prove the former. Chrysippus, he says, asserted that nothing that is infinite has 'a beginning, a middle, or an end' (1054B). He often said it was impossible and contrary to nature to think that bodies naturally tend to the middle of space, because there is no difference in the void that would attract bodies to one place rather than to another; the cause of the centripetal motion, he said, is the arrangement of the cosmos. In other words Chrysippus was arguing for something like the Newtonian theory of gravity (as Professor Sambursky (1959) is quick to point out). His view was that all the matter in the universe has a natural tendency to congregate at its own centre. He went on to argue, as Plutarch and others tell us, that this centripetal tendency is responsible both for the durability of the cosmos and for its stable position in space. For the other half of the contradiction, namely that all matter tends towards the centre of *space*, Plutarch goes to a statement by Chrysippus that if matter were not arranged round the centre the cosmos would be destroyed. This would follow, says Plutarch, only if he were speaking of the centre of space. But Plutarch is wrong; what Chrysippus probably meant was that matter must be evenly distributed or balanced round its own centre: the cosmos would be liable to destruction if the orderly concentric arrangement of earth, water, air, and fire were somewhere disrupted. This is probably the sense of the passages in *SVF* that say that for Chrysippus the light and the heavy are in balance.

We may take it to be established, then, that in Chrysippus' cosmology the four elements were naturally centripetal, and that the centre in question was the centre of the four elements themselves taken as a whole, not the centre of the infinite void. There is no reason to think that any of the early Stoics dissented from this.

But this cosmology is obviously not the target of Lucretius' criticism, but the answer to it – and an answer totally ignored by Lucretius. The Epicureans say that it is nonsense to imagine there is a centre of everything, to which the heavy elements tend, because there is no centre in the infinite void; Chrysippus takes the point, and says that nevertheless the elements are centripetal; they tend to their own centre. The Epicureans say that if air and fire are centrifugal there is nothing to stop them flying away *ad infinitum*; Chrysippus answers that they are only relatively centrifugal, so that once they have reached the outside of the heavy elements there is no reason why they should go any further.

So we return to our question: whose is the cosmology attacked by Lucretius? The last-ditch defender of orthodoxy might reply that it is after all a Stoic cosmology, not that of Chrysippus, but of a later Stoic, say Panaetius or Posidonius. But the burden of proof has now shifted on to the defence; and there is no convincing evidence for a change in Stoic theory about these points.

If not the Stoics, then who? Aristotle is the obvious suggestion. Aristotle constructed the geocentric cosmology before the Stoics, and as everybody knows his theory of motion included the proposition that earth and water are centripetal and air and fire centrifugal. Moreover, the centre in question is defined as the centre of 'the whole' (*De caelo* II.14.296 b 13), and the Epicureans would naturally interpret this to mean everything that there is – on their own theory, the infinite void and the infinitely numerous atoms. Bignone (1936) suggested the Aristotelian theory as the target for Lucretius' criticisms years ago, in his lone but lengthy protest against the universal cry of Stoicism. But there are difficulties and obscurities that were not removed by Bignone, and it may be that we can improve the situation.

The main difficulty is this. If Lucretius' target was the cosmology of Aristotle, why is there no mention of Aristotle's triumphant innovation, the fifth body (or the first body, as he always calls it in the *De caelo*)? Not merely is there no mention of it, but it actually disarms one of Lucretius' criticisms from the start. Lucretius objects that if air and fire were centrifugal there would be nothing to prevent them from dispersing at large; but Aristotle's world was bounded by shells of aether, the fifth body, which was not centrifugal but had a natural tendency to move in a circle, so that fire would have no tendency to rise beyond its proper sphere. Again, Lucretius mentions as a feature of the rival theory that heat rising from the middle accounts for the sun's heat and the stars' brightness; but Aristotle explicitly rejects the proposition that the sun is nourished from the earth in his *Meteor.* 354 b 32 – 355 a 32. The fifth body, of which the sun and the stars and their spheres are made, is something quite different from the four elements at the centre of the cosmos. A third possible objection has already been dealt with. Lucretius criticizes the rival theory on the ground that there is nothing to hold the universe together in the infinite void; but Aristotle, unlike the Stoics, rejected the idea of an infinite void outside the cosmos (*De caelo* I.9.279 a 12). It has already been seen, however, that the infinite void is an Epicurean idea introduced into the criticism here. There is no need to suppose that it was a feature of the rival theory; Lucretius was not looking for internal inconsistencies.

On the subject of the fifth body, let us consider this question: was it always in antiquity taken to be a thesis universally held by Aristotle and his school, that the heavenly bodies are made of a fifth element, different from the other four, having a natural circular motion? This thesis is the main subject of Aristotle's *De caelo* I and II. It is well known to the Doxographers and to Cicero (*Academica* 1.7.26). It became one of the most famous, if not notorious, of all Aristotelian doctrines. Yet there is good evidence that he himself did not believe it all his life, and that his immediate pupils did not accept it.

It has often been observed that the *De caelo* theory of five elements does not appear in Aristotle's *Physics*. Sometimes this observation is explained by the supposition that Aristotle was simply limiting himself in the *Physics* to the study of the principles of nature in the sublunary world, and therefore felt free to say nothing about the fifth element. But there are passages particularly in books III and IV that seem to be incompatible with the five-element theory, not merely to be silent about it (see *Physics* III.5.205 a 10–19 and 205 b 24–8; IV.7.214 a 6–9).

What is more extraordinary, there are passages in the *De caelo* itself, in books III and IV, that are strangely difficult to reconcile with the five-element theory of books I and II. Professor Solmsen has drawn attention to these (1960, p. 299):

Is it mere pedantry [he asks] to expect that Aristotle, instead of saying 'of necessity each body has either a definite weight or a definite lightness', or 'the elements must be subject to generation and destruction', should say 'each body except the first', or 'the elements other than the aether'? (301 b 16 and 305 a 13). Patience is a virtue, and we may try to be patient with Aristotle's forgetfulness; but this forgetfulness goes astonishingly far when Aristotle asserts that there are 'no more than two simple local movements' (i.e. upward and downward) (303 b 5). And when we read that a body neither heavy nor light could move only by compulsion and would thereby be carried an infinite distance (302 a 20 – b 1), our patience is beginning to be overtaxed.

Quite so. The likeliest explanation appears to be that at the time when he wrote the *Physics* (perhaps excepting book VIII), and *De caelo* III and IV, Aristotle had not yet arrived at the theory of a fifth body having a natural circular motion. Presumably at this time he believed, like most of his predecessors, that the stars and planets were made of some kind of fire.

[Two paragraphs of the original are omitted here, and a little of the wording of the surrounding context has been changed, because I no longer (in 1988) believe I was justified in claiming that the Aristotelian dialogue *On philosophy* excluded the fifth element.]

At this point it should be added that Aristotle's pupils do not appear to have received his doctrine about the fifth body with much enthusiasm. There is certainly one testimony (Taurus, quoted by John Philoponus, *De aeternitate mundi* 520.18) that tells us that Theophrastus asserted that the stars are not made of fire and adds the explanation that he thought they are made of the fifth body. But the added explanation may well be wrong, as Steinmetz has suggested (1964, pp. 163–4); in the *De igne* 4–7, Theophrastus appears to dispense with the idea of the fifth body in what he says about the sun, and inclines to the view that the sun is made of a specially pure kind of fire. When we come to Strato, the Doxographer Aëtius tells us unequivocally that he believed the heavens to be made of fire (II.11.4 = Strato fragment 84 W).

So we can answer our question now. The doctrine of the fifth element was certainly regarded as a feature of Aristotelianism by the systematic scholars who studied the school-treatises, particularly after the time of Andronicus in the late first century B.C.; and it was vaguely known to Cicero. But it was not always a feature of the cosmology of the Aristotelian school; and the Epicureans may well have directed their criticisms against an Aristotelian cosmology that worked with four elements.

The last difficulty may now be examined more briefly. It is that Lucretius' polemic is against a theory that says that the stars and the sun are fed by the *calor* that rises from the middle of the universe, and that the growth of plants is in some way connected with this. Now there is abundant evidence that both of these are Stoic doctrines; and the former proposition was explicitly denied by Aristotle once he had formed the theory of the fifth element (*Meteor.* 354 b 32 – 355 a 32). Yet it may still be Aristotelian. Aristotle certainly believed in exhalations from the earth; he certainly thought that fire is nourished by moisture; if for a while he held that the sun and the stars are fiery, he may well have believed that they are kept going by warm moist exhalations. That is precisely the view for which Cicero's Stoic spokesman claims Aristotle's support in the *De natura deorum*. According to Stobaeus I.207.16ff it appears to have been the view of Theophrastus too. I have been unable to find anything significant about the theory of plant growth mentioned here. It appears to be presupposed by the pseudo-Aristotelian *De plantis* II; perhaps it was commonplace.

It must be concluded that in this passage Lucretius may well have had in mind the cosmology of the Peripatetic school. His target is certainly not any Stoic theory known to us. This negative conclusion is an important one, and strengthens the case presented in the rest of this article. For if Lucretius ever had the Stoic philosophy in mind as a rival to his own, he should have taken note of their characteristic modifications of the Aristotelian cosmology.

II.167–183. PROVIDENCE

This subject will be discussed in connection with v.55–234, below.

II.251–293. FREE WILL AND NECESSITY

In the *Letter to Menoeceus* 134, Epicurus wrote: κρεῖττον ἦν τῷ περὶ θεῶν μύθῳ κατακολουθεῖν ἢ τῇ τῶν φυσικῶν εἱμαρμένῃ δουλεύειν. Since εἱμαρμένη is a word commonly associated with the Stoics, it may be as well to consider briefly whether it was the Stoic concept that drew the fire of the Epicureans. The idea gets some support from a similarity, pointed out by Robin, between Lucretius' description of the concept and Stoic definitions of it. 'Si semper motus conectitur omnis ...' (Lucretius II.251); 'quamquam ita sit ut ... coacta atque conexa sint fato omnia' (Aulus Gellius VII.2.7, following Chrysippus); and many other Stoic texts in *SVF* II.912–27.

However, there is good ancient authority, accepted by most modern editors, for the view that Epicurus' target was Democritus. Cicero is one who took this view: 'Epicurus cum videret ... nil fore in nostra potestate, quod esset earum [sc. atomorum] motus certus et necessarius, invenit quo modo necessitatem effugeret, quod videlicet Democritum fugerat' (*ND* 1.69). The Epicurean Diogenes of Oenoanda was another: ἂν γὰρ τῷ Δημοκρίτου τις χρήσηται λόγῳ, μηδεμίαν μὲν ἐλευθέραν φάσκων ταῖς ἀτόμοις κείνησιν εἶναι κ.τ.λ. (fragment 33, col. 2.3). One may have doubts as to whether Democritus is truly represented as a believer in εἱμαρμένη, and whether perhaps the φυσικοί mentioned by Epicurus may not be some more recent Atomists. But it is certain that there is no good reason for bringing Stoicism into the picture. This was an Atomists' dilemma, made sharper by certain ethical and psychological theories of Aristotle (discussed further in the second of my *Two Studies*, Furley (1967b)).

II.886–972. THE ELEMENTS OF SENSATION

Epicurean atoms have shape, size, and weight, and they move in the void. They have no other properties. All sensible qualities are functions of compounds of atoms.

Lucretius demolishes several objections to this theory, including the assertion that the phenomena of life and sensation cannot be derivative but must be fundamental. What is it, he asks, that makes people think that a sentient creature cannot come from non-sentient elements? (II.886). It is the fact that stones and wood and earth when mixed are (apparently) unable to produce sensation. His answer is that his own theory does not entail that the elements that can produce sensation always do so; it all depends on the invisible shapes, motions, order, position, etc. of the elements. Even logs and sods can produce worms when they are sodden, though we cannot see the crucial rearrangement of elements that brings this about (886–901).

He moves on to a positive attack on the alternative hypothesis, which may take one of two forms: (a) that what is sentient is made of sentient elements. He objects to this that the sentient parts of the body are always soft, hence the sentient elements would necessarily be soft, and being soft they could not be permanently durable (902–6; this is a conjectural interpretation of a corrupt text). Grant, however, that they could be durable, the elements must have sensation either like that of a part or like that of the whole organism, and both alternatives are objectionable and unnecessary (907–30).

The other possibility is (b) that sensation arises out of non-sentient elements by a change in the elements, 'or by some birth, as it were'. Lucretius says the way to answer this suggestion is to show that change and birth are always functions of compounds, not of elements. He produces three arguments to show that this applies to sensation, but it is hardly necessary to review them here (931–72).

The passage ends with some fun at the expense of these hypotheses. If sensation entails sentient elements, why do laughing and crying not entail laughing and crying elements, and so on? (973–90).

There are thus two alternative theories attacked here: (a) that sentient creatures are made of permanently sentient elements, and (b) that they are made of elements that either change from non-sentient to sentient, or else are 'born'. The two alternatives are incompatible. Robin (Ernout and Robin 1925) observes that it would be vain to attribute the argument to particular opponents: 'mais il me paraît difficile de douter que ces adversaires ne soient pas les Stoïciens, dont le matérialisme vitaliste s'oppose si nettement au matérialisme mécaniste des Epicuriens' (1.332). Munro, Giussani, and Bailey find a Stoic theory only in (b); Bailey sees the whole section apart from (b) as directed against Anaxagoras' theory of Homoeomereity.

The position of the editors seems particularly incomprehensible here. Lucretius is arguing defensively throughout the passage. He asserts that immutably non-sentient atoms can and do produce sentient compounds. If this assertion is false, then sentient beings are produced either from immutably sentient elements, or by the appearance of sentient elements where none had been before. He strengthens his own assertion by pointing out weaknesses in both of the logically possible alternatives. Hence there is no need to imagine that these alternatives were in fact the property of any particular schools. The words which introduce (a), 'ex sensilibus qui sensile posse creari constituunt', suggest particular adherents; on the other hand the introduction to the allegedly Stoic alternative (b) does not: 'quod si forte aliquis dicet ...' Bailey has to hedge a little: '*aliquis* will then be some Stoic writer, or possibly in view of the fut. *dicet* one of his own followers'.

What is alleged by Munro, Giussani, and Bailey to be a Stoic doctrine is that sensation arises either by a change out of the non-sentient or by 'some birth, as it were'. Munro quoted Plutarch, *SR* 1052f, according to which the embryo was said to grow in the womb like a plant, but when it was born the *pneuma* was cooled and hardened and thus changed into an animal. But this is about compounds, and is very nearly compatible with the Epicurean view. Considered as an element, the Stoic *pneuma*, as the enduring *logos spermatikos*, was more like the immutably sentient element of Lucretius' first alternative than the mutating element of the second. Giussani and Bailey rightly reject Munro's citation, but they put nothing whatever in its place. The alleged Stoic theory of the 'birth' of sentient elements, Giussani admits, is an 'obscure and fantastic theory of which we know of no other testimony'. There is no trace in Lucretius of the Stoic 'tension' doctrine, which Bailey mentions, and no evidence in the Stoic texts for the doctrine of the production of sentient particles, which he finds in Lucretius and attributes to the Stoics. It seems to be nothing but determined prejudice that finds a reference to Stoicism here.

III.307–322. CHARACTER AND PHILOSOPHY

Lucretius argues that since the soul is made of three different elements, and since the proportions of the elements make a difference to temperament, it follows that differences in temperament are to some extent given by nature. But *ratio*, by which he means the Epicurean philosophy, can eliminate all but the merest traces of these differences, so that there is nothing to prevent any man living a life worthy of the gods.

These lines, Munro says, 'have pointed reference to the great stoical doctrine of the perfect apathy of the wise or good man: Lucretius concedes much to philosophy and reason; but will not allow that they efface all distinctions of natural character'.

But this is to mistake Lucretius' emphasis. He is saying that philosophy *can* rectify deficiencies of temperament, not entirely, but for all practical purposes; we may be naturally as timid as deer, or as hot-tempered as lions, or as placid as cows, but if we read Epicurus we can all become as rationally calm as a true Epicurean. There is no reference to any Stoic doctrine here, nor to any other rival theory.

III.350–369. THE SOUL, THE BODY, AND SENSATION

The question is whether the body or only the soul has sensation. The Epicurean doctrine is that the body has sensation, though only when in conjunction with soul. A particular application of this question concerns the faculty of sight: do our eyes see, or does the mind see through the eyes as if through an open doorway? Lucretius argues against the latter alternative.

The whole section is said to be anti-Stoic by Bailey (1051–2). There is good evidence that the Stoics did hold that the soul alone has sensation, in Cicero, *Tusculans* I.46, where the sense-organs are described as 'windows of the mind', and in other passages collected in *SVF* II.850, 857–8, 861–2. But the doctrine was not regarded in antiquity as being peculiar to the Stoics. Sextus attributes it to Heraclitus, comparing the sense-organs to windows (*Adv. Math.* VII.129–30), and also to Strato (*ibid.* 350). It is possible that the Epicureans might have regarded themselves as differing from Democritus on this point, though owing to the obscurity of Democritus' theory it is hard to be sure. There is evidence that he spoke of the sense-organs as being (or having?) πόροι, which are not so very different from Lucretius' 'doors'. Lucretius criticizes Democritus by name in the section immediately following.

Whatever may be the truth about the earlier Atomists, however, it is clear that this text presents no compelling reason for thinking that the Stoics were in the forefront of Lucretius' mind.

III.425–829. THE SURVIVAL OF THE SOUL

It is claimed by Bailey (p. 1065) that Lucretius' arguments against the immortal soul are in part directed against the Stoics.

In general, however, the Stoics were not much interested in the after-life. Emotionally, as Max Pohlenz observes (1947, pp. 93, 199), they were *Diesseits-menschen*. It is unlikely therefore that Lucretius' passionate attack on ideas of survival after death would be construed by his readers as an attack on Stoicism, when there were more obvious targets, such as the Platonists and Pythagoreans. Moreover, the Stoics (with some exceptions) believed the soul to survive only for a limited time. In the doxographical tradition, Zeno and Chrysippus count as upholders of the *mortal* soul (*SVF* 1.146; 11.774). But there are no traces in Lucretius of an attack on this theory of limited survival, and his language sometimes makes it clear that he had in mind only two possibilities: either the soul loses its identity at death, or it is immortal (III.830–1).

Posidonius seems to have been an exception to the general rule that the Stoics were not much interested in the after-life, according to Pohlenz (1947, pp. 229–30). But he too accepted that the soul survives only until the *ekpyrosis*, and Lucretius does not seem to be concerned with any of the peculiarities of Posidonius' eschatology, such as the connection between the soul and the sun, and the collection of souls in the region of *pneuma* close to the moon.

III.847–861. REBIRTH

Death is nothing to us, since the soul is mortal; we shall not feel anything more after our death than we felt of the Punic War before our birth. Even if our soul *can* feel something after its separation from the body, this will be nothing to us, since we are precisely a combination of soul *and* body. Even if the same matter that now composes our soul and body is fortuitously reassembled some time, it will be nothing to us, since our memory will not be continuous. Indeed, this has probably already happened, since time past is infinite; but we do not remember.

Rebirth was a Stoic idea (*SVF* 1.109; 11.623, 627); but it is not necessary to labour the point that it was not peculiar to the Stoics. There is no reason to doubt that the Epicureans were thinking of the Pythagoreans, Plato, and perhaps early Aristotle. What was characteristic of the Stoic doctrine was that after the *ekpyrosis* the world was supposed to be reconstituted in exactly the same form, with all the same people and the same history. Lucretius could have had some fun at the expense of this doctrine. But he did not.

IV.823–857. TELEOLOGY

The Stoics were enthusiastic about final causes, as Balbus' speech in Cicero's *ND* II shows. More will be said about this subject in the next section. The passage now under discussion is less crucial, because no one doubts that the argument here is equally appropriate to Aristotle's teleology (Bailey indeed says it is more probable that it is directed against the Stoics, but he gives no reason for thinking so). The present passage is entirely concerned with the 'intrinsic' teleology that is characteristic of Aristotle's philosophy of nature: that is, the doctrine that the parts of an organism are to be explained by the good that they contribute by their function to the whole organism. Thus Aristotle asserts precisely what Lucretius denies here, that eyes are for the sake of seeing, legs are for the sake of walking, etc. It should be added also, what the editors seem to have overlooked, that all Lucretius' examples occur in another Prestoic text, namely the teleological argument put into Socrates' mouth by Xenophon in *Memorab*. 1.4: eyes for seeing (§5), legs for walking (§11), hands as tools (§11), tongue for speaking (§12), ears for hearing (§5). No doubt they were all commonplace.

v.55–234. GODS AND THE WORLD

Lucretius announces that he will now describe how the world came into being and will perish, how life originated, and speech, and fear of the gods. He will also describe the operations of the sun and the moon, lest anyone should think that they move of their own free will in order to make the crops and the animals grow, and lest we should think they move according to a plan of the gods. People tend to forget that the gods live free from all toil and trouble, and when they do so, then the mystery of the heavens tends to bring back all their old fears again (v.55–90).

He then asserts that the cosmos and all its parts will perish one day. Perhaps you have religious scruples, and believe that the earth and sun, and all the parts of the cosmos are divine and eternal, and that to doubt it is to repeat the sin of the Giants against the immortals. But in fact the heavenly bodies are a sort of paradigm case of what is inanimate and insensitive, because they have entirely the wrong kind of body. A tree cannot grow in the sky, nor clouds in salt water, nor fish in the fields, nor blood in wood nor sap in stones. So the soul or mind needs a body that consists of sinews and blood: it cannot even exist throughout the human body, let alone outside it. Hence it is quite impossible that the stars should have souls. Moreover the true nature of the gods is such that their abode must be different from this world (v.91–155).

Lucretius continues with several arguments against the thesis that the world exists for the benefit of man and therefore men ought to praise the work of the gods and recognize that it is immortal (v.156–234).

The main purpose of this passage, as described by Lucretius, is to attack the view that the cosmos is the work of the gods and is eternal (110–16). He wishes to substitute for this view the Epicurean theory that the cosmos is a natural growth, having a natural origin and end. If one thing is certain about his target, it is that it cannot be 'doubtless the Stoics', as Munro carelessly thought. For the Stoics, although they believed the cosmos to be the work of the gods, agreed with the Epicureans that it had a beginning and will have an end. This was pointed out very clearly by Robin, Bignone, and others, so that there would be no need to say much more about it if Bailey had not inexcusably glossed over everything they said on the subject. 'It is true', says Bailey's commentary (p. 1346), 'that the Stoics believed in the ultimate *ekpyrosis* of the world, but that was not held by them all, and in any case was so far distant that it did not interfere with a practical idea of its immortality.'

This is just nonsense. The traditional Hellenistic picture of Stoicism and Aristotelianism contrasted them sharply on this point. Even Cicero, who omits a Peripatetic philosopher from the team in *De natura deorum*, on the ground that the Stoic can speak for the Peripatetic as well, knows well enough that they do not agree about this doctrine. 'When your Stoic wise man has spelled all this out syllable by syllable', he says in the *Lucullus* 119, meaning by 'this' the doctrine of the World Soul and *ekpyrosis*, 'Aristotle will come, with a golden stream of oratory, to say that he is crazy: the world never had a beginning ... and will never collapse and die.'

So much is clear. The champions of the eternal cosmos were not Stoics but Aristotelians. But the immortality of the world is only one of several elements in the cosmology attacked by Lucretius in this long passage. Are all the elements Aristotelian?

One of the elements is this: the arrangement of the heavens is the work of the gods, and to doubt the eternity of the arrangement is to repeat the impiety of the Giants. This is certainly Aristotelian. Cicero's translation of Aristotle's cave simile, in *ND* 11.95–6, is famous: if there were people who had lived all their lives in well-appointed subterranean caves and were at last released to the earth's surface, when they saw the beauty and the regularity of the cosmos they would conclude at once that the gods exist and that these great works are the works of gods. Philo tells us that Aristotle condemned the frightful atheism of those who denied the eternity of the cosmos. Both quotations are probably from Aristotle's dialogue *On philosophy* (they are fragments 13 and 18 Ross).

Another element is that the heavenly bodies are living creatures, having a soul or mind. Again, this is certainly Aristotelian. Moreover, Cicero's quotation from Aristotle, probably again from *On philosophy* (it is printed as fragment 21 by Ross), shows a close connection with Lucretius' argument that is unlikely to be coincidence. Aristotle argues by analogy: earth produces its creatures, so does water, and so does air; so the fourth element, which is best adapted of them all to produce life, must have its living creatures too – and they must be the stars. Lucretius turns the analogy against him: as a matter of fact, he says, what we see is that life occurs in strictly limited conditions, and the analogy of the elements shows how *un*likely it is that the stars should be alive.

But there are several elements that are more doubtful. Lucretius argues against three propositions that most people would at once say are not Aristotelian: that the gods created the cosmos (156, 161, 174ff), that they planned its organization (80–1, etc.), and that it is organized for the benefit of mankind (80, 156ff). These three propositions are also attacked earlier in the poem (11.167–76).

Aristotle's position on these points is not free from ambiguity. It is clear that there was a certain tension in his thinking about the relation between god or gods and the world order. At his most austere, as everyone knows, he left no room at all for divine providence or planning: the divine movers of the spheres bear no relation to the spheres except that of continually provoking them to move, and they bear no relation to the changing sublunary world, the world of mortals, except that of maintaining the cycle of birth and death through the intermediary of the sun's motions, and possibly that of being objects of remote admiration.

Nevertheless, Aristotle's cosmos as a whole was dependent on the divine movers for its continued orderly existence; and it was hard for him and his supporters to describe this dependence without using language that suggested a closer, more anthropomorphic relation. This is very clearly to be seen in the pseudo-Aristotelian *De mundo*; and it was almost certainly a feature of the dialogue *On philosophy*. There is evidence of the same mode of thought scattered over the Corpus Aristotelicum. 'God and nature do nothing pointlessly' is an epitome of the attitude that Lucretius wants to criticize.

Solmsen (1951) and De Lacy (1948) have both recently defended the view that it was Chrysippus who expounded a cosmology in which man was the focus of all the teleological processes of nature, and therefore Lucretius in this passage must be fighting on his own account against the Stoics, not repeating Epicurus' polemic against the Aristotelians. I dispute this. Even in Aristotle's school-treatises, there are signs here and there of an anthropocentric teleology, notably in a well-known passage in *Politics* I.8: Aristotle concluded there that nature must have made plants and animals for the sake of man. (I am not convinced by Wieland's attempt (1962, p. 275) to set this aside: 'Denn hier geht es nicht um Naturphilosophie, sondern um die praktische Frage danach, wie sich der Mensch in der Welt einrichtet und von den Dingen dieser Welt Gebrauch macht.' It seems to me on the contrary that Aristotle's purpose in *Politics* I is to show that the *polis* is a society that is produced by nature – and by a nature that transcends human nature.) There is certainly more to be said about this point, but it must be reserved for another place. It has usually been believed that Stoic teleology was universal and anthropocentric, whereas Aristotle's was limited and specific. It can be argued that the difference was not so clear-cut after all, and that Aristotle may have come close to the Stoic position in some of the books, now lost, that he wrote for a wider public.

It cannot, however, be supposed that Aristotle ever defended the thesis that the gods created the world. It is well known that this was a subject on which he differed from Plato. He interpreted the *Timaeus* literally, as meaning a creation of the cosmos by a god, and he attacked it on this basis. Aristotle's position was well known in the Hellenistic world, too; this was not one of those doctrines that were submerged for a time and then rediscovered.

One wonders, nevertheless, how Aristotle treated this subject in *On philosophy*. Many scholars (for example Bignone (1936), II.525ff, and Untersteiner (1963), xxii) believe that Plato was a spokesman in the dialogue. It is doubtful whether this is so, but it is a more plausible thesis that Plato was a spokesman treated with respect and a large measure of agreement by Aristotle than that he was just an Aunt Sally. Most of the cosmological arguments drawn by our sources from the dialogue aim to prove that the cosmos is the work of gods and will last for ever, a point on which Plato and Aristotle agreed. It is possible that the question of its origin, which divided Aristotle from Plato (at least according to Aristotle's interpretation of Plato), was not pressed. The so-called fragments of the dialogue, collected by Ross, contain both an argument against the creation of the world (it is fragment 20, and it is actually the same argument as that used by Lucretius v. 168–73), and arguments to show that the world must be the work of a craftsman (fragments 12a and 12b, from Sextus). So it is just possible that the Epicureans regarded the dialogue as *the* major authority on Platonic–Aristotelian cosmology.

Bignone (1936, II.429) and others have written that the target of Lucretius' polemic against the creation of the world is Plato's *Timaeus*. I would rather say that it is no single work, nor any single philosopher, but a group of philosophers whom the Epicureans regarded, rightly, as their main opponents. Most of the elements attacked in Lucretius v. 55–234 are contained in the speech given to Socrates in Xenophon's *Memorab.* I.4; most of them can be found in Plato, in the *Phaedo* 96cff, in the *Timaeus*, the *Phil.* 28cff, and the *Laws* 889A–899D; most of them can be found in Aristotle's works of natural philosophy, and were probably to be found in his lost dialogue *On philosophy*. All of them can be found in all of these texts taken together. There is nothing that must be Stoic, and one major element that cannot be Stoic.

v.306–350. THE MORTALITY OF THE COSMOS

After his polemic against the eternal cosmos of the Aristotelian world picture, Lucretius offers positive arguments for the contrary view. The parts of the cosmos are mortal: hence the whole is mortal (235–46). The mortality of each of the four cosmic masses is defended (247–305). Then follows a series of subsidiary arguments, in which references to Stoicism have been seen.

First comes a straightforward, though oddly placed, reminder that nothing is so hard that it endures for ever. Next a strange argument to this effect: if the surrounding sky, as some say, gives birth to all things and receives them back again when they perish, then the whole world including the sky must be mortal; for anything that causes other things to grow must itself be diminished thereby, and it must be restored when it receives them back again (318–23).

Giussani sees in this a reference to the Stoic doctrine of *ekpyrosis*, according to which the world is assumed into the surrounding fire and then reborn from it. The Stoics believed the fire to be immortal; against them Lucretius asserts that its mortality must follow from its changeability. Giussani's view is followed, with differing degrees of emphasis, by Robin and Bailey.

The editors point out that there is a clear reference to Pacuvius' *Chryses*; indeed the verbal echoes are so close as to place this beyond doubt. The editors assume that Lucretius is aiming at the Stoics through Pacuvius – but this is no more than an assumption. There is *nothing* in the Lucretius passage that is not in Pacuvius, and not much that is distinctively Stoic in Pacuvius. If Lucretius intended a serious attack on Stoic doctrine, it must be admitted that he chose a strangely oblique approach.

If the world had no origin, Lucretius continues, why does history not go back beyond the Trojan War? Why are some of the arts still in their infancy? If you import fires or earthquakes or floods to explain this forgetfulness, you will have to concede that the same type of catastrophe will eventually destroy the world completely (324–50).

Later on, Lucretius returns to the same theme, in arguing that the balance of the strife of opposites will not always be maintained (380ff). Legend says that fire was once supreme, when Phaethon drove across the world, until Jupiter enabled Phoebus to control the sun-chariot once more (of course, the supremacy of fire, if and when it happened, would have a quite different explanation really); and that water once overwhelmed the lives of men (392–415).

Some have found references to the Stoic theory of *ekpyrosis* again here. What is remarkable, however, is how *little* it is concerned with the Stoics. The theory of periodic catastrophes is of course an old one; it is as old as Plato's *Tim.* 22C, where fire, coupled with the name of Phaethon, and flood are mentioned, and it probably found a place in Aristotle's *On philosophy* (fragment 8 Ross). The Stoic theory of *ekpyrosis* was a notable contribution to this line of speculation – yet Lucretius, when he wants an example of the triumph of fire, goes to the legend of Phaethon, who does not appear in the Stoic fragments. It seems that Lucretius might never have heard of Stoicism.

CONCLUSION

There is no single instance in these passages of Lucretius of an attack that is certainly aimed at the Stoics and could not be aimed at another school of philosophy, at several other schools, or at no school at all. Where it is clear that the attack is upon the theories of natural philosophers, rather than upon the commonplace beliefs of most men, Lucretius turns his attention to the Presocratics or the Platonists and Aristotelians. Some of the views he attacks were held by the Stoics as well as others, but we have found no reason to think that the attack has special reference to the Stoics in these cases. It may be suggested that although no particular passages can be assigned with certainty to the Stoics the case is cumulative: Lucretius attacks theories held by the Stoics in common with others – but only the Stoics held all of them, and therefore they must be the real target. But this suggestion will not stand up to examination. The accumulation of evidence points to the natural philosophy of the Platonists and Aristotelians, rather than to the Stoics. Moreover there are cases that we have pointed out where the Stoic theory is certainly and significantly ignored; I.1052–113 and V.55–234 are the most important of these.

Lucretius took very little notice of the Stoics. I believe this is a conclusion of great importance for the history of natural philosophy. It is not a new conclusion, because it was understood by the philosophers and scientists of the seventeenth and eighteenth centuries. This may well have been because they did not examine the question with the same apparatus of learning that was later employed, but whatever the reason for it, the position of Lucretius was properly appreciated at the beginning of the scientific renaissance, and has been obscured by the mistakes of the last hundred years.

For there was a major battle in ancient natural philosophy – a battle that rumbled on into the eighteenth century. There were two sides, opposed to each other (in a quite literal sense) *toto caelo*. One side consisted of the Atomists, the other side of Plato and Aristotle and their adherents. They differed from each other in that they took contradictory stands on a number of inter-related points.

The Atomists held a discontinuous theory of matter, the Aristotelians believed in a continuum. The Atomists believed in an infinite universe, the Aristotelians in a finite one. The Atomists believed in plural and perishable worlds, the Aristotelians in a single and eternal one. The Atomists tried to explain the origins of living species, the Aristotelians said they are eternal. The Atomists believed in gods who are unconcerned with the cosmos, the Aristotelians believed the cosmos to be dependent on gods. The Atomists believed in mechanical and random causes, the Aristotelians in teleology.

In the Hellenistic world, the Epicureans represented the opposition to the Aristotelian world picture. The Stoics were relatively unimportant in this struggle. They adopted most things from Aristotle; their innovations were on the whole irrelevant and retrogressive. Their characteristic theories – *ekpyrosis* and the exact, predetermined repetition of the cosmic cycle, their crude substitution of the active and passive kinds of matter for Aristotle's εἶδος and ὕλη, their materialistic account of qualities, their extreme pantheism, and its corollary, divination – these are unproductive digressions.

Lucretius, if I am right, ignored them. Wisely, or perhaps just luckily, he avoided these side issues and concentrated his fire on the main enemy: *De rerum natura* is the Atomists' answer to the Aristotelian world picture.[1]

---

[1] [Later note: The thesis of this chapter has been examined in some detail by J. Schmidt, *Lukrez und die Stoiker, Quellenuntersuchungen zu De rerum natura* (Diss. Marburg/Lahn, 1975.]

17

LUCRETIUS THE EPICUREAN,
ON THE HISTORY OF MAN

[1978]

I propose to distinguish two senses of the word 'Epicurean': (1) one who subscribes to the doctrines of Epicurus; (2) a follower of Epicurus.[1]

A distinction hardly worth making, perhaps? On the contrary, there is an important point in it. To be an Epicurean in the first sense is an attribute shared by both Epicurus and Lucretius; but Lucretius was, while Epicurus was not, an Epicurean in the second sense. If we seek to understand the individual philosophical personality of the Latin poet, it may well be useful to concentrate on something that unquestionably distinguishes him from his master. At any rate, in the hope that this is so I shall focus attention in this chapter, not on comparisons between Epicurus' and Lucretius' philosophical arguments, treated timelessly, but on Lucretius' sense of himself and his readers as followers of Epicurus.

I shall begin with a short discussion of what seem to me the difficulties and hazards of other approaches to Lucretius the Epicurean.

In the first place, it is perfectly obvious, although often temporarily forgotten, that Lucretius had access to much more of the written work of Epicurus than we have. If we seize upon some nuance, in the exposition of a piece of doctrine, that appears to differentiate Lucretius from the *Letter to Herodotus*, we must always try to rest content with frustrating conditionals, because we do not know whether Epicurus wrote with the same emphasis and the same tone in his book *On nature*.[2] There is no need to say more about this.

There is plainly more hope, if we wish to compare Lucretius with Epicurus doctrinally, in fixing upon intellectual developments that belong without any doubt to the two and a half centuries between Epicurus and Lucretius. If we can find Lucretius defending an attitude to such developments, then clearly his defence could not have been learnt directly from Epicurus, and we can begin to

---

[1] I believe the original stimulus for this chapter, which I acknowledge gratefully, came from an essay contributed to one of my graduate seminars by Dr Gregory Staley.
[2] Cf. William E. Leonard, in his General Introduction to the Leonard and Smith edition of Lucretius (1965), 32: 'The very different temperament of Epicurus, so imperturbable and unimaginative, so self-secure beyond debate or boast ... ' How does he know?

collect evidence that might reveal Lucretius' own enrichment of Epicurean doctrine.

The most significant feature in the history of philosophy in this period was the rise of Stoicism. Although Epicurus lived and taught in Athens alongside Zeno's school for many years, his philosophical doctrines appear to have been worked out before he came to Athens, and no one will suggest that Zeno was a major factor in their formation. Of developments of Stoicism by Cleanthes and Chrysippus, of course, he knew nothing. On the other hand, Lucretius wrote at a time when Stoic literature was extensive, Stoic doctrines were well known to the literate world, and to a great extent Stoicism had displaced the Academy and the Peripatos from the position of authority that they held in the time of Epicurus. If Lucretius, then, could be shown to respond precisely to Stoic positions, to show knowledge of Stoic arguments, and to frame reasoned replies to them, that would be a fairly reliable proof that he advanced beyond the position of Epicurus.

If one asks what were the peculiar physical doctrines of the Stoics – doctrines not shared by the fourth-century Academy and Peripatos – those which come to mind at once are the periodic conflagration of the cosmos and its rebirth out of the fire, the fiery creative *pneuma* that permeates everything in the cosmos, the special kind of mixture (κρᾶσις δι' ὅλου) exemplified by the permeation of *pneuma*, the tension (τόνος) imparted by the *pneuma* that gives each thing its individuality, the 'seminal formula' or 'spermatic reason' (σπερματικὸς λόγος) that accounts for the generation of each new thing, and fate. I cannot find any passage in Lucretius where one of these doctrines receives special attention.[3] If we turn to ethical questions, the list of characteristic Stoic doctrines would, I suppose, include the 'indifferents' (ἀδιάφορα), the equality of vices, the intellectual interpretation of the emotions, and the 'apathy' of the wise man. Again, I can find nothing in Lucretius that takes particular notice of these peculiarities. Lucretius' editors and commentators commonly point to particular passages of the poem with the claim that 'no doubt' he had the Stoics particularly in mind here. But on examination it appears that these passages always may, and often must, be directed at other targets.[4]

If the Stoics will not serve as a touchstone for testing Lucretius' use of his philosophical legacy from Epicurus, are there not other intellectual advances, post-Epicurean but pre-Lucretian, that might serve the purpose? The special sciences made great strides in this period, and one might perhaps expect Lucretius to take some notice of the astronomy of Eratosthenes, Hipparchus, or Archimedes, or of the physiology of Herophilus and Erasistratus, or of other similar work. In fact, we find no clear evidence in Lucretius of any acquaintance with this work. Lucretius seems to take more notice of Presocratic theories than of Hellenistic ones. The

---

[3] The doctrine of fate might appear to be an exception, because of Lucretius, *De rerum natura* II.251–93. I have tried to argue that the philosophical background of this passage is Aristotelian, rather than Stoic, in Furley (1967b), part 2.

[4] See chapter 16, where I have attempted to argue this in detail.

sixth book of *De rerum natura* evidently uses material from earlier meteorology –
but the closest connections seem to be with no one later than Theophrastus.[5]
Although the subject of astronomy – or rather of astrophysics – was important to
Epicureans, for obvious reasons, their attitude to astronomical science was
cavalier. The study of v.416–770 shows Lucretius to be a good poet and a good
Epicurean, but it does not throw any special light on the nature of his
Epicureanism.

I turn now to the main subject of this paper – to Lucretius the Epicurean in the
second sense.

It needs no long argument to show that Lucretius was indeed conscious of the
philosophical activity of Epicurus as an event in history.

> humana ante oculos foede cum vita iaceret
>
> ...
>
> *primum* Graius homo mortalis tollere contra
> est oculos ausus, primusque obsistere contra.

(1.62–7)

In just the same way, in the lines that Lucretius imitates here, Empedocles picked
out a particular event (the philosophical activity of Pythagoras, according to the
ancient source) as crucial to the growth of understanding:

> ἦν δέ τις ἐν κείνοισιν ἀνὴρ περιώσια εἰδώς ...

(D–K 31B.129)

At the beginning of book III, Lucretius reiterates the same theme:

> E tenebris tantis tam clarum extollere lumen
> qui *primus* potuisti inlustrans commoda vitae
> te sequor, o Graiae gentis decus ...

And again, climactically, at the beginning of book v (8–10):

> dicendum est, deus ille fuit, deus, inclute Memmi,
> qui *princeps* vitae rationem invenit eam quae
> nunc appellatur sapientia ...

There was a time *before*, when human life was tainted with fear and greed, then
came the teaching of Epicurus, and now *we* – Lucretius, Memmius, and all of
mankind – have been taught the wisdom (if we will listen to it) that will enable us
to live in peace and purity of mind.

Now, when Lucretius expounds the tenets of Epicurean Atomism, about the
elements of the physical world, or cosmology, or even morality, there may well be
no particular significance in the chronological distance between himself and
Epicurus. But there is one context in which it can hardly fail to be significant:
namely, in the long account, at the end of book v, of the *history* of human
civilization. It would have been difficult for Epicurus to view himself and his work

---

[5] See Reitzenstein (1924), and the Appendix to book VI in Bailey (1947).

as a point of discontinuity between earlier and later time. At least, if Epicurus made such a claim for himself (and there is no evidence that he did), he plainly could not make it with the same air of proclaiming a *fact* – a piece of good news – with which Lucretius invests it. Epicurus rarely refers to himself in the first person singular in the extant letters when he is expounding his philosophy; in the introductions, where he does refer to himself, he seems to me to adopt the tone of one who seeks for the truth along with his readers. There is, of course, a well-known tradition that Epicurus was the most ungenerous of all Greek philosophers in his treatment of his predecessors, and went to great lengths to dissociate himself from all 'influences'. But this tradition itself rests on shaky ground, and it seems to me to have been grossly exaggerated by the commentators.[6] The tradition rests very largely on Diogenes Laertius x.7–8, where the tales of Epicurus' rudeness about other philosophers are retailed along with other tales that Diogenes explicitly declares to be slanders on Epicurus; and Diogenes follows with the remark: 'But all these people [sc. who tell these tales] are crazy, since there are abundant witnesses to Epicurus' unsurpassed kindness to all men.' Moreover, where the slanders can be checked, they get no confirmation. 'Run away from all *paideia*' is quoted from 'the Letter to Pythocles', but it cannot be found in the extant *Letter*. 'Lerocritus' is said to be Epicurus' contemptuous nickname for Democritus, but this contempt finds no expression in the *Letter to Herodotus*. The evidence does not suggest that Epicurus himself claimed to be a divinely inspired prophet with a totally new message.

Lucretius, however, committed himself to such a view of Epicurus, in the passages quoted above, and thereby found himself confronted with a problem, if he was to save his consistency in his account of the development of human civilization. Following Epicurus' own doctrine, he must explain the history of man as a continuous development, wholly dependent on natural causes, from the first natural growth of men from the earth to contemporary civilizations. The important thing will be to eliminate the need for supernatural breaks in the continuity, so as to combat rival theories involving a δημιουργός or νομοθέτης. But then the happy condition of the Epicurean community, accessible to all mankind if they will only listen, needs precisely this to explain it – a break-away from previous history, produced by a kind of νομοθέτης, Epicurus himself.

To put it another way, Lucretius must show that the well-known achievements of mankind – the progressive stages of technology, political and social institutions, and so on – were learnt from nature.[7] But he must bear in mind all the time that nature *uninterpreted* or wrongly interpreted produces not Epicurean enlightenment, but only the impoverished and darkened mentality of pre-Epicurean society. As he puts it himself in a phrase that he liked well enough to use four times, the pre-Epicurean terror and darkness of mind must be dispersed by *naturae species*

---

[6] For example, Bailey (1928), 226. For a detailed criticism of the tradition, see Sedley (1976).
[7] There was of course a long tradition of imaginative histories of the development of man, beginning perhaps as far back as Anaxagoras. For bibliography and a recent account, see Cole (1967).

ratioque (1.146–8, 11.59–61, 111.91–3, VI.39–41) – that is, by looking at nature *and interpreting it*. The commentators have not always seen the point of this fully. Bailey's translation 'the outer view and the inner law of nature' does not quite get it right, and his analysis in the note on 1.51 does not justify the translation. Giussani (1896–8) glosses the word *ratio* with φυσιολογία, which is correct, and Ernout (Ernout and Robin, 1925) quotes Cicero *Fin.* 1.19.63: *omnium autem rerum natura cognita levamur superstitione, liberamur mortis metu, non conturbamur ignoratione rerum*, where the word *cognita* makes the right point.

That is not to say, of course, that Lucretius was committed to the idea of an *opposition* between the tendencies of nature and the doctrines of Epicurus. The relationship is a good deal more subtle than that. Epicurean doctrine is not unnatural or anti-natural – and of course not supernatural: *deus ille fuit* is not to be taken literally. Nature without Epicurean interpretation taught mankind how to make clothes, fires, metals, language, cities, music; and the Epicurean is not required to reject any of these things. What, then, is inadequate about nature's teaching? Chiefly, it may be that it is *endlessly* suggestive. Man is apt to pick up from nature a line of progress, without picking up the realization that the line has an end, or, to change the metaphor, that although one may continue along the same path, at a certain point one ceases to climb and starts going downhill. Thus the invention of metals is good in that it provides man with a means of security against wild beasts, but bad when it leads to a greed for gold.

Epicurus' understanding of nature, according to Lucretius, was superior in just this, that he understood the *limits* of things:

> atque omne immensum peragravit mente animoque,
> unde refert nobis victor quid possit oriri,
> quid nequeat, finita potestas denique cuique
> quanam sit ratione atque alte terminus haerens.

(1.74–7)

Nature herself is given a voice by Lucretius to protest at being misinterpreted by men who believe that life offers a *limitless* variety of pleasures:

> nam tibi praeterea quod machiner inveniamque,
> quod placeat, nihil est: eadem sunt omnia semper.

(III.944–5)

Nature speaks, and with an Epicurean accent. The good Epicurean *interprets* the message of nature. There is no clash of motives between nature and Epicurus, but nature needed the life and work of Epicurus to make its message clear.

If this idea is right, then we can conclude at once that the question so often posed about Lucretius' history of civilization, 'primitivist or progressivist?', is quite beside the point. It could hardly be, for him, either a matter of a 'natural' decline from a primitive golden age, or of a progression to higher and higher levels of prosperity and happiness. What we would expect, rather, is a step-by-step account of the growth of civilization with a mainly negative emphasis – to show that *no* step requires supernatural agencies for its explanation – together with Epicurean reflections about the spiritual impoverishment of any or perhaps each of the stages.

Let us probe a little more deeply into what we might expect of Lucretius in this situation, first stating our hypothesis somewhat more exactly.

It is, first, that Lucretius found in the writings of Epicurus an account of the growth of the institutions of human civilization, following upon the description of the origin of life on earth. It hardly needs to be proved that Epicurus would interest himself in this topic, in view of the clear indications that it had long been a point of contention between those who believed the world had an origin, like Anaxagoras and Democritus, and supporters of an eternal cosmos, like Aristotle. But in any case the very brief account in *Letter to Herodotus* 75–6 is proof enough. Some, like Giussani and Bailey, believed that a fuller version of Epicurus' theory is to be found in Diodorus Siculus 1.7–8, but this belief had already been shown to be dubious by Reinhardt, and it looks still more threadbare after Cole's careful analysis.[8] If we cannot use Diodorus to fill out our picture of Epicurus' theory, we must make the most of the slight indications that we find in the *Letter to Herodotus*.

'One is to assume', says Epicurus, 'that nature itself was instructed and constrained as to many and various matters by the very facts (ὑπ᾽ αὐτῶν τῶν πραγμάτων), and that reasoning later sharpened up and added further discoveries to the lessons passed on by nature, in some matters more quickly and in some more slowly' (*Letter* 75).

The first point that receives special emphasis here is that the opening move is accomplished by the sheer physical interaction between man and the environment: this is what provides the material for human reason to work on. With this simple move, Epicurus countered three different rival theories. There is, first, the naive idea that an Athena or a Hermes made a gift of the arts to man – the idea that is explicitly denied in the parallel passage of Diogenes of Oenoanda (fragment 10). Secondly, Epicurus' theory undermines the argument of Plato in *Laws* x that art is prior to nature and chance as a source of motion. Thirdly, it shows that the complicated hypothesis that apparently featured in Aristotle's dialogue *On philosophy* – that the cosmos is liable to periodic floods and conflagrations, after which the arts grow all over again from ideas preserved by a few survivors – is quite unnecessary.[9]

Secondly, we must notice that Epicurus distinguishes two steps in the development process: an irrational effect of the environment, and a rational use of the lessons taught by the environment. But it would be wrong to think of these as two successive chronological periods. The only point of importance is that the intelligent development of the arts presupposes the unplanned effect of the environment.

[8] See Reinhardt (1912) and Cole (1967).
[9] Aristotle, *On philosophy*, fragment 8 Ross.

Thirdly, Epicurus mentions that the contribution of reason was a gradual process that took more time in some fields than in others.

These general principles are then exemplified in the famous description of the development of languages.[10]

There are no moral reflections in this part of the *Letter*. The following sections deal with the motion of the heavens, and in this connection Epicurus frequently refers to the moral principle familiar from *Kyriai doxai* 11 and 12: that freedom from fear of the gods can come only to one who has the right philosophy of nature (φυσιολογία). There is no trace, however, so far as I can see, of the idea that this philosophy of nature is itself a feature to be fitted into the scheme of development that was sketched in §§ 75–6. Epicurus suggests neither that his philosophy of nature started from a natural impulse and progressed by stages, like other arts, nor that he himself, the inventor, was responsible for bringing about an exception to this gradualism. He simply does not consider the question.[11]

Our hypothesis is, then, that Lucretius found in his collection of works of Epicurus a fully-worked-out theory of the history of civilization and the arts, written in the same spirit as the relevant passage of the *Letter to Herodotus*. He himself worked this material into a new shape. That it was Lucretius who was the author of this new shape, and not some unknown intermediate source (the unwanted standby of those who hate to impute originality to any writer), seems to me a reasonable supposition. The focus of this reworking is the rhetorical elevation of the role of Epicurus in the history of civilization; and that is surely something that belongs to the structure of Lucretius' poem. The reworking must preserve the principles of the original – that the initial move in each process comes from the environment itself, and that the development takes place by gradual stages, as human reason deliberates about the natural facts. But the whole development is now to be studied in its relation to the discoveries (*divina reperta*) of Epicurus, which took place at a particular time in this development but stand out as an exceptional event, neither caused by the automatic necessity of the environment, like the first communicative noises of animals, nor prepared by gradual stages in earlier history, like the use of iron for ploughshares. The philosophy of Epicurus thus provides Lucretius with a new viewpoint from which to study the history of man; and it is just this viewpoint that gives the moral perspective to Lucretius' 'anthropology'.

Of course, in the Epicurean system the development of human society and technology is necessarily a progression of a certain sort. There was first a simple

---

[10] I take it that this passage *is* to be thought of as an example. A summary letter has no room for more than one example, and the general point is made more clearly by setting out one theme in some detail than by surveying many themes. There is no great significance, then, in the fact that Lucretius gives equal weight to many other matters. There may yet be significance, of course, in the detailed differences of treatment of the theme of language, but we shall not discuss that here.

[11] There are two other Epicureans whose writings in this field have been partially preserved (apart from Lucretius): Diogenes of Oenoanda, and Hermarchus, the first scholarch, whose account of the origin of laws against homicide is reproduced in Porphyry, *De abstinentia* 1.10–11. There is nothing in either of these that is similar to Lucretius' *primum Graius homo* ....

way of life, when the human species first emerged from earth, now a highly complex one, and the task is to describe the gradual progression from one to the other. But neither simplicity itself, nor complexity itself, gives a *morally better* way of life: which of the two is better is simply something that has to be determined by looking at both in the light of Epicurus' moral principles. What we should expect of Lucretius, therefore, if this hypothesis is correct, is that he would describe the development, by exercising his imagination on the theory of human history laid down by Epicurus, and take care to point out the moral inadequacies of each stage.[12] We should add that since what he describes is inevitably a progression of a sort, as we have said, we might think he would especially emphasize, to avoid misunderstanding, that this progression is not a moral one – that the later stages are not better, and can be worse, than the earlier.

The next step is to test this hypothesis by looking for confirmation or refutation of these expectations in book v of *De rerum natura*. The outcome – to anticipate – is that there is nothing in the text, so far as I can see, that falsifies our hypothesis. Furthermore, what is found in the text is accounted for more plausibly by this explanation than by any of the others that have been advanced: for example, that Lucretius was really a progressivist, because that was the teaching of Epicurus, but was inhibited from being wholeheartedly a progressivist because of his misanthropy, pathological fears, or compassionate poetic sensibilities; or that he was really a primitivist, because he was committed to the thesis that the world is now past its prime and is proceeding downhill towards ultimate dissolution, but was sometimes distracted from this thesis by the beauty of nature's lessons and the ingenuity of human art; or that Epicureanism was optimistic but Lucretius was a pessimist.

Although the whole passage must be carefully examined before we can accept our hypothesis as the best available explanation, that will not be possible within the limits of this chapter. I propose to comment on three sections only: the description of the life of primitive man (925–1010), the origin of wrong beliefs about the gods (1161–240), and the end of the book.

On the subject of primitive man, I shall be as brief as possible, since so much has already been written.[13] The first point to note is that the passage follows closely upon a description of the origin of living species from the earth, and the process of natural selection of the fittest to survive, from the large (although limited) variety of spontaneously produced creatures. Although Lucretius interposes a forty-seven-line paragraph explaining the limits imposed on this variety by the facts of nature (878–924), we should remember that initially the subject under discussion at 925ff is *survival*. We have already heard that lions survive because of their *virtus*, foxes because of their *dolus*, deer because of their *fuga*, and dogs, sheep, and cattle

---

[12] There is a stimulating tribute to Lucretius' historical imagination by Kenney (1972).
[13] See especially Robin (1916), Taylor (1947), Merlan (1950), Keller (1951), Grilli (1953), Spoerri (1959), Borle (1962), Beye (1963), Perelli (1967), and Fredouille (1972).

because their services have earned them protection at the hands of men. But man, as we can see, has none of these advantages, and it is obvious that contemporary men and women, thrust out into raw nature without any of their technology, would have a poor chance of survival. So in this case the historical imagination of Lucretius must go to work within strict limits: he could hardly do other than give primitive men a stronger, hardier constitution than men of the Roman Republic (*multo durius, solidis magis ossibus*: 925–7).

Having made this point, Lucretius stresses what they lacked: ploughing, iron, agriculture, fire, clothes, houses, politics, laws, legal marriage. They ate berries, drank water, lived in caves, slept under brushwood, mated through love, rape, or barter, defended themselves against animals with stones. There is nothing, so far, that is not an almost inevitable consequence of Epicurean physical theory. This is the first stage on the (non-moral) progression towards the complexity of civilization.

But of course there is more to it than that. A quite different picture can be presented, as many have shown.[14] Lucretius goes on to say that the first men suffered no fear that the sun would fail to return in the morning, and experienced only the same mortality rate, from wild beasts or famine, as men of the present day do from war, shipwreck, and surfeit. Moreover, much of the description of primitive conditions is deliberately contrasted with later passages. Thus primitive man was hardy (*durius*: 926), but later began to soften (*mollescere*: 1014). At first sexual desire was associated with manly strength (962–5), later with weakness (1017). At first, they could withstand cold (929), later the discovery of fire made them less tolerant (1015). Observation of such contrasts led one scholar to claim that for Lucretius 'primitive man is living the ideal existence, free of entangling human commitments; his sexual encounters can be considered auspicious by virtue of the asocial, antiseptic and atomic implications in the phrase ... "*Venus* ... *iungit corpora amantum*" ... The final contrast becomes one of innocence and serenity in ignorance, set beside viciousness and misery in knowledge.'[15]

Now, I submit that this is exaggerated nonsense. It is both ludicrous and unnecessary to think that Lucretius commends to us a life without clothes, houses, fire – or poetry; or that he wants us to return, as to a lost ideal, to fighting for our lives, in constant fear (*paventes*: 986), against wild beasts. It is notorious, of course, that he warns the reader against deep sexual feelings; but that is not to say that he wants to commend rape as an alternative, still less that he wants us to regard even friendship with disapprobation because it first arose in the 'softer' stage of human development (1019). Nor is there any contrast between 'serenity in ignorance' and 'misery in knowledge'. The lines that have been supposed to suggest such a contrast (973–81) in fact make a quite different point: namely, that primitive men lacked those *false superstitions* about the sun that might give rise to the fear that

---

[14] Especially Robin (1916), Beye (1963), and Boyancé (1963).
[15] Beye (1963), 166.

daylight would never return to earth. There is absolutely no warrant for generalizing the passage into a commendation of ignorance and rejection of knowledge.

The hypothesis that I am suggesting, on the other hand, leads to a perfectly consistent and unforced view of the passage. We find in it just that kind of texture that we should expect – on the one hand, the description of a primitive, simple state of unthinking interaction with nature, to be contrasted with more complex and more deliberate ways of life; and on the other hand, a clear moral perspective that surveys both stages, without identifying either of them as worse or better in their own nature. There is much that is morally praiseworthy about the primitive life; and Lucretius praises it in effect, as Robin and others have demonstrated. There is also much that is deplorable, and Lucretius makes that clear too: they were *miseri* (944 and 983), they were afraid (986), they died agonizingly from wounds because of ignorance (998), they suffered from famine (1007), they often died from accidental poisoning (1009). As an Epicurean, Lucretius' criterion for the good life was freedom from anxiety and pain. Admittedly, he contrasts their wounds, caused by wild beasts, with war wounds, their hunger with modern over-indulgence, their accidental poisoning with the wilful murders of modern times. But it is only dedication to a false theory about his intention that has persuaded critics to believe that he meant us to envy and emulate these poor people.

The origin of religion is discussed after an account of the development of social and political structures. In passing, it is worth observing in that account a particularly clear instance of the pattern that confirms our hypothesis – a natural development that is non-moral, assessed by moral criteria drawn from outside that development. At first, Lucretius says (1110ff), men of power distributed property to others according to their beauty, strength, or intelligence. But then property and wealth supplanted these natural talents, because the beautiful and strong people – he carefully omits intelligence this time – normally (*plerumque*) pursue wealth. Then he comments on the folly of this development from a point of view of the true philosophy of life (*siquis vera vitam ratione gubernet*: 1117). But before claiming this as another bit of evidence for the 'primitivist' interpretation, one should notice that a few lines further on the natural progression, as it continues, produces a change that must be thought of as better, when unbridled rivalry for power led to a greater reliance on law and punishment. 'Thenceforward, the fear of penalties taints the prizes of life' (1151). Bailey comments:[16] '... There arose a new disturbing influence in men's lives, the fear of punishment' – as if this were an *added* misery, another step on the downward path. But that seems to distort the sense somewhat. As an Epicurean, Lucretius would unquestionably prefer the institutions of the law to the violence of anarchy. He makes his moral comment, not by deploring the change in motivation from rivalry and anger to fear of

---

[16] Bailey (1947), 1504.

punishment, but by noting simply that because of the fear of punishment one cannot live unjustly and be happy.[17]

The notion that Lucretius intends to present some kind of steady moral progression or decline – especially one from 'innocence in ignorance' to 'misery in knowledge' – is impossible to reconcile with the way he describes the origin of religious beliefs and practices. For he puts together, in the same context, both a theory about true beliefs (according to Epicurus), and one about false beliefs. Visions, waking ane sleeping, led men to the notion of gods, in human form, everlastingly alive and supremely happy (1169–82). Beyond that, they observed the seasonal changes of the sky, and in ignorance of the true causes they attributed all the workings of the heavenly bodies and meteorological phenomena to the will of the gods (1183–93). There is no suggestion here that the second of these arguments is a decadent successor to the first, nor even that one preceded the other. Lucretius is vague about the timing: he introduces the first reason with the adverb *iam tum* (1169), which presumably means that it was contemporaneous with the early stages of civilization that he has been describing; and he continues with the second reason in the same imperfect tense with no temporal adverb but simply *praeterea* (1183).

He follows this description, morally neutral, as we have seen, with his moral comment:

> o genus infelix humanum, talia divis
> cum tribuit facta ...

(1194ff)

The structure of this passage needs some clarification: its logic has been much misunderstood.

We have first an exclamation about the miserable folly of mankind in supposing that the phenomena of the sky express the anger of the gods: they thus stored up grief for all future generations (1194–7). There is no piety in maintaining rituals at the altars: piety lies rather in being able to view everything with a mind at peace (1198–203). For (*nam*: 1204 – this is the word that has been seen as a source of trouble) when we contemplate the motions of the stars and planets, 'then into our hearts weighed down by other ills this misgiving too begins to raise up its wakened head' (*tunc aliis oppressa malis in pectora cura | illa quoque expergefactum caput erigere infit*: 1207–8) – the misgiving that perhaps there is some immense divine power that turns the stars. 'For lack of reasoning assails the doubting mind' (*temptat enim dubiam mentem rationis egestas*: 1211), that perhaps the world after all

---

[17]
> inde metus maculat poenarum praemia vita.
> circumretit enim vis atque iniuria quemque
> atque unde exortast ad eum plerumque revertit,
> ...

(1151–3)

I suggest that instead of taking this as a general comment on the folly of mankind, we take full note of *quemque* and *plerumque*, and interpret the lines thus: this is the origin of the fear of punishment, which taints all the good things in the lives of those who suffer from it; their own violence and wrong-doing has a tendency to recoil upon them.

had no natural origin and will have no end, but is endowed with eternal being by the will of the gods.

At first sight, the lines introduced by *nam* (1204ff), since they give an explanation of how human beings are led to a belief in powerful, executive gods by the movements of the stars and planets, seem to follow more naturally upon the description of this belief in 1194–7. Hence Giussani, followed by H. Diels, bracketed the intervening lines 1198–203 as a later addition. Bailey kept the lines in the text in his 1947 edition, but explained the passage as involving either an ellipse, or (Bailey's own personal favourite) 'another case of Lucretius' "suspension of thought"'. In his paraphrase (p. 1512) he ruthlessly supplanted *nam* with 'yet'.

Editors have been led astray especially, I believe, by misunderstanding two expressions: *aliis oppressa malis* (1207) and *dubiam mentem* (1211). Ernout and Robin (also Leonard and Smith) in line 1207 preferred the reading of the Italian manuscripts *in pectore* to *in pectora* (O and Q), alleging that *in pectora … caput erigere infit* tortures the sense and the grammar.[18] *Oppressa* must therefore agree with *cura*, and has to be read simply as an antithesis to *caput erigere infit*: 'cette inquiétude, étouffée jusque-là sous d'autres maux, commence elle aussi à redresser la tête'. But why should this anxiety have been hitherto suppressed in this way? And what does that idea add to the sense? Bailey, following Giussani, retains the reading *in pectora*, and takes *oppressa*, correctly, to agree with *pectora*. Yet both he and Giussani miss the point of the phrase. It is not just otiose description, but states the cause of superstitious belief: if the mind is not at peace but oppressed already by other anxieties (i.e. other than superstitious fear), then this fear too begins to raise its head. Having failed to understand this emphasis, the editors also overlook the force of *temptat dubiam mentem* (1211). We should take *dubiam* not proleptically, as Bailey does ('lack of reasoning assails our mind with doubt, whether …'), but conditionally: 'if the mind is in doubt, then lack of reasoning troubles it, as to whether …'

The logic is now perfectly straightforward. Early in their history, says Lucretius, men were led to belief in gods, firstly because of dream-images and other visions, and secondly because they could not otherwise explain the phenomena of the sky (1169–93 – all without moral comment). Wretched creatures! This belief involved them in misery and impiety. True piety does not lie in ritual observances and sacrifices, but in being able to contemplate everything with a mind at peace (1194–1203). For (*nam*: 1204) if the mind is assailed by other ills, then it is easy to fall also into terrifying *and impious* beliefs about the gods – namely, that they taint their perfect happiness with the work of rolling the heavens around and expressing their anger in thunder and lightning. For if the mind is in doubt, lack of a true philosophy of nature (*rationis egestas*) – the source of this doubt – makes one wonder whether after all the (Epicurean) theory of the

---

[18] Perhaps they were convinced by A. Brieger's astonishing comment, quoted by Bailey (1947, p. 1517): '*in pectora nihil caput erigere possit nisi infra pectus sit, i.e. in ventre*'.

mortality of the world must be wrong and the (Platonic–Aristotelian) theory of an everlasting cosmos maintained by divine powers may be right.[19]

This reading of the passage[20] reflects a normal Epicurean view of the nature of true piety and gives us a perfectly rational and coherent sequence of thought, in which the sentences introduced by *nam* in 1204 explain the thought that immediately precedes them. It is confirmed by the following lines 1218–25: it is an uneasy conscience (*ob admissum foede dictumve superbe*: 1224) that makes men fear that thunder and lightning are an expression of the gods' wrath – thus again *other* psychological troubles, of the kind that Epicureanism professes to cure, are the source of impious beliefs. Lucretius' next thoughts are similar: the admiral of a fleet – *ipso facto* disobeying the Epicurean command to live a quiet life – prays vainly to the gods in a storm. There is a certain unseen force (*vis abdita quaedam*: 1233) that frustrates the ambitions of men. I take this to be a generalizing comment: nature, of itself, brings some evils to men,[21] and if they are ignorant of the true philosophy of nature, which teaches them that these evils are limited and bearable, they allow these experiences to overwhelm them with anxiety; this anxiety makes them fall prey also to the superstitions that are the topic of the whole passage.

Now we may ask what is the relationship between this passage and our hypothesis about the composition of the history of man as a whole. There is a difference in emphasis – a slight and subtle one, but perhaps of some significance – between the rejected reading of the passage and the interpretation I have just proposed. Here is Giussani's summary of the whole section from 1181 onwards: 'Vedendo ciò e ciò, gli uomini naturalmente pensarono questo e questo; infelici! ma come poteva essere altrimenti? come mai vedendo ciò e ciò non avrebbero pensato questo e questo?' Thus he points out and attempts to make sense of the repetition of the sense of 1183–93 in 1204–25. The moral comment ('infelici!' – actually lines 1194–203) is a brief section sandwiched between two expressions of the same psychological explanation.

I suggest we should rather summarize thus: 'Observing the sky, men came to believe such and such. Poor creatures! It led them to think piety lies in placating the gods with rituals, whereas true piety is rather to be found in Epicurean philosophy, which enables one to observe the sky without forming impious beliefs.'

Thus the passage represents exactly the pattern our hypothesis leads us to expect. We have a description of a development in human society, followed by a long moral comment which explains the nature of true piety on principles drawn from outside that development. We must recall again that the whole of this theory

---

[19] It may be pointed out in passing that the everlasting cosmos was not an item of Stoic belief. See above, pp. 200ff.

[20] One interpreter who comes very close to this same reading is Waszink (1966), 308–13. But even he does not quite bring out the significance of *aliis oppressa malis*, and speaks (p. 312) of 1203–4 as 'ein allerdings nicht mit scharfer Logik konstruierter Satz'.

[21] Cf. VI.29–31.

about superstition follows an account of the origin of *true* religious belief (1169–82). Lucretius' meaning is that nature by itself suggests to the human imagination both the right and the wrong idea of gods. Which is right and which is wrong? Only the discoveries of Epicurus can teach men that.

The last twenty-two lines of book v have for a long time been a point of contention among scholars.[22] They consist, it seems, of repetitions of ideas from earlier lines, together with some scrappy and inadequate comments that do not correspond with anything earlier.[23] Repeated motifs are the fortification of cities (1440), the distribution of land (1441), the formation of alliances (1443), and the origin of agriculture (1448), of weapons (1449), of garments (1449), of poetry (1444 and 1451), and of laws (1448). The only new idea of any importance is that since writing is a recent discovery, the historian of early times has nothing but *ratio* to guide his inquiries (1445–7).

Of course, a conclusion may appropriately repeat in summary form the ideas already developed. But this list is rather unsatisfactory in that role, since it has the appearance of being an arbitrary and unco-ordinated selection.

Yet the last ten lines, taken by themselves, do look like a concluding summary. We have first a list of technological achievements, then a statement about the manner of their origin:

> usus et impigrae simul experientia mentis
> paulatim docuit pedetemptim progredientis.
> sic unum quicquid paulatim protrahit aetas
> in medium ratioque in luminis erigit oras.
> namque alid ex alio clarescere corde videbant,
> artibus ad summum donec venere cacumen.

What is striking about the last ten lines is that they present a totally *non-moral* conclusion. Without discrimination Lucretius mentions inventions that are useful in catering to human needs, such as agriculture and clothing, and superfluous ornaments such as sculpture. What he stresses is the gradualness of discovery, and the fact that its origin lies in experience (*usus*) and human ingenuity. We are back, in other words, in the world of ideas that we found in the *Letter to Herodotus* 75–6 (see above, p. 211).

But we have what looks like a different conclusion in 1379–1435, immediately before the last twenty-two lines. And this conclusion is a moral one. It is worth examining it more closely. Merlan (1950), in an otherwise valuable article on the conclusion of book v, dismisses it as one of 'two jottings' incorporated here by an editor; Bailey (1947, p. 1540) defends it against editors who called it 'incoherent', but only by allowing it to be 'discursive ... typical of Lucretius' mind with its habit of accepting one thought after another, as they occur to him'. If it is

---

[22] See for example Giuffrida (1959) and Nethercut (1967).
[23] Merlan (1950).

seen, however, as the conclusion to the history of civilization, I believe it can be shown to be one of the most carefully and beautifully composed sections of the poem.

The ostensible subject is the development of the art of music, from the first natural impulse of birdsong. But it is crucial to notice the remarkable frequency of occurrences of the idea of *pleasure*. We have *iuvare* (1381), *dulcis* (1384), *otia dia* (1387), *iuvabant* (1390), *cordi* (1391), *iucunde* (1394), *dulces cachinni* (1397), *laeta* (1400), *risus dulcesque cachinni* (1403), *solacia* (1405), *dulcedini' fructum* (1410), *suavius* and *placet* (1413), *vera voluptas* (1433). This strikes one even more significantly when one notices that in the whole preceding section 925–1378 there is no occurrence of any of these words except *dulcis* and *laetus*: *dulcis* appears once in a formula (*dulcia lumina vitae*: 989), and twice in the passage about horticulture that may be seen as preparing the way for our conclusion (1367, 1377); *laetus* appears once in the same context (1372). In all the long description of the history of civilization and the moral comment upon it so far nothing has been said explicitly about the goal of all moral endeavour according to Epicurean philosophy: pleasure. It would be superbly appropriate if, by way of conclusion, something were at last said about how much pleasure the human race had achieved.

After his discourse about the pleasures of music, Lucretius therefore generalizes his moral comment in a brief glance over the whole development. He prepares for this carefully: there is first a description of the simple pleasures of music among country people, all expressed in a past tense, then a sentence or two remarking that watchmen of the present day, seeking to keep themselves awake, stimulate themselves with pleasant music. This pleasure is constant in quantity, he observes, not any greater now than it was in early times. It is what is at hand that gives pleasure, provided that one does not remember something more pleasant that is now lost (1412–13), and the present object of pleasure drives out of mind what one used to enjoy. Thus the objects enjoyed change through the course of history, but the sum of pleasure does not grow. Once acorns and skins and beds of leaves were men's delight, then they were supplanted by other foods and clothes and more luxurious bedding. Both the simple and the more complex goods give rise to senseless rivalries and covetousness, but our fault, in modern times, is greater than that of the ancients, because the things we allow to torture us are unnecessary desires. Lucretius, the Epicurean, concludes (if this is truly the conclusion) with a comment that applies to the history of all humanity, in so far as it has failed to learn the moral lessons of Epicurus:

> ergo hominum genus incassum frustraque laborat
> semper et in curis consumit inanibus aevum,
> nimirum quia non cognovit quae sit habendi
> finis et omnino quoad crescat vera voluptas
> idque minutatim vitam provexit in altum
> et belli magnos commovit funditus aestus.

(1430–5)

This ignorance has both goaded men to seek greater technological achievement, and plunged them into wars of rivalry.

This is, of course, totally incompatible with a 'final contrast ... of innocence and serenity in ignorance, set beside viciousness and misery in knowledge' – a description that we quoted on p. 214. It is also quite incompatible, if these last few lines are read in their context, with Robin's more moderate comment: 'L'esprit de ce morceau [sc. 1408–35] est tout à fait analogue à celui du développement 925–1010: chaque progrès suscite en nous de nouveaux besoins et nous éloigne davantage de l'heureuse simplicité de la vie de nature.'[24] Lucretius explicitly rejects such an interpretation, in spite of the gloom of the last six lines, by pointing out that rivalry was just as great, in primitive times, for skins, as it is now, for purple embroidered robes (1423–7). He has just painted a charming picture of the innocent delights of a *cultivated* orchard (1370–8). He does not argue for a gradual moral decline, any more than for a gradual moral progression. He argues for a non-moral progression, and comments on it from his post-Epicurean moral standpoint.

The appropriateness of this passage (1379–1435) as a conclusion of the book convinces me that it *was* the conclusion, in Lucretius' mind. The sudden and striking emergence of the theme of pleasure (which is not noticed in the commentaries that I have consulted) shows that something different is intended here from the earlier moral comments; and the fact that pleasure is the Epicurean τέλος shows that this difference marks a climax. We finish with that crucial Epicurean moral lesson, that *vera voluptas* has a limit, in spite of its changing objects throughout the course of human history, and ignorance of this limit means the end of peace.

The presence of a second, non-moral conclusion (1448–57) tempts one to guess. That it *is* an alternative is suggested by the repetition at 1454–5 of two lines that occur in good order in the argument at 1388–9. Repetition by itself does not entail that one of the two occurrences is to be treated with suspicion, but this particular repetition seems too close and too pointless. My guess – and it is only a guess, and there may be others just as well based – is that at one time book V was of approximately the same length as the other five books; it contained a fairly brief, non-moral account of the progression of human institutions, similar in spirit to *Letter to Herodotus* 75–6, which included the two displaced scraps 1436–9 and 1440–7, and ended with 1448–57. Lucretius, the Epicurean, rewrote it at greater length, adding his own extensive moral assessments of each step in the history of man.[25]

One final comment: if my hypothesis is correct, then it is no accident that the prologue to book VI says what it does. Athens was the first to give man corn, a civilized life, laws – and then 'the pleasant comforts of life', when she gave birth to Epicurus. He understood that men had now acquired all that was necessary for life: they had security, wealth, good reputation, and worthy children – and yet they

---

[24] Ernout and Robin (1925), vol. III, p. 182.
[25] I have been greatly helped, in framing my thoughts about the conclusion of book V, by conversations with Professor John Jacobson.

were anxious. The fault lay in the mind itself, like a dirty, leaky pitcher (a picturesque way of describing the condition that we have discovered in Lucretius' account of superstition, in 1204ff: the mind *aliis oppressa malis* finds new sources of anxiety). Epicurus taught the limits of desire and fear (VI.25), and showed how the vain desires and fears that tormented mankind could be cured by the study and right interpretation of nature (*naturae species ratioque*: 41).

The moral perspective that informs Lucretius' history of civilization, set out finally in what I take to be the conclusion of book V (1430–5), is thus attributed to its author. The life and work of Epicurus came at the end of the development described by Lucretius, but it was neither a culmination nor a reversal of it. Epicurus stood above it, and shed the light of his philosophy on all that happened.

18

THE COSMOLOGICAL CRISIS IN CLASSICAL ANTIQUITY[1]

[1986]

I had better start by pointing out that the word 'crisis' in my title does not have exactly the sense usual in modern English. The modern sense derives from the Hippocratic books, in which 'crisis' is the name given to the turning-point in the course of a disease – when it is decided whether you get better or die. The author of *Epidemics* I knows that there are some fevers in which the crisis occurs on even days only: namely, the sixth, eighth, tenth, fourteenth, twentieth, twenty-fourth, thirtieth, fortieth, sixtieth, eightieth, or one hundred and twentieth day of the disease (*Epidemics* I.26): 'So one must be attentive, and know that at these times there will be a crisis resulting in recovery, or death, or a tendency for better or worse.'

But my title does not aim to imply that there was some day when ancient cosmology reached a fork in the road when it had to turn one way or the other: this is a long-term affair that I am talking about – a choice of options lasting many centuries, or even a timeless choice. I am thinking of a *krisis* of the same sort as the one posed by Parmenides at the beginning of his poem:

> ἡ δὲ κρίσις περὶ τούτων ἐν τῷδ' ἔστιν·
> ἔστιν ἢ οὐκ ἔστιν.
>
> (D–K 28B.8.15–16)

'The decision lies in this' either one thing or the other.

The *krisis* I am talking about is well expressed by Marcus Aurelius as it appeared to him in the second century A.D.

Either a medley, a mutual interlacing [of atoms], and their scattering (ἤτοι κυκεὼν καὶ ἀντεμπλοκὴ καὶ σκεδασμὸς) or unity, order, and providence (ἕνωσις, καὶ τάξις καὶ

[1] This is adapted from a lecture given at Stanford University in 1984, in memory of T. B. L. Webster. I gave it again, in modified form, to the Boston Colloquium in Ancient Philosophy in 1985. I am grateful to many fsiends who commented on the lecture on both occasions, and particularly to John Murdoch, the official commentator at Harvard, where the second version was delivered, and to John Cleary, the organizer of the Boston Colloquium, who made many helpful suggestions. In preparing the text for publication, I have decided to keep the lecture style, but I have made several changes and added notes, in response to these comments or to give fuller references.

πρόνοια). If the former, why do I desire to linger in such a messy, purposeless jumble? Why do I care about anything but how I shall some time 'return to earth'? Why do I concern myself? This scattering will be my lot too, whatever I do. But if the other is true, I bow my head, I am calm, I take courage in what orders all.

(Meditations VI.10)

The κυκεών first turns up in *Iliad* XI, where it refers to a cocktail prepared in Nestor's cup for Nestor and Machaon – an unappetising mixture of barley groats, Pramnian wine, and grated cheese. It makes its philosophical debut in Heraclitus, who says either 'the κυκεών separates when it is stirred' or 'the κυκεών separates unless it is stirred' according to the edition you read.[2] It is not very clear what he meant, whichever reading is preferred. But Marcus is clear what he means by κυκεών, and he is against it. It is a mess, a medley, a welter, and it is his word for the Atomists' universe.

At about the same time that Marcus was thus making his position clear, at least to himself in his so-called *Meditations*, an opposite point of view was being proclaimed and exhibited to the public in a remote city of the Eastern empire, at Oenoanda, where one Diogenes recorded his philosophical position on stone and had it built into the wall of a Stoa. A few years ago a new fragment was unearthed and published by Martin Ferguson Smith, in which Diogenes argues against the providential ordering of the cosmos by a planning god, almost in the manner of a western traveller complaining about an eastern hotel – the layout is inconvenient and the drinking-water is unreliable.

[The sea] occupies [excessively large] parts [of the cosmos], making a peninsula of the inhabited world, and in itself too being full of bad things, and on top of all that containing water that is undrinkable, briny, and bitter – as if it had been prepared like that by god on purpose to prevent men from drinking it. Moreover the so-called Dead Sea (νεκρὰ θάλασσα), which is really and truly Dead (for it is never sailed), even deprives the local inhabitants of part of the land they occupy; for it chases them away to a very considerable distance with its aggressive attacks and again rises and overflows, as though watching out to make sure they will not do any ploughing.

(new fragment 40)[3]

Accident or design: in the second century A.D. the cosmological debate seems to have become focused on this issue above all. Even in the first century B.C. when Cicero was writing *De finibus* and *De natura deorum* positions were already taken along these two opposing fronts in particular; it is one of the main points of contention in the *De rerum natura* of Lucretius. But the issues that divided the learned world concerning the nature of the universe were by no means confined to the opposition between accident and design. There were many more points of difference, more or less systematically linked together.

[2] Heraclitus, D–K 22B.125. It is cited without the negative by Theophrastus, *De vertigine* 9, and with it by Alexander, *Probl.* IV.42 (not III.42, as D–K says).
[3] This fragment is published with translation and commentary in Smith (1976).

The history of Greek cosmology becomes clear, I think, when we realise that it takes the form of a choice between just two fundamentally and comprehensively different ways of interpreting the cosmos. During the Presocratic period the lines of division had not yet hardened, but from the time of the death of Socrates we can distinguish quite clearly two cosmologies and not more than two, and these survived as rivals throughout the period of classical antiquity. On the one hand, the atomic theory of Leucippus and Democritus, later adopted by Epicurus and his followers; on the other, the theory of Plato, later adopted and modified by Aristotle, and again modified by the Stoics.

Now there were changes in both theories in the course of time, but I am prepared to argue that, for all the changes, the two theories remained basically intact, so that even in late antiquity someone who adopted the Aristotelian position – someone like the Neoplatonist Simplicius or the Christian Philoponus, for instance – was always much more like Aristotle than Democritus. In the following pages I shall use the names 'Atomism' and 'Aristotelianism' to refer to the two theories, conscious that this involves some over-simplification at times, but convinced all the same that the two names capture a vitally important distinction.[4]

Atomists differed from Aristotelians in a number of different ways, which can be set out schematically:

ATOMISTS	ARISTOTELIANS
accident	design (or at least order)
matter-in-motion explanations	purpose or teleological explanations
infinite universe	finite cosmos = universe
transient cosmos	eternal or repeating cosmos
our cosmos one of many	unique cosmos
matter and void	no void inside cosmos
atoms	continuum
linear dynamics	centrifocal dynamics
flat earth	spherical earth
material soul	immaterial soul (except Stoics)
evolution	creation, or eternity

The relation between the items in each column is not as strong as entailment. In principle it would have been possible to adopt a mixed position. This became perfectly obvious in later times, when Atomism was combined with Christianity. Newton gives us an example that shows everything we need to make the point. I quote a famous sentence from his *Optics*:

[4] As John Cleary has pointed out to me, there is an extremely important distinction that cuts across my simple distinction between Atomists and Aristotelians: namely, whether the order in the world is reducible to mathematical form or whether qualitative form is irreducible. This distinction separates Plato from Aristotle and the Stoics, and puts him closer to the side of Democritus, on just this one issue.

It seems probable to me that God in the beginning formed matter in solid, massy, hard, impenetrable, movable particles, of such sizes and figures and with such other properties and in such proportion to space, as most conduced to the end for which he formed them.

(*Optics*, ed. Horsley, IV.260)

From the Atomist column, we have atoms and void space; from the Aristotelian column, order and creation. Newton seems to feel little difficulty in crossing the line at these points.

In classical antiquity there was very little crossing of the dividing line. Among the Greek cosmologists it is perfectly possible to identify those who held all of the Atomist beliefs, or all of the 'Aristotelian' column, but it is hard to find eclectics. It looks as though there is some tight bond that links all of the theses of each set together. To determine how they are all related is beyond the scope of this paper.[5] My present intention is to risk some rather general observations about the two cosmologies, with a view to identifying, if possible, some basic idea that divides Atomists from Aristotelians. Is there some primary opposition that we can all recognize, which comes in some way first, and from which the others follow, no doubt with varying degrees of directness? To put it crudely, what makes an Atomist, and what makes an Aristotelian?

It is not possible just to subsume the two ancient cosmological theories under one of the well-known modern pairs of opposites. They are not opposed as Liberals and Conservatives,[6] nor as Male and Female, nor as Gardeners and Architects. They cannot be forced under the headings that Isaiah Berlin borrowed from Archilochus, Hedgehogs and Foxes, although it is amusing to try.[7] The fox, said Archilochus, knows many things, the hedgehog one big thing.[8] (Plato was a hedgehog; perhaps Aristotle was a fox trying to be a hedgehog.) Atomists and Aristotelians do not divide themselves so. Nor is it a straightforward opposition between materialists and idealists: the old Atomists from Abdera were the first to introduce the immaterial void as an important element in their cosmology, and the Stoics, from the other camp, were super-materialists.

Of course, a familiar opposition that lies close to the one we are pursuing is that between theists and atheists. The distance is short enough to make it plausible for the opponents to use these labels in their polemics against each other. This is why the Epicureans soon got the name of atheists, in spite of their sophisticated theology. The label clung for centuries. When the Atomist cosmology made a come-back in the seventeenth century, the charge of atheism was the first that the

---

[5] I am at present engaged in an attempt to survey the whole field. Vol. I of *The Greek Cosmologists* was published by Cambridge University Press in 1987, with the subtitle 'The Formation of the Atomic Theory and its Earliest Critics'. I hope vol. II, 'The Teleological World Picture and its Opponents', will follow before too long.

[6] Eric Havelock comes close to doing so (1957).

[7] Isaiah Berlin, *The Hedgehog and the Fox: an Essay on Tolstoy's View of History* (London: Weidenfeld and Nicholson, 1954).

[8] Archilochus fragment 103: πόλλ' οἶδ' ἀλώπηξ. ἀλλ' ἐχῖνος, ἓν μέγα.

new Atomists had to throw off.[9] And of course the charge with regard to the ancient Atomists was in an important sense correct. Although the Epicureans had a place for gods in their cosmology, it was not a place that involved them in the action. Lucretius' polemics on behalf of Epicureanism against active gods are notorious, and one cannot help guessing that this was a large part of the motivation of his poem.

All the same, the conflict between theism and atheism is clearly not more than part of the plot. Plato's cosmology, as set out in the *Timaeus*, does indeed involve a creator God, but even in the first generation of his students people were uncertain whether to take him seriously on this subject. The stress is on the order of the cosmos, its intelligible structure, not on the divine origin of this structure. Aristotle similarly demands a divine being as the guarantor of the eternity of the cosmos and its continuing good order; but he denies that god made the world. There is practically no trace in Plato or Aristotle of the typically Christian feeling of gratitude to God for the beauty, regularity, and well adaptedness of the physical world.[10] Aristotle could write 'when Zeus rains', but he could never write

> We plough the fields and scatter
> the good seed on the land,
> but it is fed and watered
> by God's almighty hand.

On the other side of the fence, Epicurus not only worked out and published an elaborate theology but also recognized a value in religious rituals and observances. 'Of his piety towards the gods, and his affection for his native country, it is impossible to speak adequately', says Diogenes Laertius in his biography (x.10). It is clear that the difference between an Atomist and an Aristotelian is not a matter of religious spirit.[11]

An interesting candidate for the position of first guiding principle of this controversy was suggested by Stephen Toulmin and June Goodfield in their book *The Architecture of Matter*.[12] In fact it is one of three, but the other two can be left aside for the present. I quote:

There is a contrast between two groups of theories: those that treat the development of living creatures as the pattern characteristic of all material change, and those which find the fundamental pattern in the behavior of passive, inanimate objects.

(p. 21)

---

[9] See for instance Walter Charleton, *Physiologia Epicuro-Gassendo-Charletoniana: a Fabrick of Science Natural upon the Hypothesis of Atoms, founded by Epicurus, repaired by Petrus Gassendus, augmented by Walter Charleton* (first published in 1654, rep. by the Johnson Reprint Corporation, New York, 1966).

[10] But Aristotle came closer to expressions of this type of feeling in his published works, to judge by the fragments. A famous instance is the passage from the dialogue *On philosophy* quoted by Cicero, *ND* II.97.

[11] The attitude of Democritus towards the gods does not emerge clearly from the fragments and testimonia. There is a good discussion in Guthrie II.478–82.

[12] Toulmin and Goodfield (1962).

This looks like a thoroughly plausible candidate. The atomic theory undeniably seeks to reduce everything to the movements of lifeless bits of matter, and its explanations are always couched in these terms. The Platonists, Aristotelians, and Stoics, on the other hand, regard matter in motion as at best a part of the explanations of what happens in the natural world. The tone is set in Plato's *Timaeus*, in the distinction that pervades Plato's exposition throughout the dialogue: I mean the distinction between what happens 'from necessity' and what happens 'as a result of Mind'.[13] The former category, of course, includes the unplanned motions of inanimate bodies – in other words, the whole of the basic equipment of the Atomists' universe. And Plato insists that although our understanding of the world will be incomplete without such consideration, matter in motion can never be more than an auxiliary explanation of what happens – a συναίτιον. The heart of the explanation lies in the thoughtful activity of the divine craftsman, who uses matter in motion as the material of his craft, and makes a work of art out of it. This work of art itself is not a lifeless artifact, but a living being. The model used by the craftsman in shaping the cosmos is called by Plato ὃ ἔστι ζῷον – the very model of a Living Creature (39E7); and the cosmos itself is described as if it were an animal of some kind. The whole of Plato's cosmology starts with the distinction between the soul and body of the world. If we understand the world in Plato's terms, it is because we understand what it is to be a living being, and how the parts fit together and contribute to the life of the whole.

Aristotle's use of the same model is not so obvious, and it would take too much space to spell it out. Two details will have to be enough. Aristotle's world runs, as we might say, on the twin notions of potentiality and actuality: the course of nature is a perpetual growth of the potential into the actual. These are not categories drawn from observations or speculations about lifeless matter in motion; they come from the organic world – from observations of eggs producing chickens, acorns producing oak trees, and suchlike things, all generalized into a frame for explaining everything in the world. Secondly, consider the parallel between Aristotle's ultimate cause in the natural world, the divine Unmoved Mover, and the ultimate cause of the activity of the human psyche – what he calls the νοῦς ποιητικός. The argument he uses to show that there must be such a being in the constitution of the human psyche runs parallel to the argument we find in *Physics* VIII and *Metaph.* XII for a first cause of motion in the cosmos. He does not speak of the body and soul of the world, as Plato does, but his thinking is still close to Plato's nevertheless.

This same distinction, between matter-in-motion merchants and keepers of the cosmic animal, looks even more promising and all-embracing when we extend its implications further. One of the most obvious features of an animal is that it has a skin or a shell, an outer envelope of some kind. It is pre-eminently a limited object. The cosmologists of classical times often changed the metaphor from animals with their outer skin to cities with their outer wall. They viewed the cosmos as being

---

[13] *Tim.* 48A, and many other places in the dialogue.

like one of their fortified cities, and they made themselves at home in the cosmos by thinking of it as a large-scale reflection of the familiar activities of the home town. People do different things in the city, just as the minerals, vegetables, and animals of the cosmos each have their own way of being; but just as all the different activities of the city work together for the economy of the whole, so all the performances of nature contribute to the comfortably regular cycle of the seasons and the succession of birth, flourishing, and death. The spherical shape of the whole cosmos seemed to emphasize its security, its satisfactory reliability – it is a theme that occurs in thinkers as wide apart as Cicero and Kepler.

On the other hand the Atomists were ready to accept the challenge of infinity. Maybe the Stoics modified the Aristotelian cosmos to the extent of admitting that it was surrounded by an infinite void – Aristotle had denied that it was surrounded by anything. But that void was indeed void; there was no need to worry about what was in it. There was nothing in it. The Atomists not only admitted the existence of infinitely extended void space, but they also claimed that this space was not intrinsically different from the space inhabited by ourselves: it contained matter, and indeed matter formed into worlds. They dared to claim that our world is not unique, privileged, unchallenged by competitors, but one of an uncountable number. This is indeed a difference of the utmost significance in the two kinds of cosmology. Matter in motion leads to an infinite plurality of worlds: the organic model leads to a single, finite world.

All the same, this is surely not the crucial difference; if we press it too hard, we can easily mislead.

First, a point that may seem rather obvious but is in fact often forgotten; the Atomists did not differ from the Aristotelians about the finite, closed nature of the *cosmos*. We must insist on the distinction, in ancient cosmology, between the universe and the cosmos. These are not synonyms, as they tend to be in modern English. 'Cosmos' means a finite system, with an earth at the centre and stars and other heavenly bodies encircling it. To quote the author of the pseudo-Aristotelian *On the cosmos*, 'Cosmos is a system composed of heaven and earth and the natures contained in them' (391 b 8). The outer heaven is the container, and it forms the boundary of the cosmos, just as the wall is the boundary of the city. The universe (τὸ πᾶν) is everything there is. According to Aristotle, the universe is the cosmos, but this is a synthetic statement, not a statement of equivalence. According to the Atomists, the universe contains not only our cosmos, but many, many others as well, and a lot of material and a lot of space that are not involved in the structure of any of the existing cosmoi. So for the Atomists it is the universe that is unbounded; the cosmos retains its closed, friendly, familiar structure. The Atomist Lucretius can still talk about the *moenia mundi* (1.73 and elsewhere).

More remarkably, the Atomists were still able to use the imagery of an organism, a living creature, with reference to their cosmos. This is a point that is usually forgotten, perhaps because of the temptation to bring Atomism into line with the mechanical world picture of the seventeenth century.

The best consecutive account of the beginning of the world according to

Atomist theory – the best, but still not a very good one – is from Diogenes Laertius:

The coming to be of the cosmoi is thus. In severance from the infinite, many bodies, of all varieties of shape, move into a great void. These, being assembled, create a single vortex (δίνη), in which they collide, gyrate in every way, and are sorted like to like. When because of the number they are no longer able to move round in equilibrium, then the fine ones move into the void outside, as if sifted, while the remainder stay together, become entwined, join courses with each other and bring about a first system, in the shape of a sphere. A sort of membrane comes apart from this, containing in itself bodies of all kinds. As these bodies whirl around in proportion to the resistance of the centre, the surrounding membrane becomes thin, as the bodies that are contiguous by their contact in the whirl continually flow together; and thus the earth comes about, as the bodies that are carried to the centre remain together.

(IX.31)[14]

Many details of this are somewhat mysterious, but the external membrane (ὑμήν) stands out rather clearly. This is the caul that surrounds the embryo. From this alone we can see that the origin of the cosmos is not being contrasted with an organic birth, as a mechanical interaction of lifeless material bodies might be contrasted with the processes characteristic of life. Cosmogony is the story of a birth, even for an Atomist.

This single detail can be reinforced, fortunately, by a revealing parallel in the little treatise on embryology that was attributed in antiquity to Hippocrates under the title *The nature of the child* (it probably dates from the fourth century B.C.). The author describes the first stages of growth as the mixing of the seed of both parents in the womb, the condensation of the mass through heat, and its acquisition of a kind of breathing process. He then continues:

As it inflates, the seed forms a membrane around itself; for its surface, because of its viscosity, stretches around it without a break, in just the same way as a membrane is formed on the surface of bread when it is baked; the bread rises as it grows warm and inflates, and as it is inflated, so the membranous surface forms. In the case of the seed, as it becomes heated and inflated, the membrane forms over the whole of its surface, but the surface is perforated in the middle to allow the entrance and exit of air. In this part of the membrane there is a small projection, where the amount of seed inside is very small; apart from this projection the seed in its membrane is spherical.

(para. 12, trans. Lonie)[15]

The author claims to have seen a six-day human embryo himself, when he caused a dancing-girl to abort by getting her to jump vigorously up and down, touching her buttocks with her heels.

[14] Printed in Diels–Kranz as 67 (Leucippus) A.1. There is a good study of this text by Kerschensteiner (1959). See also Guthrie II.406–13. This text should not be taken as the pure doctrine of Leucippus: there are echoes of Epicurus, *Letter to Pythocles* 88–90, in it too.
[15] This text is not included in the four volumes of the Loeb edition. I. M. Lonie's translation of it is included in Lloyd (1978), 324–46, and his edition of it is announced as forthcoming in the Ars Medica series from De Gruyter (Berlin).

He continues with his theory in a few paragraphs. The embryo draws in blood, along with breath, and this blood coagulates and begins to form new flesh:

As the flesh grows it is formed into distinct members by breath. Each thing in it goes to its similar – the dense to the dense, the rare to the rare, and the fluid to the fluid. Each settles in its appropriate place, corresponding to the part from which it came and to which it is akin ...

Now the formation of each of these parts occurs through respiration – that is to say, they become filled with air and separate, according to their various affinities. Suppose you were to tie a bladder on to the end of a pipe, and insert through the pipe earth, sand, and fine filings of lead. Now pour in water, and blow through the pipe. First of all, the in- gredients will be thoroughly mixed up with water, but after you have blown for a time, the lead will move towards the lead, the sand towards the sand, and the earth towards the earth. Now allow the ingredients to dry out and examine them by cutting around the bladder: you will find that like ingredients have gone to join like. Now the seed, or rather the flesh, is separated into members by precisely the same process, with like going to join like.

(para. 17, trans. Lonie)

The Atomist cosmogony appealed to the sorting action of the vortex to account for the formation of the parts of the cosmos, and the Hippocratic embryologist uses a similar model of sorting materials by agitating them in a liquid to explain the formation of the parts of the body. So it is no surprise after all to recall that Lucretius can talk about the *maxima membra mundi* – the great limbs of the cosmos (v.243).[16]

Democritus himself was said to have been the first to call man a microcosm – μικρὸς κόσμος. But the attribution to Democritus is not certain. Galen is the source, and he attributes the idea to 'the Ancients, pretty good on nature' (ἀνδρὲς παλαῖοι περὶ φύσιν ἱκανοί). Since the passage offers an excellent, if bizarre, example of the argument about teleology in nature, it is worth quoting at some length. It occurs in the context of a description of the adaptive features of the human foot:

It is time now for you, my reader, to consider which chorus you will join, the one that gathers around Plato, Hippocrates, and the others who admire the works of Nature, or the one made up of those who blame Nature because she has not arranged to have the bodily wastes discharged through the feet. Anyone who dares to say these things to me has been spoiled by luxury to such an extent that he considers it a hardship to rise from his bed to

---

[16] It may be objected that these passages do not establish the point that the Atomists are not wholly committed to the matter in motion frame for explanation, as opposed to the 'world animal', because when they speak of the world in biological terms they nevertheless reduce biological processes to matter in motion. This is an objection raised by John Murdoch, and it is a good one. In reply I should have to call in more evidence from the Atomist literature, and especially from Lucretius, *De rerum natura* v, where many analogies from biology are offered in explanation of cosmological phenomena, without any attempt to show the possibility of a reduction to matter in motion. A good example would be the description of the aging of the cosmos in v.821–36.

relieve himself, thinking that man would be better constructed if he could simply extend his foot and discharge the wastes through it.

(*Use of the parts* III.10; 1.173.11–21 Helmreich; trans. May, adapted)[17]

He goes on to argue that the feet are well designed as they are: they do the necessary job and they are in the right place.

Who will deny that the foot is a small, ignoble part of an animal? But we know full well that the sun is grand and the most beautiful thing in the cosmos. Consider this, however: where was the right position for the sun in the whole cosmos and for the foot in the animal? In the cosmos the sun had to be set in the midst of the planets, and in the animal the foot must occupy the lowest position. How can we be sure of this? By assuming a different location for them and seeing what would follow. If you put the sun lower down where the moon is now, everything here would be consumed by fire, and if you put it higher, ... no part of the earth would be habitable because of the cold. ... Observe that the same skill has been employed in locating both sun and foot. I am intentionally comparing the noblest of the stars with the lowliest member of the animal body. What is more insignificant than the heel? Nothing. But neither could the sun be better located anywhere else in the whole cosmos.

What is the grandest and most beautiful of existing things? The cosmos. Who could deny it? But the animal is like a little cosmos, as the ancients say, men who are well-versed concerning nature, and in both you will find the same skill on the part of the craftsman (δημιουργός). Then show me, I hear you cry, a sun in the body of an animal. What a thing to ask! Are you willing to have the sun made of the substance of blood, so prone to putrefy and so full of mire? Wretched fellow, you are mad. This, and not the failure to make offerings and burn incense, is true sacrilege. I will not, indeed, show you a sun in the body of an animal, but I will show you the eye, a very brilliant instrument, and most like the sun.

(*Use of the parts* III.10; 1.176.9–177.20 Helmreich; trans. May, adapted)

Then he realizes that he has been rather carried away, and returns to the subject: 'It is, however, my present intention to speak of the foot.'

Thus Galen's use of the analogy between the macrocosm and the microcosm, and he attributes it to 'the Ancients'. It is a late Christian writer who says the first to call man by the name of microcosm was Democritus – one David, an Armenian of the sixth century.[18] If it is right, it will serve to underline what I have been trying to demonstrate by other means: namely, that the ancient Atomists did not seek to draw a sharp distinction between the inanimate and animate realms of the cosmos. The nerve of Atomism does not lie in a preference for inanimate models for explanation in cosmology, as opposed to Plato's and Aristotle's use of basic ideas drawn from the animate world.

The mechanical philosophy was a later product. The Atomist philosophy of the classical period anticipated it in many respects, but we should be wary of equating it too exactly with its successor. The Atomists of the fifth century B.C. were not so

---

[17] References are to *Galeni de usu partium libri XVII* rec. Georgius Helmreich (Leipzig: Teubner, 1907; repr. Amsterdam: Hakkert, 1968); and to *Galen on the Usefulness of the Parts of the Body*, trans. Margaret Tallmadge May (Ithaca: Cornell University Press, 1968).

[18] David, *Prolegomena philosophiae*, ed. Busse (*Comm. in Arist. Graeca* XVII.2; Berlin, 1904), XXXVIII.14 = D–K 68B.34.

very far removed from Thales, Anaximander, and Anaximenes in the sixth century. Those men were materialists, in the sense that they sought for the explanation of things in the matter from which they emerged, but their materialism is rightly called 'hylozoism', the theory that matter has qualities of life in it. If Thales said 'all is water', he did not mean that H₂O is the basic molecular constituent of all material compounds; as Aristotle tells us, he was thinking of the moisture of the seed. So was Anaximander, probably, when he talked about the primitive γόνιμον, the generator of the Hot and the Cold. Anaximenes changed the basic matter from moisture to air, but he meant the breath of life; and his idea was repeated by a contemporary of Democritus, Diogenes of Apollonia. There was never a clear-cut division, in Presocratic cosmology, between the animate and the inanimate world, and even the Atomists Leucippus and Democritus belong in this tradition.[19]

After rejecting several possible ways of selecting a primary element in the difference between Atomism and Aristotelianism, it is time that I tried to say something positive about it. If the difference is not theism versus atheism, nor the closed world versus the infinite universe, nor mechanism versus animism, nor any of the other oppositions we have tried so far, then what is it? I suggest that the primary opposition is after all a very obvious one: it is that the Platonists, Aristotelians, and Stoics have in common a way of giving priority in explanation to whole forms, whereas the Atomists regard whole forms as something to be explained by reducing them to their component parts. To put it at its simplest, for an Aristotelian, it is because this dog is a dog that he has four paws, a sharp nose, and a tail, and it is because he must have four paws, etc., that he contains bone and blood and skin and fur, and it is for the sake of this bone and blood that the animal contains earth and water and air and fire in such and such proportions. The Aristotelian is content when he has shown why a dog must have these components if it is to lead its proper canine life. At each level, the more complex thing explains the presence of the less complex, rather than vice versa.

For the Democritean or Epicurean Atomist, it is the other way round. His basics are atoms and void, and they have the minimum characteristics built into them. The Atomist is content when he has shown why it is that certain combinations of atoms of certain shapes and sizes make up blood, or bone, or skin, and how it is that these again make up a dog or a cat or a cow or a human being. Aristotle could speak of the Atomic Form (ἄτομον εἶδος), meaning the form of the natural species. That is atomic, indivisible, by contrast with the generic form, such Animal, or Mammal, which can be divided into species. But of course it is nothing like what an Atomist would call atomic. Of course it is divisible, the Atomist would say, in the sense that it is analysable into component parts, and its component parts are what must be understood before you understand the form.

---

[19] References in this paragraph are as follows. Aristotle on Thales: *Metaph.* 1.3.983 b 20–6. Anaximander: pseudo-Plutarch *Stromateis* 2 = D–K 12A.10. Anaximenes: Aëtius 1.3.4 = D–K 13B.2. Diogenes of Apollonia: D–K 64B.4.

Obviously there is a great deal to be said about this distinction, of which I have given the merest sketch, in the hope that this will be enough for the purpose of this lecture. The purpose is to see whether this distinction is primary with respect to the others that I listed at the beginning, and whether it is related to them in the right way. Some of them fall into place quickly and easily, others with more of an effort. It is not hard to see why the Aristotelian, committed as he is to taking whole forms as his data, has to adopt either the view that natural forms belong to an eternal order that has always been in place in the world, or else that the world was created after a pre-existing pattern of forms, in the manner of Plato's *Timaeus*. If the Forms are not eternal, then they have an origin, an ἀρχή, and then the ἀρχή is prior to them; they are no longer the things that explain, but join the class of thing to be explained. The Aristotelian is also pretty well committed to the belief that order is prior to accident: if the forms of the natural world were a matter of accident, they might be infinitely numerous and varied, and there would be no knowing them.

Something similar can be said about the opposition between the closed world and the infinite universe, although the logical connections are not so tight. The Stoics show how much room the basic hypothesis allowed in this respect. Their universe was infinite – but empty, except for the single cosmos. Their universe was transient, not eternal – but endlessly repeated itself. So neither in space nor in time was there any necessity to consider new forms, or to entertain the idea of an origin of the world order from some prior condition. The Atomist hypothesis, on the other hand – the claim that things are explained by their minimal components – did not merely allow them to entertain the notion of an infinite universe: it virtually forced it upon them. I have tried to show in another place what the connections are in this case – how they came to think that only an infinite universe would give them a theory of motion capable of explaining how the cosmos grew out of atomic elements.[20] The alternative open to them was the alternative adopted in the quotation from Newton that I gave earlier in this lecture: a creator god, who made atoms just when and as he needed them to make a world. But this alternative was hardly open to the Atomists of classical antiquity, because of a prior decision that if God did make the world, either he made it out of pre-existing materials, like a potter with clay, or else he (or rather she) gave birth to it. But both of these possibilities were ruled out for them, because both assume the prior existence of the form that is supposed to emerge. The craftsman already knows what he is going to make, and parents produce offspring of the same kind as themselves.

What about the opposition between linear dynamics and flat earth on the one hand, and centrifocal dynamics with spherical earth on the other? The Aristotelians got the answer right, and their reasoning was good; so there is no need to seek for a further explanation of their choice in this case. But why did the Atomist doggedly adhere to the flat earth? It is not clear who first suggested that

[20] See chapter 1 of this volume.

the earth is spherical and that falling bodies fall towards the centre of the earth's sphere; the first certain occurrence of the idea is in Plato's *Phaedo* (108cff). Possibly this option was not open as a serious possibility to Democritus. But it was quite certainly open to Epicurus and his followers. So what induced Lucretius to put in that disastrous passage at the end of book I, in which he made fun of the idea of the antipodes, where living creatures walk head downwards, like the reflections that we see in water (1.1060–1)? If the universe is infinite, it has no centre; so we cannot have a universal centrifocal dynamics on the Aristotelian model. But why not the Stoic version, in which the earth's sphere forms its own dynamic centre in the infinite void? And how did the Epicureans manage with a flat-earth theory, after the astronomers had shown how everything fits if the earth is spherical? To some extent these questions can be answered, but not briefly and not without some detailed textual interpretation, which must be postponed to another occasion.

I have been arguing that the primary opposition that distinguished the Atomists from the Aristotelians, from which their other differences were derived with more or less logical stringency, lay in an epistemological preference for the bits and pieces of things on the one hand, and for whole forms on the other: the Theory of Atoms versus the Theory of Forms. Some may want to seek for a derivation of this primary difference itself at a deeper level in the human psyche – for example, from an irrational preference for sight or touch as the favoured way of making connections with the outside world. But that is a different enterprise from the one outlined in this lecture.

BIBLIOGRAPHY

Alfieri, V. E. 1953. *Atomos idea: l'origine del concetto dell' atomo nel pensiero greco*. Firenze: Le Monnier

Allen, R. E. *See* Furley, D. J., and Allen, R. E.

Anton, John P., and Kustas, George L. (eds.). 1971. *Essays in Ancient Greek Philosophy*. Albany: State University of New York Press

Arrighetti, G. 1960. *Epicuro: opere*. Torino: Einaudi, 1st ed.; 2nd ed. rev., 1973

Bailey, Cyril. 1928. *The Greek Atomists and Epicurus*. Oxford: Clarendon Press. Repr. New York: Russell, 1964

1947. *Lucretius*. Oxford: Clarendon Press

Balme, D. M. 1939. 'Greek Science and Mechanism: 1. Aristotle on Nature and Chance'. *Classical Quarterly* 33: 129–38

1941. 'Greek Science and Mechanism: 2. The Atomists'. *Classical Quarterly* 35: 23–8

1965. *Aristotle's Use of the Teleological Explanation*. Inaugural Lecture. University of London: Queen Mary College

Barnes, Jonathan. 1979. *The Presocratic Philosophers*. London/Henley/Boston: Routledge and Kegan Paul

Benardete, S. 1963. 'The Right, the True, and the Beautiful'. *Glotta* 41: 54–62

Berti, E. 1962 *La filosofia del primo Aristotele*. University of Padua: Facoltà di Lettere e Filosofia, 1962

Beye, C. R. 1963. 'Lucretius and Progress'. *Classical Journal* 58: 160–9

Bignone, E. 1936. *L'Aristotele perduto e la formazione filosofica di Epicuro*. Florence: La Nuova Italia

1938. 'Le idee morali di Antifonte Sofista'. *Studi sul pensiero antico*. Napoli. Repr. in German trans. by Frank Regan in Classen (1976), 493–518

Bollack, Jean. 1959. 'Lukrez und Empedokles'. *Die neue Rundschau* 70: 656–86

1965, 1969. *Empédocle*. Paris: Éditions de Minuit. Vol. I, vols II–III

Bollack, Jean, and Laks, André (eds.) 1976. *Études sur l'Épicurisme antique*. Université de Lille III, n.d.

Bollack, Jean, and Wismann, Heinz. 1972. *Héraclite ou la Séparation*. Paris: Éditions de Minuit

Borle, J. -P. 1962. 'Progrès ou déclin de l'humanité?' *Museum Helveticum* 19: 162–76

Boyancé, P. 1965. *Lucrèce et l'épicurisme*. Paris: Presses Universitaires de France

Brentlinger, John. 1972. 'Incomplete Predicates and the Two-World Theory of the *Phaedo*'. *Phronesis* 17: 61–79

Brieger, A. 1884. *Die Urbewegung der Atome bei Leukippos und Demokritos*. Halle: Heynemann

Burkert, Walter. 1963. 'Iranisches bei Anaximandros'. *Rheinisches Museum* 106: 97–134

1969. 'Das Proömium des Parmenides und die Katabasis des Pythagoras'. *Phronesis* 15: 1–30

1970. 'La genèse des choses et des mots: le papyrus de Dervéni entre Anaxagore et Cratyle'. *Les Études Philosophiques* 4: 443–55

1972. *Lore and Science in Ancient Pythagoreanism*. Cambridge, Mass.: Harvard University Press. English trans. by E. L. Minar of *Weisheit und Wissenschaft: Studien zu Pythagoras, Philolaos und Platon*. Nuremberg: Verlag Hans Carl, 1969

Burnet, J. 1945. *Early Greek Philosophy*. 4th ed. London: Black. 1st ed. 1892.

Calogero, Guido. 1967. *Storia della logica antica*. Bari: Laterza

Carteron, Henri. 1923. *La notion de force dans le système d'Aristote*. Paris

Charlton, W. 1970. *Aristotle's Physics books I and II, Translated with Introduction and Notes*. Oxford: Clarendon Press

Cherniss, H. F. 1935. *Aristotle's Criticism of Presocratic Philosophy*. Baltimore: The Johns Hopkins University Press. Repr. New York: Octagon, 1964

1944. *Aristotle's Criticism of Plato and the Academy*, vol. I. Baltimore: The Johns Hopkins University Press

1976. *Plutarch's Moralia*, vol. XIII. Loeb Classical Library. London: Heinemann, and Cambridge, Mass.: Harvard University Press

Classen, C. J. 1970. 'Anaximandros'. In Pauly–Wissowa, *Realencyclopädie* Supp. 12: 30–69

(ed.). 1976. *Sophistik*. Darmstadt: Wissenschaftliche Buchgesellschaft

Cohen, Morris R., and Drabkin, I. E. 1966. *A Source Book in Greek Science*. Cambridge, Mass.: Harvard University Press

Cole, T. 1967. *Democritus and the Sources of Greek Anthropology*. American Philological Association Monographs 25

Cooper, J. M. 1982. 'Aristotle on Natural Teleology'. In *Language and Logos: Studies presented to G. E. L. Owen*. Ed. M. Schofield and M. C. Nussbaum. Cambridge University Press. Pp. 197–222

Cornford, F. M. 1930. 'Anaxagoras' Theory of Matter'. *Classical Quarterly* 24: 14–30 and 83–95. Repr. in Furley and Allen (1975), 275–322 (page-references to this)

1952. *Principium Sapientiae: The Origins of Greek Philosophical Thought*. Cambridge University Press

Coutant, V. C. B. 1936. 'Alexander of Aphrodisias' Commentary on Book IV of Aristotle's *Meteorologica*'. New York: Columbia University Dissertation

Coxon, A. H. 1968. 'The Text of Parmenides 1.3'. *Classical Quarterly* 18: 69–70

Davison, J. A. 1953. 'Protagoras, Democritus, and Anaxagoras'. *Classical Quarterly* 3: 33–45

De Lacy, P. H. 1948. 'Lucretius and the History of Epicureanism'. *Transactions of the American Philological Association* 79: 12–23

De Lacy, P. H. and E. A. 1941. *Philodemus: On Methods of Inference*. 1st ed. American Philological Association Monograph. 2nd ed. rev. Naples: Bibliopolis, 1978

Dicks, D. R. *Early Greek Astronomy to Aristotle*. Ithaca, N.Y.: Cornell University Press, 1970

Diels, H. 1893/1968. 'Ueber das physikalische System des Straton'. *Sitzungsberichte der Kgl. Pr. Akademie der Wissenschaften zu Berlin*. Pp. 101–27. Repr. in his *Kleine Schriften zur Geschichte der antiken Philosophie*. Ed. Walter Burkert. Darmstadt: Wissenschaftliche Buchgesellschaft. Pp. 239–65.

Dolin, Edwin F. 1962. 'Parmenides and Hesiod'. *Harvard Studies in Classical Philology* 66: 93–8

Düring, I. 1944. *Aristotle's Chemical Treatise: Meteorologica Book IV*. With Introduction and Commentary. Göteborg: Acta Universitatis Gotoburgensis

Dyroff, A. 1899. *Demokritstudien*. Munich: Dieterich

1904. 'Zur Quellenfrage bei Lukretius (v. Gesang)'. *Programm ... der Universität König Friedrich Wilhelms III*. Bonn

Easterling, H. J. 1964. 'Quinta Natura'. *Museum Helveticum* 21: 73–85

1966. 'A Note on *De anima* 413 a 8–9'. *Phronesis* 11: 159–62

Edelstein, L. 1934. 'Cicero, *De natura deorum* 2'. *Studi Italiani di Filologia Classica* 11: 131–83

1940. 'Primum Graius homo: Lucr. 1.66'. *Transactions of the American Philological Association* 71: 78–90

Eichholz, D. E. 1965. *Theophrastus: De lapidibus*. Edited with Introduction, Translation and Commentary. Oxford: Clarendon Press

Ernout, A., and Robin, R. 1925. *Lucrèce, de la Nature: Commentaire*. Paris: Les Belles Lettres, 2nd ed. 1962

Ferguson, John. 1971. 'DINOS'. *Phronesis* 16, 97–115

Festugière, H. J. 1946. *Épicure et ses Dieux*. Paris, 1946

1949. *La Révélation d'Hermès Trismégiste: II Le Dieu Cosmique*. Paris: Gabalda, 1949.

Flashar, Hellmut. 1962. *Aristoteles: Problemata Physica*. Darmstadt: Wissenschaftliche Buchgesellschaft

Fränkel, Hermann. 1955. *Wege und Formen frühgriechischen Denkens*. Munich: Beck

Fredouille, J. C. 1972. 'Lucrèce et le double progrès contrastant'. *Pallas* 19: 1986. 11–27

Freudenthal, Gad. 1986. 'The Theory of Opposites and an Ordered Universe: Physics and Metaphysics in Anaximander'. *Phronesis* 31, 197–228

Furley, D. J. 1967a. 'Parmenides of Elea'. In *Encyclopedia of Philosophy*. Ed. Paul Edwards. New York: Macmillan and Free Press

1967b. *Two Studies in the Greek Atomists*. Princeton University Press

Furley, D. J., and Allen, R. E. (eds.). 1970, 1975. *Studies in Presocratic Philosophy*. London/ New York: Routledge and Kegan Paul, vol. I; vol. II

Furley, D. J., and Wilkie, J. S. 1984. *Galen on Respiration and the Arteries*. Princeton University Press

Furth, Montgomery. 1968. 'Elements of Eleatic Ontology'. *Journal of the History of Philosophy* 6: 112–32

Gatzemeier, Matthias. 1979. *Die Naturphilosophie des Straton von Lampsakos*. Meisenheim: Hain

Gershenson, Daniel E., and Greenberg, Daniel A. 1964. *Anaxagoras and the Birth of Physics*. New York

Gigon, O. 1952. 'Aristotelesstudien I'. *Museum Helveticum* 19: 113–36

1953. *Kommentar zum ersten Buch von Xenophons Memorabilien*. Basel: Reinhardt

1959. 'Cicero und Aristoteles'. *Hermes* 87: 143–62

Giuffrida, P. 1959. 'Il finale (vv. 1440–1457) del v libro di Lucrezio'. In *Epicurea in memoriam Hectoris Bignone*. Genoa. Pp. 129–65.

Giussani, Carlo. 1896–8. *Lucrezio: De rerum natura*. Turin: Loescher

Gomperz, T. 1865. *Herkulanische Studien, I: Philodem über Induktions-schlüsse*. Leipzig

Gotthelf, Allan. 1976. 'Aristotle's Concept of Final Causality'. *Review of Metaphysics* 30: 246–9

Gottschalk, H. B. 1961. 'The Authorship of *Meteorologica* Book IV'. *Classical Quarterly* 11: 67–79. Trans. into German, with 'Nachtrag 1973', in *Die Naturphilosophie des Aristoteles*, ed. G. A. Seeck. Darmstadt: Wissenschaftliche Buchgesellschaft, 1975. Pp. 114–38

1965. *Strato of Lampsacus: Some Texts*. Edited with a Commentary by H. B. Gottschalk. Proceedings of the Leeds Philosophical and Literary Society, Literary and Historical Section 11. 6. Leeds: Maney

1980. *Heraclides of Pontus*. Oxford: Clarendon Press

Grant, Edward. 1964. 'Motion in the Void and the Principle of Inertia in the Middle Ages'. *Isis* 55: 265–92

Grilli, A. 1953. 'La posizione di Aristotele, Epicuro, e Posidonio nei confronti della storia della civiltà'. *Rendiconti dell' Istituto Lombardo, Classe de Lettere* 86: 3–44

Guthrie, W. K. C. 1952. 'The Presocratic World Picture'. *Harvard Theological Review* 45, 87–104

1953. *Aristotle: On the Heavens*. Loeb Classical Library. London: Heinemann, and Cambridge, Mass.: Harvard University Press

A History of Greek Philosophy. Cambridge: Cambridge University Press. Vol. I: 'The Earlier Presocratics and the Pythagoreans', 1962. Vol. II: 'The Presocratic Tradition from Parmenides to Democritus', 1965. Vol. III: 'The Fifth Century Enlightenment', 1969

Hammer-Jensen, I. 1915. 'Das sogenannte IV. Buch der Meteorologie des Aristoteles'. *Hermes* I: 113–36

Happ, H. 1971. *Hyle*. Berlin: De Gruyter

Hartman, Edwin. 1977. *Substance, Body, and Soul: Aristotelian Investigations*. Princeton University Press

Havelock, Eric A. 1957. *The Liberal Temper in Greek Politics*. London: Cape

1958. 'Parmenides and Odysseus'. *Harvard Studies in Classical Philology* 63: 132–43

Heath, Sir Thomas. 1913. *Aristarchus of Samos: The Ancient Copernicus*. Oxford; repr. 1959

Heidel, W. A. 1937. *The Frame of Ancient Greek Maps*. New York: American Geographical Society, Research Series 20

Heinimann, Felix. 1965. *Nomos und Physis: Herkunft und Bedeutung einer Antithese im griechischen Denken des 5. Jahrhunderts*. Basel: Reinhardt

Heitsch, E. 1962. 'Die nicht-philosophische Ἀλήθεια'. *Hermes* 90: 24–33

Hölscher, Uvo. 1965. 'Weltzeiten und Lebenszyklus'. *Hermes* 93: 7–33

1968. *Anfängliches Fragen*. Göttingen: Vandenhoeck and Ruprecht

1969. *Parmenides: Vom Wesen des Seinden*. Frankfurt: Suhrkamp

Jaeger, W. 1934. *Aristotle: Fundamentals of the History of his Development*. Oxford: Clarendon Press

Joachim, H. H. 1922. *Aristotle on Coming-to-be and Passing-away (De Generatione et Corruptione): A Revised Text with Introduction and Commentary*. Oxford: Clarendon Press

Jobst, F. 1907. *Über das Verhältnis zwischen Lukrez und Empedokles*. Erlangen

Jöhrens, O. 1939. *Die Fragmente des Anaxagoras*. Bochum

Joly, R. 1960. *Recherches sur le traité pseudo-hippocratique Du Régime*. Paris: Les Belles Lettres

Kahn, Charles H. 1960a. *Anaximander and the Origins of Greek Cosmology*. New York: Columbia University Press. Repr. Philadelphia: Centrum, 1985

1960b. 'Religion and Natural Philosophy in Empedocles' Doctrine of the Soul'. *Archiv für Geschichte der Philosophie* 42: 3–35

1966. 'The Greek Verb "to be" and the Concept of Being'. *Foundations of Language* 2: 245–65

1967. 'Anaximander'. In *The Encyclopedia of Philosophy*. Ed. Paul Edwards. New York: Macmillan and Free Press. Pp. 117–18

1968. Review of Bollack (1965). *Gnomon* 40: 439–47

1969. 'The Thesis of Parmenides'. *Review of Metaphysics* 22: 700–24

1979. *The Art and Thought of Heraclitus*. Cambridge University Press

Keller, A. C. 1951. 'Lucretius and the Idea of Progress'. *Classical Journal* 46: 185–8

Kember, Owen. 1973. 'Anaxagoras' Theory of Sex Differentiation and Heredity'. *Phronesis* 18: 1–14

Kenney, E. J. 1972. 'The Historical Imagination of Lucretius'. *Greece and Rome* 19: 11–24

Kerferd, G. B. 1959. 'The Moral and Political Doctrines of Antiphon the Sophist: a Reconsideration'. *Proceedings of the Cambridge Philological Society*, 26–32

1969. 'Anaxagoras and the Concept of Matter before Aristotle'. *Bulletin of the John Rylands Library* 52: 129–43. Repr. in Mourelatos (1974), 489–503, to which references are given.

Kerschensteiner, J. 1959. 'Zu Leukippos A 1.' *Hermes* 87: 441–8

Kirk, G. S. 1954. *Heraclitus: The Cosmic Fragments*. Cambridge University Press

1955. 'Some Problems in Anaximander'. *Classical Quarterly* 5, 21–38. Repr. in Furley and Allen (1970), 335–40

Kirk, G. S., and Raven, J. E. 1957. *The Presocratic Philosophers*. Cambridge University Press, 1st ed., 2nd ed. rev. by Malcolm Schofield, 1983

Kleve, Knut. 1963. *Gnosis Theon. Symbolae Osloenses*, Suppl. 19

Konstan, David. 1972. 'Epicurus on "Up" and "Down" (*Letter to Herodotus* 60)'. *Phronesis* 17: 269–78

Koyré, Alexander. 1957. *From the Closed World to the Infinite Universe*. Baltimore and London: The Johns Hopkins University Press; repr. 1968.

Kranz, W. 1944. 'Lukrez und Empedokles'. *Philologus* 54: 68–107

Landels, J. G. 1978. *Engineering in the Ancient World*. London: Chatto and Windus

Lanza, Diego. 1963. 'Le omoiomere nella tradizione dossografica anassagorea'. *La Parola del Passato* 91: 256–93

1966. *Anassagora: testimonianze e frammenti*. Firenze: La Nuova Italia

Lee, H. D. P. 1952. *Aristotle: Meteorologica*. Loeb Classical Library. London: Heinemann, and Cambridge, Mass.: Harvard University Press. 1st ed.; 2nd ed. rev. 1962

Lefèvre, C. 1978. 'Sur le statut de l'âme dans le *De anima* et les *Parva naturalia*'. In Lloyd and Owen (1978), 21–67

Leonard, William E., and Smith, Stanley B. 1965. *Lucretius*. Wisconsin University Press

Lesher, J. H. 1984. 'Parmenides' Critique of Thinking'. *Oxford Studies in Ancient Philosophy* 2: 1–30

Lesky, Erna. 1950. *Die Zeugungs- und Vererbungslehren der Antike und ihr Nachwirken*. Mainz: Akademie der Wissenschaften und der Literatur, Abhandlungen der geistes- und sozialwissenschaftlichen Klasse 19

Liepmann, H. C. 1886. *Die Mechanik der Leukippisch-Demokriteischen Atome*. Leipzig: Fock

Lloyd, G. E. R. (ed.). 1978. *Hippocratic Writings*. Harmondsworth: Penguin Books

Lloyd, G. E. R., and Owen, G. E. L. (eds.). 1978. *Aristotle on the Mind and the Senses: Proceedings of the 7th Symposium Aristotelicum*. Cambridge University Press

Long, A. A. 1963. 'The Principles of Parmenides' Cosmology'. *Phronesis* 8: 90–107

Louis, P. 1956. *Aristote: Les Parties des Animaux*. Paris: Les Belles Lettres

Luria, S. 1964. 'Zwei Demokrit-Studien'. In *Isonomia*, ed. J. Mau and E. G. Schmidt. Berlin Akademie-Verlag. Pp. 27–54

1970. *Democritea*. Leningrad

McDiarmid, John B. 1960. 'Theophrastus' *De sensibus* 61–62: Democritus' Theory of Weight'. *Classical Philology* 55: 28–30

Mansfeld, Jaap. 1964. *Die Offenbarung des Parmenides und die menschliche Welt*. Assen: Van Gorcum

1971. *The Pseudo-Hippocratic Tract* Περὶ ἑβδομάδων *ch. 1–11 and Greek Philosophy*. Assen: Van Gorcum

Mansion, A. 1946. *Introduction à la physique aristotélicienne*. Louvain: Institut Supérieur de Philosophie, and Paris: Vrin

Marcovich, M. 1967. *Heraclitus: Greek Text with a Short Commentary*. Merida, Venezuela: The Los Andes University Press

Mates, Benson. 1961. *Stoic Logic*. Berkeley/L.A.: University of California Press

Mathewson, I. R. D. 1958. 'Aristotle and Anaxagoras'. *Classical Quarterly* 8: 67–81

Mau, J. 1954. *Zum Problem des Infinitesimalen bei den antiken Atomisten*. Berlin: Akademie-Verlag

Merlan, P. 1950. 'Lucretius, Primitivist or Progressivist?' *Journal of the History of Ideas* 11: 364–8

Mesnard, P. 1947. 'Antifinalisme et finalité chez Lucrèce'. *Revue des Sciences Humaines* 45: 97–105

Mondolfo, R. 1956. *L'infinito nel pensiero dell' antichità classica*. 2nd enlarged ed. of *L'infinito nel pensiero dei Greci*. Florence, 1936

Moraux, P. 1963 'Quinta Essentia'. In Pauly–Wissowa, *Realencyclopädie* 24

Morrison, J. S. 1955. 'Parmenides and Er'. *Journal of Hellenic Studies* 75: 59–68

1959. 'The Shape of the Earth in Plato's *Phaedo*'. *Phronesis* 4: 101–19

1963. 'The Truth of Antiphon'. *Phronesis* 8: 35–49. Repr. in Classen (1976), 519–36

Moulton, Carroll. 1973. 'Antiphon the Sophist: On Truth'. *Transactions of the American Philological Association* 103: 329–67

1974. 'Antiphon the Sophist and Democritus'. *Museum Helveticum* 31: 129–39

Mourelatos, A. P. D. 1969. 'Comments on [Kahn's] "The Thesis of Parmenides"'. *Review of Metaphysics* 22: 735–44

1970. *The Route of Parmenides*. New Haven and London: Yale University Press

(ed.). 1974. *The Pre-Socratics: A Collection of Critical Essays*. Garden City, N.Y.: Anchor/Doubleday

Mueller, Carl W. 1965. *Gleiches zu Gleichem*. Wiesbaden: Harrasowitz

Mugler, C. 1953. 'Sur quelques particularités de l'atomisme ancien'. *Revue de Philologie* 27: 141–74

Munro, H. A. J. 1866. *T. Lucreti Cari De rerum natura libri sex*. 2nd ed. rev. Cambridge: Deighton Bell

Nethercut, W. R. 1967. 'The Conclusion of Lucretius' Fifth Book: Further Remarks'. *Classical Journal* 63: 97–106

Nussbaum, Martha Craven. 1978. *Aristotle's De motu animalium: Text with Translation, Commentary, and Interpretive Essays*. Princeton University Press

O'Brien, D. 1968. 'The Relation of Anaxagoras and Empedocles'. *Journal of Hellenic Studies* 88: 93–113

1969. *Empedocles' Cosmic Cycle*. Cambridge University Press

1981. *Theories of Weight in the Ancient World: Four Essays on Democritus, Plato and Aristotle: A Study in the Development of Ideas*, vol. I: 'Democritus: Weight and Size: an Exercise in the Reconstruction of Early Greek Philosophy'. Paris: Les Belles Lettres and Brill

Osler, M. 1979. 'Descartes and Charleton'. *Journal of the History of Ideas* 40: 445–56

Owen, G. E. L. 1957–8. 'Zeno and the Mathematicians'. *Proceedings of the Aristotelian Society*, 199–222. Repr. in Furley and Allen (1975), 143–65

1960. 'Eleatic Questions'. *Classical Quarterly* 10: 84–102. Repr. in Furley and Allen (1975), 48–81

Pease, A. S. 1955. *M. Tulli Ciceronis De Natura Deorum*. Cambridge, Mass.: Repr. Darmstadt: Wissenschaftliche Buchgesellschaft, 1968

Peck, A. L. 1931. 'Anaxagoras: Predication as a Problem in Physics'. *Classical Quarterly* 25: 27–37 and 112–20

1937. *Aristotle: Parts of Animals*. Loeb Classical Library. London: Heinemann, and Cambridge, Mass.: Harvard University Press

Pepe, L. 1978. 'A proposito del IV libro dei Meteorologica di Aristotele'. *Atti dell' Accademia di Scienza Morale e Politica, Napoli* 89: 503–23

Perelli, L. 1967. 'La storia dell' umanità nel V libro di Lucrezio'. *Atti della Accademia delle Scienze di Torino* 101: 117–285

Philippson, R. 1909. 'Zur Wiederherstellung von Philodems sog. Schrift Περὶ Σημείων καὶ Σημειώσεων'. *Rheinisches Museum* 64: 1–38

1910. 'Zu Philodem Περὶ Σημειώσεων'. *Rheinisches Museum* 65: 313–16

Pohlenz, M. 1947. *Die Stoa*. Göttingen: Hubert

Popper, Karl R. 1959. *The Logic of Scientific Discovery*. London: Hutchinson

Rankin, H. D. 1963. ''Α-λήθεια in Plato'. *Glotta* 41: 51–4

Raven, J. E. 1954. 'The Basis of Anaxagoras' Cosmology'. *Classical Quarterly* 4: 123–37

Regenbogen, O. 1940. 'Theophrastos'. In Pauly–Wissowa, *Realencyclopädie* Supp. 7

Reinhardt, K. 1912. 'Hekataios von Abdera und Demokrit'. *Hermes* 47: 492–513

Reitzenstein, E. 1924. *Theophrast bei Epikur und Lukrez*. Heidelberg

Robin, L. 1916. 'Sur la conception épicurienne du progrès'. *Revue de Métaphysique et Morale* 22: 697–719

1925. See Ernout, A., and Robin, L.

Robinson, John Mansley. 1971. 'Anaximander and the Problem of the Earth's Immobility'. In Anton and Kustas (1971), 111–18

Rodier, G. 1890. *La physique de Straton de Lampsaque*. Paris: Alcan

Roscher, W. H. 1913. 'Die hippokratische Schrift Περὶ ἑβδομάδων'. *Studien zur Geschichte und Kultur des Altertums* 63–4. Paderborn. Repr. New York, 1967

Ross, W. D. 1936. *Aristotle's Physics: A Revised Text with Introduction and Commentary*. Oxford: Clarendon Press

Samburgsky, S. 1959. *Physics of the Stoics*. London: Routledge and Kegan Paul

Saunders, Trevor J. 1978. 'Antiphon the Sophist on Natural Laws'. *Proceedings of the Aristotelian Society*, 216–35

Schilling, Robert. 1954. *La religion romaine de Vénus*. Paris

Schofield, Malcolm. 1975. 'Doxographia Anaxagorea'. *Hermes* 103: 1–24

1978. 'Aristotle on the Imagination'. In Lloyd and Owen (1978) 99–140

Schwabl, Hans. 1953. 'Sein und Doxa bei Parmenides'. *Wiener Studien* 66: 50–75

1963. 'Hesiod und Parmenides: Zur Forschung des parmenideischen Prooimions'. *Rheinisches Museum* 106: 134–42

Sedley, D. 1976. 'Epicurus and his Professional Rivals'. In Bollack and Laks [1976], 119–59

Seeck, G. A. 1964. *Über die Elemente in der Kosmologie des Aristoteles*. Munich: Beck

1965. '*Nachträge*' *im achten Buch der Physik des Aristoteles*. Abhandlungen der Geister- und Sozialwissenschaftlichen Klasse, Akademie der Wissenschaften und der Literatur. Mainz

Skemp, J. B. 1978. ' Ὄρεξις in *De anima* 3.10'. In Lloyd and Owen (1978), 181–9

Smith, Martin Ferguson. 1976. 'More New Fragments of Diogenes of Oenoanda'. In Bollack and Laks [1976], 279–318

Solmsen, F. 1951. 'Epicurus and Cosmological Heresies'. *American Journal of Philology* 72: 1–23

1953. 'Epicurus on the Growth and Decline of the Cosmos'. *American Journal of Philology* 74: 34–51

1960. *Aristotle's System of the Physical World*. Ithaca, N.Y.: Cornell University Press

1965. 'Love and Strife in Empedocles' Cosmology'. *Phronesis* 10: 109–48

1971. 'Plato's First Mover in the eighth book of Aristotle's *Physics*'. In *Philomathes: Studies in Memory of Philip Merlan*. The Hague. Pp. 171–82

Sorabji, R. R. K. 1980. *Necessity, Cause, and Blame: Perspectives on Aristotle's Theory*. London: Duckworth, and Ithaca, N.Y.: Cornell University Press

1983. *Time, Creation, and the Continuum*. London: Duckworth

Spoerri, W. 1959. *Späthellenistische Berichte über Welt, Kultur, und Götter*. Basel: Schweizerische Beiträge zur Altertumswissenschaft 9

Sprague, Rosamund Kent (ed.). 1972. *The Older Sophists*. Columbia, S.C. University of South Carolina Press

Steinmetz, P. 1964. *Die Physik des Theophrast von Eresos*. Bad Homburg/Berlin/Zürich: Gehlen

Strang, Colin. 1963. 'The Physical Theory of Anaxagoras'. *Archiv für Geschichte der Philosophie* 45: 101–18. Repr. in Furley and Allen (1975), 361–80, to which references are given.

Strohm, H. 1970. *Aristoteles' Meteorologie*. Berlin/Darmstadt

Stückelberger, Alfred. 1984. *Vestigia Democritea: Die Rezeption der Lehre von den Atomisten in der antiken Naturwissenschaft und Medizin*. Schweizerische Beiträge zur Altertumswissenschaft 17. Basel: Reinhardt

Tarán, Leonardo. 1965. *Parmenides: A Text with Translation, Commentary and Critical Essays*. Princeton University Press

Taylor, M. 1947. 'Progress and Primitivism in Lucretius'. *American Journal of Philology* 68: 180–94

Theiler, W. 1965. *Zur Geschichte der teleologischer Naturbetrachtung bis auf Aristoteles*. 2nd ed. Berlin: De Gruyter

Thesleff, Holger. 1973. Review of Mansfeld, *The Pseudo-Hippocratic Tract. Gnomon* 45: 232–6

Tigner, Steven S. 1974. 'Empedocles' Twirled Ladle and the Vortex-Supported Earth'. *Isis* 65: 433–47

Toulmin, S., and Goodfield, J. 1962. *The Architecture of Matter*. London: Hutchinson

Untersteiner, M. 1963. *Aristotele: Della Filosofia: introduzione, testo, traduzione, e commento esegetico*. Rome: Edizioni di Storia e Letteratura

Vlastos, Gregory. 1946. 'Parmenides' Theory of Knowledge'. *Transactions of the American Philological Association* 72: 66–77

 1950. 'The Physical Theory of Anaxagoras'. *Philosophical Review* 59: 31–57. Repr. in Furley and Allen (1975), 323–53, to which references are given.

 1959. 'One World or Many in Anaxagoras?' from a review of Fränkel (1955) in *Gnomon* 31: 199–203. Repr. in Furley and Allen (1975), 354–60

 1965a. 'Degrees of Reality in Plato'. In *New Essays on Plato and Aristotle*. Ed. R. Bambrough. London: Routledge and Kegan Paul. Repr. in G. Vlastos, *Platonic Studies*. Princeton University Press, 1973. Pp. 58–75

 1965b. 'Minimal Parts in Epicurean Atomism'. *Isis* 56: 121–47

 1983. 'The Socratic Elenchus; and Afterthoughts'. *Oxford Studies in Ancient Philosophy* 1: 27–58 and 71–4

Vos, H. 1963. 'Die Bahnen von Nacht und Tag'. *Mnemosyne* 16: 18–34

Wagner, H. 1967. *Aristoteles' Physikvorlesung*. Berlin: Akademie-Verlag

Walzer, R. 1934. *Aristotelis Dialogorum Fragmenta*. Florence: Sansoni

Waszink, J. H. 1966. 'Zum Exkurs des Lukrez über Glaube und Aberglaube (5.1194–1240)'. *Wiener Studien* 79: 308–13

Waterlow, Sarah. 1982. *Nature, Change and Agency in Aristotle's Physics*. Oxford: Clarendon Press

Wehrli, Fritz. 1969. *Die Schule des Aristoteles: V. Straton von Lampsakos. VII. Herakleides Pontikos*. Basel/Stuttgart: Schwabe and Co., 2nd ed.

West, M. L. 1971a. 'The Cosmology of [Hippocrates] *De hebdomadis*'. *Classical Quarterly* 21: 365–88

 1971b. *Early Greek Philosophy and the Orient*. Oxford: Clarendon Press

Wieland, Wolfgang. 1962. *Die aristotelische Physik: Untersuchungen über die Grundlegung der Naturwissenschaft und die sprachlichen Bedingungen der Prinzipienforschung bei Aristoteles*. Göttingen: Vandenhoeck and Ruprecht

Woodbury, Leonard. 1958. 'Parmenides on Names'. *Harvard Studies in Classical Philology* 63: 145–60. Repr. with additional notes in Anton and Kustas (1971), 145–64

Wright, W. A. (ed.). 1900. F. Bacon, *The Advancement of Learning*. Oxford: Clarendon Press

Zeller, E. 1879. *Die Philosophie der Griechen*. 3rd ed. Leipzig

INDEX LOCORUM

Presocratic philosophers appear in this index under their own name: 'fr. nn' = 'B nn' in Diels–Kranz, Vorsokratiker. *Doxographers and Commentators on the Presocratics also appear generally under their own name, rather than as 'A' references in Diels–Kranz.*

Aeschylus		Antiphon, fr. 44	66–76
Persae 419	35n	Aquinas, *De physico auditu*	
Supplices 822	91n	2.12	115n
Aëtius		Archilochus, fr. 103	226
1.3.4	233n	Archimedes, *Arenarius* 1.4	3n
1.3.5	53n	Aristophanes	
1.3.18	8on	Clouds	116
1.4.2.	94	Frogs 1365, 1407	91n
1.12.6	8on, 93n, 94	Thesmophoriazusae 549	31
1.25.1	21n	fr. 488.4	91n
11.2	99n	Aristotle	
11.11.4	195	*Analytica Posteriora*	
11.13.3	96	11.12.96 a 2ff	119
111.10	99n	*De anima*	
111.10.5	8on, 99n	11.1.413 a 8	123
111.11.3	23n	11.4.416 b 33	127
111.15.7	100n	11.5.417 a 14–16	127
Alexander of Aphrodisias		11.5.417 b 19–21	127
Metaph. 36.26–7	108n	11.7.418 b 4	153
Meteor. 226.23	135n	111.2.426 b 29–31	127
Problemata IV.42	224n	111.10	129ff
Quaestiones 11.23	154n	111.10.433 a 17 – b 28	126
Anaxagoras		*De caelo*	
fr. 1	55	1.5–7	111, 114
fr. 3	49, 60f, 185	1.5.271 b 28ff	2
fr. 4a	56, 57n	1.7.274 b 30	81n
fr. 4b	55, 63	1.7.275 b 29ff	87n
fr. 5	60, 62	1.7.275 b 29 – 276 a 14	101
fr. 6	55	1.275 b 32	88n
fr. 10	48ff, 51ff, 57–8	1.9.279 a 12	193
fr. 12	56	1.9.279 a 14	113n
fr. 17	48	11.1.284 a 18–24	97
Anaximander, fr. 1	29n	11.3.286 a 25	139
Anaximenes, fr. 2	21	11.13.293 a 17–18	99n

245

II.13.294 b 13–14	95n, 100n	II.8	146
II.13.295 a 10	98n	*De motu animalium*	
II.13.295 a 13–22	97	698 a 7–9	125
II.13.295 a 32 – b 9	98–9	700 b 23–4	126
II.13.295 b 10–16	17	701 a 5	127n
II.14	80n	701 b 17–18	127n
II.14.296 b 13	193	702 a 17–19	130
II.14.296 b 20	92	703 a 4–5	126
II.14.297 b 19	92n	*De somno*	
III.1.300 b 8–16	101	3.457 b 2	140
III.2.300 a 29	88n	3.457 b 31ff	119
III.2.300 b 11	81n	3.458 a 27	140
III.2.300 b 8–16	88n, 100–1	*Ethica Eudemia* II.16	125
III.2.301 b 16	194	*Metaphysics*	
III.2.301 b 29	86	I.3.983 b 20–6	233n
III.3.302 a 20	194	I.3.984 b 17	100
III.4.302 b 32	109	I.4.985 a 4 – b 3	100
III.4.303 a 18	109	I.4.985 b 19	89n
III.4.303 a 4ff	109	I.4.985 b 20	100
III.4.303 b 5	194	I.9.990 b 14	185
III.5.304 a 1–7	102	III.5.1002 a 18	111
III.6.305 a 13	194	XII.6.1071 b 32	100
III.8	133	*Meteorologica*	
IV.1.308 a 11	89n	I.4.341 b 35 – 342 a 16	138
IV.2.308 b 9	80n	I.9	137
IV.2.309 a 1–2	93	I.11.347 b 12ff	118
IV.3.311 a 12	124n	I.12.348 b 6	140
IV.5.312 b 5ff	157	I.12.348 b 16	140
De generatione animalium		II.2.354 b 32 –	
I.8.716 b 18	147n	355 a 32	193
I.17ff	147n	II.2.355 b 10	145
II.1	134	II.9.369 a 20–30	138
II.1.734 b 27 –735 a 2	146	II.9.369 b 5	138
II.2.735 b 26	147n	III.1.371 a 18	138
II.2.735 b 35–7	147n	III.6	145
II.4.739 b 5ff	147n	IV.1.379 a 22–6	136, 144, 147n
II.5.741 b 10–15	148	IV.3.380 b 17–24	136
II.6.742 b 17–24	100	IV.3.380 b 22	144
II.6.743 a 1–17	142n	IV.3.381 a 5	134
II.6.743 a 7	132n, 147n	IV.3.381 a 33 – b 3	137
II.6.744 a 5–11	143	IV.3.381 b 4	134
IV.3.769 a 7–35	57	IV.4.382 a 7–13	139
V.3	139	IV.4.382 a 11–14	145
V.3.783 a 16	139	IV.5.382 b 8–10	140
V.3.783 a 33	143	IV.6.383 a 7	137
De generatione et corruptione		IV.6.383 a 13–19	137
I.2.316 a 13ff	104	IV.6.383 a 20	139
I.3.318 b 16	139	IV.7.383 b 25	134, 147n
I.7.323 b 10ff	79n	IV.8–9	141, 155
I.8	132, 141, 155	IV.8.386 a 29 – b 7	155
I.8.325 a 4	167n	IV.9.386 a 29 – b 7	140
I.8.325 a 15	111	IV.9.387 a 15–17	155
I.8.325 a 23ff	78n	IV.10.389 a 22	147n
I.8.326 a 8	93	IV.12.390 b 2–14	134–5
I.8.326 a 9	80n, 102	*Nicomachean Ethics*	
I.8.326 b 21–8	142	III.1.1110 b 9–15	128
II.2	146	III.1.1111 a 22	125
		III.5	125

III.5.1113 b 17 | 128
III.5.1114 a 3ff | 128
III.5.1114 a 31ff | 128
On Democritus | 88n
On Philosophy | 194, 202, 227n
  fr. 8 | 204
  fr. 8 | 211
  fr. 12a | 203
  fr. 12b | 203
  fr. 13 | 201
  fr. 18 | 201
  fr. 21 | 201
  fr. 20 | 203
Parts of Animals
  II.1.646 a 14–17 | 146
  II.2.649 a 17 | 139
  II.2.649 a 20 | 146
  II.2.649 a 33 | 132n
  II.3.649 b 12 | 143
  II.4 | 139
  II.4.650 b 16 | 143
  II.4.651 a 9 | 139
  II.7.653 a 2ff | 119
  III.10.672 b 29 | 145
  III.11.673 b 8 | 145
Physics
  II.1.192 b 13–33 | 121
  II.2.192 b 21 | 84n
  II.7.198 b 4–9 | 119
  II.7.198 b 29ff | 179
  II.8 | 114
  II.8.198 b 16 – 199 a 8 | 115–20
  III.4–5 | 111
  III.4.203 a 19ff | 105
  III.4.203 b 15–30 | 110, 112
  III.5.204 a 20ff | 185
  III.5.205 a 10–19 | 194
  III.5.205 b 24–8 | 194
  III.6.206 a 18 | 105
  III.6.206 b 7 | 105
  III.8.208 a 9–11 | 112
  III.8.208 a 10–14 | 111
  III.8.208 a 14–19 | 110
  IV.1 | 81n
  IV.1.209 a 20 | 85, 86n
  IV.4 | 150
  IV.4.211 b 15–29 | 81n
  IV.4.211 b 18–19 | 82n
  IV.4.211 b 20–9 | 82n
  IV.6.213 b 2–29 | 154
  IV.6.213 b 14–18 | 141
  IV.6ff | 132
  IV.7 | 82, 150
  IV.7.214 a 2 | 87n
  IV.4.214 a 6–9 | 194
  IV.7.214 a 16–26 | 111
  IV.7.214 a 26 – b 11 | 111
  IV.7.214 a 28–32 | 154

IV.7.214 a 32 | 153
IV.7.214 a 32ff | 141
IV.8 | 111
IV.8.214 b 14ff | 78n
IV.8.214 b 28ff | 86n
IV.8.215 a 6–9 | 102
IV.8.215 a 14 –
  216 a 11 | 83n
IV.8.215 a 20–2 | 87n
IV.9 | 111, 141, 155
IV.9.216 a 11–21 | 83n
IV.9.217 a 26 b 11 | 141
VI.1–2 | 84n
VI.1.231 a 28 | 107
VI.2 | 108
VI.10.240 b 17 –
  241 a 26 | 108
VII.1.241 b 34 | 85
VIII.1.251 b 15 | 103
VIII.1.251 b 20 | 111
VIII.1.252 a 32 | 89n
VIII.1.252 a 34 | 100
VIII.1.253 a 11–21 | 123ff
VIII.4 | 85
VIII.4.254 b 14–33 | 122
VIII.4.255 a 5–10 | 121, 125
VIII.4.255 a 30 – b 15 | 127
VIII.4.255 b 29 | 124
VIII.4.256 a 19–27 | 122
VIII.4.256 b 3ff | 122
VIII.5.258 a 22–27 | 122
VIII.5.258 b | 125
VIII.6.259 b 1–20 | 123ff
VIII.7.260 b 7–13 | 134
VIII.10.266 b 27 –
  267 a 12 | 87n
VIII.10.267 a 2ff | 86
[Aristotle]
  De mundo | 202
    2.391 b 8 | 229
    6.397 b 9ff | 84n
  De plantis II | 195
  On indivisible lines | 107
    968 a 2ff | 185
  Problemata physica
    XI.33 | 153n
    XI.49 | 153
    XI.58 | 153 and n
    XXIII.8 | 153n
    XXV.9 | 153n
    XXV.22 | 153n
Aulus Gellius VII.2.7. | 196
Bacchylides
  fr. 9.85 | 41
  fr. 14.4. | 41
Censorinus
  5.2ff | 58n
  5.4 | 58n

6.8	58n	fr. 9	48
Cicero		fr. 11	49
Academica 1.7.26	194	fr. 12	49
Ad Quintum Fratrem		fr. 17	48n
II.9.3	176	fr. 20	51n
De finibus		fr. 21	48n
1.19	90n	fr. 22.2	174n
1.19.63	210	fr. 23	52
V.9	172	fr. 26	48n
De natura deorum		fr. 35	51n
1.69	196	fr. 57	179n
II	199	fr. 61	179n
II.42–3	195	fr. 82	179n
II.95–6	201	fr. 96	49
II.97	227n	fr. 112	181
Lucullus 119	201	fr. 129	180, 208
Tusculan disputations 1.46	198	fr. 137.1–4	181
David, *Prolegomena*		Epicurus	
philosophiae		*Kyriai Doxai*	
XXXVIII.14	232n	11–12	212
Democritus		24	170n
fr. 34	232	*Letter* 1 (*Letter to*	
fr. 164	79n	*Herodotus*)	206
Demosthenes L.22	35n	1.35	170n
Derveni papyrus	62n	1.38	166, 170n
Diels–Kranz, *Vorsokratiker*		1.41–2	111–12
12A.10	21n	1.42	157
12A.11	21n	1.46	157
12A.25	21n	1.48–9	163n
12A.26	21n	1.49	163
44A.17	23n	1.50–1	163ff, 170n
64A.16a	23n	1.56–9	168
68A.1 = 1.81.10	21	1.56	106
68A.1 = 1.82.9	21	1.58	108
68B.167	11n	1.59	108
Diodorus Siculus 1.7–8	211	1.60	89n
Diogenes of Apollonia fr. 4	233n	1.61–2	83n
Diogenes Laertius		1.61	108
1.16	59n	1.62	84n, 169
V.43	176n	1.72–3	184
V.59	150	1.75–6	211–12, 219, 221
IX.21–2	24	*Letter* 2 (*Letter to*	
IX.30ff	80ff	*Pythocles*)	
IX.31	230	2.87	162n
IX.31–2	79n	2.88–90	230n
IX.32	94n	*Letter* 3 (*Letter to*	
IX.57	23n	*Menoeceus*)	
X.7–8	209	3.134	195
X.10	227	*On Nature*	
X.25	176n	21–2	177
X.32	170n	29.14–15	165, 170n
Diogenes of Oenoanda		Eudemus, fr. 145 W	21
fr. 10	211	Galen	
fr. 20, col. 2	112	*An in arteriis* 7	158
fr. 33, col. 2.3	196	*De nat. fac.*	
n. fr. 40	224	II.4	158
Empedocles		II.6	158
fr. 8	49	*De usu partium* III.10	231–2

De usu respirationis 3 — 140n
Gregory of Nazianzus, schol. — 57–8
Heraclitus
  fr. 94 — 29n
  fr. 125 — 224
  fr. 125a — 44
Hero, *Pneumatica* — 150ff, 156ff
Herodotus
  I.24 — 42
  I.82 — 25
  II.115 — 42
  II.21ff — 42
  II.65 — 92n
  II.115 — 42
  III.104 — 23
  IV.18 — 41
  VI.100 — 27
Hesiod
  Theogony
    123ff — 29
    722–5 — 14
    728 — 14n
    740ff — 29
    748–57 — 30n
  Works and Days 714 — 40
Hippocratic Corpus
  Airs, waters, places — 75
    VII.86 — 70
    X.84 — 70
  Ancient Medicine
    9 — 91n
    22 — 144
  De carnibus VI.13 — 144n
  De flatibus
    10 — 144n
    15–18 — 144n
  De morbis
    II.3 — 144n
    II.11 — 144n
  Epidemics I.26 — 223
  The nature of the child
    12 — 230
    17 — 231
  On fractures XIX — 40
  Regimen
    II.57–8 — 144n
    II.62 — 144n
    II.64 — 144n
[Hippocrates], *De hebdomadibus* 6 — 4n
Homer
  Iliad
    VIII.69 — 91n
    IX.522 — 39
    XI.641 — 224
    XII.434 — 91n
    XXII.209 — 91n

  Odyssey — 91n
    x.86 — 30n
    XI — 28n
Horace, *Odes* III.11.1 — 175n
Irenaeus II.14.2 — 57n
Leucippus A7 — 78n
Lucretius, *De rerum natura*
  1.1–43 — 172ff
  1.55–7 — 178
  1.62–7 — 208
  1.62–101 — 179–82
  1.73–5 — 2
  1.73 — 229
  1.74–7 — 210
  1.146–8 — 210
  1.215ff — 186
  1.335ff — 188
  1.370–97 — 168
  1.370ff — 84n
  1.449–82 — 183
  1.599–634 — 168
  1.611–12 — 108
  1.615–27 — 107, 185
  1.635 — 187
  1.635–704 — 185f
  1.645–64 — 186
  1.665–74 — 186
  1.712–33 — 176
  1.763–829 — 174
  1.782–802 — 187
  1.834–42 — 53n, 54n
  1.835–6 — 49
  1.875 — 53n
  1.951ff — 188
  1.960 — 111
  1.968–79 — 7n, 110
  1.1014–20 — 112
  1.1052–113 — 187, 204
  1.1052–82 — 113
  1.1060–1 — 235
  1.1102 — 4n
  II.59–61 — 210
  II.62–332 — 10n
  II.167–76 — 201
  II.167–83 — 195
  II.216–50 — 90n
  II.221–4 — 101n
  II.225–39 — 83n
  II.251–93 — 195, 207
  II.434 — 161
  II.886–972 — 196
  II.1077 — 9n
  II.1144 — 4n
  III.1–17 — 180
  III.1–3 — 208
  III.16 — 4n
  III.91–3 — 210
  III.307–22 — 198

III.350–69	198	Melissus	
III.425–829	198	fr. 1	36
III.830–1	199	fr. 4	36
III.847–61	199	fr. 7	36, 78n
III.944–5	210	fr. 7.7	167
IV.416–31	13	fr. 8	36
IV.722–922	163n	Mimnermus, fr. 10 (Diehl)	14
IV.732–3	165	Pacuvius, *Chryses*	203
IV.750–1	166n	Parmenides	
IV.757–9	166	fr. 1	27ff
IV.823–57	199	fr. 2	33ff
IV.1037ff	178	fr. 2.1	29
V	12	fr. 3	35
V.1–54	180	fr. 6	33ff
V.8–10	208	fr. 6.3–4	44
V.55–234	195, 200, 204	fr. 7.5–8.2	33, 38ff, 44
V.91–109	178	fr. 8.1–21	49
V.168–73	203	fr. 8.9–10	26
V.243	231	fr. 8.15–16	223
V.245	174	fr. 8.39	30
V.251–60	174	fr. 8.42–9	25
V.261–72	174	fr. 8.44–5	31
V.273–80	174	fr. 8.53–4	30–3
V.281–305	174	fr. 55–9	31
V.306–50	203	fr. 9	31n, 32
V.371	4n	fr. 16	31
V.380–415	204	Philodemus, *On signs*	
V.416–770	208	VIII.32–IX.3	167, 168n
V.422ff	113	Philoponus	
V.432–3	174	*De aeternitate mundi*	
V.433–508	174	520.18	194
V.458	174	*Physics*	
V.466	174	571.9ff	159
V.509–33	10n	675–95	155
V.513–16	16	840.5	134n
V.534–63	190	Pindar	
V.540–7	22	*Isthmian*	
V.614–782	10n	III.14	40
V.783–820	178	VIII.65	40
V.788ff	179n	*Nemean*	
V.821–36	231	III.15	40
V.837–41	179n	VIII.20	41
V.878–924	213	VIII.38–9	41
V.925–1010	213ff	X.45	43
V.925–1378	220	*Olympian*	
V.1161–240	214ff	VIII.19	40
V.1194–217	216ff	X.52–5	43
V.1218–25	218	*Pythian*	
V.1346–57	219ff	II.90	91n
V.1379–435	219–22	VIII	39
V.1436–57	219–22	XI.49	40
VI	162n, 208n	Plato	
VI.1–42	221	*Apology* 19C	18
VI.29–31	218n	*Gorgias*	
VI.39–41	210	473B11	46
Lysias XIV.5	28	483C–D	67
Marcus Aurelius,		493A2	18n
Meditations VI.10	224		

Laws
VII.815A8 — 158
X — 211
x.889A–899D — 203
Lysis 215C4 — 18n
Parmenides
127A–C — 59
137D — 108n
Phaedo
96ff — 59
96Cff — 203
97C–D — 119–20
103Cff — 64, 139
108E–109A — 18
108E — 99
109Cff — 235
Phaedrus 274C5 — 18n
Philebus 28Cff — 203
Protagoras 329D–E — 54
Timaeus — 143
22C — 204
39E7 — 228
48A — 228n
59A — 87
79A–80C — 156
79E — 139, 144
Republic — 76
I, 348C–D — 67
II, 359A — 73
VII, 533A3 — 45
Symposium 201Dff — 18n
Plautus, *Trinummus* 1070 — 172
Pliny, *Natural History*
II.1.14 — 6
Plutarch
Adversus Coloten 1113A–8 — 48n
De communibus notitiis
38, 1079A — 185
41 — 184
49, 1085C — 158
De Stoicorum repugnantiis
41, 1052F — 197
42–4 — 192
43, 1054B — 192
44, 1054E — 98n
Lysander 12 — 96
Platonic Questions 7,
1004Dff — 144n
Stromateis 2 — 233n
Porphyry, *De abstinentia*
I.10–11 — 212n
Seneca, *Epistulae* CXVII — 184
Sextus, *Adversus*
Mathematicos
VII.129–30 — 198
VII.350 — 198
Simonides IV.13D — 35n

Simplicius
De caelo
295.9 — 101
530.30f — 94n
531.32ff — 20n
723.22–32 — 157n
Physics
28.8–25 — 109
28.25ff — 79n
374.18ff — 115n
407.35 — 110
453–67 — 105n
459.25–6 — 105n
460.2–4 — 105
467.16 — 113
467.25ff — 110, 113n
467.26ff — 7n
492.14ff — 105
573.2–27 — 82n
577.24ff — 83n
597.1–5 — 86n
601.14–24 — 149
1153.22 — 103
1208.30ff — 123
Sophocles, *Electra* 1353 — 42
Stesichorus
fr. VI.1–4 — 14
fr. VIII — 29
Stobaeus
1.207.16ff — 195
Stoicorum Veterum
Fragmenta
I.93 — 184
I.99 — 191
I.109 — 199
I.146 — 199
II.331 — 184
II.379 — 186
II.413 — 186
II.482 — 185
II.509–21 — 184
II.597 — 186
II.609 — 186
II.618 — 186
II.619 — 186
II.623 — 199
II.627 — 199
II.774 — 199
II.850 — 198
II.857–8 — 198
II.861–2 — 198
II.912–27 — 196
Strato
fr. 32 — 150–52
frr. 32–6 — 159
frr. 33–5 — 132n
frr. 42–8 — 159

frr. 50–2   159
frr. 54–67   132n, 150
frr. 54ff   141n
fr. 55   83n, 149
fr. 56   157f
frr. 60–3   154
fr. 65a   151ff
fr. 82   159
fr. 84   159, 194–5
Theognis 157   91n
Theophrastus
 De causis plantarum I.5.2   57n
 De igne
   4–7   194
   14–15   139
   17   139
 De sensibus
   3   31n
   61   80n
   71   101

De vertigine 9   224
Historia Plantarum III.1.4   57n
Physicorum opiniones fr. 1   186
Thucydides
 I.131   42
 II.37   32n
 III.53   43
 III.61   43
 III.64   44
 IV.94   25
 VI.86   43
Xenophanes, fr. 28   16
Xenophon
 Anabasis I.2.24   28
 Memorabilia I.4   200, 203
Zeno of Elea
 fr. 1   62n
 frr. 1–2   36, 60
 fr. 3   60

INDEX OF MODERN SCHOLARS

Alfieri, V. E.   8on
Arrighetti, G.   163n, 164n

Bailey, Cyril   54n, 8on, 161ff, 172, 175n, 183ff, 208n, 209n, 211, 215, 217, 219
Balme, D. M.   115
Barnes, Jonathan   39
Benardete, S.   170n
Bentley, Richard   13
Bergk, T.   181n
Berlin, Isaiah   226n
Beye, C. R.   213n, 214n
Bignone, E.   72, 75, 193, 200, 202
Bollack, Jean   44n, 176n, 177n
Borle, J. -P.   213n
Brentlinger, John   51n, 62n
Brieger, A.   94, 100
Burkert, Walter   3n, 21n, 22n, 24, 27n, 28n, 29, 62n
Burnet, J.   8on, 94

Calogero, Guido   60n, 61n
Carteron, Henri   127n, 144n
Chadwick, John   91n
Charlton, W.   115n, 117–18
Cherniss, H. F.   50, 57n, 8on, 93n, 144n
Classen, C. J.   17n
Cleary, John   223n, 225n
Cole, T.   209n, 211
Cooper, J. M.   115n, 120n
Cornford, F. m.   17n, 55n, 57n, 162, 166, 171
Coutant, V. C. B.   136
Coxon, A. H.   29

Davison, J. A.   59n
De Lacy, P. H.   167, 202
Dicks, D. R.   17n
Diels, H.   28, 44n, 159n, 181n, 217
Dyroff, A.   94

Easterling, H. J.   123n
Edelstein, L.   180

Eichholz, D. E.   132
Ernout, A.   172, 187, 210

Ferguson, John   11n, 79n, 96n
Flashar, Helmut   153
Fredouille, J. C.   213
Freudenthal, Gad   22n
Fritz, K. von   17n
Furth, Montgomery   34n, 37n, 65n

Gatzemeier, Matthias   149ff
Giuffrida, P.   219n
Giussani, Carlo   172, 183, 187, 190, 197, 203, 210, 211, 217, 218
Gomperz, T.   167
Goodfield, J.   227 and n
Gotthelf, Allan   115n
Gottschalk, H. B.   3n, 132, 141, 143, 149ff, 155n
Grant, Edward   87n
Grilli, A.   213n
Guthrie, W. K. C.,   4n, 11n, 17n, 25n, 27n, 28, 31, 34n, 50, 52n, 54n, 55n, 59, 60n, 72, 74, 8on, 87n, 92n, 93n, 94, 177n, 181n, 227n, 230n

Hammer-Jensen, I.   132
Hampshire, Stuart   129n
Happ, H.   142
Hartman, Edwin   121n
Havelock, Eric A.   28n, 72–3, 226n
Heath, Sir Thomas   3n
Heidel, W. A.   17n, 23
Heinimann, Felix   69
Heitsch, E.   170n
Humphries, Rolfe   176n

Joachim, H. H.   133
Jobst, F.   176n

Kahn, Charles H.   4n, 17n, 20n, 27n, 35n, 37n, 44n, 177n, 182n

Kember, Owen   57n, 58n
Kenney, E. J.   213n
Kerferd, G. B.   52n, 54ff, 68ff
Kerschensteiner, J.   230n
Kirk, G. S.   4n, 17n, 44n, 79n, 80n, 92f, 177n, 186
Kleve, Knut   165n
Konstan, David   89n
Kranz, W.   24n, 176n

Lachmann, K.   188
Landels, J. G.   10n
Lanza, Diego   53n
Lee, H. D. P.   32, 140, 144, 145n, 155n
Leonard, William E. D.   172, 206n
Lesher, J. H.   38n
Lesky, Erna   58
Liepmann, H. C.   94
Lloyd, G. E. R.   230
Long, A. A.   31n
Lonie, I. M.   230n
Louis, P.   146
Luria, S.   110n

McDiarmid, John B.   80n
Mansfeld, Jaap   24n, 27n, 29n, 31, 32n
Mansion, A.   115n
Marcovich, M.   44n
Martin, J.   188
Mates, Benson   167
Mathewson, I. R. D.   54n
Mau, J.   103
Merlan, P.   219
Mondolfo, R.   111
Moraux, P.   149
Morrison, J. S.   27n, 68, 74
Most, Glenn W.   91n
Moulton, Carroll   73
Mourelatos, A. P. D.   27–37
Mueller, Carl W.   79n
Mugler, C.   110n
Munro, H. A.   172, 183, 187, 197
Murdoch, John   223n, 231n

Nethercut, W. R.   219n
Nussbaum, Martha Craven   115n, 121n, 130n

O'Brien, D.   91–102, 177n
Owen, G. E. L.   25n, 35n, 37n, 56n, 62n

Peck, A. L.   54n, 55n, 62ff, 146
Pepe, L.   132
Perelli, L.   213
Philippson, R.   167
Pohlenz, M.   199

Popper, Karl R.   43, 166

Rankin, H. D.   170n
Raven, J. E.   55n, 60n, 79n, 177n
Reinhardt, K.   211
Reitzenstein, E.   208n
Robin, L.   172, 183, 195, 197,200, 203, 213n, 214n, 221
Robinson, John Mansley   17n
Rorty, Amelie   74n
Roscher, W. H.   24n
Ross, W. D.   110, 113n, 115n, 123n, 134

Sambursky, S.   192
Saunders, Trevor J.   70, 75–6
Schilling, Robert   175n
Schofield, Malcolm   53n, 121n, 130n
Schwabl, Hans   31
Sedley, D.   209n
Seeck, G. A.   124n
Skemp, J. R.   126n
Smith, Martin Ferguson   224
Solmsen, F.   121n, 124n, 143, 177n, 194, 202
Sorabji, R. R. K.   115n, 121n, 159n
Spoerri, W.   213n
Steinmetz, P.   145n, 194
Strang, Colin   60n, 62n
Strohm, H.   135, 144, 145n

Taylor, Charles   129n
Taylor, M.   213n
Thesleff, Holger   24n
Tigner, Steven S.   11n, 79n, 96n
Toulmin, S.   227

Untersteiner, M.   202
Usener, H.   158

Ventris, Michael   91n
Vlastos, Gregory   4n, 45n, 50, 52n, 55n, 106n, 170n
Vos, H.   30n

Wagner, H.   119, 134n
Waszink, J. H.   218n
Waterlow, Sarah   120n
Webster, T. B. L.   223n
Wehrli, Fritz   149ff
West, M. L.   17n, 47
Wieland, Wolfgang   111, 116, 202
Wilkie, J. S.   158n
Woodbury, Leonard   32n

Zeller, E.   35n, 81n, 94, 100

GENERAL INDEX

This index supplements the Table of Contents on pp. v–vi

Academy 185, 207
aether 96; *see also* fifth element
air *see* elements; in Anaximenes 233
Anaxagoras 4n, 20, 23, 47–65, 134, 179, 185, 197, 209n, 211
    chronology of 59
    compared with Empedocles 100
    criticized by Aristotle 109
    on infinite divisibility 106
    on Mind 13
    see also change; meteorite; *and under* elements; mind
Anaximander 4n, 14–26, 36–7, 99n, 112, 140, 233
Anaximenes 16, 19f, 233; on elements 102
Andronicus 195
animal, world compared to 4, 227ff
animals, movements of 121–31
antiperistasis 140ff, 144n, 145ff
antipodes 188–91, 235
ants, gold-digging 23
apathy 198, 207
apodeixis 167
Archimedes 207
Archytas 113n; argues for infinity 7, 110
Aristarchus 3, 17
Aristotle 211, 225ff
    argues against void 6–8
    condemns atheism 201
    cosmology of 1, 178–9
    evidence for Democritus 12
    founder of medieval Christian cosmology 1
    geocentrism of 193f
    on motion 9
    on place 81ff, 149
    and providence 201ff
    on syllogisms 45
    teleology of 199f
    see also under elements

Asclepiades 145
astronomy 208, 235
atheism 226
Athena 211
Atlas 96
Atomists, contrasted with Strato 152, 159
atoms 78ff, 225, 233–5;
    speed of motion of 169
    see also soul, atomic; swerve of atoms; *and under* weight
Atticus 78
attraction 136ff, 179; Plato's explanation of 144

Bacon, criticizes Aristotle 116
balance, to measure weight 91f
barbarians and Greeks 74–5
Boundless, the 22

Callicles 66f
catastrophe 204, 211
centre
    of the universe 188–93, 235
    of vortex 98ff
centrifocal dynamics 7–12, 15, 79f, 99, 159, 189ff, 234–5; *see also under* Parmenides
change, Anaxagoras' theory of 16–2
Charleton, Walter 5–6, 13, 227n
Chrysippus, 184, 185, 192, 199, 202, 207; on fate 196
Cicero 78, 195, 224, 229
Cleanthes 207
combustion 142ff
coming-to-be 55ff
compression 154ff
conflagration *see ekpyrosis*
continuity 143ff, 152, 169, 186, 205, 225
contraries in Parmenides 33
Copernicus, Nicolas 5
cosmic cycle 205, 234

cosmogony 230
cosmos
    contrasted with universe 2, 229
    mortality of 200, 218
    shape of 99–100
craftsman 203, 228, 232, 234; divine 178
creation 225, 227; in *Timaeus* 202
creator 234
cycles, cosmic 177

Damascius on place 149
Dead Sea 224
death 199
demiurge 209
Democritus 4, 20, 154n, 159, 167, 179, 198,
    209, 211, 225ff, 231, 235
    arguments for infinity 6
    on fate 196
    on gods 227
    on infinite worlds 4
    on place 149
    on position of earth 100n
    on skin of the world 4
    theory of motion 8–13
desire 125ff
dianoia 125ff
Diogenes of Apollonia 23, 233
Diogenes of Oenoanda 212n
down *see* up and down
doxa 163–70
dreams 163ff, 170, 216
dualism of linear and circular motion 8–13,
    15

earth 29, 49, 54, 188, 229
    at rest 1–2, 94–7
    drum-shaped 21
    flat 10, 90
    movement of 21
    position of 86, 100n
    shape and position of 14–26, 80, 86, 92,
        100n, 225, 234–5
    stability of 190
eidola 163ff
ekpyrosis 186, 199, 200ff, 203, 207
elements 56, 135ff, 172ff, 176ff, 185
    in Anaxagoras 47–65
    in Aristotle 51ff
    in Empedocles 48ff
elenchos 33ff
embryology 230
Empedocles 20, 116, 134, 142, 185
    compared with Anaxagoras 47–51, 64–5,
        100
    on Love and Strife 13
    Purifications 181–2
    on survival of fittest 114
    vortex supports earth 96

    see also under elements
enlightenment 28
Ennius 181
epibolê 162ff
Epicurus 159, 179ff, 225ff, 235
    on infinite worlds 4
    on motion 10, 81, 83ff, 89, 101
    on place 149
    praised by Lucretius 2
    purpose of physics 5
    on religion 227
    on weight 80, 94
    see also under mind
epimartyresis/antimartyresis 163n
Epimenides of Crete 28
epistemology, Aristotelian and Epicurean 107
Erasistratus 145, 158ff, 207; on void 150ff
Eratosthenes 207
eternity 178–9, 201, 211, 225, 227, 234
eudaimonia 129
Eudemus 113n; on infinity 105–7, 110
Eudoxus 17
evaporation 136ff
exhalations 195

falling bodies 11–12
fate 195ff, 207
fifth element 13, 15, 159, 193ff
fire 177
    in the centre of the world 3
    of the heavens 172ff
    see also elements
focus of natural motion 7–8; *see also*
    centrifocal dynamics
form 233–5
friendship 214

Galen 142, 145, 158; on place 82
Galileo 5
Gassendi, Pierre 5
geocentric motion 89; *see also* centrifocal
    dynamics
geometrical atomism 104
Giants 200f
gods 175, 179, 205, 212, 216ff, 224, 227, 234;
    in Epicureanism 163
gravity, theory of 7–8, 192

Helen 184
Heracleides of Pontus 3; on star-worlds 4
Heraclitus 185ff, 198
Hermarchus 176, 212n
Hermes 211
Hero 140
Herophilus 207
Hipparchus 207
Hippocrates 142, 231

homoiomerous bodies 51ff, 63, 133ff, 146ff, 197
horror vacui 156ff
Huygens, Christian 99n
hylozoism 233

illusions 163ff, 170
imagination 163
India 23
indifferents in Stoicism 207
indivisibles, motion of 84
inertia 87
infinite divisibility 61–2, 152, 168; *see also under* Anaxagoras
infinity 225, 229, 234, 235; five arguments for 6
intention 125ff
Iphigeneia 181
Italy, visited by Plato 23

Jupiter 204
Justice (goddess) 29

Kebes 23
Kepler, Johann 3n, 5, 229

Laestrygonians 30
language, development of 212
law 68ff, 215
Leucippus 167, 179, 225ff, 230n
    on infinite worlds 4
    on skin of the world 4
light
    Aristotle's theory of 153
    and knowledge 31
like to like 19, 139, 147, 179, 230–1
Linear B 91
logos 146
logos spermatikos 197, 207
Love and Strife 100, 176ff
Lucretius 172ff, 183ff, 206ff

magnetism 144, 154ff
Mars 175
mathematics 104, 225n; contrasted with physics 11
mechanical philosophy 225–32
Melissus argues for infinity 6
memory 165
meteorite, predicted by Anaxagoras 59
meteorology 162, 208
microcosm 231–2
mind 228
    in Anaxagoras 56, 64, 100
    in Epicureanism 163
minimae partes 106–9, 168, 185
moon 199, 200, 232; motion of 14
mortal belief, in Parmenides 30ff

Mover, Unmoved *see* Unmoved Mover
movers of spheres 100
music, development of 220
mythology 162

names, in Parmenides 32ff
natural motion 84ff
nature
    and justice 66ff
    source of morality 66ff
    source of technology 210ff
necessity 115–20, 212, 228
Newton, Isaac 5, 225–6, 234
Night, house, of 27ff
nutrition 52ff, 53

Ocean 14, 42
opposites 54, 63–5, 133ff, 204
orexis 125ff
Orpheus 28

Panaetius 193
pangenesis 58
parallax 3
Parmenides 76
    against void 78
    on centrifocal dynamics 23–6
    on position of earth 100n
    on shape of earth 23–6
    see also Justice; mortal belief; names; night; roads of Day and Night; sun, daughters of, home of
perception 127ff, 161ff
periosis 144, 156
Peripatos 207
Phaethon 204
phantasia 126ff, 163
Philolaus 23
Philoponus 225
Phoebus 204
physis/ technê 135
piety, Epicurean 216, 218
place 111–12, 149ff
    Aristotle's idea of 81ff, 149
    Strato on 83, 159
    see also Proclus
planets, motion of 14
Plato, 199, 225ff, 226, 231
    cosmology of 1, 178–9
    on demiurge 13
    on motion 9
    on place 149
    spokesman in Aristotle's dialogue? 202
    theory of Forms 45f, 62–5
    Timaeus 202–3, 227, 228, 234
    on World Soul 13
pleasure 175, 220–2

pneuma 186, 197, 199, 207; *see also under*
  Stoics
pores 132ff, 151ff
Posidonius 193, 199
potentiality 127ff, 147, 153, 185, 228, 106, 113
powers, physical 33
primitivism/progressivism 210, 213
Proclus, on Place 149
progressivism *see* primitivism
projectile, motion of 86–7
prolepsis 165n
providence 224
Ptolemy, world picture of 1
punishment 215ff
Purifications of Empedocles 181–2
Pythagoras 180n, 182n
Pythagoreans 17, 23, 199; and central fire 3

qualities 142ff, 159, 196ff, 205, 225n

rarefaction/condensation 186
ratio 210, 219, 221
religion, origin of 215ff
responsibility 127ff
rest, natural and forced 88
roads of Day and Night 27–30

sacrifice 181
Sallustius, *Empedoclea* 176
sea 179
seed 166, 230–1, 233; in Anaxagoras 55ff, 63
sensation 161ff
sight 198
Simmias 23, 37
Simplicius 18–150, 154, 225
size of the world 1
skin of the world 4
Socrates 17, 203, 225
  his 'autobiography' 59
  vs Thrasymachus 66
soul 56, 121–31, 198, 200, 225, 228; atomic
  166, 180
sphere *see* earth, shape and position of
sphere of stars 1
stars 162, 173f, 189, 191, 216, 229
  made of rock 96
  not infinitely distant 2
Stoic logic 44ff, 167
Stoics 107, 207, 218n, 225ff, 234
  centrifocal theory of 98n
  cosmology of 178
  dynamics of 235
  on extracosmic void 4, 78
  on *pneuma* 85
  on tension 158
  theory of natural motion 8
  see also Zeno
Strato 132, 140, 142, 198
  on place 83, 159
  see also Atomists

sufficient reason, principle of 17, 22, 26
sun 173, 177, 189, 191, 194, 199, 200, 204,
  214, 232
  daughters of 27–8
  home of 29
  motion of 14
  nourishment of 193, 195
survival of fittest 179, 213f
swerve of atoms 90, 178–9

Tartarus 14, 16, 29
technology 115,–20, 179, 205, 225, 231
telescopes 2
tension 158ff, 186, 197, 207
Thales 16, 19f, 233
Theophrastus 21, 132, 155n, 158, 160, 195,
  208
  on Empedocles 176
  on fifth element 194
Thrasymachus 66f
time 184
tissues 56, 158; organic 50–1
tradition in Lucretius 175
transmigration 181
transparent 153

universe
  centre of 7–8
  distinguished from world 2, 229
  infinite 2
Unmoved Mover 13, 85, 89, 122ff, 159, 202,
  228
up and down 15, 24, 91ff, 188

vector 89
Venus 175ff, 214
void 104, 140, 186–93, 188, 225, 226, 229,
  233–5; extracosmic 4–6
voluntary/involuntary 129ff
vortex 11–12, 79ff, 94ff, 230–1

water 16
  in Thales 233
  see also elements
water-wheel 15
weight 187–8; of atoms 178–9
windmills 10n
world, finite 2
worlds, plural 4, 205, 229

Xenophanes 20

Zeno (Stoic) 184, 191, 199, 207
Zeno of Elea
  Achilles argument 62
  antinomies of 76
  chronology of 59
  dichotomy argument 62
  relation to Anaxagoras 58ff